General Editor'

MW00638618

Asbury Theological Seminary Series in
World Christian Revitalization Movements

This volume is published in collaboration with the Center for the Study of World Christian Revitalization Movements, a cooperative initiative of Asbury Theological Seminary faculty. Building on the work of the previous Wesleyan/Holiness Studies Center at the Seminary, the Center provides a focus for research in the Wesleyan Holiness and other related Christian renewal movements, including Pietism and Pentecostal movements, which have had a world impact. The research seeks to develop analytical models of these movements, including their biblical and theological assessment. Using an interdisciplinary approach, the Center bridges relevant discourses in several areas in order to gain insights for effective Christian mission globally. It recognizes the need for conducting research that combines insights from the history of evangelical renewal and revival movements with anthropological and religious studies literature on revitalization movements. It also networks with similar or related research and study centers around the world, in addition to sponsoring its own research projects.

Albert Hernandez's study of medieval expressions of the biblical theme of Pentecost represents a creative and little perceived use of this theme in the history of Christianity as well as the history of Western culture in the medieval era. He demonstrates the appeal of Pentecost to key figures in the making of modern science, suggesting ways in which this central motif of revitalization within Christianity was influential in suggesting alternative paradigms for interpreting the natural world as well as salvation history. This study is the fruit of longstanding research by Hernandez, who also serves as Vice President for Academic Affairs at Iliff Seminary.

J. Steven O'Malley
Director, Center for the Study of World Christian Revitalization Movements
General Editor, The Asbury Theological Seminary Series in Christian Revitalization Studies

Sub-Series Foreword

Medieval and Reformation Studies

In the pages that follow, readers will be delighted to discover themselves drawn into a compelling account that aims to recover the story of Pentecost as narrated by author Albert Hernandez. While providing a substantive study in religious, intellectual, and cultural history treating both familiar and unfamiliar figures, events, and movements from the twelfth to the seventh century, this book may be even more important in giving serious attention to the way such study may be itself a subversive undertaking. Hernandez reminds us that remembering the Christian past may "offer much nourishment for academic, as well as ordained and lay readers interested in the story of Christian spirituality and related themes like Pentecostalism (xi).

This task is accomplished by a skilled story teller. Hernandez' carefully crafted narrative demonstrates that strong interest in the story of Pentecost is not just a recent phenomenon; and that an untold story of men and women in medieval and early modern Europe awaits the liberation of our imaginations from the restrictions imposed by modernity's visions of history and reality. For this reason, *Subversive Fire* may be read not only as an important contribution to the study of revitalization but also as a highly relevant guide for our own ecclesial, spiritual, and cultural concerns. This book will serve as an exemplary model of the kind of post - modern, interdisciplinary scholarship we yearn for in our attempts to think and live into what its author describes as the "ever approaching, not - yet of the future," a future which, paradoxically, is discerned as we listen to and learn from the resources of the past.

Michael Pasquarello III, PhD
Medieval and Reformation Sub - Series Editor

Subversive Fire

The Untold Story of Pentecost

Albert Hernández

The Asbury Theological Seminary Series in
World Christian Revitalization Movements in
Medieval and Reformation Studies No. 1

EMETH PRESS
www.emethpress.com

Subversive Fire: The Untold Story of Pentecost

Library of Congress Cataloging-in-Publication Data
Hernández, Albert.
Subversive fire : the untold story of Pentecost / Albert Hernández.
    p. cm. -- (The Asbury Theological Seminary series in world Christian revi-
talization movements in medieval and Reformation studies ; no. 1)
Includes bibliographical references (p.   ) index.
ISBN 978-1-60947-005-0 (alk. paper)
    1. Pentecost season--Europe--History. 2. Holy Spirit--History of doctrines. 3.
Pentecost--History of doctrines . I. Title.
BV61.H47 2010
263'.94094--dc22   2010027307

The photo on the front cover is a copy of a painting *Pentecost* by El Greco, a Greek artist
who migrated to Spain where he became the arhictect of the Spanish Renaissance. Public
domain. Source: http://www.bestpriceart.com/painting/?pid=90558 (used by permission).

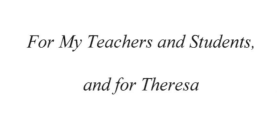

For My Teachers and Students,

and for Theresa

CONTENTS

wrote
this 1st

PREFACE

During the past few decades there has been a resurgence of pneumatology and curiosity about the Third Person of the Trinity; a renaissance of interest in both the academic study of the Holy Spirit and in the role of the Holy Spirit in Christian worship and personal piety. This renewed emphasis on *personal religious experience* is noticeable among almost all contemporary Christian denominations, while a new emphasis on the *academic study of spirituality* has emerged in numerous seminaries and theological schools across North America and other parts of the world. In the early twentieth century, Christianity witnessed the birth and growth of Pentecostalism, first as a localized movement in the days of the Azusa Street Revival (1906-ca.1915), and, then gradually as a broader, worldwide phenomenon which now, in the early years of the twenty-first century, is the fastest growing sector of global Christianity. While this book is not about Pentecostalism, nor specifically about pneumatology, its focus on the historical recovery of Western European conceptions of Pentecost and the Holy Spirit from the 1100s through the late 1600s will offer much nourishment for academic, as well as ordained and lay readers interested in the history of Christian spirituality and related themes like Pentecostalism. A number of the figures and movements examined throughout this book were well known among earlier scholars who read and studied their works during the 1900s from the perspective of apocalypticism and millennialism. However, despite familiar stories about Pentecost, along with well-known biblical references to the Holy Spirit, some of the names and information discussed in the following chapters will seem unfamiliar, even uncanny at times. But the relevance of the story of Pentecost throughout the history of Christianity, especially among the medieval and early modern men and women whose life stories and religious imaginations form the core of this book's material, remains as important for contemporary Christian revitalization and theological reconstruction as it was centuries ago, an enduring inheritance whose relevance transcends denominational boundaries.

This volume is the beginning of a line of research on often neglected themes in the modern and postmodern study of the history of Christianity, themes with direct relevance for the study of pneumatology, ecclesiology, and church revitalization studies. Readers bewildered by this mixture of "unknowing knowing," as Saint John of the Cross described his encounter with the Holy Spirit, would do well to hold the following question in mind until all of this volume's figures and movements have made their cameo appearances: Why do Pentecost, and the Holy Spirit, show up in such astonishing and creative ways throughout the history of Christianity? This is the question that ignited my initial curiosity about medieval and early modern understandings of the Pentecost story. This is the question that fueled my initial forays into the social logic within which these theological conceptions, local and trans-local religious traditions, and annual commemorations of Pentecost functioned for centuries before being eclipsed by the rise of modernity and the decline of the liturgical calendar in the lives and daily labors of Western European Christians.

I humbly confess at the outset that, although in the book's conclusion I offer some historical and theological reflection on this larger question, my thoughts remain in the process of assessing the historical meaning and theological implication of these research results. More work is needed to further map and recover the significant number of references to personal transformations and supernatural visions just before, during, and after the Feast of Pentecost, which can be found throughout a wide variety of extant primary and secondary sources from the medieval and early modern periods of Christian history.

This book represents the culmination of nearly five years of research and writing on a topic and a span of years, which easily could have filled several volumes. It emerged out of a series of glimpses into the religious sensibilities of now distant medieval and early modern Christians who lived from the 1100s through the 1670s. In some of the medieval sources, there was a curious sense of wonder and reverence with which many of the men and women serving the Church regarded the presence of the Holy Spirit in the natural world and in the potential for spiritual "gifts" among all Christians, a sacred presence that also called them to hold the laity and leadership of the Church accountable to its essential mission dating back to the outpouring of wisdom through the Third Person of the Trinity at the first Pentecost. As I read some of the early modern sources, from the Italian Renaissance to just before the Enlightenment, I noticed a very similar, if not identical, mingling of wonder and reverence for the empowering presence of the Holy Spirit in calls for pedagogical reform and innovation, scientific speculation, and general Christian reformism. In addition, there was a gradual waning of these traditions and practices by the end of the seventeenth century and the beginning of the eighteenth century. These "little wonders" in the works of so many medieval and early modern Christian writers and visionaries suggest there was a way of thinking about Pentecost and the Holy Spirit, in the midst of living the Christian liturgical calendar, practicing daily devotions, and participating in annual commemorations of Pentecost, that "quickened" one's religious imagination with a longing for "deep prayer" and contemplation, and which opened the heart of the believer to a wide range of visionary experiences. The fruits of this mystical, inner journey during the seven-times-seven days from Easter Sunday to Pentecost Sunday (Whitsuntide) sparked ecclesiastical and socio-political revitalization efforts, which, over the

|| 0⁰⸍0𝘶
   ᵢ ᶜₒ0𝘶

centuries also generated more than a few transformative, personal religious experiences.

Since these ways of thinking about the Holy Spirit and Pentecost are now largely forgotten by most Roman Catholics and Protestants, and remain relatively unknown among contemporary clergy and scholars of Christian history, I offer this book as a preliminary series of vignettes from the lives and works of Christian authors whose religious vocations were inspired, and whose careers were set into dynamic motion, by some personal insight or revelation dealing with the Feast of Pentecost or with the presence of the Holy Spirit in their lives. The period covered herein stretches from the late 1100s to the late 1600s, or roughly from the time of Hildegard of Bingen and Joachim of Fiore to the rise of the Scientific Revolution's "chemical phase" when trailblazers like Francis Bacon, Jan Baptiste van Helmont, and Robert Boyle moved away from their initial fascination with magic, alchemy, and the "*ethereal fire*" of the Spirit realm to a more rationalistic and process-oriented way of understanding "the secrets of Nature."

Any historical narrative spanning five centuries runs the risk of either covering too much ground or of not including and discussing enough primary materials for a balanced treatment of its major themes. However, in the task of recovering the historical reality of these forgotten yet foundational and enduring aspects of the story of Christianity, it was precisely this trajectory that needed to be measured and mapped, a trajectory whose ecclesiology began with the story of the first Pentecost as recorded in the New Testament. Thus, rather than providing comprehensive portraits of each period, author or movement, I compressed them into one volume by offering selective vignettes from each period, writer, or movement. Indeed, as indicated above, a more comprehensive account of these medieval and early modern conceptions of Pentecost and the Holy Spirit would have required writing a multi-volume work.

This book is not intended for the sole use of other historians of Christianity. Indeed, academic specialists in either medieval or early modern studies, or history, or theology seeking micro-studies of historical periods will be sorely disappointed. The present volume does not follow the familiar Scholastic ground of medieval pneumatological speculation from Augustine and Basil the Great to Bonaventure and Thomas Aquinas. I did not set out to write that sort of book. I also set out in hopes of finding an editor and publisher who would allow me the freedom needed to explore the divergent aspects of this book's central questions and thesis, and I was fortunate to have found that among the staff and leadership of the Center for the Study of World Christian Revitalization Movements at Asbury Theological Seminary. Some of the names and movements examined in this book have been relegated to the heretic or lunatic fringe of the medieval and early modern periods. Big mistake, —especially since that long-forgotten and so-called heretic or lunatic fringe now bears such an amazing rhetorical resemblance and "equivalence of experience" to the eruption of Pentecostalism in the early 1900s, an ongoing robust global manifestation of Christianity's *subversive fire* which most of our mainline seminaries, schools of theology, and denominational governing bodies seem incapable of fully understanding. My academic colleagues and I will debate the accuracy of some of the findings and conclusions offered in this book, while other fellow historians will want to unearth the voices of those writers and visionaries whom, for the sake of time and space limitations, I intentionally left out of the narrative. But in the academic marketplace of historical and theological studies, this is as it should be.

On the other hand, I sincerely hope that clergy and laity who read this work will ponder its relevance to their contemporary spiritual concerns and ecclesiastical circumstances while, no doubt, lamenting the loss of such imaginative ways of thinking about Pentecost and honoring the presence of the Holy Spirit in Nature, in the Church, and in the human heart. My caution to some of those potential readers is: Beware of nostalgia for the past; it often gets in the way of perceiving the ever-approaching *not-yet* of the future, which can only be discerned if we posses full mastery and understanding of the resources of the past while listening to the silences of our own world and peeking into the blind spots of the present age.

Nonetheless, as both a historian of Christianity and a practitioner of its traditions, I recognize that the on-going work of Christian revitalization necessitates juxtapositions of past, present, and future, for as Ecclesiastes (1:9) reminds us: "There is nothing new under the sun." We who live in the present are charged with remembering the lessons of our ancestors, as well as with healing the ruptures between their past and our anxious present. And this, too, is as it should be — even as *we* live into the unfolding of our own uncertain future.

For this volume, I have chosen the title, *Subversive Fire* because the pneumatological dreams and personal piety of the authors and movements surveyed in the following pages motivated them to work endlessly for justice and liberty among their brothers and sisters in the Church, while advocating for various types of ecclesiastical, socio-political, and educational reforms across the varied times and places that make up the story of Christianity. But the story of Pentecost and the Holy Spirit surveyed herein is also a tale touching upon questions of transformative leadership, Christian education and learning, and Trinitarian traditions of relationality, as well as on issues of sacred and miraculous communication between the human and the divine realms of being. Thus, the sending forth of the Holy Ghost at the first Pentecost, and the annual remembrance of this sacred event as the birth of the Church, led many medieval and early modern followers of Christ's teachings to reflect, each year around the Feast of Pentecost, on the vitality, moral integrity and future well-being of the institution founded by Jesus and the Apostles in the Book of Acts — the Christian Church. In other words, the Holy Spirit inspired and empowered them "to subvert" dominant ecclesiastical and political paradigms for the betterment of society and for the emancipation of God's children, a task sometimes opposed by stubborn, recalcitrant contemporaries so set in their ways that living out the content of these visions cost some of this story's protagonists their ecclesiastical careers and others their earthly lives.

ACKNOWLEDGMENTS

A project of this size and breadth could only be possible with the generous support, academic encouragement, and fellowship of a number of people. First and foremost, I thank my wife Theresa and our children Steven, Sara, Christina Maria, and Anthony, for their patience and sense of humor during all those days, nights, and weekends away from them while locked in the basement researching and writing about what they irreverently, but in a friendly way, referred to as "all those dead people Dad hangs out with." Others will surely benefit from buying and reading this book, but each one of you, my dear family, paid the highest price of all while waiting for the completion of this volume and my return to the rhythms and patterns our family life. Theresa's help preparing the final camera-ready copy of this manuscript, during a particularly busy time in each of our careers and at home, was enormously helpful and deeply appreciated. My thanks are due also to my in-laws, "Flo" and "Bear" Gradzki, for offering me a very peaceful and productive writing retreat at their lovely seaside home on the Jersey shore in December 2006.

I owe a great debt to my mother, Doris Hernández-Perez, for her invaluable advice and prayers when this project was still in search of a publishing contract. My sensitivity and awareness to the presence of the Spirit in Nature was nurtured from the day of my birth by her earthy wit and wisdom, and especially by my maternal grandmother's personal blend of Afro-Cuban folk wisdom and Roman Catholic piety. Maria Fermina Arencibia-Hernández raised me. She taught me to listen passionately from the moment I awoke each morning of my childhood to Nature's earthly voice in the simple daytime rhythms of life and death, and then to listen with deep reverence to Her divine silence in the darkness of night.

I am grateful to my graduate students at the Iliff School of Theology who responded in considerably large numbers to a new course on the "Holy Spirit in Christian History and Tradition," which I taught there several times from 2006 through 2009. My student research assistant for several years during the early phases of this project, Ellen Rosenthal, provided help with early Christian and traditional Jewish understandings of Shavuot. My student research assistant during the final stages of research and writing, Adriana Tulissi, also provided invaluable assistance and astonishingly rapid turnaround time whenever I sent her off tracking down more reference and library materials for me or while helping me with the book's indexing. I especially wish to hold up the constructive feedback and critiques of the Roman Catholic and Protestant female students in each of these classes who encouraged me again and again to listen to the lost voices of medieval female saints inspired by the Holy Spirit, and to the voice of *Dame Nature* speaking across the centuries through our primary sources. I also thank all of the former engineers, physics and chemistry majors, and "scientists-turned-pastors," who enrolled in my classes at the Iliff School of Theology and encouraged me to persevere in my fledgling attempts at fathoming the relation of the Holy Spirit and the quest for *ethereal fire* among the scientific pioneers discussed in Chapter Five, the early modern trailblazers whose fascination with electromagnetism and Nature's Spirit I could not ignore while completing this volume.

A huge debt of gratitude goes to my Iliff masters students John Gray and Demian Wheeler who, way back in 2002, made me aware of how my approach to historical studies reminded them of certain historicist and pragmatic themes in Delwin Brown's *constructive historicism*, Sheila Davaney's *pragmatic historicism*, and William Dean's works. I was then a first year, assistant history professor while Del, Sheila, and Bill were my senior colleagues at the Iliff School of Theology. However, it was John's and Demian's "enthusiasm" for the historical and theological implications set forth in the publications and divergent teaching styles of these three, long-time Iliff theologians that led me to assess how careful attention to theories of *tradition, radical historicism*, and *theological reconstruction* might help me make sense of the curious and often bizarre ways that Pentecost and the Holy Spirit showed up in the medieval primary sources and documents I was then researching. It is precisely the historicist perspective of these notions of *tradition* and *theological reconstruction*, which I hope will offer both academic specialists employed in theological education and concerned clergy in different denominations a unique opportunity to discuss the importance of *revitalization studies* for the study of the history of Christianity. As so eloquently and simply stated throughout the pages of Delwin Brown's *Boundaries of Our Habitations*, and his 2003 essay "Limitation and Ingenuity: Radical Historicism and the Nature of Tradition," religious traditions do, after all, reconstruct themselves over and over from the resources of the past. Features of historic Christianity that both liberals and conservatives would do well to ponder as both camps have had their progressive voices through the centuries.

There are several colleagues at the Iliff School of Theology whose support and friendship were highly significant for me during the conception, research, and writing stages of this book project. After some very insightful conversations with New Testament scholar, Richard Valantasis, I realized it was possible to approach topics like pneumatology, historical understandings of Pentecost, and visionary texts about the Holy Spirit from a literary and historicist perspective, while not succumbing to the sort of postmodern relativism that ignores the spiritual realities addressed in such texts. As my faculty mentor for a couple of years before leaving Iliff, Richard reminded me the Holy Spirit is actually that aspect of the Trinity embodied in and manifesting through the particularities of time, place, and culture. In the words of Jürgen Moltmann: "The Spirit of life is present only as the Spirit of this or that particular life." As my faculty mentor, Richard also chided me that there were easier ways of achieving tenure than by writing a book covering five hundred years. To my family's great dismay, I did not listen to his advice, but I did listen when he very wisely suggested condensing the scope and breadth of the proposed book's content into a series of vignettes from each period or movement capable of holding the entire cast of characters and spiritual themes together in one volume. Whatever shortcomings the present volume holds, are my entire responsibility.

Although there were ongoing discussions and offers from a couple of editors for writing a multivolume work, I chose instead to keep it all together in one volume regardless of the critique this might garner from historians with a penchant for micro-studies of medieval and early modern history. Such micro-studies might emerge later, from the work of other scholars or from me. For *Subversive Fire*, however, I intentionally chose figures, movements, materials and texts with a larger trans-local scope and breadth from across European Christianity. I stand by its ambition to recover a few glimpses of long forgotten ways of commemorating and experiencing Pentecost and the Holy Spirit by reaching across historical periods from the late 1100s to the mid-1600s. I also humbly stand by and accept the critiques that such an approach is bound to conjure up from the short-sighted professional assumptions of other historians.

I am also deeply grateful to my Iliff colleagues Miguel De La Torre, Ted Vial and Jacob Kinnard for providing me with the very best pre-tenure advice and editorial suggestions that I received on this entire project, especially when it mattered the most. Edward Antonio and Jean Miller Schmidt read an early draft and outline of this work and provided useful feedback and encouragement. Debbie McLaren, my Administrative Assistant, helped me by proofreading the manuscript, securing permissions, reviewing bibliographic entries, and occasionally keeping me sane when what I really wanted most was to abandon the loneliness of the long distance writer and just be present in the company of colleagues or family.

I also thank my employer, the Iliff School of Theology, for a generous research and writing leave during the 2005 Winter Term, and our Dean, Jeffrey Mahan, for much needed course teaching reductions during the final stages of work on the manuscript. The staff at both the University of Denver's Penrose Library and Iliff's Taylor Library helped me enormously throughout the entire period of my research and writing. Research visits to the Drew University Library, Princeton University Library, the Speer and Henry Luce III Libraries at Princeton Theological Seminary, and to the Rosicrucian Research Library at Rosicrucian Park in San Jose, California, provided much assistance with older texts and secondary sources, as well as access to rare book collections.

Lastly, I thank my editors, J. Steven O'Malley, Lawrence Wood at Emeth Press, and the staff of the Center for the Study of World Christian Revitalization Movements at Asbury Theological Seminary in Wilmore, Kentucky, for their assistance and for selecting this book for publication in the *Revitalization Series*. Special thanks are due to J. Steven O'Malley who, providentially, sat next to me in San Francisco at the "First National Conference on Building A Wesleyan Theology of Peace for the 21st Century," and then took such a genuine interest in how the story of Pentecost informed my historical presentation on that late September afternoon in 2006.

Denver, Colorado--Pentecost 2008

CHAPTER 1
RECOVERING THE STORY
OF PENTECOST

And they were all amazed, and were in doubt, saying one to another *"What does this mean?"*

Acts 2:12

The elucidation of meaning requires a story, the stuff of religion.

Kanan Makiya[1]

Throughout history, powerful Spirit movements have challenged the conventional doctrine and practice of the church . . . Not only did they question the pneumatological understanding of the church but also its ecclesiology and view of revelation.

Veli-Matti Kärkkäinen[2]

The conceptual reconstruction of a tradition's past is inextricably tied to the affective life of that tradition. If history cannot live without creativity and creativity without history, neither can live long apart from the affections, for feeling and thought in interaction serve as the vehicle of a tradition's recovery and innovation.

Delwin Brown, *Boundaries of Our Habitations*[3]

THE PROBLEM: "WHAT DOES THIS MEAN?"

One of the earliest stories of Greek mythology was about how Prometheus stole fire from the gods after a banquet at which he tricked Zeus, the father of the Olympian deities, and gave fire to humans. Zeus punished Prometheus by chaining him to a rock in the Caucasus Mountains while a vulture fed daily on his liver until Hercules freed him many years later by shooting the bird with an arrow. This mythic story probably dates back to prehistoric times long before the invention of writing and written languages. The story of Prometheus stealing fire from the Olympian gods reveals something primordial and seminal about humanity's fascination with *fire*. We are always amazed and captivated by this mysterious and transformative energy, which humanity has been using for millennia as a source of light, in cooking, purification, and melting, for sterilization and healing, as well as for manufacturing, warfare, and so forth. Every adult can recall his or her childhood fascination with fire, whether sitting around a camp fire, gazing at a warm and alluring fireplace, staring into a candle flame, or witnessing the sparks set off from lighting a match, instances which were usually followed by our elders wisely reminding us: "don't play with fire." According to the Book of Acts, Pentecost was a moment in which the disciples began a new life after the flames of the Holy Spirit burst into their hearts in a miraculous form of communication giving birth to a new creation, the Christian Church. God's fiery presence was seen, felt, and heard through a mighty wind and the miracle of the tongues of fire that descended on the Apostles and everyone who was present in the upper room on Pentecost. The persons gathered together that day did not have to steal this fire from their God because this powerful energy was freely sent forth upon them through the intercession of their Lord, Jesus Christ, who promised before the Ascension that he would be sending them the Holy Spirit as a Comforter or Intercessor. This outpouring of divine mercy and grace has been understood and commemorated by Christians through the centuries as a spiritual and miraculous "event" that gave rise to Christ's earthly Church as a distinct community and institution empowered by the Spirit to carry out the work of God in the world. Just as fire transmutes all things into something else, the invocation and presence of this fiery Spirit of Pentecost has been responsible for some of the most intriguing and contested transformations in the history of Christianity, which more often than not has manifested as a *subversive fire* of divine presence and vitality propelling people, institutions, and Nature towards the spiritual fullness of their particularity. This book aims to recover the story of Pentecost, as interpreted and commemorated by a small sampling of Christian writers, visionaries, and reformers from the late 1100s to the late 1600s, from the scholarly and ecclesiastical neglect generated by modern and postmodern readings of pneumatology in the history of Christianity.

Since by entering the domains of pneumatology and Pentecost we are in the realm of spiritual power and religious experience let us begin by making a few things very clear at the outset of this study. First, the concrete historical reality of the "events" and "experiences" recorded in the Book of Acts about the first Pentecost is not a concern of the present study. Regardless of our contemporary amnesia about the imaginative ways that Christians conceived, and practiced, the diverse commemorations and celebrations of this story, which they understood as one of the foundational moments of their religious tradition, by 1100 the story of Pentecost, and its fifty-day festal season from Easter Sunday to Whitsunday, had taken on a life of its own at both the local and trans-local levels of medieval Christendom. Throughout this study, we will read the *story* of Pentecost from the perspective of the visionary men and women whose voices and personal stories this study seeks to recover. Men and women whose supernatural claims and reactions to their particular encounters with the Divine during the annual season of Pentecost, were understood at both a surface level of literal cognition and at a deeper level of allegorical or figurative interpretation that had profound implications for the Church and society to which each of them belonged. These pneumatological sensibilities and pietistic tendencies were compounded by monastic prayer practices and the rhythmic celebration of feast days in the Christian liturgical calendar, which served to embed medieval and early modern followers of Christ's message in an extended meditation, or spiritual journey, through the stages of his earthly life that culminated each year on the Feast of Pentecost before the calendar returned to ordinary time en route to the next Advent season when the cycle of sacred time and spiritual unfolding resumed all over again. Thus, Christ's life story became the meditative and practical basis for how clergy, and many among the laity, ordered the story of their lives and labors through the seasons of the year. The promise and power of faith, is found in the old dictum that "the magic of believing, is believing." In the act of suspending judgment, we enter the narrative flow of storytelling, a feature of human ideality which is true of every story we hear or read from different times and locations around the world. But, it is the sense of wonder and awe sparked in our minds and hearts by certain stories that results in our being captivated, and indeed being *played* by the powers that reside in the stories themselves. The magic of storytelling is similar to our childhood fascination at "*playing with fire*," or like the wonder of sitting around a campfire with family and friends telling and retelling stories. We may be rational beings, but, without a doubt, the process of narrative flow holds uncanny possibilities for the human heart and mind.

While researching some of the figures and texts featured in this volume, I realized the *story of Pentecost* held potentialities for personal transformation and transformative leadership that scholars of Christian history, trained, as I was, in the postmodernist historiography of the 1990s, were ill-equipped to recover, and interpret. Indeed, in order not to violate the spiritual realities and contextual integrity of the medieval and early modern pneumatological conceptions and sensibilities preserved in these primary sources, I realized the interpretive and thematic lenses that earlier generations of church historians had applied to some of these figures and movements suffered from an excessive emphasis on apocalypticism and millennialism. This is not to claim that pneumatology, and visions of Pentecost, do not possess an eschatological dimension for the Holy Spirit clearly leads all things to their potential temporal and cosmic fullness in relation to the Father and the Son. But it appeared to me that what some of these writers and visionaries had originally stated about how and when the Holy Spirit poured forth upon them with apocalyptic and/or millenarian visions, was not being read and accepted at face value in earlier studies of these figures and movements. In other words, something about the social logic of these texts as convergent sites for ecclesiastical and pneumatological concerns had been overlooked.

In the mid-1990s historiography, in general, was still exorcising the spirits of logical positivism and modernist meta-narratives. Therefore, in order to allow the past to speak for itself, and not miss the effects of this enduring story of Pentecost on countless generations of Christian writers, visionaries, and reformers since early Christian times, it became clear to me that it was necessary to take the story at face value and suspend our urge to concretize its historicity or merely allegorize its possible meanings. With this attitude in mind, we can begin to fathom the profound and creative impact of this fiery and mysterious *story of Pentecost* on Christian tradition and the religious imagination throughout the past two millennia, a huge span of recorded Christian memory out of which the present volume surveys a hefty but manageable five centuries.

While the first Pentecost cannot be separated from its location in the multi-cultural milieu of the Hellenistic-Roman world, or from its Jewish cultural context as the festival of Shavuot, for centuries thereafter Christian theology and liturgical practice upheld and amplified the legacy of that engendering moment as fixed-in-time yet ever open to new possibilities. The historical record reveals that in the Middle Ages authors such as Wolfram von Eschenbach (ca. 1200), and visionaries like Joachim of Fiore (ca. 1145-1200), whose idea of a *"plena spiritus libertas"* foretold the transformation of the cosmos and of the Church in the coming "Age of the Holy Spirit," looked back to that pneumatic moment in Acts 2 for inspiration in their own endeavors. On Saturday May 19, 1347 the Italian revolutionary Cola di Rienzo sat through an estimated twenty to thirty masses dedicated to the Holy Spirit in the Church of Sant'Angelo in Rome. The next morning, Pentecost Sunday, Cola roused the populace and nobility into revolting against the French Papacy and the Holy Roman Empire as he and his followers declared a new era of justice and peace, and liberty for all Italians based upon the gifts of the Holy Spirit. Although Cola's successes and failures over the next eight years proved the world was not yet ready for his republican ideals, Cola's Pentecostal dream of liberation, justice and equality for all lived on in Italian history and bore fruit in modern times.

Despite Lutheran and Calvinist cautions against "enthusiast" factions, a similar yearning for the unfinished dimensions of the biblical event of Pentecost holds true for Reformation period authors, and even more so in pneumatological works by leading radical reformers like Thomas Müntzer's "Prague Manifesto" (ca. 1521) and Michael Servetus' *Christianismi Restitutio* (ca. 1553). The Roman Catholic Reformation of the 1500s and early 1600s was no exception to these pneumatological sensibilities. While recovering in a hospital bed, on Tuesday May 20th of Pentecost week 1521, after a cannon ball nearly ripped his legs off in battle against an invading French army, the Catholic reformer Ignatius of Loyola received a vision of the person and piety of Jesus Christ that became the basis for his founding of the Jesuit Order. Among the early-modern reformist works associated with the "Rosicrucian Renaissance" such as Johann Valentin Andreae's *Christianopolis* (1619) and Francis Bacon's *The New Atlantis* (1627),[4] we find a proto-scientific fascination with the Holy Spirit and "the Laws of Nature" that culminated in Robert Boyle's studies of "those invisible" yet "ponderable fire particles." Bacon even called for a "Second Pentecost" whereby the gifts of science and a deeper understanding of Nature's laws would help reform education and society. And John Wesley's famous "Aldersgate experience" occurred three days after Pentecost Sunday on Wednesday May 24th, 1738.

Indeed, in almost every period of Christian history we find similarly rich yet mysterious manifestations of this highly imaginative Pentecostal visionary legacy. The pneumatological movements, visionary texts, and mystical figures examined in this study labored under the Holy Spirit's inspiration, and in some instances under penalty of execution, with the steadfast conviction they were protecting the Church against misguided ecclesiastical and political leaders. As recently as 1970, novelist, and alleged U.S. naval cryptographer, Thomas Pynchon's *The Crying of Lot 49* (1966) set the standard for the postmodern novel by creating a disjointed narrative which undermined interpretive efforts on almost every page while critiquing modernist, technological assumptions about language and meaning using the linguistic mysteries of Pentecost as the story's underlying structure. These tantalizing yet little known traces of Pentecost across the pages of Western literary, theological, and intellectual history beckon us to revisit the question posed in the upper room on that fateful day by the first century Jewish author of Acts: *"What does this mean?"*

In his comprehensive introduction to the study of contemporary pneumatology, Veli-Matti Kärkkäinen describes the recent surge of academic interest in the Holy Spirit as a "pneumatological renaissance concerning the doctrine and spirituality of the Holy Spirit" generating "much interest and even enthusiasm from all theological corners."[5] However, not all corners of the theologically interested profession and its cognate disciplines share his optimism. Within the fields of church history, European intellectual history, and medieval religious history comprehensive academic studies of pneumatology from a postmodernist perspective have yet to be written.[6] Kärkkäinen argues that for theologians and philosophers:

> Approaching the topic of the Spirit and pneumatology from the perspective of experience is the only way to do justice to the 'object' of our study. It is one of the rules of scientific inquiry that the methodology has to fit the object, not vice versa.[7]

But, for historians, "experience" is neither a viable "object" of inquiry, nor a theoretical "construct" that one can extract or retrieve from an "ancient document" or from a "medieval text." Experience is simply not a datum of historical evidence for the historian. Perhaps the legacy of logical positivism that influenced the historical profession from the early 1900s through the 1970s remains operant in the theoretical assumptions shared by contemporary historians. And perhaps the old positivist prejudice against the spiritual subtleties of pneumatology as the domain of "unverifiable subjectivities" still hampers our methodological and contextual choices. Medieval or Early Modern conceptions of Pentecost and the Holy Spirit, however, are far from merely unverifiable, static visions posited by foolish men and women who believed their spiritual experiences stood as testimony of the Spirit's unifying and universalizing possibilities. As Jürgen Moltmann reminds us: "Whatever we may say in general about ourselves and other people in the light of eternity, the Spirit of life is present only as the Spirit of this or that particular life."[8] And Kärkkäinen vividly asserts: "talk about the Spirit must always be contextual and therefore culture specific."[9] Although the experiential component of texts describing revelatory mystical states often remains veiled in the language of feeling and ecstasy, the historical and cultural inflection of the *story of Pentecost*, overflowing with the rich possibilities exemplified among the various movements of the Holy Spirit, is quite open to academic study and investigation.

This book offers a historical survey and analysis of the ways that medieval and early-modern European Christian writers and visionaries conceptualized the meaning of the Pentecostal narrative found in the New Testament. While the primary aim of this study is the recovery and examination of the various meanings of Pentecost as envisioned by Christian thinkers during these two historical periods, the relationship of such ideas and concepts to pneumatology in their respective contexts is also discussed in this book. Pneumatological foundations form the core of numerous Christian doctrines in soteriology, ecclesiology, and eschatology. However, rather than attempting a detailed survey of topics and themes already covered in other histories of pneumatology, my approach presents a series of vignettes describing Christian conceptions of Pentecost and pneumatology from the late 1100s to about 1670 while examining related questions of theological discourse. What is it about Pentecost and the Western imagination that allows Pentecost to show up in a variety of literary and theological forms throughout Christian history? Why have so many Christian visionaries revisited the story of Pentecost as an act of *theological reconstruction* often aimed at subverting dominant ecclesiastical paradigms? What is the relationship between the miraculous pneumatic communication signified in the biblical story of Pentecost and the empowering voice and gifts of the Holy Spirit?

The genesis of the present study occurred at Drew University's Caspersen School of Graduate Studies while writing my doctoral dissertation on Wolfram von Eschenbach's Middle High German poem *Parzival.* Wolfram's famous poem is an allegorical romance about the quest for the Holy Grail whose breadth and status among the corpus of Christian literature from the High Middle Ages is often compared with Dante's *Divine Comedy.*[10] Wolfram organized his epic tale of love and adventure around an uncanny chronology spanning seven years "from a first Pentecost when Parzival is made a knight in name to a seventh Pentecost when he becomes truly a knight in spirit."[11] Although my earlier focus was on Wolfram's allegorical method and his use of Hispano-Arabic sources transmitted to the Latin West via Toledo, it was then that I began wondering about the various meanings of Pentecost among medieval Christian authors and visionaries like him. Why would a twelfth-century poet-knight in Germany select "Pentecost" as the underlying structure for such a complex allegorical saga, particularly when his treatment of chivalry and knight errantry was at odds with that of his contemporaries and with much of the heroic individualism that subsequent nineteenth century Romanticism and German nationalism ascribed to Wolfram's story? As I spent time with these questions, Hildegard of Bingen's reflections on Pentecost, written in her *Scivias* about fifty years before Wolfram's *Parzival,* came to mind. Hildegard's visions, however, signified a very different set of naturalistic concerns more in line with her notion of *viriditas* or the "greening" of the Holy Spirit than with a pneumatological subversion of the status quo. Given the preponderance of references to Pentecost throughout the enormous corpus of works known as the "Arthurian Tradition" and its sub-genre of "Grail-Quest" romances, the primary sources suggest an uncanny mixture of pre-Christian, Celtic, and Germanic traditions of Nature-worship and annual fertility cycles with Christian conceptions of Pentecost and the Holy Spirit.

The encounter between early Christianity and Europe's pre-Christian pagan tribes was accentuated by the fall of the Western Roman Empire in the late fifth century CE. This "clash of cultures" and the conversion process experienced over centuries by Celts, Franks, Saxons and Normans, Angles and Danes, Welsh and Scots, and a host of other Germanic and Scandinavian peoples left its signature in the folkloric oral traditions of the region and eventually found its way into the popular literature of the Middle Ages. The varied European stories and legends about King Arthur and the Quest for the Holy Grail became a convergent site for the syncretistic blending of pre-Christian beliefs about Nature with Christian conceptions about the Holy Spirit during the springtime holy season or "fifty-day-cycle" of Pentecost. Modern Christians, for whom Pentecost is a "feast day" or "holy day," are unfamiliar with the conception of Pentecost as a seven-week cycle from Easter Sunday to Whitsunday that both coincided with the arrival of spring across Europe and intersected with almost all pre-Christian fertility festivals in May and June. In the context of introducing the Celts and other native European peoples into a twelve month solar calendar aimed at replacing their thirteen month lunar calendars associated with Druidic sacred groves and Nature's gifts of "greening" and regeneration, medieval Christian leaders faced the question of allowing for a syncretism of time-reckoning practices and sacred calendars celebrated by almost all pre-Christian peoples in their various May and June feast days. This constellation of topics and themes is the subject of Chapter Two. Thus, for saints like Hildegard of Bingen or chivalric bards like Wolfram von Eschenbach and Thomas Malory, ancestral beliefs about nature and agrarian practices coincided rather harmoniously with the meditative dimensions of the seven-times-seven days of the Pentecost cycle. By 1200 this amplification of the *imitatio Christi* was as rooted in Nature's act of regeneration following winter's starkness as in Jesus' promise of going to the Father and sending forth the Holy Spirit as the "Comforter" and "Intercessor" between heaven and earth.

Hence pneumatological sensibilities blending medieval agrarian cycles with pre-Christian fertility traditions, paralleled in the Church's liturgical calendar, can be juxtaposed with Joachim of Fiore's dramatic Pentecost Sunday visions at the Abbey of Casamari (ca. 1183 or 1184), and the turbulent thirteenth century ecclesiastical reactions to his prophesied "Age of the Holy Spirit." The fate of the so-called "Franciscan Spirituals" who, following Joachim's lead, called passionately for church reform in the mid-1200s and 1300s, only to be silenced by imprisonment, torture, or execution at the hands of their inquisitors, also come into focus. As I delved deeper into the intellectual and cultural history of this period, the suppression of pneumatological movements simultaneously alongside the growth of movements promulgating naturalistic pneumatological concerns across Medieval and Early Modern Europe appeared intriguingly complex. This complexity between prophetic utterances and a somewhat recalcitrant religious leadership resonated with postmodernist readings of the relation between language and identity, and between alterity and power. But on the subject of "spiritual power" or "pneumatology in historical context," the general academic discourse among intellectual and cultural historians in the late 1990s seemed bereft of theoretical constructs for *recovering* these stories of Pentecost.

It was about this time that I read Peter Brown's *Authority and The Sacred*[12] in which this distinguished scholar of early Christianity revisited his highly influential article on "The Rise and Function of The Holy Man" published twenty-five years earlier.[13] In his own words: "I am far less certain than I once was . . .as to how exactly to fit the holy man into the wider picture of the religious world of late antiquity."[14] A couple of my church history professors at the time were perturbed by Brown's reversal in this piece. But having read all of Brown's hagiographic studies, what struck me most about this frank admission was its emphasis on reassessing the role of "spiritual power" in terms of the holy man's interiority and knowledge of the invisible world. Brown reassessed these themes as significantly underestimated factors in the important social roles holy men and holy women performed in the late antique and early medieval periods as "arbiter(s) of the holy."[15] The key point for me was Peter Brown's statement:

> Filled with the Holy Spirit and more certain than were most other Christians of enjoying the support of a whole hierarchy of heavenly powers, in alliance with whom they upheld the claims of Christ, their God, holy men (unlike most of us who study them) knew spiritual power when they saw it.[16]

Indeed, "most of us who study" pre-modern holy men or holy women have little or no understanding of the affective ground over which their supernatural longings trod; longings which, in most cases, articulated an eloquent though sometimes cryptic "theology of wonder" with echoes of the pre-Christian fascination with Nature and fertility. This theological commerce with the unseen world is one, which in our limited post-Enlightenment, postmodern academic vocabulary, at best, we can only identify as "mystical theology," and one, which, at worst, we often dismiss as an "unverifiable subjectivity." Peter Brown's bold re-evaluation of the reality of "spiritual power" in the cultural history of early Christianity suggested to me that a similar oversight might be at work in the discrepancy between medieval or early modern conceptions of Pentecost and the apparent displacement of academic discourses about Pentecost and pneumatology among scholars during the past two centuries of the modern academic enterprise.[17]

It is not that histories of Christian pneumatology are unavailable, for Charles Williams' *Descent of the Dove* examined this domain in the 1930s, while Yves Congar and Stanley Burgess have published recent surveys of pneumatology spanning the periods from antiquity to modernity.[18] But the postmodernist fascination with linguistics and communication, and with "power-relations" between signified and signifier, apparently overlooked the parallels between medieval and early modern visions of Pentecost and our postmodern desire to subvert dominant paradigms in the name of liberation and empowerment. This oversight represents a "gap" or "blind-spot" in academic discourses on Christian pneumatology and especially church history, a gap obscuring long standing medieval and early modern meanings of Pentecost.

Reading and analysis of the primary sources available from each of these periods reveals that this Pentecostal legacy functioned in two complementary ways. First, Pentecost manifested as a recurring *literary or prophetic trope* in certain symbolic and canonical traditions dealing with pneumatological concerns and containing great creative and liberative importance. Secondly, it served as a *source of inspiration* or *repository of Christian tradition* for ecclesiastical reformers and visionaries across the varied times and places of Christian history.

First, as a *literary or prophetic trope,* the story of Pentecost functioned as a biblical reminder and historical marker of the sending forth of the Holy Spirit and birth of the Church on the first Pentecost. In this way, the biblical story of Pentecost served as a convergent site for a myriad of visions, hopes and reflections on the unfinished work of ecclesiology and soteriology in the world. This, in turn, had the effect of turning the *story* into an imaginal *repository of tradition* with endless possibilities for either reinterpreting or re-creating diverse elements of Christian tradition. In other words, a virtual storehouse for the affective, aesthetic, intellectual, or prophetic "reconstruction" of any or all of the principal elements of Christian tradition, such as canon, symbol, ritual and liturgy, or theology and ecclesiology, etc. Furthermore, as the founding moment of Christ's earthly, temporal *ecclesia* the biblical account of Pentecost served as a "sacred time" to which Christian reformers looked back whenever they believed that an ecclesiastical or prophetic *renovatio* was needed for the moral health and continued viability of the Church. In other words, the Pentecost story has been always open to new possibilities. And, as evidenced by the worldwide growth of Pentecostalism since the early 1900s, the story of Pentecost remains open today for all Christians as a pneumatically inspired inheritance of divine grace. The Spirit of Pentecost empowers some with voice, others with special gifts for leadership, while others receives visions and dream dreams about the reform and revitalization of the church and God's people.

This seems to have been part of the dynamic at work in the case of Joachim of Fiore's eschatological visions about the coming "Age of the Holy Spirit," and among the Franciscan Spirituals and Cola di Rienzo, who were influenced by the controversial Calabrian abbot's prophetic warnings that the Church of their times would soon give way to a new church and world order not witnessed since the day of the first Pentecost. Although studies of Joachim's life and works have tended to focus on the apocalyptic aspects of his visions, or on the influence of his ideas for Western European conceptions of history and millenarian movements, our discussion of the Calabrian Abbot in Chapter Three will focus on the Pentecost Sunday revelations (ca. 1183 or 1184) that sparked Joachim's major exegetical and prophetic works through which he integrated his visions and ideas concerning God's future plans for the Church and society. Chapter Three will treat Joachim of Fiore as the starting point for the pneumatological subversion that readers and adherents of his Pentecostal visions aligned with their own pneumatological convictions and prayers for a better world.

Secondly, as a *source of inspiration* for Christian reformers and visionaries, I contend that Pentecost and its images of the Holy Spirit's descent, accompanied by the linguistic miracle of those fiery tongues, served as a resource of genuine "spiritual power" for the liberation of the oppressed and for the empowerment of what Joachim of Fiore referred to as the *vir spiritualis*, a prophesied order of Christian spiritual leaders who would help usher in the new era of the *ecclesia spiritualis*, the Church of the Holy Spirit. Indeed, for those seeking to subvert dominant theological vocabularies or loosen oppressive ecclesiastical structures across medieval and reformation Europe, the affective "spiritual power" of the biblical event of Pentecost infused their imaginations and intellects with interpretive possibilities by which they could reclaim and renovate Christian tradition. Such tendencies are evident in the tone of radical reformer Thomas Müntzer's "Prague Manifesto," in ways very similar to their manifestation in Wolfram von Eschenbach's innovative and unique treatment of the Muslim "other" in his thirteenth century Grail saga, *Parzival*, as well as in Francis Bacon's bold portrayal of a Second Pentecost uniting the nations of the world through the "gifts" of the scientific enterprise depicted in his early seventeenth century utopian novella, *The New Atlantis*.

Since visions of Pentecost are almost always accompanied by references to the Holy Spirit as the Paraclete (*paraklētos*), or Intercessor and Comforter, the exposition that follows in this book includes relevant material on pneumatology relating to the historical periods or topics covered in each chapter, with specific emphasis on the relationship of ecclesiology and pneumatology. Chapter Four surveys the conceptual and affective reconstruction of this pneumatological legacy during the Protestant and Catholic Reformations of the 1500s and 1600s, and among so-called "radical reformers" like Servetus and Müntzer who personified the "subversive fire" theme in ways similar to Joachim of Fiore and the spiritual movements influenced by his *Psaltery of the Ten Strings*.

In Chapter Five we will explore the strange world of *Christian magical theology* from its medieval roots in alchemy and Hermetic philosophy to its popularity during the Italian Renaissance, which then culminated in the Scientific Revolution of the 1600s. This part of our story is perhaps the one least known today among professional scholars, Christian clergy and laity, and the general public. The first few generations of modern scientists tried to "read" and "decipher the Book of Nature" by focusing on experiments aimed at understanding and harnessing what for centuries was known among religious scholars and natural philosophers by names and terms like "*ethereal fire*," "*The Quintessence*," "*those ponderable fire particles*," or simply as the mysterious "powers of the Holy Spirit" sent forth at Pentecost. Francis Bacon's vision of a Second Pentecost already mentioned above, or the Rosicrucian designations of their movement as the "House of the Holy Spirit" are two examples of how scientific thinking and Christian spiritual tradition intersected at the dawn of modernity. While this may sound like the Promethean hubris of a mad scientist in an English novel, contemporary Christianity would do well to revisit and recover this highly fruitful and creative fascination between *Dame Nature* and *scientia* as an act of Christian revitalization aimed at integrating the mind and the heart.

Finally in Chapter Six, entitled "The Ecstasy of Communication" (a phrase I borrow from postmodern philosopher Jean Baudrillard), I offer several concluding reflections concerning the temporal, linguistic, epistemological, and theological issues raised by the figures and texts examined throughout the book's historical narrative.

Seeking a *via media* between the affective (and aesthetic) dimensions of the human encounter with the unseen realm of the Spirit, and the more well-known intellectual modes of medieval and early modern pneumatological speculation, this attempt at recovering the untold story of Pentecost relies on Delwin Brown's theory of tradition (*constructive historicism*) as a useful lens for the sort of focus necessitated by the primary sources examined herein. I will return to questions of theory and method concerning my use of Brown's theory of tradition after a brief overview of the transit from the first Pentecost to our current historical amnesia about the rich assortment of meanings and manifestations of Pentecost throughout the history of Christianity.

HARVESTING THE SPIRIT:
FROM PENTECOST TO THE ENLIGHTENMENT

Despite making a liturgical comeback in recent years, Pentecost often passes without much notice among most contemporary Christian denominations. While this is surely not the case among Pentecostal or charismatic churches, conversing with churchgoers and clergy from different denominations around the country one notices a profound lack of knowledge about the type of traditional and historic practices formerly associated with the Feast of Pentecost.[19] Some churches today do not even follow the traditional liturgical calendar while other churches miss Pentecost altogether since their pastors and congregation begin a summer recess in late May or early June, which usually does not end until after Labor Day in September. There was a time in the not too distant past, however, when Pentecost served along with Easter as two of the most important primary feast days commemorated in the liturgical calendar. For ancient Hellenized Christians, *Pentekosté* literally meant "the fiftieth day." Roman and Byzantine Christians for centuries regarded Pentecost as the culmination of the entire Easter season with Christ's redemptive labors reaching their zenith, nine days after commemorating and celebrating the Ascension, in the sending of the Holy Spirit at Pentecost.

In Jewish tradition Pentecost was known as Shavuot or "the festival of weeks" because it fell on the fiftieth day at the end of seven times seven weeks after the Sabbath of Passover.[20] Christian commemorations of the fifty-day cycle leading up to the outpouring of the Holy Spirit and birth of the Church at the first Pentecost date back to the second century CE, and there is evidence that by the early fourth century CE the Council of Elvira in Spain opposed a proposal to change the Easter-to-Pentecost celebration of thanksgiving from a fifty-day (*Quinquagesima*) cycle to a forty-day (*Quadragesima*) cycle. The 43rd Canon of the Council of Elvira explicitly threatened charges of heresy if the fifty-day cycle was not upheld and celebrated according to the traditional manner.[21] In Jewish tradition Shavuot was originally an agricultural festival associated with the barley and wheat harvest, but by the end of the second century CE the festival became associated with the giving of the Torah and the Decalogue to Moses on Mount Sinai.[22] Hence, the words in the Jewish liturgy marking this special day: "*zeman mattan toratenu*," which translates as "the time of the giving of our Torah." In medieval Judaism Shavuot marked the time of year when children who were about five years old began their formal instruction in the Hebrew alphabet. An interesting feature of the celebrations set aside for children at this time of year was the preparation of cakes and treats covered with honey and inscribed with verses from the Torah. Another noteworthy feature of Shavuot concerns the Jewish tradition of counting the days of the Omer as both individuals and the community prepare for the commemoration of the sending forth of the Law at Sinai and for communal reflection on the meaning of this Providential act for the whole tenor of salvation history.[23]

In the Medieval Latin Church, the Feast of Pentecost ranked after Easter as the second most important feast day on the liturgical calendar and tended to be treated as a separate feast day. The Medieval Latin Church also tended "to make this day an independent entity and thus a more or less isolated feast day of the sending of the Holy Spirit."[24] Hellenistic-Roman customs concerning calendar cycles and time reckoning considered the day after a sacred or transforming "event" as the first day of that new cycle or period. This may account for the inclination of the late ancient and medieval Latin Church to conceptualize Pentecost in the Roman liturgy as an "act" of the Holy Spirit, which by giving birth to the Christian Church necessitated a separate feast day from the Easter cycle. This leads to notions of a "Whitsuntide" marking the seven-times-seven-days from Easter Sunday to Pentecost Sunday (Whitsunday) and hence the notion of a Pentecost cycle that I contend had the meditative and sacramental effects on both clergy and laity suggested by the figures and movements discussed throughout this book.

Indeed, even the "red" vestments worn by clergy on Pentecost, in contrast with the "white" vestments of the Easter cycle, were understood by Innocent III in the early 1200s as signifying the "tongues of fire" from the biblical event recorded in Acts 2, and further attests to the practice of a separate festal day and culmination of a cycle of days in the liturgical calendar. The different colors selected for the vestments "may be regarded as a holdover from the time when the feast was treated as an isolated entity."[25] The contemporary Roman Catholic and Episcopal denominations, in order to treat the whole cycle of the paschal mystery as a single entity, have revised the Medieval Latin Church's practice of treating the commemoration of Pentecost as a separate feast day.[26]

One of the most interesting features of Medieval and Early Modern conceptions of Pentecost, yet today rarely known or remembered, was the association of the seven-times-seven days of the Pentecostal season and festival with the completed arrival of spring and the annual renewal of Nature's warmer agricultural cycles of the spring and summer months. Given their location in the northern latitudes, and the devastating effects of the so-called "Little Ice Age" of the Northern Hemisphere that lasted for centuries, most medieval and early modern Christians lived through many Easter Sundays on which snow still covered the ground and forest vegetation whether Easter fell in late March or sometime in April. This gives us a much clearer picture of why Pentecost, which usually took place in May or early June, became associated from the 1100s through the early 1700s more with the annual rebirth of spring than Easter Sunday. In addition, Celtic folk traditions and "old-time-religion" have a longevity and persistence all their own as pre-Christian Europe's ancient agricultural beliefs and practices combined over time with the Feast of Pentecost in the Christian liturgical calendar for the months of May and June.

During the Reformation period, the legacy of Pentecost and the role of the Holy Spirit in theological discourse served to inspire both Martin Luther and John Calvin to re-construct Christian pneumatological understandings in the areas of canon, soteriology, and ecclesiology in ways that looked backward to a "tradition" derailed by corrupt politics and hierarchical oppression, while looking forward to a renewed era of pneumatological empowerment.[27] This early Reformation outlook remains true despite the later Lutheran and Calvinist suspicion and criticism of "Enthusiast" (*Schwärmer*) factions and libertine "mystical" tendencies. Voicing their discontent with the trajectories of the mainline reformer's vision for the church, and feeling that the Lutheran and Calvinist reforms had not gone far enough, the Radical Reformation revisited the story of Pentecost and opened yet another *theological reconstruction* just a few years later. In the hands of leaders like Thomas Müntzer or Michael Servetus, and in movements such as the Anabaptists and the German Pietists, this second wave of reformers relied upon the Pentecostal legacy as both prophetic trope and repository of Christian tradition amidst their respective cultural and historical locations, and unleashed a fiery *renovatio* in the 1500s and early 1600s.

The final stages of these radical Pentecostal visions may be seen in the pneumatological innovations of early modern figures like Francis Bacon, or J. V. Andrea and the Rosicrucians, whose investigations of the mysteriously elusive *pneuma* and *Spiritus* leads to the empiricism of Isaac Newton and Robert Boyle when the late medieval and early-modern spiritual sensibility yielded to modern rationalism in the late 1600s. Unfortunately, after the English Revolution and the Thirty Years War, a fissure developed between ontological and pneumatological understandings of the cosmos, between Church and self, and between religion and society. Widespread mistrust of "enthusiast" factions and the emotive instability of radical pneumatological movements during the epistemological and political revolutions of the seventeenth, eighteenth, and nineteenth centuries also contributed to the enthronement of Reason above Spirit. This fissure, although refreshing and liberating at first, in time revealed a deep rupture between religious practices and Euro-Western thought, which I contend accounts for a large part of the *pneumatological deficit* observed by twentieth century theologians and philosophers such as Hendrikus Berkhof, Moltmann and Kärkkäinen, Kilian McDonnell, Alister McGrath, and others.

WESTERN CHRISTIANITY'S PNEUMATOLOGICAL DEFICIT

Kärkkäinen and McGrath's identification of a "pneumatological deficit"[28] in Western Christianity is not just the result of theological or institutional differences rooted in the medieval split between the Latin Church of Western Europe and the Greek Church of the East. Assessing this "pneumatological deficit" in modern theological discourse requires an overview of certain anti-ecclesiastical trajectories in modern intellectual life and of the vocabularies of emancipation from religious superstition fostered by Enlightenment modernism and secularism. In my opening comments above, I suggested that the academic study of Pentecost was eclipsed by the philosophical and methodological assumptions of Enlightenment modernism, and by subsequent nineteenth and early twentieth century shifts to the model of logical positivism among the humanities and social sciences, of which the history of Christianity is a related field. While a comprehensive survey of the broader implications of these issues is beyond the scope of this book, before proceeding further, I offer this brief analysis of how the various meanings of Pentecost and pneumatology examined herein may have arrived at their present state of scholarly and theological neglect.

Questions about historical representation, as well as questions about structures of power and exclusion, abound among the silences, omissions, lost voices, and discursive gaps of the story of Christianity. However, I too, am aware that my own narratological effort to re-cover some of the traditional meanings and conceptions of Pentecost represents yet another reconstruction of a "past" whose essential details we can only know approximately. French historian Fernand Braudel often reminded his students: "The past is about the present." The historical materials examined herein were not waiting in the archives to be unearthed and reconstructed like archaeological artifacts, but were well known to visionaries and holy persons living in the medieval and early modern contexts revisited in this book. Indeed, the "blind-spot" mentioned in my opening comments above, is not located in the temporal field of past eras, but in the discourses and unexamined assumptions by which modern and postmodern scholarship identified that which was worthy or unworthy of academic study.

Ecclesiastical responses to the rise of science in the 1600s, coupled with English, French, and German cultural attitudes towards the Catholic Reformation and the Spanish Inquisition, had profound effects on how "religious tradition" came to be both interpreted and maligned in subsequent periods. Although a detailed survey of engravings included in Reformation period Bibles printed between 1525 and 1600 reveals that all contained illustrations of the sending of the Holy Spirit on Pentecost, many European intellectuals after 1650 increasingly moved away from traditions and symbols that bore the aroma of Roman Catholicism, radical prophesy and enthusiasm, and pneumatological traditions perceived as perpetuating an outmoded "medievalism." When the Puritans seized control of England in 1640, they banned all the May and June celebrations that connected Pentecost with the lingering traditions and revelry of pre-Christian, lunar and solar fertility rites. For example, in 1644 the Puritans ordered that all May-poles in England be destroyed, and by the time of the Stuart Restoration of Charles II in 1660 an entire generation of people across Britain had been raised without the syncretistic experience of celebrating Pentecost alongside the revelry of "May-pole dances" and the sacred Hawthorne tree rituals that once took place in the "merrie, merrie month of May" and early June. When local merchants and townspeople tried to resurrect their ancestral festivals and Pentecost celebrations in the late 1660s, few remembered the old traditions of honoring *Dame Nature* alongside the presence of God's Holy Spirit in the natural world. After more than two decades of religious warfare, severe winters, cooler than normal springs, and occasional outbreaks of deadly plague, even fewer people responded with public reverence and support for these vestiges of the pre-Christian past. The strict moral and scriptural legalism of the Puritans penetrated deeper into the conscience of the populace than anyone ever imagined, and, as the Restoration era unfolded into the Age of Reason, England's new, "modern" rational attitude about Nature became its steadfast and secure response to the spiritual fancies and radicalism of recent memory.

Furthermore, suspension of such ancient rituals and customs for more than two decades was a very long time in an era when people were quite lucky to reach forty-five years of age. After the failure of the Puritan Revolution there was also a backlash against "Enthusiast Dissenters" claiming any sort of special insight or revolutionary zeal from the Holy Spirit. By 1663 even the "Royal Society of London for Improving Natural Knowledge," whose Baconian beginnings as the "Invisible College" twenty years earlier included a number of scholars quite sympathetic to the rational examination of esoteric mysteries, was discouraging its fellows from certain speculations on the border between religion and science. By the time Isaac Newton served as President of the Royal Society in 1710, he was very careful to keep his alchemical studies and experiments in the privacy of his home and cellar. John Locke's *Essay Concerning Human Understanding* (1689) was sharply critical of those for whom revelations of the Holy Spirit derived from "individual experience" or "prophetic enthusiasm." He also stressed the need to downgrade such fanciful and dangerous claims in favor of a more rationally oriented temperament in essays like *The Reasonableness of Christianity* (1695).

The secularization of knowledge in the eighteenth, nineteenth, and twentieth centuries had intense and far-reaching effects upon how Western civilization would treat religious and theological subjects, both within and beyond its Eurocentric sphere of activity. Most scholars working in the fields of philosophy, theology, or intellectual history would argue that the implications of Rene Descartes' epistemological and metaphysical ideas led to the whole tenor of modern, post-Cartesian thought as emancipation from the truth claims of religious tradition. When Descartes "resolved to strip himself of 'all opinions and beliefs formerly received' and to create truth claims on his own, much as a spider spins a web from its own substance," he opened a chasm with Christianity that widened considerably after his death in 1650.[29] However, despite objections from colleagues in related fields, I am not sure that we have been fair in our willingness to place so much of this responsibility at Descartes' doorstep. It is worth noting that when this Jesuit-trained French sage breathed his last *cogito*, the emergence of the Enlightenment as a self-conscious, clearly defined movement was still a hundred years in the future.

As a philosophical movement, the European Enlightenment became conscious of itself around 1752 when Denis Diderot and Jean d'Alembert issued the first volumes of the *Encyclopédie*. Voltaire began work on his *Philosophic Dic-*

tionary shortly thereafter. Diderot's deep suspicion of ecclesiasticism and authoritarian hierarchy maintained: "Men will never be free till the last king is strangled with the entrails of the last priest,"[30] not exactly the kind of sentiment that fostered dialogues of mutual edification between revolutionary secular leaders and conservative religious leaders. Then, around 1754, Voltaire unleashed his scathing attack by proclaiming the rallying cry of the Enlightenment's anticlericalism: "*Ecrasez l'infame!*" "Crush the infamy," of ignorance, superstition, and ecclesiasticism. But the emergent French *philosophes* along with the movers and shakers of the German *Aufklärung* already stood atop a century of scientific and rational discourse upon which to build an even stronger case against medieval, ecclesiastical superstition and the "unverifiable subjectivity" of Christian pneumatology.

On the other hand, the Enlightenment's closely related opposing movement, Romanticism, sought to balance the scales by emphasizing the affective and aesthetic dimensions of human existence against the enthronement of Reason, while further expanding the critique of ecclesiastical and political authority. In the early 1800s, Friedrich Schleiermacher and Immanuel Kant became the principal exponents of the epistemological implications of this counter-Enlightenment movement. While other Romantic strains influenced poetry and literature, as well as the visual arts and music, in radically imaginative ways, the humanities veered off in a quixotic quest for the lost innocence of the world in the Greco-Roman revival known as Neoclassicism. It may seem that Romanticism, and its contemporaneous Christian revivalist movements of the 1700s and 1800s, offered a corrective to the enthronement of reason and objective science by the Enlightenment, but one cannot deny that some of the counter measures served to further radicalize the estrangement of Western culture from the themes and genres in which Romanticism sought expression, genres among which the recovery of the Spirit and preservation of the aesthetic imagination were priorities.

We should bear in mind that, even in the midst of this Enlightenment project and the emergent sensibilities of Romantic modernism, there were voices such as William Blake and John Wesley who, in their own divergent ways, argued for the metaphysical reality and epistemological validity of the Spirit. Wesley's famous Aldersgate Street experience occurred at a London prayer meeting three days after Pentecost Sunday on May 24, 1738, while John Fletcher's theology of Pentecost set the stage for much of the spiritual tone of early Methodism.[31] And, at a little known barn meeting held on Pentecost in 1767 near Baltimore, Maryland the German Reformed pastor Philip William Otterbein and the Mennonite preacher Martin Boehm declared themselves "*Wir sind Brüder*" (We are brethren) and founded the Church of the United Brethren in Christ.[32] Even the Calabrian Abbot, Joachim of Fiore, whose Pentecostal visions are so important to the periods and themes examined in this book, continued to influence pneumatological thinkers and movements in the modern era.[33] The demise of the Christian liturgical calendar as a meditative and practical guide to the hours and days, weeks and months of the year was accompanied by the rise of nationalist ideologies of ethno-genesis and historiogenesis that constructed glorious racial and imperial origins among the modern nation-states. Even those nations recognized as predominantly Roman Catholic moved away from their ancient festivals and holidays rooted in the liturgical calendar, which affected the way these Christian communities commemorated time and recalled the great feast days of the medieval religious calendar. Although during the eighteenth and nineteenth centuries, Europe witnessed the interplay of these and many more intellectual movements for which the materialist and nationalistic discourses of the times necessitated an innovative reaffirmation of Christian pneumatological traditions, pneumatology underwent a period of consistent decline and increasing academic neglect and was often referred to as the "Cinderella of Theology."[34]

Ironically, in the midst of the positivist and materialist challenge, pneumatological sensibilities echoing Pentecost traditions and legacies discussed in this book resurfaced on the European intellectual scene at the dawn of the twentieth century. One cannot deny that society and the individual benefited greatly from the scientific optimism and discoveries stimulated by the modernist enterprise of the 1800s and early 1900s. But, perhaps it was the alleged perfectibility of human nature and the unfulfilled promises of unlimited industrial and technological progress, which led some European intellectuals to their initial doubts and then to an eventual revolt against positivism in the 1890s.[35] For example, in 1907 French philosopher Henri Bergson published a speculative treatise expanding his 1889 *Essay on the Immediate Data of Consciousness* into a mystical philosophy, entitled *Creative Evolution*, while the sociologist Emile Durkheim cautioned colleagues in the new "human sciences" against threats to empirical progress from such a "renascent mysticism."[36] In the early 1900s, around the same time Sigmund Freud was preoccupied with reigning in his protégé Carl Jung from too much talk about psyche and Spirit, the founder of anthroposophy, Rudolf Steiner, was hard at work promoting the emergence of a creative and egalitarian Christian spirituality, which he called "World Pentecost."[37] Although Bergson and Jung were specifically interested in the empirical "recovery of the unconscious,"[38] Steiner's pneumatic reconstructions of reality relied on individuals calling forth and activating the temporal intervention of the Holy Spirit and locate him along a continuum of reform minded visionaries stretching back to the medieval and early modern Christian visionaries discussed in the following chapters.

Collectively, however, the post-Enlightenment and post-Romantic epistemological debates fostered a mindset that sought verifiable solutions to concrete human problems amidst an academic community eschewing all sorts of traditional elements from the immediate "past" epoch of the Christian Middle Ages. In the "brave new world" of modern universities and seminaries, the demise of pneumatology as a significant sub-field of theological education during the late-1800s and early 1900s reflected this paradigmatic shift toward the integration of positivist principles into the frameworks by which the modern humanities and social sciences were being crafted, a shift that over time led to both academic and popular amnesia about the creative role Pentecost and the Holy Spirit had played throughout the history of Christianity.

In the aftermath of the historical profession's infatuation with logical positivism, and subsequent disdain for so-called "unverifiable subjectivities," to which pneumatological concerns and claims are of necessity surely predisposed, how do we recover the historicity of pneumatological traditions like those associated with Pentecost in ways acceptable and useful for postmodern historical, literary, and theological scholarship? Which methodological approaches should one apply to *recover* the *story* of how Christians imagined and reinvented Pentecost through the centuries? The basic repertoire of methodologies available to the twenty-first century historian is not much different from those available to the first generation of historians in the 1850s. We still expect each other to conduct primary source research with full understanding of the languages of our respective texts or manuscripts. Despite a continued commitment to objectivity, tempered by a sobering and liberating postmodernism, we also acknowledge our participation as creators of historical narratives. The "past" is not waiting there as a datum of human experience, nor as an artifact awaiting discovery. The "past" is constructed and interpreted from the vantage point of the historian's temporal, cultural, and affective "present." Nonetheless, we must inquire about those unexamined assumptions by which so many voices and topics were left out of the writing of the history of Christianity, as well as the history of religions. Every item left out of the picture of the past, every voice left out of the story, eventually finds its way back to historical consciousness as the present unfolds into the "*not-yet*" of the future.

At the dawn of the twenty-first century, historians, as always, would like very much to write works of lasting value. Having emerged from the fount of nineteenth century German historicism in the works of Ranke, Herder, Burckhardt, Harnack and Droysen, the historical profession has been shaken as much by the twilight of Enlightenment modernism as by the postmodernist linguistic and theoretical challenge. While completing my doctoral studies and considering the historical questions about pneumatology examined in this book, one of my graduate professors jokingly chided me: "I wonder about you sometimes. You're interested in that religious stuff. I thought we outgrew all of that stuff in the Nineteenth Century." Well, the post-September 11th public appetite for religious issues and theological bestsellers renders its own verdict on that colleague's positivist quibble. However, we must guard against relapsing into such intellectual prejudices, for by excluding certain themes or topics from academic inquiry, postmodern church history runs the risk of continuing the myopic tendencies of modernism in such a way that its research agenda becomes a mere extension of the exclusionary modernist project.

In the interest of full disclosure, I thought it best to bring these issues to the table in this introduction rather than waiting until the concluding chapter. If recovering the rich and varied conceptions of Pentecost and the Holy Spirit from the 1100s to about 1670 is the primary historiographic task of the present volume, then the task of offering a useful interpretation on the subject's applicability for church history studies, and theological education in general, might be enhanced if the larger issues and constituencies affected in the mix are named at the outset.

In *Pragmatic Historicism: A Theology for the 21ˢᵗ-Century*, theologian Sheila Davaney offers a convincing critique of the empowering values Enlightenment modernism bequeathed us while arguing against those Enlightenment values which obscured certain aspects of the broader range of human existence and calls for a widening of the "field of theological inquiry and debate."[39] She identifies an increasing number of philosophers and theologians who are working on the implications and meaning of the historicity of human life. Davaney identifies this emergent *theological historicism* as *pragmatic historicism*. Historians have always labored under the conviction that "past" events both inform and influence social structures and cultural tendencies in the "present." For the intellectual historian or cultural historian of the early twenty-first century it is no longer possible, nor wise, to teach and write as if the events of the "present" have no impact upon our construction of the "past" or on our choice of research topics. Furthermore, the "cognitive crisis" to which Davaney alludes in her book has had deleterious effects on all historians, but none more so than those working in the history of Christianity or in the history of religions. The truth claims of religion as discussed above were one of the principal targets of the modernist project. Davaney encourages scholars to take the liberating insights of the past and move forward in ways that incorporate the demands of the present. She boldly insists:

> We must ask our questions not only at the center of traditions but at their margins, not only in terms of one tradition but also in terms of other traditions, not only for practitioners but also for all, believers or not, who experience its impact daily.[40]

It might be objected, that such a critical, historicist perspective will lead to relativism or to the denigration of perspectives with ontological and essentialist commitments about the Holy Spirit. But even most scholars and believers with charismatic or Pentecostal commitments would agree with Moltmann and Kärkkäinen that, despite its mysterious provenance from the realm of the unseen, the "Spirit of Life" manifests and is experienced within the temporal field of cultural and individual activity in specific times and locations.[41]

The "social logic" through which the language of Christian conceptions of Pentecost served the socio-cultural realities of their contexts and locations is worth pondering further, for here was a "social logic" rooted in a particular view of tradition as fluid and dynamic.[42] Because of my training in the cultural roots, continuities and dislocations that involved the transit from the medieval world to the early modern era, I found myself wondering about the interplay between religious tradition and historical change. The "traditioned" character of religious culture with its deep awareness of sacred-time and sacred-space, as well as of canon and ritual, was the subject of theologian Delwin Brown's work on *"constructive historicism."* And, it was actually Brown's particular version of *theological historicism,* which first caught my attention when pondering the possible meanings of the various medieval and early modern manifestations of Pentecost. To that subject, we now turn.

CONSTRUCTIVE HISTORICISM & THE PENTECOSTAL LEGACY

Why does the story of Pentecost and the outpouring of the Holy Spirit appear in such varied ways across the different times and places of Christian history? This persistent fascination with Pentecost signifies something vitally important, yet elusive, about language and the spiritual power of a religious tradition to re-create itself from the resources of the past. What exactly do these stories and visions of Pentecost reveal about communication and literary interpretation, about human temporality and historical memory, and about the creativity inherent in religious traditions? In *Boundaries of Our Habitations: Tradition and Theological Construction* (1994), Delwin Brown offered an analysis of culture and historicity, canon and ritual, and imagination and innovation that significantly parallels the creative manifestations of the Pentecostal and pneumatological legacies, which are the focus of this book's medieval and early modern sources.[43]

The Hebrew author of Ecclesiastes understood something crucial about the nature of religious tradition and culture when writing: "What has been is what will be, and what has been done is what will be done; and there is nothing new under the sun." (1:9). Given modernity's and postmodernism's fascination with novelty and exotic forms of expression, such thinking about tradition and the legacy of the "past" upon the "present" have not been very popular among most academic experts or educated laypersons of recent times. Our society delights in a consumer-oriented popular culture of novelty, while academics, like me, build our careers upon the novelties of the academic marketplace and of the professional guilds to which we subscribe. This is not such a bad thing. After all, in just a few centuries humanity has gained great personal and social benefits from advancements in the natural sciences and from the new inventions generated by our consumer economy. But religious traditions are not the closed, static systems most academic experts and laypersons, and religious skeptics believe them to be. Spiritual power is not about Christian exclusivity or upholding the status quo of ecclesial elites. And, as Brown points out, "reconstruction" is neither reduplication, nor a mere imitation of conservative, idealized, symbolic, and canonical systems.[44] Traditions and canons can be simultaneously very progressive and very dynamic as the medieval and early modern texts in this study will show.

The cultural and theological innovations of the Italian Renaissance and of the Protestant and Catholic Reformations were another instance of the creativity that is possible from the seminal roots and cultural resources of a tradition. It is in this way that Delwin Brown's *constructive historicism* serves as a theoretical lens by which to read and interpret the pneumatological movements and texts examined in this historical study; movements and texts, writers and visionaries spanning the period from the 1100s through the late 1600s whose leaders and authors labored in some instances under penalty of execution with the steadfast conviction that they were revitalizing the Holy Spirit and protecting the Church against misguided ecclesiastical and socio-political hierarchies in their day. An act of subversion, which in their displeasure with the status quo, they offered up to Christ, their God, and to their contemporaries as a creative reconstruction of their community's canonical and theological symbols.

As Brown discusses in *Boundaries of Our Habitations*, the process of recovery and innovation for any religious tradition rests upon affective and intellectual tinkering with its historical accretions:

> The viability of a tradition is the vastness of its collected resources, unified enough to sustain needed continuity and diverse enough to create something new for new times. The power of a tradition is the worth of its space, the productivity of its complementary and competing voices, as it progresses through the novelties of history.[45]

This should in no way be confused with a narrow conservatism, nor in the case of the present study with Christological exclusivity based on the truth claims of Christian pneumatology. Brown eloquently states:

> To affirm the positive, constitutive role of the past for the creation of a viable future does not in the least imply the use of the past that is uncritical, on the one hand, or simply critical, on the other. Accordingly we should say that ours is a *constructive historicism.* Its principal claim is that the past creatively appropriated, imaginatively reconstructed, is the material out of which the future is effectively made.[46] (Emphasis added)

It might be objected that applying such historicist sensibilities to the unseen, metaphysical elements of a biblical event like Pentecost threatens its canonical and ecclesiastical viability. But, conceptions of Pentecost and pneumatology are undeniably also constructions arising out of particular historic and geographical locations, constructs from a "past" holding numerous interpretive and visionary possibilities that one must ponder in order to recover the rich and varied meanings ascribed to Pentecost through the centuries.

Where I find the greatest utility for Brown's constructive historicism is in the recognition that far from any sort of universalizing closure, the divergent narratives and creative visions of Pentecost examined in the following chapters suggest a dynamic openness within the biblical text as well as among Christian writers, reformers, and visionaries across time and place. As Brown contends: "The dynamism of a tradition is its contestability and therefore its perpetual contest."[47] In the specific case of Christian conceptions of Pentecost, a good portion of that "perpetual contest" has been waged in the pages of Western literary, philosophical, and religious history. Hence the inclusion of literary texts deploying Pentecostal or pneumatological tropes such as Wolfram von Eschenbach's medieval Grail saga *Parzival* examined in Chapter Two, and Francis Bacon's *New Atlantis*, alongside Johann Valentin Andrea's *Christianopolis* discussed in Chapter Five. The Bacon and Andrea material is particularly intriguing since both these men have been linked with the so-called "Rosicrucian Renaissance" of the seventeenth century, a quasi-mystical reformist movement with historical ties to Christian alchemy and Hermeticism. This material presented a bit of challenge as each figure produced both conceptual and literary texts calling for a number of pedagogical and epistemological reforms in the early 1600s. Rosicrucianism developed its own proto-scientific discourse signifying the reality of the Holy Spirit throughout the universe, a discourse that culminated after more than a century of empirical observation and experimentation in the re-signification of their beloved yet elusive "ethereal fire" as "electromagnetism."

Delwin Brown describes the role of tradition throughout Christian history in a tripartite expression as "an advocate, as well as a gift and task:"[48]

> The creativity of a tradition is the tensive character of the life lived within, and sometimes against, its boundaries. The viability of a tradition is the vastness of its collected resources, unified enough to sustain needed continuity and diverse enough to create something new for new times. The power of a tradition is the worth of its space, the productivity of its complementary and competing voices, as it progresses through the novelties of history. The dynamism of a tradition is its contestability and therefore its perpetual contest.[49]

The empowering voice and presence of the Holy Spirit in the lives of the Christians discussed in the following chapters parallels Brown's concept of *tradition* and his dynamic understanding of *theological construction* with remarkable accuracy and significance, even as we extend our survey of these writers and movements across European Christendom from the twelfth through the late seventeenth centuries. Brown concludes:

> The relevance of a tradition is its contemporaneity, what it brings to and receives from the discourse of truth in every age. But the life of a tradition, its vitality as a real way of being in the world, is the assumption of its own resources as one's own. Tradition is canon lived, —the negotiation of corporate and personal identities with/in canonical space.[50]

In summary, the re-telling and re-creation of the story of Pentecost throughout Christian history cannot be divorced from its historical and cultural contexts, a critical stance insightfully enhanced by applying the theory of tradition articulated by Delwin Brown as *constructive historicism*. This critical stance in no way ignores or rejects the pneumatic dimensions of the Pentecostal inheritance. On the contrary, Brown's theory of tradition serves as an appropriate lens offering us a particular focus on the historical issues in this study, the interpretation of text and artifact, and the writing of a history of Pentecost in the Medieval and Early Modern eras. Given the "traditioned" yet open character of Pentecost throughout Christian history, Brown's understanding of the contested and creative aspects of "tradition" offers an equally useful and promising perspective for assessing the various ways Pentecost shows up across the long span of Christian tradition: "unified enough to sustain needed continuity and diverse enough to create something new for new times."[51]

Thus, by *re-covering the story of Pentecost* from the forgotten pages of Western literary and theological history, we also "*widen the field*" of historiographic inquiry and debate. Recovering a coherent picture of the historical meanings of Pentecost will be important for historians of Christianity, theologians, pastors and laity, and religious educators. What follows in these chapters is a glimpse into a wide range of texts dealing with the *story of Pentecost* and its *conceptual legacy* from the late 1100s to about 1670 and before the advent of Enlightenment modernism. Religious tradition, and the cultural expressions generated by tradition, is grounded in *story* and *narrative*, both oral and written stories of the human encounter with the Divine. The biblical event of Pentecost is one of the most enduring of the many Christian stories contained in the New Testament. Brown's theory of tradition sheds light on the aesthetic and affective dimensions of Pentecost as Christians continually retold and reread this familiar story across time and place while re-creating and revitalizing their pneumatological relationship with God and with each other as members of Christ's earthly church.

NOTES

1. Kanan Makiya, *The Rock: A Tale of Seventh-Century Jerusalem.* (New York: Vintage Books, 2002), 16.
2. Veli-Matti Kärkkäinen, *Pneumatology: The Holy Spirit in Ecumenical, International, and Contextual Perspective.* (Grand Rapids: Baker Academic, 2002), 38.
3. Delwin Brown, *Boundaries of Our Habitations: Tradition and Theological Construction* (Albany: SUNY Press, 1994), 118-119.
4. For a comprehensive overview of the seventeenth and eighteenth century Rosicrucian movement see Frances A. Yates' classic study *The Rosicrucian Enlightenment* (London, 1972).
5. Kärkkäinen, 11.
6. Elizabeth A. Dryer's *Holy Power, Holy Presence: Rediscovering Medieval Metaphors for the Holy Spirit.* (Mahwah: Paulist Press, 2007) was released just as this volume's final draft was being prepared for publication, and for this reason I did not have sufficient time to completely assess its contents and significance. However, from what I was able to digest of Dreyer's new book, my preliminary assessment is extremely favorable, and I believe her book will stand as an important contribution in the on-going academic work of recovering and interpreting the diverse range of medieval and early modern traditions of pneumatology. Many more book length studies are needed and hoped for in this neglected area of the history of Christianity.
7. Kärkkäinen 15.
8. Jürgen Moltmann, *The Spirit of Life: A Universal Affirmation.* Trans. M. Kohl (Minneapolis: Fortress Press, 1992), 8.
9. Kärkkäinen, 9.
10. Albert Hernández, *Islam and The Holy Grail: 'Convivencia,' Allegorical Transformation, and Ecumenical Visions in Wolfram von Eschenbach's 'Parzival.'* (UMI Dissertation Services, 2001).
11. Helen M. Mustard and Charles E. Passage, Trans. and Ed., "Introduction" to *Wolfram von Eschenbach, 'Parzival:' A Romance of the Middle Ages* (New York: Vintage Books, 1961), l.
12. Peter Brown, *Authority and The Sacred: Aspects of the Christianisation of the Roman World.* (New York: Cambridge University Press, 1996), 59-74.
13. P. Brown, "The Rise and Function of the Holy Man in Late Antiquity," *Journal of Roman Studies* 61 (1971), pp. 80-101; republished in *Society and The Holy in Late Antiquity* (Berkeley: California University Press, 1982).
14. P. Brown, *Authority and The Sacred*, 59.
15. Ibid. 60.

16. Ibid. 67.

17. Despite the paucity of academic studies on the historicity of Pentecost and the decline of pneumatology as a sub-field of Christian theological education since the late nineteenth century, those scholarly currents, representing educational institutions and professional guilds with essentialist or confessional orientations of either Pentecostal or Charismatic origins have not ignored the idea of Pentecost as an "event" chronicled in the New Testament with significant ecclesiastical import and symbolic power. But the professional and academic guilds of the USA, with their deeply rooted commitments to post-Enlightenment and Postmodern evaluative and methodological criteria, have neither paid attention to, nor engaged works on Pentecost by scholars with Pentecostal or ultra-conservative, confessional commitments. This trend was increasingly evident during the latter half of the twentieth century, which ironically also coincided with the global expansion of Pentecostalism as the fastest growing sector of Christianity across Latin America, Africa, and Asia, a trend that was still quite evident and vibrant while I was writing this book.

18. Charles Williams, *The Descent of the Dove: A Short History of the Holy Spirit in the Church* (Grand Rapids: Eerdmans, 1939); Yves Congar, *I believe In the Holy Spirit* (New York: Crossroad/Herder, 1997); and Stanley M. Burgess' three volume series, *The Holy Spirit: Ancient Christian Traditions* (Peabody: Hendrickson, 1984); *The Holy Spirit: Eastern Christian Traditions* (Hendrickson, 1989); *The Holy Spirit: Medieval Roman Catholic and Reformation Traditions* (Hendrickson, 1997).

19. For readers familiar with the demands of liturgical scheduling and the ministerial profession, the following brief discussion will be useful, as it sheds some light on our modern amnesia concerning Pentecost traditions. While the professional systematization of ministerial training from the late 1800s to the present may partly account for this lack of awareness, extremely busy pastoral and congregational schedules during the contemporary Lenten and Easter seasons should not be ruled out as a factor on this issue. Indeed, the increased level of expectation among the laity, along with an increased ministerial workload, is highest across all contemporary Christian denominations precisely from Ash Wednesday through Resurrection Sunday. Ministers and priests, pastors and deacons scarcely have enough energy left after Easter for leading the laity in the type of theological reflection and heartfelt piety during the seven-times-seven-days of the paschal cycle as the Christians of bygone centuries described in this study. Pastoral workloads and congregational demands, however, are not the reason more contemporary scholars have not written about the history of Christian conceptions of Pentecost. This oversight needs to be accounted for in other ways, which seem to be rooted in the empirical program and philosophical assumptions of Enlightenment modernism and as a by-product of the historical positivism that gripped church historians and historians in general, during the late nineteenth and early twentieth century.

20. See Exodus 34:22; Leviticus 23:11-21; Numbers 29:35; and Deuteronomy 16:10.

21. For more on the Council of Elvira, which probably took place between 306 CE and 310 CE, see Maurice Meigne, "Concile ou collection d'Elvire," *Revue d'histoire ecclésiastique* 70 (1975), 361-387; or Samuel Laeuchli, *Power and Sexuality: The Emergence of Canon Law at the Synod of Elvira* (Philadelphia: Temple University Press, 1972).

22. See Exodus 19.

23. Although there is no equivalent or comparable work on "Pentecost" from a Christian perspective, for a comprehensive compendium and overview of this rich and varied Jewish tradition see *The Shavuot Anthology* (Philadelphia: JPS, 1974).

24. Adolf Adam, *The Liturgical Year: Its History & Its Meaning After the Reform of the Liturgy.* Trans. M. J. O'Connell (Freiburg, Germany: Verlag Herder, 1979; New York: Pueblo Publishing, 1981), 89.

25. Ibid. 91

26. For a complete discussion see Ibid. 11, 84-91.

27. On the question of whether or not Luther and mysticism belong in opposite domains see Bengt R. Hoffman, *Theology of the Heart: The Role of Mysticism in the Theology of Martin Luther* (Minneapolis: Kirk House Publishers, 1998), 189-263; for a study of the aesthetic and spiritual aspects of popular and intellectual culture during the Reformation see Peter Matheson, *The Imaginative World of the Reformation* (Minneapolis: Fortress Press, 2001), 77-140; for information on Calvin's sixteenth century pneumatology, and subsequent Calvinist understandings of the Holy Spirit and personal piety, see Paul Chung, "Calvin and the Holy Spirit: A Reconsideration in Light of Spirituality and Social Ethics," *Pneuma* (Vol. 24, No.1: 2002) pp.40-55; and Peter de Klerk, *Calvin and the Holy Spirit: Papers and Responses Presented at the Sixth Colloquium on Calvin and Calvin Studies* (Grand Rapids: Calvin Studies Society, 1989).

28. See Kärkkäinen, 16-19; and Alister McGrath, *Christian Theology: An Introduction. 2nd Ed.* (Cambridge: Blackwell, 1997), 279.

29. R. Descartes as cited in Delwin Brown's opening comments in *Boundaries of Our Habitations*, 1.

30. As cited in Will Durant, *The Story of Philosophy* (New York: Simon & Schuster, 1961), 176.

31. For more on Fletcher and his theology of Pentecost see the superbly written pioneering study by Laurence W. Wood, *The Meaning of Pentecost in Early Methodism: Rediscovering John Fletcher as John Wesley's Vindicator and Designated Successor;* Pietist and Wesleyan Studies, No. 15. (Lanham: Scarecrow Press, 2002).

32. J. Steven O'Malley, "The Warmed Heart in the German Idiom," in Richard B. Steele, Ed., *"Heart Religion" In The Methodist Tradition and Related Movements* (Lanham: Scarecrow Press, 2001), 67-70.

33. For a detailed discussion of Joachimist influences after 1650 see Marjorie Reeves and Warwick Gould, *Joachim of Fiore and The Myth of the Eternal Evangel in the Nineteenth Century* (Oxford: Clarendon Press, 1987); Marjorie Reeves, *Joachim of Fiore and The Prophetic Future* (London: Sutton Publishing, 1999), 166-179; and Norman Cohn's revised and expanded edition of *The Pursuit of the Millennium: Revolutionary Millenarians and Mystical Anarchists of the Middle Ages.* (New York: Oxford University Press, 1970), 108-126.

34. For more on this "pneumatological deficit" see Kärkkäinen, 16-19; and Alister McGrath, *Christian Theology: An Introduction. 2nd Ed.* (Cambridge: Blackwell, 1997), 279.

35. For a concise discussion of the themes and concerns of the generation of the 1890s see H. Stuart Hughes, *Consciousness and Society: The Reorientation of European Social Thought, 1890-1930* (New York: Vintage, 1961; Rev. Ed. 1977), 33-66.

36. Ibid. 35.

37. For more on Steiner's use of Pentecostal imagery see Richard Leviton, *The Imagination of Pentecost: Rudolf Steiner & Contemporary Spirituality.* (Hudson: Anthroposophic Press, 1994).

38. See H. Stuart Hughes' fine chapter on "The Recovery of the Unconscious" in *Consciousness and Society,* 105-160.

39. For more on the contemporary shift in attitudes towards the Enlightenment among theologians and philosophers see Delwin Brown's "Introduction" to *Boundaries of Our Habitations,* 1-7; and Sheila Davaney's chapter "Histories and Contexts" in *Pragmatic Historicism: A Theology for the Twenty-First Century* (Albany: SUNY Press, 2000), 1-22.

40. Davaney, 161.

41. In my own areas of specialization as a historian of medieval and early-modern Christianity, I have tended to follow the methodological considerations outlined in Gabrielle Spiegel's highly influential essay first published as "History, Historicism, and the Social Logic of the Text," *Speculum* 65 (1990), 59-86, reprinted in Gabrielle M. Spiegel, *The Past as Text: The Theory and Practice of Medieval Historiography* (Baltimore: Johns Hopkins University Press, 1997), 3-29.

42. As I was researching and writing this book, Elizabeth A. Clark's *History, Theory, Text: Historians and The Linguistic Turn* (Harvard University Press, 2004) was released. Writing from the perspective of a historian of early Christianity, her first two chapters (pp. 9-41) offer an analysis of the birth and growth of the historical profession that resonates with many of the modernist and postmodern discourses to which I have called attention in my introduction. Clark also examines the implications and the promise of Gabrielle Spiegel's methodology for contemporary challenges in the study of premodern texts facing the fields of cultural and intellectual history and for the wider field of the history of Christianity (156-186).

43. Although Delwin Brown later expanded this theory of tradition in an essay published in 2003, in which he began describing the development of his ideas about culture and tradition by reference to the term "radical historicism," my use of his theory of "constructive historicism" throughout this volume relies primarily on his initial formulations in the 1994 publication of *Boundaries of Our Habitations.* For Brown's expansive reflections and a very effective and concise summation of his views on the matter this 2003 essay is an excellent resource: "Limitation and Ingenuity: Radical Historicism and the Nature of Tradition," *American Journal of Theology and Philosophy,* Vol. 24, No. 3 (Sept 2003): pp. 195-213.

44. Delwin Brown, *Boundaries of Our Habitations,* 120-21.

45. Ibid. 89.

46. Ibid. 118.

47. Ibid.

48. Ibid. 88.

49. Ibid. 89.

50. Ibid.

51. Ibid.

CHAPTER 2
"THE MERRIE MONTH OF MAY:"
NATURE, PENTECOST, &
THE HOLY GRAIL

In the beginning God created the heavens and the earth. The earth was without form and void, and darkness was upon the face of the deep; and the Spirit of God was moving over the face of the waters.

Genesis 1:1-2

Bewilderment begets curiosity and seeks a solution, and over the last hundred years, scholars and would-be scholars have tried to discover the secrets of the Grail, with such contrasting results that the reading public, eager for enlightenment, may well feel more puzzled than ever.

Roger Sherman Loomis, 1963[1]

There are twelve months in all the year, as I hear many men say. But the merriest month in all the year, is the merrie month of May.

Fourteenth Century English Ballad

Why begin a study on medieval and early modern Christian traditions of Pentecost and the Holy Spirit by looking at the legends of King Arthur and the quest for the Holy Grail? Why not begin with pneumatology among the great Scholastic theologians or even with the experiences of the Holy Spirit witnessed in the works of medieval mystics and saints? For no other reason than the deeply intriguing and extremely numerous references to Pentecost scattered throughout the literary corpus of King Arthur and the Holy Grail, a body of evidence whose bardic story-telling foundations rest upon much older pagan and pre-Christian traditions. Historians usually focus their research around a set of tentative questions, but, if we are to be intellectually honest, it is the historical documents and primary texts available to us that, more often than not, alter and shape the trajectory of our inquiry into a dimly remembered yesterday which can only be known by approximation. In his study of tradition and theological construction, Delwin Brown observes:

The diversity of Christian canon, or of any canon in which story predominates, may have as much to do with the character of stories as the diversity within the material the stories are about. It is easy to see how in telling and retelling stories people can again and again renegotiate their identities through the pluralities of rushing time.[2]

Similarly, an examination of the diverse references to Pentecost and the Holy Spirit in so many of the Arthurian and Grail stories of the Middle Ages confounded my initial curiosity and suggested a slightly different starting point for understanding this *quest* and its historical *quaestiones*. What role did the image of the Holy Spirit play in converting pagan rites of spring and natural transformation into the Christian cosmology and feast days of medieval society? Although the literary traditions of King Arthur and the quest for the Holy Grail have almost nothing to do with official Christian canon or doctrine as understood in the Middle Ages, these literary and symbolic traditions, "in which story predominates," exerted a profound influence on the religious imaginations of European Christians for over a thousand years.

Today, at the start of Christianity's third millennium, the story of King Arthur and Christ's fabled chalice of immortality still influence a new generation of mythmakers and storytellers. Popular novels, like Dan Brown's *The Da Vinci Code* and Kate Mosse's *Labyrinth* blur the realms of fact and fiction by drawing on these legends, and Hollywood movies like Jerry Bruckheimer's *King Arthur* (2004) and Dino De Laurentiis' *The Last Legion* (2007) blend archaeology with literary history to reinvent the legendary king's story as that of a Roman commander protecting Britain during the barbarian invasions that followed the fall of the Roman Empire. The *quest* for Arthur and the Grail has always been about a set of both spiritually mysterious and politically practical *questions*. The "Matter of Britain," as the genre of Arthurian and Grail romances was known in the Middle Ages, is about relating the human person to Nature as well as about building a just society in which human agency operates in relation to Christ and the Holy Spirit. By taking into account local and trans-local aspects of the Arthurian and Grail literary traditions related to both the medieval liturgical calendar and Christian conceptions of Nature (*Natura*),[3] this inquiry into the historical and spiritual dimensions of Pentecost offers the possibility of representing our medieval forbears' pneumatological sensibilities more accurately.

However, centuries after the conversion and migration period of the Early Middle Ages, when the syncretism between pre-Christian practices and Christian beliefs initially occurred, *Natura* was reinterpreted for the resurgent Christian discourse of the High Middle Ages in works like Bernardus Silvestris' *Cosmographia* (ca. 1147)[4] and Alain of Lille's *De planctu Naturae* (ca. 1160-1165).[5] Although little about his biography is known with certainty, Silvestris (ca. 1085-1178) was one of the most enigmatic and influential figures of the Twelfth Century Renaissance. The highly erudite Alain (ca. 1128-1202), was known to his contemporaries as *doctor universalis*, and was one of the most revered figures of the same Christian revival of classical learning of the 1100s as Silvestris. According to Barbara Newman it is in and through such fine works by these two authors that: "The birth of Natura, the most enduring of all medieval goddesses, can be precisely dated."[6] Newman's masterful analysis of the persistence of goddess figures in medieval Christian culture and theological discourse, in *God and the Goddesses*, exposes how it was in the works of Bernardus Silvestris and Alain of Lille that *Natura* came to be personified as that procreative vitality of the cosmos, for which Peter Abelard and William of Conches had recently been criticized when they equated the Platonic *anima mundi* with the Holy Spirit of the Trinity:

> Bernard and Alan succeeded remarkably well in establishing Natura's dominion within her own distinct realm. Once she had settled into cordial but rather distinct relations with her Father, the goddess emerged as one of medieval literature's most fruitful and evocative means for exploring ethical questions related to sexuality and gender, and for articulating and testing ideas of the normative. After 1200, fine-tuning the relationship between Nature and Nature's God becomes a matter for the theologians; secular and vernacular poets who portray the goddess make a decisive turn away from cosmology toward the human world of gender, generation, and desire.[7]

Although I am taking these continuities and discontinuities concerning the goddess and the Trinity in a different direction, Newman's outstanding two chapters on representations of the goddess in Christian theological, philosophical, and literary constructions during the 1100s and 1200s,[8] remind us of the twists-and-turns of *theological reconstruction* that were already underway in the Christian imagination of those times "...as either an alternative or complement to the rising tide of scholasticism."[9] This little recognized, and barely perceptible, pneumatological revitalization during the Twelfth Century Renaissance sparked the popular literary inventiveness that burst on the scene in the late 1100s with the first Arthurian romances of Chrétien de Troyes, Wolfram von Eschenbach, Marie de France, and so many other poets who, in divergent local and trans-local ways, portrayed King Arthur and his gallant knights amidst pre-Christian Celtic elements mingled with numerous references to the month of May and the Feast of Pentecost.

Scholarly acknowledgement of pre-Christian and Celtic influences on the Arthurian and Grail sagas is a well known and thoroughly documented area of investigation. However, the role of Pentecost in diverse examples of these literary and historical materials, while not entirely new, is precisely where I want to draw attention. This chapter contends that the numerous examples of Pentecost referenced throughout the stories of King Arthur and the quest for the Holy Grail, references echoed even in the climactic moments of the lives of knights serving the Round Table fraternity, we find the syncretistic convergence of pre-Christian religious traditions concerning the months of May and June with medieval Christian traditions of pneumatology and the Feast of Pentecost during the same period of the liturgical year. Hence, as sung in a familiar fourteenth century English ballad, it was in "the merrie, merrie month of May" that the Pentecost story from the Book of Acts became the basis for medieval festivities capable of holding pre-Christian fertility traditions alongside the annual Christian commemoration of God's gracious outpouring of the Holy Spirit nine days after the Ascension of Christ. This syncretistic blending of pagan and Christian traditions around Pentecost were essentially at odds with each other, yet each tradition was convinced that in Nature's assorted acts of generation and rebirth, something ineffable about humanity's place in the order of creation was revealed for the greater good of all living creatures.

CELTIC CHRISTIANITY AND THE MONTH OF MAY

Richard Barber rightly contends "the convergence of literary imagination and religious ideals made the stories of the Grail possible."[10] The stories of the Grail are also closely related to the stories of King Arthur and his Knights of the Round Table, and together their strands represent a convergence of medieval Christian and earlier pre-Christian elements. But, in which cultural contexts and under what sort of historical forces did such a convergence occur? If we limit our historical understanding of pneumatology to the writings of medieval mystics and Scholastic theologians, then the cultural history and social logic within which medieval men and women actually lived the seasons of their lives through the seasons of the Christian liturgical calendar will never be fully understood, nor will the silenced memories of the medieval world's pre-Christian ancestry speak to us if we limit our inquiry to the trans-local views of a Christianized, elite European culture.

The influence of pre-Christian beliefs about Nature and pagan religious practices on the emergence of Western European Christianity has been documented recently by Bernadette Filotas in her groundbreaking study, *Pagan Survivals, Superstitions, and Popular Cultures in Early Medieval Pastoral Literature.*[11] From uncanny pagan beliefs about animals and trees to anomalous beliefs about Christian saints; from practices of magical healing to intercessory Christian prayers on behalf of the sick and dying, Filotas' research furthers our understanding of the syncretistic Christianization process that took place throughout Europe from the sixth through the eleventh centuries as the Celtic and Germanic peoples converted to the monotheistic and ethical paradigm of the Judeo-Christian tradition. Her work relies on the vast number of extant texts of ecclesiastical law, sermons, and fragments of other forms of written expression by early medieval bishops and pastors admonishing their flocks against practicing the "old ways" of their ancestors. The medieval Church Fathers employed the language of prohibition against idolatry (*cultores idolorum*), and used the accusative forms of Latin verbs, as they sought to gain power over the pagan past. It is clear from the evidence Filotas presents that trees, springs, ponds and lakes, along with stones, fire, earth, and sacred groves all played a special role in the personal piety and religious practices of the Celtic and Germanic tribes who became the people of medieval European Christendom.[12] In one instance we learn of the mixing of pagan ritual with Christian supplication as prayers were offered in sacred groves "to God, His Saints, and Holy Mother Church."[13] The intermingling of Christian beliefs and practices about Easter and Pentecost with pre-Christian beliefs and practices about fertility and Nature's regeneration during the months of May and June, while not specifically examined by Filotas, were also part of the syncretistic comingling that occurred in the Christianization process spanning the centuries known to contemporary historians as the "Dark Ages," the "Migration Period," or the "Early Middle Ages." Modern scholars have been studying the literary history of the Arthurian and Holy Grail traditions since the late 1700s, and today it is widely acknowledged that although the highpoint of popularity for these stories dates to the late 1100s and 1200s, their origins reside in the much more ancient oral traditions of Celtic sages and bards.

In his pioneering study of early medieval Irish theology, Thomas O'Loughlin argued for a historical re-evaluation of Christianity in Celtic lands and suggested that "those who are interested in the evolution of western Christian theology need to pay closer attention to the theological products of the insular region" of Ireland and the British Isles "for they are fully a cog in the intellectual history of the Western church."[14] He maintains that, regardless of the peripheral location of these Irish and Anglo-Saxon islands to the rest of Europe, "several of their innovations entered the mainstream of Latin theology" and describes these as "part of the tapestry of medieval theology."[15] Discussing the need among theologians and historians for "keeping company with each other," O'Loughlin's emphasis upon the importance of the particulars of time and place echoes the historicist sensibilities of theologians like Delwin Brown, whose historicist and pragmatic insights on Christian tradition inform my own historiographic approach in this study. Indeed, O'Loughlin shares a similar concern with Brown for the pairing of theology and history as expressed by his conviction in the "growing awareness of how theology is tied to culture/place/time/society."[16]

While critically mindful of the flurry of "New Age" books and neo-pagan euphoria promoting popular reconstructions of Celtic Christianity during the past couple of decades, O'Loughlin's work also highlights the aversion earlier generations of historians and theologians, interested solely in the exotic world of the Druids or in the heretical doctrines of Pelagius, developed toward the study of religious place and culture among the medieval societies of Ireland and Wales. In contrast, he emphatically reminds us that "Ireland saw itself as having received Christianity from the British (i.e. the Welsh)" and that "there was much interchange of ideas and people" from the sixth through the eleventh centuries.[17] Precisely the same historical period during, which the oral legends and bardic sagas about the Holy Grail and the famous *Rex Arcturus* were being generated. Scholarly debates for and against the existence of a "Celtic Church," or of a "Celtic Christianity" notwithstanding, the socio-cultural and syncretistic tendencies presented in O'Loughlin's theological study have their counterpart in the poetic and religious representation of Irish and Welsh traditions we find echoed in the Arthurian and Grail stories that began appearing in written form after the eleventh century, stories which might be considered the local and courtly equivalents of the monastic lives and primary sources O'Loughlin believes attest to the existence of a Celtic theology.

The various stories of King Arthur and the Grail quest were often read and understood in the Middle Ages as synonymous with the so-called *"merrie month of May."* The cycle of days and weeks from Easter Sunday to Pentecost Sunday, also known as "Whitsuntide," usually occurred as well in the months of May or early June and it was experienced as a joyous time in the medieval Christian liturgical calendar. Indeed, centuries before Sir Thomas Malory wrote his famous narrative poem *Le Morte d'Arthur* in 1485, lords and knights had been going "A-maying" at this time of year. This was a pre-Christian Celtic tradition whereby horsemen rode out either on May 1st or on the eve of May's first full moon in celebration of the Great Goddess' sexual union with Belenus, god of the sun, light and healing. It was a time of rejoicing over the conclusion of winter's cold, gray bitterness and the revived cycle of fertility brought on by the arrival of the spring and summer growing seasons. Hence, for medieval Europeans, Pentecost almost always arrived in the months of May or early June, as it does today across the world.

Some of these medieval calendar traditions date back to ancient Greece where the spring months of March and April coincided with better weather conditions for the start of military campaigns. Others may be traced back to the Roman Empire where the god of war, Mars, was honored each year in March with a military procession and festival known as the *Campus Martius.* In her richly illustrated and highly informative volume, *Medieval Calendars,* Teresa Pérez-Higuera assembled and analyzed an impressive selection of medieval calendar manuscripts, relief sculptures, zodiac wheels, and illustrations for the months of the year ranging from about 975 to the late 1500s.[18] Even a cursory glance at extant illustrations on medieval calendar pages for the month of May reveals myriad images of knights on horseback galloping through verdantly lush, flowering fields. Pérez-Higuera explains that these illustrations and depictions for the month of May changed over time as medieval society went through various historical transformations, and that these depictions of the mounted knight surrounded by *floralia,* Latin for abundant flowers and greenery, became more or less a fixed image during the 1100s and 1200s.[19] She traces these iconographic embellishments of "exuberant vegetation" in both medieval Spanish and French calendar pages for the month of May, respectively, as *floresta* and *verdure.*[20] In the late 1300s, the French King Charles V even gave members of his court "gifts of green garments, known as *livré de maï*" in honor of the spring celebrations associated with the first of May, known as "May Day."[21] One of Pérez-Higuera's most intriguing images included in her book was found on the capital of a column from the cloister of Spain's Santa María la Real de Nieva, in which both the months of April and May are signified by men on horseback dressed in the upper class clothing styles of the 1100s to the 1300s. The horseman for April carries a flowering branch, while the rider for May holds falcon in one hand and carries a small flowering tree over his right shoulder, which represents a direct allusion to the Celtic and Germanic Maypole celebrations of pre-Christian Europe.[22] While Pérez-Higuera identifies this as "a unique case of iconographic interference,"[23] I contend this syncretistic blending of Christian religious traditions with elements from pre-Christian religious beliefs about the spring months were a significant aspect of the parallels that emerged between the Feast of Pentecost and the much older rebirth, or "greening," festivals of May and June that found their way into the Arthurian and Grail romances.

These fertility rites, and the traditions through which they were commemorated and transmitted to subsequent generations by poets and shamans, took on many local variations across Britain, Ireland, Scotland and Wales, Normandy, and the German Rhineland. Green was the favorite color of the Celtic and Germanic traditions for this time of year. It comes as no surprise then that among some modern Christian denominations "Pentecost green," symbolizing Nature's "greening," is still used alongside the more traditional "red" colors, symbolizing the outpouring of the Holy Spirit as "tongues of fire," advocated by Pope Innocent III around 1200. Over time, these folk-myths and stories, and the feast days marking their annual passage, became assimilated alongside Christian conceptions about May Day, the Virgin Mary, and the Feast of Pentecost.

As far back as Geoffrey of Monmouth's *History of the Kings of Britain* (ca. 1138) we read that King Arthur pulled the sword from the Stone on Pentecost Sunday, a Christian feast day that almost always occurs in the "merrie month of May." While writers of medieval romances regarded him as the earliest and greatest chronicler of Britain's royal histories, Geoffrey's haphazard methods for recounting the past would not qualify him as a bona fide professional historian today. William of Malmesbury's *Gesta Regum Anglorum* (1125) and Henry of Huntingdon's *Historia Anglorum* (1129) appeared before Geoffrey's work and sought to separate historical fact from fiction on the question of King Arthur's origins. Still Geoffrey's account of the young king's exploits is one of the earliest examples of the so-called "Matter of Britain," more popularly known as the "Arthurian Tradition." Cloaked as they are in the storied legends of pre-Christian, pagan chroniclers and Celtic poets, the religious origins of this literary tradition will never be fully known, as the stories themselves represent tribal beliefs and traditions about sacred vessels (the Grail) and magical weapons (Excalibur) reaching back millennia to a time before the Roman conquest of Gaul, Celtic Spain and Britain. The syncretism of ancient Celtic symbols and beliefs with certain aspects of medieval Christian spirituality raises a number of questions about the origins of these stories and their religious meanings.

How and why did the Feast of Pentecost become such a common trope in the oral traditions and literary narratives of King Arthur and the quest for the Holy Grail? What is the relationship of pre-Christian fertility rites associated with the "Maypole," once celebrated widely across Ireland, Scotland, Wales, Normandy and Germany, to the Pentecost cycle of the Christian liturgical calendar? What does all of this cross-cultural fertilization amidst the sixth century "clash of civilizations" between pagans and Christians have to do with the Holy Spirit and with traditional commemorations of the Feast of Pentecost? Why does there seem to be a connection between medieval reverence for the Holy Spirit with pre-Christian nature-worship embodied in the idea of the "Goddess" as the Divine Feminine? Why would a thirteenth-century German poet-knight like Wolfram von Eschenbach write a story about an oracular Grail-stone from heaven with a plot structure spanning seven Pentecosts? The answers to such questions lay not in the types of pneumatological inquiry that church historians or theologians have taken on before, but rather in a multidisciplinary line of inquiry that will shed light on the so-called "greening" of the Holy Spirit mentioned by church figures like Hildegard of Bingen, or in the special reverence for flora and fauna memorialized in the annals of early medieval Irish and Welsh hagiography. Again, like the narrator in the Acts of the Apostles, our hearts wonder at these parallels as our minds echo the Pentecostal inquiry: *What does this mean?*

TIME-KEEPING IN THE CHRISTIAN LITURGICAL CALENDAR

Calendars can be wonderful tools for planning all manner of labor and activities, commemorating significant events or sacred holidays, and organizing the days, weeks and months, and years of our lives. Calendars are to time reckoning like maps are to traveling, and in cosmological systems a calendar functions much like a "cosmological map" of the year by highlighting both the terrestrial and heavenly aspects of human ideality and ways of life. Our notion of dividing the day into "hours" derives from the Latin term, *horarium*, which in medieval holy rules also signified the routines prescribed for certain days, or for portions of each day, and the prayers or practices that accompanied each segment of sacred time. Hence, what happened in the prayer life of medieval monks, and other clergy who followed these practices, placed them in a meditation about the course of the year through the *lectio divina* of the Daily Office. Whether discussing a solar calendar charting the sun's transit across the sky as it generates the seasons, or examining a lunar calendar charting the reappearance of the moon in its various stages each month, or whether pondering the cosmological syncretism evident in so many different calendar systems, one thing is certain: calendars have been deployed as tools of domination just as often as they have been deployed as markers of sacred time, or as marking new eras in a society's understanding of its place in the universe. This section examines the cultural encounters that generated a deep confluence of pre-Christian Celtic elements concerning the May-June cycle of fertility feasts with Christian elements concerning the seven-week cycle of Pentecost during the same period of the liturgical calendar.

Within the astronomical dimensions of a twelve month solar year comprised of 365.25 days, the early medieval Roman Church organized the months, weeks and days of the Julian calendar based upon the major events or stages of Christ's earthly life as incorporated into the liturgy. Hence the trajectory of the major periods, Holy Days, and feast days in the Latin Church's liturgical calendar: Advent; the twelve-day Christmas season culminating on December 25; the Feast of the Epiphany on January 6 followed by the forty days of the Lenten Season; the Easter season (also known as Passiontide or Eastertide) culminating on Resurrection Sunday at the end of Holy Week; the Feast of the Ascension forty days after Easter Sunday; and the final feast of the year closing with Pentecost Sunday; after which the Christian believer entered a period of "ordinary time" (from *ordinal* meaning "the counted weeks"). This ordinary time lasted from five to six months depending on the annual cycles of the Easter *computus* while en route to the next liturgical year with the return of Advent by the end of

November or the beginning of December. Despite denominational variations concerning the observance of particular feast days among Roman Catholic, Eastern Orthodox, Protestant and Episcopal traditions, along with regional and local differences governing special festal observances, and minor changes resulting from the Gregorian calendar reforms of 1582, the Christian liturgical year has remained relatively the same since Christianity emerged from its seminal roots in Antiquity and the Middle Ages.

If contemplated prayerfully and experienced ritually as a pietistic journey from mere human temporality through the eternity of God's love and mercy, then one's experience of sacred-time was surely enhanced and blessed by the indwelling of Jesus Christ's Holy Spirit in the hearts and minds of believers, a pneumatological empowerment whose possibilities were felt each year on or about the day of Pentecost. This benevolent and caring Spirit of Christ, in turn, bestowed numerous "fruits and gifts" among the people of the one, true God, whether clergy or laity, "gifts of the Spirit" and "fruits of the Spirit" intended for the benefit and service of the church. Commenting on the textual evidence for the strict time-patterns of medieval Irish monasteries, Thomas O'Loughlin writes:

> For the people whose religious texts we have been examining, time was at the heart of Christianity: to be a believer was to fit oneself ever more precisely into an externally determined schedule. Just as today a worker in a time-sensitive occupation is expected to fit his or her whole time around the schedule of the organization, and indeed is expected to surrender his or her own control of that time, so medieval Christians were expected to merge their time not only with the ineluctable cycles of weather and agriculture, but also with those of religion.[24]

The convergence of Christian practices and beliefs with agricultural cycles and religious beliefs about Nature was a typical feature of medieval piety among the clergy and the laity, especially in the rural and remote areas of medieval Europe. This was essentially the *experience of time* documented in countless saints' lives and rules for monastic orders throughout the medieval world, and which somehow made it into many of the Arthurian and Grail stories.

In the early middle ages, however, such conceptions of time must have also represented a cultural fault line between the Roman Church of Western Europe and older, pre-Christian time-reckoning methods more akin with lunar and agricultural cycles than with the *imitatio Christi* of the Christian liturgical calendar. "Moreover, the more one sought Christian perfection" behind the walls of a monastery or even in the earthy sanctum of a monastic garden "the more one was expected not to have a personal schedule at all."[25] During the conversion period of the late fifth century, the future Patron Saint of Ireland, Patrick, observed the increasing numbers of high-ranking pagan male and female youths converting to Christianity throughout the Irish countryside.[26] As late as the eleventh century, we hear of laws in England forbidding people in the countryside and rural villages, as well as in the larger towns and cities, from taking any sort of religious or spiritual advice from a Druid priest or priestess. This example gives us a sense of how rapidly the demise of pre-Christian beliefs and practices, and pagan cosmologies, must have set in following the end of the migration and invasion periods of the Dark Ages.

Commenting about the legacy of early medieval astronomies on the medieval monastic sense of time and calendars, Stephen McCluskey notes a certain dissonance between the temporal conceptions of the clergy and those of the laity. "The divine lawgiver's dominion over nature, and nature's ultimate dependence on Him, arise in monastic prayer as well." He describes the predawn office of lauds based on Psalms 148-150, and celebrated in Gregory of Tours' sixth century work *De cursu Stellarum*, as characteristic of an attitude to nature and the heavens whereby "monks began each day by calling upon the heavens and all creation to praise God for his dominion." Calling upon the sun and moon, and the waters above the heavens, and the shining stars in the highest heavens, the Psalmist shouts out in glory:

> Let them praise the name of the Lord! For he commanded and they were created. And he established them forever and ever; He fixed their bounds, which cannot be passed. (Psalm 148:5-6)

McCluskey rightly contends that medieval commentators interpreted such scriptural passages "as referring to an unchanging natural order" across the terrestrial and cosmic planes of Creation." However, he also contests the mistaken assumptions that such totalizing, biblical views of God and Nature also held sway over the social logic of the larger society's syncretistic Christianity, because outside these medieval monasteries "the divine dominion was still questioned among the rustic population of Gregory's time who, like their Germanic and Celtic forebears, continued to address the Sun and Moon as 'lords'."[27]

Adomnán's *Vita Columbae* and the allegorical voyages of St. Brendan in the *Nauigatio sancti Brendani* are both superb examples of the importance of liturgical time in the medieval monastic environment. Spread over a period of seven liturgical years, in the *Nauigatio sancti Brendani* Saint Brendan (ca. 460-577) and his companions sail from Advent to Christmas and through Lent and Easter to Pentecost in their penitential journey towards spiritual perfection as an *imitatio Christi* whose by-product will also be their complete transcendence beyond terrestrial temporality. Curiously enough, St. Brendan's feast day also occurs during the calendar cycle discussed herein on May 16th. Patricia Rumsey's recently published book on "sacred time" in early Irish monasticism contrasts the *Nauigatio sancti Brendani* with the Rules of the Celí Dé to show that more than one understanding of "sacred time" operated in the liturgical and monastic practices of early Christian Ireland.[28] The first conception understood "sacred time" as both "source" and "gift" related to all that was "good" and "holy" in the Order of Creation, and facilitated the flow of ideas and traditions between the pagan "past" and the emerging Christian "present." The second understanding of "sacred time" was more concerned with the "future" and tended to perceive time as part of a fallen world requiring eschatological redemption and sanctification.[29] This second conception of time proved decisive in the cultural, cosmological, and theological mechanisms by which Christian understandings of time and Nature gained power over the pre-Christian past and replaced the world views of Europe's indigenous peoples, a pattern of conquest and conversion that would be played out wherever and whenever Christianity identified itself against its divergent "others."

From Late Antiquity through the Middle Ages, the Christian liturgical calendar was superimposed upon the indigenous peoples of Europe with the aim of converting them, and in the hope that they might abandon their "wild ways" and "pagan customs." Although these changes were sometimes characterized by alleged mass conversions, or by armed force when alleged heretics posed an acutely political or economic threat, the Church's strategy of converting tribal leaders, or so-called "war lords," while educating their children, had the concomitant effect of producing a feudal elite with a rather shallow and "unschooled" Christian identity. As for the rank-and-file members of these tribal groups, the net result was probably one of resentment over their leaders' abandonment of the old gods and goddesses. As late as the eleventh century, Muscovite and Kievan popular opinion advocated that when encountering an approaching priest in town, one should spit on the ground and step aside so as to cast off any bad influences from this adversary of one's beloved ancestors and ancient traditions. Such sentiments both mask and reveal the deep pain and sense of loss that must have accompanied the process of Christianisation in Europe from the sixth to the twelfth century. Over time, the cultural lag inherent in such processes produced two types of cultural orientations across much of medieval Europe: a feudal aristocracy in close association with ecclesiastical leaders and structures, and an uneducated, mostly rural and agrarian population, for whom Christian faith and reason were not the only acceptable ways of knowing and being in relationship with Nature and with their cherished ancestors.

However, the transformation of pagan societies and entire cultural histories through the creation and imposition of new calendar systems was nothing new in the history of Europe or of the world. The Celtic and Germanic peoples had been dealing with Latinization since the Roman army began expanding outside the Italian peninsula around 300 BCE, which by early-Christian times had led to the emergence of a dynamic Romano-Celtic hybrid culture. As he became more attracted to Christianity during the years leading up to the Council of Nicea in 325 CE, Constantine the Great instituted the seven-day week throughout the Roman Empire. In his study of the great empires of the ancient world, *The Ecumenic Age*, the German sociologist Eric Voegelin examined the relationship between imperial systems and the emergence of universalizing religious or philosophical movements that often arise out of such imperial expansions and collapses. He coined the term *historiogenesis* as a means of describing the processes by which universalizing empires like those of the Persians, Alexander the Great, China's Han dynasty, the Romans, and Islam often reinterpret the cosmological story of their respective time and place by generating new calendar systems and universal myths that look back to their particular regime's appearance on the stage of world history as the starting point for a new era or a new world order. Voegelin called these imperial systems *ecumenic empires*. He also discussed the simultaneous appearance of religious and philosophical movements alongside the growth of these imperial systems, which sought and/or posited an ethical and universalizing view of "the ties-that-bind" peoples and cultures into homogeneity. Some of these were movements of faith, like Zoroastrianism, Christianity, or Islam, and others were movements of thought, like Stoicism, Skepticism, or Epicureanism. In each instance, such *ecumenic movements* looked back to their particular beginning moment with special reverence like Islam did with Muhammad's *Hejira,* or "exodus" from Mecca to Medina, as year one in the Muslim calendar. Other movements re-interpreted the birth of a religious founder or messianic figure with the start of a new historical eon as in the birth of Jesus Christ and the *Anno Domini* dating system.[30]

Roman *historiogenesis* dated their civilization's history from the founding of Rome at the beginning of Romulus' reign as sole King of Rome on April 21, 753 BCE. Events after this date were followed by the designation AUB, *ab urbe condita,* meaning, "since the founding" of Rome. In 395 CE Emperor Theodosius I of Byzantium made Christianity the official religion of the Roman Empire, and although the Western Roman Empire collapsed in 476 CE as the Goths overran Italy, it was not until 523 CE that Dionysius Exiguus, a Scythian monk and canon in the Roman Curia of Pope Boniface II, was officially charged with the task of improving the method for calculating the dates of Easter. By the sixth century, it had become customary for the papal see to count the years from the massive restructuring of Roman imperial protocols and provincial structures carried out by Emperor Diocletian two centuries before. Dionysius, on the other hand, understood Diocletian as the last major pagan persecutor of Christians prior to the rise of Constantine the Great so, instead of numbering the years of this new calendar since the founding of Rome (AUC) or since the reign of Diocletian, he chose to renumber the years from the birth of Christ, which he calculated as 753 *ab urbe condita* or *Anno Domini* year 1. Thus, Dionysius fixed the Incarnation of Christ as occurring during the reigns of King Herod and the Emperor Augustus around the presumed date of the first Christmas on the 25th of December, 753 AUC, and decreed the following day as January 1st, 754 AUC, and henceforth 1 AD. Though now widely acknowledged as a miscalculation because we are not certain that Dionysius Exiguus realized that Diocletian actually reigned a little over a thousand years after Romulus' mythical founding of Rome (ca. 1037-1058 AUC; 284-305 CE), in these clear examples of *historiogenesis* we see the power of calendars to shape and determine not only conceptions of religious and national origins, but subsequently the unconscious power of the cycle of days, weeks, and months by which people order their lives and labors.

Following the fall of the Western Roman Empire in 476 CE, and given its understanding of temporal power and eschatological time, the Christian *ecclesia* of the late fifth and sixth century CE bequeathed its Romano-Celtic descendants the universalizing assumptions of forging a new *Respublica Christiana* out of those lost centuries known to us as "the Dark Ages," an endeavor which lasted until after the conversion of the Carolingian Franks around 800 CE. "To be human is to exist in time, and to be a Christian is to see time as an inherently sacred dimension, for the Word has become flesh in history. This belief was impressed in the Christians of the first millennium every time they deliberately chose to use AD dating, and it was supported by the recognition of the order of the seasons, the recurring cycles of life and the march of time towards death."[31] In such a worldview, the theocentric miracle of the first Pentecost must have been understood as a powerful scriptural example of the overarching apostolic and ecumenical mission of the church to "make disciples of all nations" by bearing witness to the Incarnation of the Word and the outpouring of the Holy Spirit at Pentecost.

On the distinction in the church's liturgical calendar between "ordinary time" and "festal time," O'Loughlin's insights are quite useful. While the hours of the day and the weeks were significant units of time each with their own holy duties and prayer observances, "there were periods which were larger than a week which had their own character." As examples of this, he discusses the forty penitential days during the period of Lent and the fifty-day period after Easter leading up to the Feast of Pentecost. He also highlights the "constant references to these longer sessions in saints' lives and monastic documents," before finally reminding us, his modern colleagues and readers, that these historical clues "show they had a significance we do not give to any such periods."[32] Thus, the distinctions between "ordinary time" and "festal time" in the medieval Christian experience of living through the cycles and festivals of the liturgical calendar were significant precisely because of the eschatological dimension of God's merciful intervention in human history in "festal events" like Advent, the Incarnation at Christmas time, the Resurrection at Easter, the Ascension of Jesus forty days after Easter, and the descent of the Holy Spirit at Pentecost.

Hence, the various commemorations built into the liturgical calendar functioned at the collective level of Christian culture and tradition as an extended act of remembrance of the Savior's life and ministry, but at the individual level of personal piety and spiritual practice helped induce a meditative state of recollection among both clergy and laity. This sheds light on the hard to understand cycle of seven Pentecosts chosen by Wolfram von Eschenbach as the underlying structure of his epic poem for Parzival's seven-year quest after the Holy Grail, discussed later in this chapter. It also helps us understand the rhythmic cadence of contemplative prayer and fasting amidst the alternating passage of ordinary time and festal jubilation while living through the liturgical calendar that led so many visionaries like Joachim of Fiore and reform minded clergy like Ignatius of Loyola, and dissenters like Cola di Rienzo and Thomas Müntzer to experience the liberating flames of the Holy Spirit in the particular ways each claimed to have received the Spirit. In other words, living the monthly cycles of the sun and moon through the Christian liturgical calendar was like living in an extended, existential meditation on the *imitatio Christi*. In the eloquent words of Thomas O'Loughlin: "To pass through the year was an act of recollection, and this was a holy task in its own right."[33]

TIME-KEEPING IN PRE-CHRISTIAN EUROPE

In contrast, "passing through the year" for pre-Christian or pagan men and women was quite different from the passage of time experienced in the ecclesiastical year of the liturgical calendar. For most literate medieval Christians, the story of Pentecost was synonymous with the Third Person of the Trinity and, since the Spirit gave both birth and voice to the Church for its task of transforming the world, in the minds of "educated" laity and clergy ecclesiology was synonymous with pneumatology. However, among the "simple devotees" (*simples devotos*) of the countryside and the far-off highlanders who resisted Christian conversion and assimilation, "literacy" or "being educated" might be more accurately and fairly described as being conversant with and reverently steeped in the *wisdom of one's ancestors*. While being careful not to romanticize this sector of the medieval populace, it is worth noting that for those living outside the direct influence of the cathedral-based medieval urban centers and large manorial estates, many of the religious beliefs and practices of their Romano-Celtic, Germanic, Saxon, or Anglo-Norman ancestors survived well into the fifteenth and sixteenth centuries. Although a comprehensive discussion of the pre-Christian agricultural and fertility festivals that influenced the Christian calendar is beyond the scope of this book, our analysis of how these influences intersected with conceptions of Pentecost and the Holy Spirit will benefit from a brief survey of Celtic myths and time-keeping beliefs.

It would be imprudent to draw a strict distinction between the medieval urban populace and the rural agrarian populace. Such rigid lines of demarcation are almost always illusory since ritual observances and religious identity affected by deep cultural syncretism are often more fluid and open than usually interpreted by modern historians and archaeologists. An example of the persistence of religious memory and tradition are the Maypole celebrations and references to the sacred Hawthorne tree that were still in effect throughout the British Isles in the 1600s before the Puritan Revolution banned these and other lingering traces of pre-Christian beliefs and practices. Over time, and due to its proximity in these two different, yet related calendar systems, the Feast of Pentecost became synonymous with pagan religious observances and fertility celebrations occurring between the first of May and the middle of June.

Although shrouded in various Celtic myths of highly uncertain origins, and obscured by nineteenth century inaccuracies bred from the nationalist dreams of amateur historians, a blatant fabrication of facts by Robert Graves in *The White Goddess* (1946), and further complicated by decades of appropriation among "New Age" neo-pagans, the so-called "Celtic Tree Calendar" could have served as a useful explanation for the connections perceived between Pentecost and so many of these medieval fertility celebrations.[34] Unfortunately, we cannot follow this line of research since Robert Graves' historical claims have been weighed-in-the-balance and found quite wanting by contemporary researchers. It would have been a nice exercise in historical analysis to vindicate the tribal legacies of one's Celtic or Hiberno-Saxon ancestors by proving that the "Celtic Tree Calendar" months named Alder (or *Fearn*, March 18–April 14), Willow (or *Saille*,

April 15-May 12), Hawthorn (or *Huath,* May 13-June 9), and Oak (or *Duir,* June 10-July 7) all coincided with the Christian liturgical calendar's "Great Fifty Day Cycle" from Easter Sunday to Pentecost Sunday, which fell sometime between early May and mid-June. But this controversial tree calendar, and the fictitious Celtic astrology that goes along with it, both of which are now quite famous among "New Age" lovers of Celtic lore, yet academically infamous among reputable scholars of Celtic history, appears to have been the result of Grave's poetic misuse of error laden, irresponsible works by now forgotten eighteenth and nineteenth century amateur scholars.[35]

Nonetheless, the archaeological and historical evidence indicates that "trees" were indeed used as markers of time by the ancient Greeks and early Romans who understood something about the significance of tree-rings as indicators of yearly agricultural cycles. This technique was known in Renaissance Italy as well and was mentioned by Leonardo Da Vinci. Trees were also revered as sacred objects among European pre-Christian tribal cultures like the Celts and their holy men and holy women. Peter Berresford Ellis has documented how the word for Druid derives from the Celtic god of the sacred oak, Bíle, and that "because they were not allowed to speak his holy name, they called the oak *draoi* and those learned in such knowledge were said to possess oak *(dru)* knowledge *(vid)* and thus were known as *Druids*."[36] Once the processes and travails of Christianisation began in the Late Roman and Early Medieval periods, these and other ancient Celtic beliefs about Nature's sanctity and the role of the Druids in religious life and sacred learning coalesced with Christian beliefs about naturalistic festivals and time reckoning methods that somehow seems to have kept the thirteen-month lunar calendar functioning for centuries alongside the twelve month Romano-Christian solar calendar. This would account for the association of Hawthorne trees and sacred Hawthorne groves with various fertility beliefs and practices that survived across England into the mid-1600s, as well as the Maypole festivals that survived until the same period in England and in many parts of continental Europe as far as the German Rhineland.

In addition, it is believed that many of these Celtic tree myths and legends also corresponded to certain letters of the *Ogam alphabet,* the origins of which are ascribed to Ogma, the Irish god of writing and poetry. Ogam probably originated as a system of magical symbols among continental Druids around 500 BCE, possibly living as far eastward as the German Rhineland. Anne Ross notes that this type of script was similar to the "Latin alphabet and consisting of strokes or notches which were cut into wood, bone, or stone,"[37] while David McManus indicates that it was clearly in use by the fourth century CE.[38] The Druids believed that humans were descended from two primordial elements of Nature: the sacred waters of heaven personified as the life-giving Mother Goddess, Danu, goddess of the Danube River; and the sacred oak that grew from the nourishment offered by Danu's waters personified as the tree god, Bíle.[39] They also believed that certain trees had magical and spiritual properties, which had both generative and curative influences on people, as well as providing many useful applications for more mundane tasks such as teaching and communicating their sacred Druidic wisdom.

Given the close association among tree spirits, magical writing, and religious Ogam oaths, either uttered from ear-to-ear or scripted on wood, bone or stone, it is easy to see how the Christian church associated these with spells and sorcery. Kelly reports how in the sixth century at the First Synod of Saint Patrick it was "ordained that a Christian who swore before a Druid in the pagan manner had to do a year's penance."[40] Stones with Ogam inscriptions have been found all over Ireland, England, Scotland and Wales, with some of the ciphers actually recording the names of Christian ecclesiastical officials on "bilingual stones" in both Ogam and Latin. Ogam thrived until about the end of the eighth century or ninth century CE when an increasingly Christianized clergy and nobility discouraged the rustic population's attachment to the pagan past. Nonetheless, Mark Redknap maintains that Celtic mystical beliefs associated with Ogam and the natural world "may have continued to some degree in the Lives of the Saints" and "suggest an association between magic and Christianity in relic pagan form, still evident in folklore today."[41]

In summary, based upon the Easter *computus* of Dionysius Exiguus in the sixth century, and the use of his *Anno Domini* dating system in the Venerable Bede's *Ecclesiastical History of the English People* (ca. 731), and then finally augmented by the simplified Easter *computus* worked out by Abbo of Fleury in 988 CE, the Julian calendar of the Middle Ages was in standard use until the Gregorian calendar reforms of 1582. In this system, that saw such widespread use during the Christian Middle Ages, March 22 was the earliest date for Easter while April 25 was the latest date Easter could occur. Counting "seven-times-seven-days" from March 22 and April 25, as the early and outer limits for Easter Sunday observances, we arrive at May 5 and June 13, respectively, as the earliest and latest possible dates for Pentecost in the medieval Julian calendar, dates which coincide almost precisely with the months of Huath and Duir in the alleged Celtic "tree calendar." But, even if this calendar has been exposed as a poetic fabrication, or as the passing fad of "New Age" dreamers, there are still the undeniable pre-Christian celebrations of the Feast of Beltane and the veneration of sacred Hawthorne groves that coincided with the cycle of days passing through the Romano-Christian months of May and June, a convergence that might explain the abundant references to Pentecost alongside allusions to the Mother Goddess and *Dame Nature* scattered throughout the stories of King Arthur and the Holy Grail.

MEDIEVAL CALENDARS AND CLIMATE PATTERNS

Another key point worth considering is the relationship between the calendar systems just discussed and European climate patterns during the medieval period, climate patterns that indeed held sway as well during the five centuries of Western European religious history surveyed in this book.

Therefore, as already established from the preceding discussions and analyses, and given the syncretism of pagan and Christian traditions common then, it is fair to say that pagan fertility festivals celebrated in May and early June intersected with the Christian Feast of Pentecost. This was especially so whenever Whitsunday occurred in "the merrie, merrie month of May." These patterns and parallels may have influenced the symbolic use of Pentecost "green" by some clergy, as opposed to the traditional "white" and "red" priestly garments still common to this day in most parts of the Christian world. Visionaries, like Hildegard of Bingen, referred to the role of the Holy Spirit in Nature and in the traditions of the church as one of "greening" because of its regenerative and positive attributes leading all things to their fullness by divine Grace. Thus, it was the Feast of Pentecost, arriving usually in May or early June, and not Easter, that became synonymous with the onset of spring and spiritual rebirth through the descent of the Holy Spirit, a fact attested to in a wide range of medieval calendar illustrations, Pentecost sermons, and literary works dealing with chivalry.

Regional climate patterns and local pagan time-reckoning systems also account for a wide range of differences as to how the trans-local Feast of Pentecost and local fertility festivals were commemorated across a European realm that, at best, was only marginally Christian until just before the onset of the High Middle Ages. Although in some medieval European communities the practices and rituals attached to Pentecost were as important as those associated with Easter, whether Easter arrived in March or April, much of medieval Western and Northern Europe had late winter snow on the ground during Holy Week. Spring still arrives later across Continental Europe than across most of North and Central America.

Furthermore, although completely beyond the scope of the present study, the relationship between the "Little Ice Age" that gripped Europe and much of the Northern Hemisphere from the fourteenth century until about 1850, most likely affected temperature cycles during the five centuries covered in this book and surely reinforced the close association of Pentecost with the actual onset of springtime among the European peoples of the High Middle Ages and the Early Modern period because the ground was almost always snow covered during Eastertide. Thus when compared with our contemporary experience of Earth's climate during the annual Easter to Pentecost cycle of days, the contrast with the Middle Ages seems so stark that the effects of the alleged "Little Ice Age" on European temperature patterns, and medieval understandings of Pentecost as the actual onset of spring-time, warrants further investigation by scholars interested in the effects of climate on social history and cultural patterns.

NATURE AND THE HOLY SPIRIT IN SCRIPTURE

For the Hellenistic Greek and Roman cultures of the ancient world, the presence of "spirits" (Latin: *daemons*; Greek: *daimones*) was recognized everywhere in the physical and cosmic realms. These were the supernatural entities or ghosts that existed in the imaginal realm between mortals and the gods, and which could take on either evil or good forms. But, for the Hebrews and the emerging Christian culture of those times, the discernment of these "spirits" was an important distinction between their monotheistic convictions and the polytheistic superstitions of their "spiritually inferior" opponents in the wider world of Antiquity. Although a great deal of Christian assimilation had taken root among the citizens of the Roman Empire before the collapse of its western half in 476 CE, Europe went through the entire cycle of conversion and acculturation into the Christian worldview again during the great tribal migrations and nomadic invasions of the Early Middle Ages (ca. 450 to ca. 900 CE). Given the Biblical understanding of God's omnipotent role in *Natura* (Nature), along with a theological anthropology in which this powerful Creator gave humans dominion over the natural world, it is worth reviewing the perception of Nature expressed in the Judeo-Christian scriptures, for this view apparently had a lasting effect on medieval and early modern Christian conceptions of Pentecost and of the Holy Spirit's presence in the natural world.

At this point several different, but related, questions emerge. As a feast day commemorating God's act of sending forth the Holy Spirit and the birth of the Church, Pentecost was one more example in the Scriptures of God's intervention in the physical world as an act of mercy for the salvation of humanity. What traditioned elements might there be in the Hebrew and New Testament canons that predisposed medieval conceptions about Pentecost and the Holy Spirit in favor of such close associations with ideas about *Natura* (Nature) and Creation? How might the sending forth of the Holy Spirit be equated with "acts of generation" in the physical and natural realms through the will of God? And, if hybrid creations are a common feature of the natural world over which God reigns and humans seek mastery, then how might a pneumatological understanding of hybridism, or mixing, find a place within a Christian natural philosophy so averse, since the time of Justin Martyr, to the many spirits and disembodied energies with whom non-Christian peoples and cultures conversed with on a daily basis?

These questions were apparently more common among medieval Christian attitudes toward the natural world than has been assumed by modern and postmodern investigators. Throughout medieval Christendom, and until about the seventeenth century, clergy and laity associated the seven weeks from Easter Sunday to Pentecost Sunday with five major theological reflection themes: 1) The Gifts of the Holy Spirit; 2) Deep prayer or contemplation; 3) Ecclesiology; 4) Sporadic attempts at dialogue with non-Christian communities; and 5) The promise of healing and redemption through God's "*act of regeneration*" or "*greening*" with the onset of spring. In his commentary on Acts, *The Gospel of the Spirit*, church historian Justo Gonzalez suggests an interpretation of the first generation of the Christian community as inspired and empowered by the "Acts of the Holy Spirit" rather than the more familiar reading of this New Testament book as the "Acts of the Apostles."[42] From a pneumatological standpoint, and based upon the interdependence among the three Persons of the Trinity, such a stance points to God's dynamic and creative participation in the physical realm of human temporality, first through the Incarnation, and then through the abiding presence of the Holy Spirit in the here and now of the sensorial world, and for all time after being poured out upon all flesh at the first Pentecost. From a theological standpoint, however, we must recall that the Christological controversies of the various Early Christian movements stemmed in no small measure from the great challenge of harmonizing the earthy and relational theology of Jesus with the abstract metaphysical postulates of Greco-Roman thought about the Highest God as the Divine Logos. This existential and metaphysical tension, derived from Christianity's Hebrew roots, accounts for a sizable portion of the Church Father's output of philosophical and theological treatises.

Psalm 104 speaks of God as Creator and Provider to all kinds of creatures of earth and sea, "living things both small and great," who look to God "to give them their food in due season." This passage implies that animals may share their life-Spirit with God, the Creator, for "when thou takest away their breath, they die and return to their dust. When thou sendest forth thy Spirit, they are created; and thou renewest the face of the ground" (25-30). But, it is clear from the way other passages in the Hebrew Scriptures and in the New Testament were interpreted and deployed through the centuries that human beings are regarded as superior to all other creatures of earth and sky and sea. After all, as beings created in the image and likeness of God (Genesis 1: 26-27), humans had dominion over the land and over nature's other inhabitants, which is precisely the interpretation of Genesis 1:28 from whence the prevailing Christian view of Nature was derived: "Be fruitful and multiply, and fill the earth and subdue it; and have dominion over the fish of the sea and over the birds of the air and over every living thing that moves upon the earth."

As Jeremy Cohen observed in his history of Rabbinic and Christian interpretations of Genesis 1:28, the changing interpretive patterns of biblical texts reveal much more about the interpreter's time and place than about the actual intent of the biblical author.[43] Cohen's work reminds us that the Jewish, Patristic, and Medieval understanding of Nature and Genesis 1:28 was seen as a primordial blessing from a God who desired to be in relationship with humanity, while reminding the human race that, in order to fulfill its special place in the order of Creation, the sacred duty of procreation should not and could not be ignored. For Judaism, this always conferred a deep sacredness on human sexuality and the act of procreative generation, regardless of the patriarchy inherent in the Hebrew tradition. As Cohen points out, "To reproduce and fill the earth, on the one hand, and yet to master it on the other hand, suggested that humans are situated on a cosmic frontier, between terrestrial and supernal realms of existence."[44] This produced a creative tension on matters of sexuality and dominion over the natural world that Cohen argues was most effectively expressed among the medieval Jewish Kabbalists[45]

Early Christian and Medieval exegesis of Genesis 1:28, however, had difficulty balancing the view of the human body and sexuality, derived largely from Platonism and partly from Gnosticism, with the sexual and procreative implications of this biblical verse. This dichotomous situation was probably complicated more after Pope Gregory VII tried to abolish clerical incontinence by enforcing the "rule of celibacy" as a traditional vow and practice with solid apostolic foundations and required of all bishops, priests, and deacons seeking ordination. Gregory's position on clerical celibacy, and his ardent desire to end the practice of married clergy appointing their sons to ecclesiastical office, was emphatically upheld in 1139 at the Second Lateran Council. The populace and some of the married clergy who were in positions of church leadership did not respond well to these measures, as there were threats of violence and local resistance to these Roman decrees across European Christendom.

However, such passionate opinions over the celibacy issue in the eleventh and twelfth centuries also masked deep rooted and prevailing Christian structures of patriarchy. These structures perpetuated deplorable views of women, sexuality, and the private lives of nuns, while disdaining the feminine aspect of the deity mirrored in Nature (*Natura*). These were structures that, although never fully dismantled, would resurface and reassert patriarchal supremacy during the infamous "witch-craze" of the 1500s and 1600s. Even the extensive deforestation generated by an ever expanding demand for construction wood throughout Europe from about 1000 to the late 1600s was connected with this patriarchal and autocratic lack of veneration for the spirituality of Nature. Imagine the impact of clearing the forests on ancestral ritual patterns and religious traditions connected to pre-Christian nature mysticism, or to the rich lore of tree spirits and forest entities that abounded among the Celts, Normans, Anglo-Saxons and Welsh.[46]

Cohen disputes some of Lynn White's (1907-1987) presumptions on medieval views of "mastery over Nature" in the latter's now famous 1967 essay, "The Historical Roots of Our Ecologic Crisis."[47] Although Lynn White was a fully credentialed medievalist, who specialized in the history of medieval technology and its impact on Western society and the natural environment, he did overlook some of the more positive aspects of the medieval attitude toward Nature, while very accurately pointing out how some Western intellectuals through the centuries invoked Genesis 1:28 to support both the exploitation of the natural environment and the cultural subjugation of non-Christian peoples deemed "pagan," "savage," or "uncivilized." While early medieval tribal groups, like the Celts or the Normans, revered and worshipped Nature as the source of fertility and human sustenance, in time it was Christianity's monotheistic view of an omnipotent and loving God, who, as the Creator of all that is seen and unseen in the natural world, also required a loyalty and piety that allowed no room for the gods of wood and stream, or the spirits of bird and beast and flower: "You shall have no other gods before me" (Exodus 20:3-4). Cohen's critique of Lynn White's historic thesis is well founded since, among the surviving original sources, we find multiple examples of how medieval Christians revered Nature and delighted in the contemplation of God's presence in Nature through the mystery of the Holy Spirit.[48]

Nonetheless, the conception of God suggested in the verses from Genesis, Exodus, and the Psalms cited above, had unmistakable implications for the development of Western European ideas about God and Nature, and for the trajectory of Christianisation later preached by Romano-Christian clergy as they encountered a greater number of Celtic, Anglo-Saxon, Germanic and Norman tribes on the European frontier from the sixth to the late tenth century.[49] Although the New Testament offers rich, naturalistic imagery for both the Blessed Mother of Jesus and for the Holy Spirit, imagery which surely appealed to most pre-Christian European peoples, its metaphysical conception of God as Logos, along with the Doctrine of Original Sin as worked out by theologians from Augustine to the early Scholastics, ~~was incompatible with the cosmologic~~al worldview of non-Christian indigenous groups. The idea of God as Logos offered an immutable and distant deity estranged from such earthy experiences as farming and gardening, sexuality and procreation, or midwifery and herbal folk medicine.

On the other hand, the idea of Jesus as the Incarnate Logos was slightly more palatable to non-Christians raised on a hearty diet of semi-divine spiritual intermediaries who could converse with the gods, as well as command the forces of Nature for the benefit of the human community. From our vantage point, it was Christ's Holy Spirit that took on a special significance in the Early Middle Ages as most favored divine intermediary between the physical and the spiritual realms. As God's abiding presence in *Natura*, the Holy Spirit's propensity towards the fullness and plenitude of all things facilitated a sacred view of the natural world of flora and fauna deemed so essential in the worldviews of all indigenous peoples, past and present. We see these tendencies in the theological naturalism of Hildegard of Bingen, Albertus Magnus, Francis of Assisi, and in the much-misunderstood lore of medieval Christian alchemy (see Chapter Five for a discussion of alchemy and natural philosophy). This type of pneumatological sensibility is difficult for modern and postmodern Euro-Western scholarship to comprehend. This affective tendency to view Nature as both vibrant with generative power and conscious with spiritual power, accounts for the bewildering syncretism that took root over the centuries between the fifty-day Pentecost cycle of the liturgical calendar and the two month cycle of days from May to June surrounding the pre-Christian springtime fertility festivals of the Celts and many of the other commonly known non-Christian tribal groups of the early middle ages.

Medieval Christianisation must be understood as an on-going, complex process in which the ideal of forging a *Respublica Christiana* never quite bridged the gap between feudal aristocracy and ecclesiastical dominion, nor one that ever completely banished the old fertility rites and folkways from the hearts and practices of the populace. As H. Paul Santmire observes, "the metaphor of migration to a Good Land," inherent in the Hebrew Scriptures and the New Testament, led to a highly ambiguous and morally complex Christian position on questions of conquering the non-monotheistic Other and on mastery over Nature,[50] which Santmire identifies as "the travail of Nature" at the hands of Western civilization.[51] In addition, the natural philosophy that emerged from centuries of mixing Greco-Roman ideas with Judeo-Christian concepts of Nature stopped far short of the pantheism and nature-worship needed to appreciate *Dame Nature's* acts of generation each year. As a fecund deity, so dear to the pre-Christian peoples who became the people of "Medieval Europe" by the twelfth century, it seemed as if Christendom had fallen in love with her again in her new guise as Mary, the Blessed Mother of Jesus Christ. Indeed, for three centuries, the new Christian cult of the Virgin Mary inspired the construction of grander and grander church buildings, the Gothic cathedrals of the Middle Ages, all dedicated to "*Notre Dame*," "*Nuestra Señora*," "Our Lady." It is to the intersection of her story with the story of Pentecost that we turn next.

THE GODDESS AND THE MONTH OF MAY

The vast majority of the early medieval populace regarded the Divine Feminine and her annual winter and spring fertility rites as the cornerstone of their ancestral pre-Christian religious traditions. The ideas, practices, and feast days of this ancient cultural system, and its close ties with various folk traditions associated with agriculture, exhibited an amazing tenacity in the hearts and minds of medieval Europeans who lived and worked both inside and outside the direct influence of the Christian church. When the long process of Christianisation across Western and Northern Europe, and the British Isles was completed during the High Middle Ages, vestiges of the religious ideas and ritual practices of these pre-Christian traditions lingered until the late 1600s. Some modern New Age groups would argue that this tradition never died out, and this is especially so with regard to their affectionate reverence for the Divine Feminine, also known as the Goddess or *Dame Nature*. For better or for worse, depending on the degree of cultural purity one's religious affiliation demands, a fascinating syncretistic congruence of traditions between the pre-Christian worship of the Mother Goddess and the Christian celebration of Pentecost occurred in early medieval Western Europe, and which was then passed on to subsequent medieval periods and cultures with diverse and specific regional variations.

Numerous examples of this mixed heritage have survived into modern times, but the contemporary penchant for tourist revenues has obscured the historical reality behind many of the festivals that occur each year across Western Europe. Although virtually unknown today outside of France, one of the earliest examples of this syncretism of pagan and Christian traditions still celebrated each year on May 24 and 25, is the Festival of Saintes-Marie-de-la-Mer in the Camargue region of Bouches-du-Rhône on the Mediterranean coast of Provence. According to local legend, sometime between 40 and 45 CE, fearing for their lives under threat of Roman persecution after the Crucifixion of Jesus, Mary Magdalene and her siblings Martha and Lazarus, together with Mary Salome and Mary Jacobe, their young servant Sara, and several other disciples set off in a boat without oars or sails, and with very few supplies, across the Mediterranean Sea. After a dangerous journey, God's loving Grace led the boat to land in a marshy area on the south of France where the Rhone River meets the sea. Most of the passengers lived out their lives spreading the message of Christ in Roman Gaul. Other legendary accounts report that Mary Magdalene went to St. Baume, and Martha to Tarascon. Some tales go so far as to claim that Joseph of Arimathea was with the seafarers when he brought the Holy Grail through France on his way to Glastonbury. Mary Salome, Mary Jacobe, and Sarah, however, stayed in the Camargue region and became the central figures in the local cult of veneration surrounding the early medieval church dedicated to the "Saint Marys of the Sea." All three women were buried there and thus, the medieval seaside town that grew up around the church was named, St. Marie de la Mer.

The three original tombs and church sanctuary, dating back to the sixth century, are relatively small with an odd fortress-like exterior that was probably added during the barbarian invasions of the eighth and ninth century or perhaps during the partial reconstruction of the site in the mid-1100s by local monks. The church site, known as "Notre-Dame-de-la-Mer" throughout the medieval period, also housed the three saints' relics until a much larger church was built in the late 1400s. The veneration of Saints Mary Salome and Mary Jacobe in this region of France on May 25 during the medieval period is well known. At some point in the late Middle Ages, an annual celebration began when the Roma Gypsies claimed Saint Sara-la-Kali (Sara the Black), also known as "the Black Madonna," as their patron saint.[52] According to some accounts, Sara was the Egyptian servant of Mary Salome and Mary Jacobe who converted and became one of the earliest teachers of the Gospel message in this area of Roman Gaul. According to other accounts, she was the servant of Mary Magdalene, while the more fantastic tales claim she was the daughter of Jesus and Mary Magdalene.

The annual pilgrimage festival on May 24, in which thousands of Gypsies descend upon Saintes-Marie-de-la-Mer, honors Sara-la-Kali, but the Roman Catholic Church has not officially recognized her as a local saint. The following day, May 25, witnesses a procession carrying the statues of Sts. Mary Salome and Mary Jacobe in a boat from the church to the sea and back in a symbolic commemoration of Christianity's arrival in Western Europe after the Crucifixion and Resurrection of Jesus Christ. One can only wonder at the special significance of the two-day festivities in years when the Feast of Pentecost coincided with the dates of May 24 or May 25. The sense of wonder and awe at the Holy Spirit's role in guiding the small boat safely across the Mediterranean Sea, at a time of Roman Imperial persecution, must have been a comforting symbolic experience in both story and iconography for medieval Christians in the region.

In this example from Les Saintes-Marie-de-la-Mer, the syncretistic aspects come into clearer focus as we consider ancient local legends and archaeological excavations indicate this was also the site of a sacred spring dedicated to a threefold Celtic water goddess of uncertain identity. The holy spring was known in late-Roman times (ca. 350-450 CE) as "Oppidum Priscum Ra," but the archaeological evidence suggests the spring had been in use since the Celtic-Ligurian period.[53] Water goddesses, in triadic and double form, were extremely popular among the Celts and represented one of their favorite ways of venerating the Mother Goddess, from whose sacred waters and wells sprang the origins of all animals and plants, and human life as well. These aspects of the site's sacred pre-Christian origins overlap rather well with the medieval veneration of three Christian female figures that arrived by "water" as the heralds of a new message of human sustenance and wholeness, an unfathomable syncretism that, although muted by centuries of change and forgetfulness, still echoes and comes alive each May in the little Provençal seaside town of Saintes-Marie-de-la-Mer.

Another example of the intersection of the goddess tradition with the Pentecostal season is highlighted in Joseph Goering's bold and innovative book, *The Virgin and the Grail: Origins of a Legend*, which explores the possible connections between Chrétien de Troyes' Arthurian romances and a virtually unknown iconographic tradition from northern Spain, in which the Virgin Mary is depicted holding fiery vessels and grail-objects.[54] Goering recounts his fascination and bewilderment when he realized that most of the churches containing these frescoes and wooden altar images of the Virgin with a chalice were done in the Romanesque style of the late eleventh and early twelfth centuries, which pre-dates the appearance of Chretien's and Wolfram's grail sagas by fifty to seventy years.[55] His findings are significant for my project of recovering medieval con-ceptions of Pentecost and the Holy Spirit because some of the most intriguing images included in his book are of the Virgin Mary and the Apostles gathered together in the upper room on the day of Pentecost.[56] One group of frescoes, in particular, originally located in the apse of an obscure Catalan church in the Py-renees highlands, attributed to the Master of St. Clement of Taüll, shows the Ascension of Christ, Christ in Majesty, Pentecost, and the Virgin Mary Holding a Grail with an enigmatic light radiating outward from the chalice and blending with other representations of light and fire depicted in the rest of the group of paintings. Goering concludes that the theological focus or spiritual meaning of these paintings must have been the Ascension of Christ and the subsequent "grace of the Holy Spirit poured out at Pentecost,"

> Since this grace is multivalent, so too is the Virgin's vessel; it might represent the Spirit's presence in the tongues of fire at Pentecost, or in the supernatural light of a lamp, or in the burning incense that fills the Church and purifies it. Because the grace of the Holy Spirit is manifested especially in the Church's tangible sacraments, the vessel might be thought to contain the holy water of baptism and of ritual cleansing, the holy chrism of consecration and confirma-tion, the holy oils of exorcism and of extreme unction, or the body or the blood of Christ in the Eucharist, to name only the most obvious possibilities. . . .so, too, can the Virgin's holy and radiant vessel be seen to represent any and all of the gifts of the Holy Spirit given to the Church.[57]

Another fine example of the blending of pre-Christian goddess and fertility traditions with medieval Christian springtime celebrations and symbolism is represented in the enigmatic figure of the Lady of the Lake found in Arthurian literature. Every connoisseur of the legends of King Arthur knows of the sorcer-er Merlin's symbolic association with the Druids and King Arthur's role as a Christ-symbol. What are less often understood in the academic study of Arthu-rian literature are the syncretistic elements that constellated around the mystify-ing figure of the Lady of the Lake and her uncanny relation to King Arthur's magical sword, Excalibur. As the various stories of the boy-king attest, Arthur's mentor, Merlin, already had a relationship with the Lady of the Lake. In some versions of the story, Merlin and the Lady of the Lake, known as Nimue, share a love interest, while in other versions of the legend she is an enchantress that tries to detain Merlin from his destined work.

In Thomas Malory's epic tale, *Le Morte D'Arthur,* the sword that King Ar-thur drew from the stone on Pentecost Sunday was later broken in battle. Merlin goes to the Lady of the Lake on behalf of King Arthur, and then, for the sake of peace and harmony among all of the peoples of Britain, he prays that she might grant Arthur the privilege of wielding Excalibur for the greater good of all who dwell in his kingdom. Although the twelfth century Welsh chronicler, Geoffrey of Monmouth, was the first to identify King Arthur's magical sword as "Cali-burn" or "*es Calibor,*" meaning "cut steel" and most likely derived from late

Latin, by the mid-1400s the Lady of the Lake was connected in Malory's version with this mythical "sword of power," which as we shall see shortly was not a new idea.

Renowned Celtic archaeologist and writer, Barry Cunliffe once stated "since water came from the earth, it was appropriate for the deity of the source to be female reflecting one of the powers of the earth mother."[58] The close association of Celtic conceptions of the goddess with lakes and ponds, rivers and streams is thoroughly attested to by archaeologist Miranda Green, who points out that "the Celtic mother-goddesses may also have influenced early Christian cults, such as those of the Virgin Mary and certain female saints."[59] Ancient swords, along with many other ritual offerings, have been found in bodies of water throughout Europe, especially in sacred wells and springs dedicated to the Celtic water-goddess Coventina, who is often accompanied by three water nymphs linked with healing and maternal nurture, and possibly signifying the three stages of human life: birth, adulthood, and death.[60] These Celtic triple goddesses offer an interesting contrast with the masculine designation of the three Persons of the Holy Trinity.

In addition, it is entirely possible that Malory's narrative twist in which Merlin intercedes on King Arthur's behalf, and helps procure Excalibur from the Lady of the Lake in *Le Morte D'Arthur,* is based on the ancient Celtic legends and ritual practices of figures like Coventina. The name of Arthur's half-sister, "Morgana" or "Morgan le Fay," might also allude to both a fairy-nymph and a water-deity of some sort since in Welsh "Morgan" means "sea-dweller." After the Battle of Camlann, Malory's King Arthur entrusts Sir Bedivere with his last wish before dying, that he take Excalibur and cast it into a pool of water ensuring its safe return to the Lady of the Lake. As Malory's epic adventure closes, readers catch a glimpse of King Arthur's body resting majestically on a boat with *three queens,* one of whom is his sister Morgan le Fay, all bound for the sacred Island of Avalon where the women will heal his mortal wounds and restore him to life. Thus, long before the migration and conversion period, a close association among sacred bodies of water, healing, and regeneration seems to have been in place among the Celts of the sixth to eighth centuries, and which was then transmitted to the various strains of Celtic Christianity that flowed into the literary construction of the Arthurian and Grail traditions in subsequent centuries.

Another example of these continuities and discontinuities dates to the beginnings of the Feast of Corpus Christi in the early 1300s, which was usually celebrated on the second Sunday after Pentecost or on the Thursday after Trinity Sunday. This late medieval feast day celebrating the Eucharist, which usually takes place sixty days after Easter Sunday in either May or June, was hailed at the Council of Trent in 1551 as a "victory over heresy." Although there was no officially approved celebration of Corpus Domini or Corpus Christi until Pope Clement V authorized and mandated it in 1311 at the Council of Vienne, the actual papal impetus for the celebration originated in 1264 by Pope Urban IV who died before the new Holy Day took root in the practices and beliefs of Latin Christendom.

The Feast of Corpus Christi, however, has even deeper roots than those ascribed to the two popes whose names became associated with its ecclesiastical endorsement and promotion. The story has come down to us that an Augustinian nun from Liège, known today as Saint Juliana of Mount Cornillon (1193-1258), began having an intense and recurring dream about a church under a full moon with a disturbing black spot on the moon. One day Christ appeared in the dream, and he interpreted its meaning to her. Juliana explained to her bishop that, according to Jesus, the moon in the dream signified the Church's calendar of festivals and that the black spot signified the absence of a festival celebrating the Eucharist. Tradition records that St. Juliana's local bishop, Jacques Pantaléon, began honoring the festival in 1246 until he ascended the papal throne as Pope Urban IV and mandated it as an obligatory feast of the church before his untimely death. At the famous Cistercian Abbey of Casamari, which will figure very prominently in Chapter Three's discussion of Joachim of Fiore, by the time of the Council of Vienne (1311-1312) local custom seems to have already been assembling the *infiorata* displays, meaning "flower tapestries," that spectacularly adorn the nave of this abbey each year during the Feast of Corpus Christi. Other towns and cities across Europe celebrated the feast with Eucharistic processions in which rose petals were cast before the feet of people carrying the ceremonial vessel, called a monstrance, on a pallet. While some have claimed that these "flower tapestries" and annual processions were in existence as early as the eleventh century, the juxtaposition of Christ's *Corpus Domini* alongside the flowering months of May and June, two weeks after Pentecost Sunday harkens back to earlier pre-Christian times when celebrations of Nature now lost in the mists of the early medieval period still marked the passage of time, a time for marriage and fertility rites, and the advent of the agricultural growing season.

The spiritual syncretism of Celtic and Christian elements noted above in the annual May festivities of the French town of Saintes-Maries-de-la-Mer, and in the symbolic figures of the Lady of the Lake and Morgan le Fay preserved in the annals of medieval Arthurian literature, and in the beautiful *infiorata* displays associated with the first celebrations of the Feast of Corpus Christi in the 1300s, are only a few examples from among a vast number of similar vignettes which further illustrate this chapter's main points. Celtic mother-goddesses, and the procreative Earth-Mother principle they represented, were known across pre-Christian Europe by a variety of trans-local names: "Great Mother," "White Goddess," "Mother Earth," "Lady of the Lake," and "Goddess of the Moon." While a comprehensive account of these examples, and many other similar stories from Medieval and Early Modern Europe, is beyond the reach this book, there is little doubt that their concern with healing and regeneration, along with diverse beliefs and rituals concerned with revering Nature and the spirit world, coalesced with Christian understandings of the Virgin Mary and the rapidly growing cult of Christian saints in the centuries from the Migration Period of the early middle ages to the building of the great Gothic Cathedrals in the twelfth and thirteenth centuries.

During the Dark Ages that followed the fall of Rome, a rapidly spreading Christian movement reached out to convert and educate the warrior-elites among

Europe's Celtic peoples and other pagan tribes which formerly had been left alone by the Romans to worship their local gods and goddesses. By the ninth century ascension of Charlemagne as King of the Franks, Christianity was well on its way toward superseding these primordial traditions at both the local and trans-local levels. For the priests and priestesses who served these agrarian, fertility traditions spiritual power resided in both understanding and mediating the pathways between the domain of the living and the mysterious world of the Unseen, the realm of the spirits. Although we are focused on the medieval period, the cultural situation and the social logic in which these stories and symbols functioned is analogous to the late ancient holy men and holy women described by Peter Brown as "arbiters of the holy" in a time of fragmentation and transition to a new *ordo spiritualis* based on Christian monotheism and its abstract Trinitarian theology. At this point in our exposition and analysis of such wide ranging historical data, it is wise to interject the usual postmodernist academic caution that all of our theorizing about pre-Christian fertility traditions, pagan and Christian notions of the goddess or the Divine Feminine does not equate with, nor support an elevated status for women's roles and agency in the patriarchal societies of medieval Christianity.

On the other hand, it does suggest, rather forcibly, as highlighted in Barbara Newman's studies of goddess figures and women's spirituality in medieval religious history, that, despite the misogyny and rigidly defined gender roles in place throughout medieval Europe, women had access to forms of agency and power that modern scholarship has only recently begun to perceive and recover.[61] Surveying the course of Western conceptions of Nature from Platonism to the Scholastic High Middle Ages, while focusing her research on "those goddesses who function within overtly Christian schemes of representation,"[62] Newman points out, "that Natura first emerges as a mediatrix between God and the world."[63] This feature of Natura's cosmic relational activity in relation to our embodied terrestrial existence and female fertility predisposed her in the minds of medieval visionaries and poets towards an affinity with the Holy Spirit's manifestation in the natural world and in the particularities of human life as the intermediary between the Trinity and human temporality. Just as one of the functions of the Incarnate Son is in restoring humanity to the Father, one of the functions of the Holy Spirit, therefore, is to infuse particularity with divinity as the breath of God through the Son, which thereby reminds the human creature of its relation to animals, plants, the oceans, the fecundity of the earth, and the *anima mundi*. Such a stance is perhaps a necessity in a monotheistic version of a Three Person godhead devoid of an overtly feminine person, and hence the popular veneration and eventual elevation of the Virgin Mary (along with certain female saints) throughout the Christian Middle Ages as a means of recalling and honoring Natura's concern with fertility and "the production of bodies."[64] Even the contemplative practices of deep prayer and other forms of meditation, like staring meditation or ritually "walking the labyrinth," happen through bodily actions aimed at stilling the mind and allowing the voice of the Holy Spirit to speak through the human heart. Given the Holy Spirit's other manifestation as Divine Wisdom (Sophia), the association of this pneumatological principle with the order of creation, as reflected in Natura, makes all the more sense regardless of whether or not it is specifically named as such in the majority of medieval primary sources.

As suggested by Peter Brown in his studies of early Christian monasticism,[65] we can assume, with more than a little confidence, that in the early Middle Ages there were pagan holy men and holy women who resisted the march of the Christian ethos in accord with a mighty host of tree spirits and procreative goddess energies, and life-filled bogs, lakes, rivers and streams. Others from these same pagan traditions felt called to the service of the one God who came to drive out the many gods of their ancestors, and their numbers increased as Christianization gained momentum through local converts. In either instance, the devotees of the pre-Christian past and the devotees of the Christian future wielded profound *spiritual power* over their communities as intermediaries between the living and the dead, between the Church-men of Scholasticism and the folk-wisdom of Mother Earth, and between the *past* and the *not-yet* of the future. These mediators were also storytellers and poets of the religious imagination who, no matter which side of the Christian-pagan divide they were on, showed others "how in telling and re-telling stories people can again and again renegotiate their identities through the pluralities of rushing time," as attested in Delwin Brown's theory of tradition.[66] The coming together of pagan conceptions regarding the May-June cycle of fertility feasts with the Christian liturgical calendar's forty-nine day cycle of Pentecost may have as much to do with the creative vitality of Romano-Celtic and Germanic influences as with Christianity's historic predisposition to syncretistic accretions from the cultures it coexisted with, or conquered and converted.

In her survey of the millennium long history of Celtic religious traditions, Miranda Green concludes:

> It is important to acknowledge pagan Celtic religion as a dynamic force, which was constantly changing and responding to the stimuli of new concepts and ideas, whilst still retaining a core of conservatism. It is indeed the tension between tradition and innovation, which gives Celtic religion its essential character of diversity and enigma.[67]

Therefore, the convergence of Pentecostal elements with pre-Christian fertility traditions, as exemplified in the Arthurian and Grail-quest traditions is not just a function of the conquest and domination of pagans by the Church and it's newly Christianized feudal aristocracy. The pneumatological and Pentecostal continuities we detect in the primary sources, as well as the discontinuities we sense, must also be a function of those creative features allowing Celtic religion and Christian traditions to constantly change, adapt, and renegotiate individual and communal identities. As theologian Delwin Brown suggests in his theory of tradition: "feeling and thought in interaction serve as the vehicle of a tradition's recovery and innovation."[68]

PENTECOST IN THE ARTHURIAN & HOLY GRAIL TRADITIONS

Richard Barber describes the Grail as "a mysterious and haunting image, which crosses the borders between religion and spirituality, and which, for eight centuries, has been a recurrent ideal in Western literature."[69] Such a notion of the Holy Grail as an object on the borderlands of the human spirit, forever poised between heaven and earth, parallels the notion of the Grail as a sacred object poised between Europe's pre-Christian Celtic traditions, and the dynamic role of Pentecost and the Holy Spirit in the medieval Christian imagination. There is no doubt that long before the first legions of Roman centurions crossed the English Channel, the people of Celtic Britain told stories of magical cauldrons and enchanted swords, while their holy men and holy women celebrated their culture's most sacred rituals honoring the Goddess and Nature's rebirth each May and June. In Britain and across continental Europe, many of these celebrations survived the fall of Rome and later were assimilated into the emerging Christian culture of the Early Middle Ages. Barber rightly refers to the heroic figure of Arthur and the rich symbolism of the Grail as "a construct of the creative imagination," just as I contend throughout this book that the story of the Pentecost event, preserved in the Book of Acts, functioned as a repository of spiritual power and creativity open to all imaginative Christians across the varied times and places of church history. In this section, and in the chapter's remaining sections, we will examine the rise of the Arthurian and Grail traditions with the aim of seeking out some of their forgotten Pentecostal sensibilities, cultural legacies, and religious meanings.

After four centuries of Roman rule, the Romano-Celtic peoples of the British Isles were invaded during the late fifth, sixth, and seventh centuries, by successive waves of warrior tribes from across the sea. First arrived the Saxons and the Angles, who were then followed by the Danes and other Scandinavian invaders, referred to by chroniclers mostly as the Vikings. Finally in 1066 came the Normans, led by King William the Conqueror, whose arrival and assimilation produced the very rich and influential Anglo-Norman culture of medieval England. However, in the early stages of this "Invasion Period," a legend arose about a gallant and brave Roman commander, Ambrosius Aurelianus, who united the people of Britain against the Saxons and led them to a great victory at a place called "*Mons Badonicus*," from which both hero and place came the raw material for the legends of King Arthur and the Battle of Baden Hill. Mention of King Arthur's role in these events occurs in Bede's *Ecclesiastical History* (ca. mid-700s), and it is now well-known that Bede relied considerably for much of his content on the earlier Welsh chronicle by Gildas, *De Excidio et Conquestu Britanniae* (ca. 550). While the *Annales Cambriae* chronicle places this battle around the years 516 or 517, scholarly opinion has tended to downplay the historicity of the events.

Nonetheless, Peter Hunter Blair recognizes Gildas as an eyewitness at the battle and concludes:

Despite these obscurities we must accept as historical fact the winning of a major British victory over the invaders and the consequent enjoyment by the victors of a respite which lasted for half a century or more,. . . A much later tradition ascribed a prominent part in this victory to Arthur. This we must treat with caution, though not with caution so extreme as to deny all historical existence to that same Arthur, for Arthur's fame was great in the sixth century, though we do not know why.[70]

Similarly, in affirmation of the religious and literary origins of the Arthurian and Grail sagas from ancient Celtic and Welsh story-telling traditions, Rodney Castleden observes:

> The transmission of information in the Celtic world was mainly oral, so we have to accept that the history of the sixth century will be likely to survive to later centuries mainly in the form of recited ballads, songs, funeral   panegyrics, elegies and triads, in other words, in poetic and musical forms that were relatively easily committed to memory. The memorizing was done by highly trained bards and when the material was eventually written down, in the seventh, eighth, ninth or even later centuries, much of it will have arrived in little-altered condition.[71]

Although I disagree with Castleden about such transmissions arriving in "little altered condition," the larger process he describes is essentially accurate. Castleden's views of Celtic cultural transmission during the Dark Ages (ca. 476-950) are supported by opinions and conclusions expressed in the comprehensive, international collaboration of Celtic scholars and archaeologists assembled in Miranda Green's *The Celtic World,* and with the now classic literary and historical insights of Roger Sherman Loomis.

With an academic career spanning over four decades, Roger Sherman Loomis was the twentieth century's leading authority on Arthurian literature and Grail romances until his death in 1967. Four years before his passing, Loomis summarized his life's work in *The Grail: From Celtic Myth to Christian Symbol.* Of particular interest, for the assimilation of pre-Christian Celtic beliefs with medieval Christian spirituality, is Loomis' contention that the Grail stories combine "earthy magic and sacramental miracle,"[72] which is precisely the issue to be fathomed if we are to understand the range of pneumatological consciousness open to the medieval writers and readers of these numinous tales.

Ironically, despite the origins of the historical King Arthur in foggy memories of the sixth century, the vast majority of the court romances about Arthur and the Grail, and the Knights of the Round Table, surfaced in France and Germany from about 1170 through 1250. This may seem ironic to modern readers, given that so much of the legendary background material for these stories came from much older Celtic sources in Ireland and Wales, but it also attests to the persistence of Celtic cultural and religious traditions on the European continent during the twelfth and thirteenth centuries.[73] And, it also substantiates the popularity of King Arthur as a trans-local symbol for medieval ideas about peace and justice, prosperity, and successful kingship. During the 1200s and 1300s, "Round Tables" became a stylistic fad among European nobility eager to reflect some of this aura of just and stable leadership garnered from the Arthurian legends, while itinerant Arthurian poets and storytellers proliferated from England to Spain and eastward to Italy.

It was the popular appeal of Chrétien de Troyes' Arthurian romances, composed between 1160 and 1185, which started the widespread proliferation of French poets and troubadours composing epic tales based upon the older Celtic sagas circulating then in Brittany, and already known as the "Matter of Britain" featuring King Arthur and his legendary knights. Today he is widely regarded by many to be the creator of Arthurian romance. Chrétien served as herald-at-arms for about twelve years at the court of his literary patroness Marie de France, Countess of Champagne (1145-98), daughter of the French King Louis VII and Queen Eleanor of Aquitaine.[74] As an author herself, Marie also relied on magical tales from the Breton and Celtic past, which in her famous poetic series, known as the *Lais*, challenged patriarchal and traditional Christian perspectives on the role of women, while portraying positive views of Nature, and all manner of flora and fauna, as embodying a legacy of spiritual freedom and human love misunderstood by church and society. Very little is known about Chrétien's life story or about his education and how he learned so much about the Welsh, Irish, and Breton stories he translated into Old French verse. We know that he was familiar with Geoffrey of Monmouth's *Historia regum Britanniae* (1138) and probably knew of Wace's Anglo-Norman *Le Roman de Brut* (1155), which provided much literary inspiration for later poets seeking to bring the wondrous adventures of Arthur and his reign of peace and generosity to the attention of court audiences in France. Beyond these bits and pieces, and a few other details, very little else is known about the family origins and life story of this twelfth century literary genius.

One thing is certain, however, that with Countess Marie de France as his patroness, Chrétien composed some of the most important Arthurian romances and courtly love lyrics of the High Middle Ages.[75] Among these are *Érec and Énide*, *Lancelot, Cliges*, and *Yvain, The Knight of the Lion*. In the opening lines of his famous *Lancelot, The Knight of the Cart*, Chrétien honors Marie by describing her as a lady who "surpasses all others who are alive, just as the south wind which blows in May or April is more lovely than any other wind."[76] On or about May 14, 1181, during that year's Pentecostal cycle of days, Marie de France entered into a military alliance with Count Philip of Flanders, who soon became Chrétien's next patron and who would soon be leaving on Crusade to the Holy Land. Shortly thereafter, Chrétien began composing an epic poem for Philip of Flanders entitled *Perceval, Le Conte du Graal*, which although left unfinished due to the poet's death around 1191, influenced almost every subsequent medieval and modern retelling of King Arthur's reign and the quest for the Holy Grail.

The association of King Arthur with Pentecost was well known before Chrétien wrote his Arthurian romances, and the plot sequences in most of his romances feature allusions akin to Pentecost or Whitsuntide amid narrative settings in the late spring or early summer months of May and June. *Le Conte du Graal* is mainly about Perceval who, following his father's death, was raised by his mother as far away as possible from his ancestral homeland in Wales. One day he meets a group of proud knights passing through, and is so captivated by the sight that, against his mother's stern wishes, he decides to visit King Arthur's court and become a knight. Along the way he meets the character of the Wounded Fisher-King, fails to ask the healing question, and begins his search for the Grail. The narrative also features lengthy sections on the adventures of Arthur's kinsman and bravest knight, Gawain, but overall the plot meanders here and there as it was never finished due to Chrétien's death.

Nonetheless, Chrétien sets up Perceval's spiritual transformation to take place within the symbolic realm of the Christian worldview, and, although unfinished, the saga ends with Perceval and Gawain looking forward to the upcoming "Whitsuntide Court" convened each year by King Arthur at the culmination of the seven-times-seven-days of Pentecost. Given that some knights are prone to prideful and often violent misconduct when Arthur holds court, there seems to be a moral clue imbedded within this Pentecostal setting. As the commemoration of God's gracious outpouring of the Holy Spirit on the first Pentecost, and as signifying God's Grace through the gifts of the Holy Spirit, perhaps the two most significant knightly virtues of the Feast of Pentecost then were those of Christian charity and forgiveness. Hence, chivalric misbehavior involving selfishness, greed, and dishonesty among members of the Round Table fraternity was a serious sin against these Christian ideals and God's commandments.

After Chrétien's death, admirers of *Le Conte du Graal* tried, for better or for worse, over the next fifty years to complete the narrative verse he had begun in a series of so-called "continuations," of which there were four.[77] While these attempts to finish Chrétien's story about the Grail interest modern scholars, none of the continuators succeeded in capturing the intermingling of religious ideals and chivalric elements that made Chrétien's earlier Arthurian romances such a popular form of courtly entertainment during the poet's lifetime. The task of reinventing the story of King Arthur and the quest for the Holy Grail would be taken up by new generations of poets and storytellers in the thirteenth century, some of whom also understood and amplified the legend's Pentecostal and pneumatological aspects.

For example, in the *Didot Perceval* (ca. 1210) King Arthur orders a great feast on Pentecost leading to the formation of the chivalric fraternity later known as the Round Table. In Robert de Boron's *Joseph of Arimathea*, *Merlin*, and *Perceval* sagas (ca. 1200-1210), we find similar accounts referencing Pentecost and the month of May in relation to the Round Table, with Merlin serving as the mouthpiece for what appear to be much earlier oral legends about other pre-Christian "sacred tables." Wolfram von Eschenbach's *Parzival* saga (ca. 1200) depicted a naïve young knight's seven-year quest for the Holy Grail set around an eerie chronology of seven Pentecosts, while Malory's famous work, *Le Morte D'Arthur* (ca. 1470), more than two centuries later, also featured the major turning points in King Arthur's career during the Pentecostal cycle of the liturgical calendar. The influence of ancient Celtic mythology filtered through Irish, Welsh, and Breton sources is clearly evident in many medieval versions of the Matter of Britain.

However, the influence of Christian beliefs and doctrines is equally evident in the vast corpus of stories about King Arthur and the Holy Grail. This pattern is noticeable in the time-sequences and forest settings employed by many writers of these Arthurian tales, such as the numerous references to the major feast days of the liturgical calendar, or the references to the "Canonical Hours" of the monastic lifestyle wherein periods of prayer alternate with the labors of the day. Another example of a more pronounced Christian perspective, quite contrary to the Celtic elements discussed above, is found in *The High Book of the Grail* (ca. mid-1200s), which begins with the following prologue:

> The high book of the Grail begins in the name of the   Father, Son, and Holy Spirit. These three are one substance, and that substance is God, and from God comes the noble story of the Grail; and all those who hear it must be attentive and forget all their baseness, for those who hear it with their hearts will find it most profitable.[78]

Likewise the tendency among some of the narratives to depict King Arthur as drawing a magical sword from a stone on either Easter Sunday or Pentecost Sunday are further indications of the legend's gradual Christianisation and literary adaptation to a changing audience.

In summary, the imaginative possibilities and liminal spaces of the Grail romances allowed for both overtly Christian expressions of the relation among the Three Persons of the Holy Trinity and overtly pre-Christian expressions of the relation among Nature worship and the spirit realm to live together in these stories and epic poems. An act of generation, attesting as much to the pluriform possibilities of Christian pneumatology as to the pluriform vitality of the Divine Feminine, which a male-dominated church leadership thought it could silence but who won the day when the emerging *Respublica Christiana* of the twelfth century began dedicating those magnificent Gothic cathedrals to her as "Notre Dame," "Nuestra Señora," "Our Lady." In the 1100s and 1200s, men and women across Europe became devotees of the cult of the Virgin Mother of God who, clothed in robes of azure blue and adorned with heavenly stars and precious gems, stood atop an ancestrally familiar crescent moon more akin to the cosmological and agrarian traditions of pre-Christian Europe than to the rapidly growing urban centers and swiftly rising Christian cathedrals of the High Middle Ages. None of the stories about King Arthur or about the quest for the Holy Grail make more vivid use of Pentecostal imagery than Wolfram's fantastic story about Parzival, to which we now turn.

PENTECOST IN WOLFRAM'S PARZIVAL, CA. 1200

Sometime around the year 1200, a German poet-knight by the name of Wolfram von Eschenbach composed an epic adventure about a foolish youth's quest for the Holy Grail.[79] The poem totals 24,810 lines of rhymed couplets in Middle High German divided into 827 thirty-line sections arranged into sixteen chapters or "Books." These divisions, although based upon the available medieval manuscript copies of the poem, are largely the work of nineteenth century German scholars and literary critics. The narrative weaves numerous subplots into the poem's vast geography and within the perplexing genealogies of the story's two chivalric families: the Grail-family and the Arthurian fraternity of the Round Table. The young protagonist's unexpected initiation into the violent world of knight-errantry and the possibilities of spiritual redemption through love and compassion lead him through a steadfast seven-year quest for the Holy Grail. Wolfram's *Parzival* legend must have confounded its medieval audiences and readers then as much as it perplexes modern readers today by depicting the Grail as a "stone" that fell from the sky on Good Friday, and which was nourished each year during Holy Week by a dove bearing a communion wafer. The Holy Grail depicted as a stone? Surely this must be an impostor to the much more familiar magical dish, or another pretender to the famous chalice used by Christ at the Last Supper. This extraordinary Middle High German tale of love (*minne*) and adventure (*âventiure*) spans seven years, or more precisely, seven Pentecosts that encompass Parzival's spiritual transformation from a naïve boy in search of chivalric glory to King of the Grail Family as the compassionate and just leader of his kinfolk at the Grail Castle.

Chivalry and love are not the only themes depicted through the lives of the characters in this engrossing saga.[80] Even in the late 1200s, while more than a few European Christian writers depicted mosques as "mahommeries" and denigrated Muhammad's name, Wolfram was recognized for his tolerant views and humane portrayals of Muslims, Arabs, and Moors in his works. Unlike Chrétien de Troyes' unfinished romance *Le Conte du Graal* (ca. 1181-1191), Wolfram's version of the Grail legend intertwines a rich and complex tapestry of elements from Islamic Spain with elements from Arthurian romance and chivalric lore. As demonstrated by Arthur Groos, the *Parzival* presents a decentered narrative that employs a variety of literary styles and devices, while keeping its readers constantly guessing and rethinking the direction in which the story is headed.[81] These complexities are further convoluted by the poem's enormous geographical breadth as Parzival's quest is played out under the aegis of the so-called Grail-family, whose ties stretch beyond Western Europe to the Islamic kingdoms of Iberia and the Middle East, reaching as far away as Baghdad.

Since the rediscovery of forgotten medieval manuscript copies of the work in the late-1700s by Swiss and German scholars, no researcher has succeeded in providing a comprehensive analysis of Wolfram's complex narrative, and no such attempt will be made in the following pages. In the 1960's, Henry and Renée Kahane very aptly described the *Parzival* as a work "at the frontier of religion,"[82] and while the interpretive complexities of that literary and religious "frontier" were the focus of my unpublished doctoral thesis, the pneumatological dimensions of Parzival's seven year journey of transformation spanning seven Pentecosts will be the primary focus of the analysis and discussion offered herein.[83]

One of the challenges confronting both literary and historical studies of *Parzival* has always been the extremely scanty information available about his particular region of Germany during the period coinciding with Wolfram's life and works (ca. 1165-1220). Scholarly analysis of the place names mentioned throughout his works led researchers in the 1800s to conclude that Wolfram was from the Upper Main valley town of Ober-Eschenbach, located then between Ansbach and Nuremberg. In medieval times this was the region known as Central Franconia, although he himself claimed to be a Bavarian. This discrepancy is probably a result of the feudal conflicts of those times, which caused the lands in the region to change hands frequently between the kingdoms of Bavaria and Swabia. In honor of Wolfram's stature within the canon of German literature, a statue of him was erected at Ober-Eschenbach in 1861. Then in 1917, after much scholarly debate and civic posturing as to questions of origins, the town's name was changed to Wolframs-Eschenbach.[84] Furthermore, we know the Eschenbach family was a member of the lower nobility as attested to by archival evidence bearing their coat of arms. Archival records also identify a "von Eschenbach" family, presumably related to the poet, living in that region from about 1268 through the late 1300s. At various times over the years, different graves in the region caught the attention of scholars and interested laymen as being the burial site of Wolfram von Eschenbach, but reliable evidence for such a site has remained inconclusive. Regardless of how we situate both author and text within the literary and historical landscape of his times, we lack a complete picture of his life.

Equally unclear are other details that could help us weave a more complete biographical picture of this medieval poet, who is regarded today as meriting a place beside Dante, Chaucer, and Petrarch. Details such as his education, his marital status, and the names of any children he might have had would be useful. We suspect the *Parzival* was dedicated to a woman (Bk. XVI, sec. 827), and at another point in the narrative Wolfram offers us an aside that implies that he was married (Bk. IV, sec. 216). We are further confused by his admission elsewhere in the narrative that he was wronged in an act of "disloyalty" by a certain lady, whom he was presumably courting (Bk. II, sec. 114-116). Thus, Wolfram's statements about himself in *Parzival*, and in his other works, while stimulating much scholarly speculation over the years, have only added to our often confusing, incomplete picture of his personal life.

We do know, however, that beyond his talents as a poet, he also served proudly as a knight who was as well versed in the use of arms as he was in the realm of courtly love poetry (Bk. II, sec. 115). As both *Minnesanger* (minstrel) and knight, he seems to have been in the service of several different royal patrons, as he states in *Parzival* (Bk. IV, sec. 184) and in his other epic *Willehalm*. Among these patrons were such historical figures as the Landgrave Herman of Thuringia (died ca. 1217) and the Counts of Wertheim, Poppo I (died ca. 1212) and Poppo II (d. 1238).[85] He might even have been connected with the highly traveled and colorful Count Rupprecht von Durne (died ca. 1197-1200). As a typical poet-knight of that era, Wolfram used his travels and knightly adventures as the *prima materia* for his courtly songs and epic poems. His knowledge of the place names and the geography of Bavaria, Thuringia, and Wertheim are well attested and accurately reflect our historical understanding of those regions of medieval Germany in the late 1100s and early 1200s. His other source of information for tales of love and chivalry seems to have derived from traveling minstrels and troubadours, such as the Kyot de Provence believed to have been the historical William of Tudela, whom Wolfram credits with telling him this unusual story about Parzival and the Grail as an "oracular stone" that fell from heaven.

Issues of origins and transmission aside, how Wolfram von Eschenbach became interested in composing stories like *Parzival* and *Willehalm* is uncertain and may never be known. The prevailing opinion is that his patron, Herman of Thuringia, gave Wolfram a copy of the *chanson de geste,* known as the *Bataille d'Aliscans*, which became the basis for his other great work *Willehalm.* Although it appears to have been left unfinished after chapter nine, *Willehalm* weaves together the legends and heroic exploits of Count William of Toulouse in his struggle against the "Saracen" (Arab) invaders in the days of Charlemagne (ca. 780–815). Wolfram's sense of tolerance and empathy towards Muslims is evident here as in the *Parzival* by the compassionate treatment of the so-called "heathen" characters in the poem. Wolfram's only other work, known as *Titurel* among German medievalists, was never finished beyond a few minor fragments of verse.[86]

One of the great difficulties in comprehending the sources for Wolfram's inspiration is that, during the Protestant Reformation, his *Parzival* epic seems to have been forgotten, as laity and clergy in the 1500s across the German hinterland developed a disdain for the literary, liturgical, and symbolic traces of what they considered the Roman Catholic past. Indeed, from 1520 to the late 1600s, there is a sharp decline in courtly, public, and ecclesiastical interest in the romance literature and sagas of the High Middle Ages. The Spanish mystic Teresa of Ávila tells us that she derived much pleasure from reading chivalric romances as a pastime, while the Spanish novelist Miguel de Cervantes portrayed Don Quijote as a knight whose madness was precipitated by reading too many chivalric tales. Judging from the number of surviving manuscript copies of *Parzival* dated to the thirteenth, fourteenth, and fifteenth centuries, we are quite certain that Wolfram's masterpiece continued to be popular after the poet's death in the early 1200s.

For almost three centuries, medieval manuscript copies and late fifteenth century printed copies of Wolfram's *Parzival* languished in libraries, monasteries, and private collections in Europe. Then, in the mid-1700s, a Swiss poet and literary critic from Zurich, J. J. Bodmer, uncovered several manuscripts in Berlin attributed to a then relatively unknown poet-knight calling himself Wolfram von Eschenbach, manuscripts which told the fantastic tale of a young knight in search of a Grail-object which seemed neither ecclesiastically holy nor a chalice, but which was instead a *"steine"* (stone) brought down from heaven by the neutral angels when Lucifer waged war in heaven against God. When Bodmer realized how many late medieval manuscripts and Renaissance print copies of this story were scattered across Germany, he realized it must have been a very popular work in its own time. Edwin Zeydel cited a folio volume produced at Strasbourg in 1477 as evidence of the poem's persistent appeal centuries after Wolfram's death.[87] Bodmer began identifying, collecting, cataloging, and editing some of these manuscripts and texts. In 1784, Bodmer collaborated with Christoph Heinrich Myller, a fellow Swiss antiquarian and grammar school teacher, in an editorial project for circulation among a small circle of scholars living in Berlin. The German philologist Karl Lachmann published the first modern, critical edition of Wolfram's Parzival in 1833.[88] Other contemporary voices motivated more by the concerns of national identity and racial hegemony than by a medieval author's fascination with Pentecost and the Holy Spirit would soon see different possibilities in the story of Parzival.

Also noteworthy among this first generation of literary critics and scholars engaged in reassessing the importance of Wolfram's work were the Grimm brothers, Jacob and Wilhelm, and Karl Bartsch. In the opening decades of the nineteenth century, the cultural forces that would impel Germany to become an industrial, military, and academic leader were just taking shape. Writers like the Brothers Grimm, and scholars like Karl Bartsch, must have felt Parzival's heroic quest for the Grail reflected something of the dynamism and courageous vitality emerging in Germany at that time and simultaneously being advocated by the prevailing Romantic artists and thinkers of their day. Jacob Grimm referred to Wolfram as "den an Gedanken und Gemut reichsten Dichter unserer Vorzeit,"[89] while Karl Bartsch believed Wolfram was more than just a great German poet, but instead a poet of universal significance comparable in medieval history only to Dante.[90] We need not limit such interest to the perceived heroic dimensions of Wolfram's work, for the *Parzival's* pneumatological aspects surely appealed to German intellectuals familiar with the rich legacies of German pietism, or to avant-garde intellectuals pondering the historicist significance of Hegel's Universal *Geist*. Commenting on the "spiritual" value and meaning of such stories for the people, Wilhelm Grimm wrote that: "The mythic element resembles small pieces of a shattered jewel lying strewn on the ground all overgrown with grass and flowers, and can only be discovered by the most far-seeing eye."[91] In the wake of Goethe's literary triumphs and Wagner's *Parsifal*, and with the very popular recovery of "*volkisch*" folklore tales by the Brothers Grimm, the search was on for national literature and intellectual culture capable of embodying the noblest ideals of a people with a great spiritual and political future, the German race. One wonders if anyone at that time of the "*Sturm und Drang*" (Storm and Stress) movement actually understood the deeply existential ontological and pneumatological questions Wolfram's thirteenth century sensibilities were already grappling with and perhaps even warning future European Christians about.

Thus, after three centuries of neglect, Wolfram's *Parzival* legend was recovered. This rebirth, although wrapped in the incarnation of an academic enterprise, would eventually raise Wolfram's narrative poem as the most studied work of the medieval German literary canon, as well as a very popular and troublesome nineteenth century symbol of the *Volksgeist* or Spirit of the German race.[92]

The long and rich discourse of *Parzival* scholarship that sought to situate Wolfram's text in relation to Chrétien de Troyes' *Le Conte du Graal* has never succeeded in answering the question of the narrative's origins.[93] Chrétien claimed that he based his version of the Grail story on a book given him by

Count Philip of Flanders, but this mysterious *livre* has never been successfully identified. Although Count Philip served as a crusader in the Holy Land, there are no Arabic source references in Chrétien's account of Perceval's quest for the Grail, and Philip, we are certain, died of fever or dysentery at Acre on 1 June 1191, followed by Chrétien's death a short time later. As a result, one would suspect that Chrétien's unknown source was probably based upon the Celtic, Welsh, or Breton tales his former patroness, Marie de France, shared with him. This is further complicated by Wolfram's very direct, parting jab at Chrétien's credibility in the final lines of his narrative's conclusion:

> If Master Chrétien von Troyes did not do justice to this story, that may well vex Kyot, who furnished us the right story. . . From Provence to Germany the true facts were sent to us, as this adventure's final conclusion. I, Wolfram von Eschenbach, shall tell no more of it than the master told there. (Book XVI, 827)[94]

The hypothesis that Chrétien's version of the quest for the Holy Grail is the so-called "pre-text" of the *Parzival* does not account for the fact that Wolfram's German version of the story is filled with many more pneumatological symbols and references to Pentecost than his bardic sparring partner from the French court. Given the numerous associations among King Arthur's reign, the Knights of the Round Table, and Pentecost, it is not surprising that regardless of the sources that inspired Wolfram's masterpiece, his particular version of the story is so deftly tinged with pneumatological references and allusions.

The differences between Wolfram's account of Parzival's adventure and Chrétien's version are numerous, especially with respect to the story's alleged connections with Islamic Spain. Indeed, Wolfram's references to Toledo and Seville suggest a familiarity with those places, which lends further credibility to Wolfram's professed connection with a mysterious, Arabic book from Toledo that Kyot de Provence then transmitted to him.[95] It is worth noting that Wolfram is incredibly consistent with regard to the issue of his version's origin in Islamic Spain and its transmission through Kyot de Provence. Indeed, he specifically states that he did not write the story, but committed to German verse a tale, which Kyot de Provence translated from Arabic into French after reading it in a book by a Moor named Flegetanis of Toledo, who, in turn, we read was descended from the legendary King Solomon. No doubt a convoluted mess! But nonetheless, a fascinating conundrum that has generated many fanciful ideas and theories about the origins of Wolfram's *Parzival.*

Although I believe the so-called "Kyot problem" is unsolvable, one is often puzzled by whether this medieval minstrel was balancing the demands of artistic expression with historical representation (always a daunting feat for poets and novelists), or whether Wolfram was just playing with the imaginations of his audiences and readers. In all my years of carefully reading Wolfram, and spending time with this magnificent and entertaining text, I realize that he was a genuine comic wit with a rare gift for ironic, subtle humor.

Wolfram's delight in tantalizing his audience is evident from the very beginning of the story, wherein we are offered a most mystifying Prologue that was sure to ignite the imaginations of both hearers and readers of this tale:

> Never have I met a man so wise but that he would have liked to find out what authority this story claims and what good lessons it provides. On that score it never wants for courage, now to flee, now to charge, dodge and return, condemn and praise. Whoever can make sense out of all these turns of chance has been well treated by Wisdom, or whoever does not sit too tight, or walk astray, but in general understands. (Bk. I, sec. 2-16)[96]

Suggesting at the outset that his audience should seek to unravel the "authority" upon which the story is based, the poet warns us not to get distracted by the twists and "turns of chance" of the journey we are about to undertake. At this stage one might assume that Wolfram's antecedent "authority" is Chrétien's unfinished Grail story *Le Conte du Graal*, but when we get to Book IX of Wolfram's narrative, we discover that his story's Grail-object is neither holy chalice, nor sacred dish (as in the Celtic, Welsh and Breton sagas documented by R. S. Loomis), but a confounding stone called *"lapsit exillis."* We then learn of the two obscure seekers from Spain and France whom Wolfram credits with writing and transmitting the story: Flegetanis of Toledo and Kyot de Provence.

We are thus forced to question the starting point of this adventure's sources and objectives, a cultural dissonance that would not have gone unnoticed by Wolfram's contemporary hearers and readers. The *"quaestio"* then becomes a series of allegorical *"quaestiones"* leading up to Parzival's enigmatic question that heals the wounded Fisher-King of the Grail-Castle and secures Parzival's ascension as the next Grail-King on Pentecost: *"What ails you uncle?"* This mysterious turn of events reminds us of the perplexity echoed in the Pentecostal inquiry from Acts 2: *"What does this mean?"*

The tripartite structure of Wolfram's plot causes one to wonder which portion of the action leads to the true meaning of the story. These "turns of chance," as the author refers to them, focus on three broad areas of narrative action and character development: the parentage of Parzival and his Moorish half-brother, Feirefiz (Books I and II); the beginning of Parzival's career as a knight around a first Pentecost when he stumbles upon the Grail Castle, but fails to ask the wounded Anfortas the healing question (Books III-VIII); and Parzival's transformation into a mature knight and humble servant of God who stops short of killing his Muslim half-brother, Feirefiz, in combat on the afternoon of the evening before Pentecost, then attains the Grail and heals the wounded Fisher-King (Books IX-XVI). This basic outline is further complicated by the Gawan episodes in Books VII and VIII, which seem to function like a story-within-the-story alongside Parzival's quest and spiritual formation. I believe, however, that Wolfram probably intended the Gawan sequence as highlighting the dichotomous aims of the *chivalric realm* represented by King Arthur, Gawan and the other knights of the Round Table fraternity versus the *spiritual realm* represented by both the Grail-Family at Munsalvæsche and Parzival's personal quest that is fulfilled over a period of seven years, or more precisely, over a span of seven Pentecosts.

It is as if Wolfram was encouraging his audience to "question" the very nature of these two "quests" (Parzival's and Gawan's), which run parallel to each other for two-thirds of the narrative. If Wolfram offers us Parzival as a Christ-symbol, then what are we to make of his Muslim half-brother, Feirefiz, who joins him at the Grail Castle on the eve of the narrative's seventh and final Pentecost when Parzival becomes the next King of the Grail-family? Was Wolfram making a statement about kinship ties based upon the Biblical theme of the Children of Abraham? In so doing, we too, join the "quest" for the Holy Grail as readers and interpreters of the spiritual values signified by the Grail-Family versus the worldly and militaristic values of King Arthur's court.

Wolfram's unique rendition of the story is quite different from the way other chroniclers and poets depicted the Arthurian realm. Given Wolfram's concern for religious toleration of Muslims and Jews, his understanding of the kinship of all believers, in a narrative spanning seven Pentecosts, recalls the pneumatological and theocentric miracle of the first Pentecost, at which representatives from all over the Hellenistic-Roman Empire heard the Word of God in their own tongues, a multi-religious and multilingual group of people from all over the known world brought together and touched in an ineffable way by the power of the Holy Spirit. Might this be one of the deeper meanings or spiritual lessons Wolfram intended by altering the story of the Grail and Arthurian romance so creatively? *What does this mean?*

There are a few significant differences in Wolfram's use of symbols and in his divergence from some of the better-known details among the Arthurian and Grail traditions. Before proceeding with a brief summary of the plot, it will be helpful to discuss a few more of these deviations. Among these are six major symbols or motifs deployed by Wolfram in his own imaginative and original style: 1) The Grail-stone; 2) The location of Arthur's Court; 3) The omission of Merlin, the Lady of the Lake, and Excalibur from *Parzival*; 4) The Grail Castle; 5) The heraldic symbol of the turtle-dove emblazoned on the shields and saddles of the Grail-family; and 6) The etymology of Parzival's name and eventual discovery of his surname.

The first and most obvious of these, Wolfram's Grail as a mysterious, oracular stone called "*lapsit exillis*," has previously been mentioned. What we have not highlighted, however, is the Grail-stone's connection with the Word of God. As the plot unfolds, we learn that the names of the men, *and women*, chosen by God to join the Grail Family and serve humanity appear on the side of this enigmatic stone whenever the Will of God decrees it. We also learn that this mysterious stone is no bigger than a human eye, yet is capable of multiplying food and drink to feed the multitudes, and has the power to bestow immortality on those who serve God faithfully. Parzival's uncle, the Hermit Trevrizent, informs him that the Grail was brought down from heaven by the neutral angels who did not participate in the war between God and Lucifer. Each year during Holy Week, a lovely, gentle white dove brings a Communion wafer to the stone, from which the sacred stone derives its sustenance and vitality. The pneumatological dimensions of this miraculous stone are as bewildering today as they must have been to Wolfram's contemporaries in the early 1200s, but within the context of the seven-times-seven days of Whitsuntide, these symbolic dimensions attest to the special reverence Wolfram and his audiences held for the Person of the Holy Spirit and its mysterious yet abiding relationship with the Triune God.

Secondly, King Arthur's court is not the familiar Camelot or Caerleon of Welsh and Breton Arthurian lore, but instead is located in the heart of Normandy at Nantes. Third, neither the "sword of power," Excalibur, nor the sorcerer Merlin, nor the Lady of the Lake are featured here. Although there are no magical weapons in the narrative, the role of mystical mentor for the protagonist is fulfilled by Parzival's uncle, the Hermit Trevrizent, who teaches him about the symbols and mysteries of the Grail-quest. By personal example and wise counsel, he leads him to reconcile his anger at God and return to his Christian faith. As for the portrayal of the Divine Feminine, symbolized by the Lady of the Lake or Morgan le Fay in other versions of the Arthurian and Grail sagas, this is not a feature of Wolfram's version. But, the women in his rendition of the legend are among the most independent and noteworthy of the Arthurian and Grail literary tradition, for it is through their voices and suffering that Wolfram critiques the all too frequent medieval tragedy of separation and death caused by feudal militarism, knight errantry, and religious intolerance. The women in Wolfram's *Parzival* reflect the reality of upper class females in late-twelfth and thirteenth century France and Germany so closely that this poet probably had no use for idealized and mythological figures like Morgana or the Lady of the Lake.

Fourthly, Wolfram's Grail Castle contains a bewildering cast of noble characters, while being attended to by more women than men. As the home of the Grail Family, the Grail Castle seems to signify both the Church founded by Christ and God's gift of the Son's Holy Spirit on the day of Pentecost and the broader kinship of all true believers as understood by Wolfram. This castle, we learn, is called "*Munsalvæsche*," which as a Middle High German variation of Latin and French words could mean either "Wild Mountain" or "*Mons Salvationis*." Quite literally, this "Mount of Salvation" could be read as a subversive and liberative symbol created by Wolfram and signifying his hope for a kinder, gentler society that truly stood against militarism and abuses of power. We also learn through Parzival's hermit uncle, that both his hermitage and the Grail Castle are located in the forest known as "*Terre de Salvæsche*," which again appears to offer a double-meaning as a "Savage Forest" of perils and trials one must pass through on his/her way to redemption versus its image as a blessed "Land of Salvation" to be attained after the seeker develops a self mastery that is firmly rooted in the Christian faith.

A significant fifth symbol, yet nearly imperceptible within the narrative, is the turtle-dove image portrayed on the banners, shields, and saddles of the Templar knights who guard the secret approaches through the forest to the Grail Castle. Turtledoves are universal symbols of peace and of the coming of spring. This gentle bird was a well-known medieval symbol for the Holy Spirit, and a popular medieval symbol of both human and divine love. In the Hebrew Scriptures, the turtle-dove appears as a symbol of love and heralds the passage of time and the coming of spring (see Jeremiah 8:7 and Song of Solomon 2:11-12). In *Parzival* a combination of all these rich meanings is probably the intent, but especially so, given the Grail-family's commitment to peace and justice and the plot's Pentecostal and springtime imagery.

Finally, although Wolfram's protagonist is intentionally based upon the English and Old French name, "Perceval," usually meaning "innocent fool," Wolfram intentionally alters this accepted convention in Book III when Sigune, a maiden related to the young knight, informs him that he is the son of Angevine nobility and tells him his name: "In truth, your name is Parzival, which signifies 'right through the middle.'"[97] Herzeloyde, Parzival's mother, wanted to protect her son so desperately from the militaristic and misogynist ways of courtly life that she raised him without ever calling him by his first name, nor does the young lad know his family's surname, which as we shall discuss later is another symbol of great significance in this story. The French etymology for Parzival's name could thus be the equivalent of the phrase: "*perce à val*," which in Middle High German also means, "pierced through the middle" (MHG: *der nam ist rehte enmitten durch*).[98] Scholarly opinion suggests this etymology refers to the manner in which Parzival broke his mother's heart when he left home against her wishes to become a knight. However, the etymology might also be an allusion to Parzival as a Christ-symbol since there are two significant scriptures where we read about Jesus being "pierced" (see Luke 2:35; and John 19:34-35). We will return to the question of Parzival's unknown family name later.

Seeking an understanding of the chronology of events Wolfram incorporated into the poem's plot structure, some scholars Like Helen Mustard and Charles Passage observed that the *Parzival* follows a "joy-sorrow-joy" pattern, while others like Herman Wiegand detected a "spring-autumn-spring" pattern in the rhythmic unfolding of the plot and the main character's adventures. By applying this three-fold pattern to the *Parzival's* plot structure as "Initiation-Purgation-Fulfillment," Herman Wiegand's research on the "Spring-Autumn-Spring"[99] pattern of the narrative's time sequence makes even more sense than it did when Helen Mustard and Charles Passage described "the joy-sorrow-joy pattern of the poem as a whole."[100] From this perspective, it is highly plausible that Parzival's quest for the Grail and the narrative's tripartite structure was intended as an allegory of the three stages or levels of mystical transformation.

These stages are a common cultural and philosophical feature of most mystical traditions around the world and can be sequentially and variably identified as: 1) Initiation or *nigredo*; 2) Purgation or *albedo*; and 3) Perfection, or *rubedo*. The Latin terms: *nigredo* (meaning "darkness" or confusion), *albedo* (meaning "whitening" or purgation), and *rubedo* (meaning "reddening" or completion) are derived from medieval Christian alchemy. The last term, *rubedo*, is particularly noteworthy in this discussion, for its medieval association with the planet "Mercury" and with the Holy Spirit. As a planet, Mercury was associated with spiritual knowledge and creativity. As an element, mercury was associated with transformative chemical operations and medical tinctures. Mercury as "quicksilver," or as *the spirit Mercurius*, was also associated, among medieval mystics and alchemists, with supernatural communication and the transcendent powers of the Holy Spirit, whose quintessential color in medieval symbolism was always "red" just as the tongues of fire from the first Pentecost gave the Feast of Pentecost its particular predisposition towards red vestments and red decorations.

Furthermore, the *Parzival*'s "joy-sorrow-joy" pattern detected by so many literary critics and Wolfram scholars over the years may be summarized as follows: The naïve and impetuous young Parzival leaves his mother Herzeloyde in search of chivalric adventure because he wants to become a knight. He achieves great and unexpected victories, bravely faces numerous challenges, and marries the beautiful Princess Condwiramurs, whose name means, "leading love," and she becomes the leading light of his soul. One night he miraculously finds his way to the Grail Castle, and later he receives an invitation to join King Arthur's Round Table. Thus, despite being raised by a mother who intentionally kept him in ignorance of knighthood and courtly manners, and even his surname, Parzival begins his quest in a "joyous" mood of winsome anticipation and chivalric success. His immaturity and arrogance, however, lead him into trouble with certain knights and ladies at Arthur's court. In defense of King Arthur's honor, and to win both armor and a battle horse by jousting, he kills Ither, the Red Knight, but he simultaneously sins against God and the rules of chivalry for Ither turns out to be his kinsman. At the Grail Castle of Munsalvæsche, he fails to act with compassion and humility by asking King Anfortas the healing question, which would have earned him the Grail and restored the Grail-family's honor. The sorceress Cundrie then denounces him at Arthur's court as a disgrace to the Grail-family and a failure in the annals of chivalry. By the time he returns to his uncle, Trevrizent's hermitage in the forest of Terre de Salvæsche in Book IX, Parzival is weary, disillusioned, and angry with God for his misfortunes. Thus, he experiences a lengthy period of "sorrow" as he proceeds through the Initiation (*nigredo*) and Purgation (*albedo*) stages of his spiritual journey.

Parzival's arduous quest for the Grail is actually a quest for his own spiritual transformation and purification. Indeed the purgation stage of mystical transformation is depicted splendidly in a cryptic passage from Book VI with rich Pentecostal imagery:

> Now will you hear where his journey has taken Parzival the Waleis? That night fresh snow had fallen thick upon him. Yet it was not the time for snow, if it was the way I heard it. Arthur is the man of May, and whatever has been told about him took place at Pentecost or in the flowering time of May. What fragrance they say is in the air around him! But here this tale is cut of double fabric and turns to the color of snow.[101]

Wolfram clearly was aware of the stages of the liturgical calendar and wanted his audience and readers to ponder the meaning of King Arthur's association with the flowering "merrie month of May" as Parzival's spiritual purification (*albedo*) unfolded throughout the rest of the narrative. Near the story's end there will be a magnificent revelation on the day before Pentecost before the assembled leaders of both the Grail-family and the Arthurian fraternity.

While in the woods at Trevrizent's hermitage, his uncle offers an exposition on the qualities and lore of the Grail-stone, while also preaching about humanity's unbreakable bond with God through Adam and Jesus Christ. This inspires Parzival to resume his quest for the Grail, make amends with the lords and ladies whom he has offended, and seek reconciliation with God, whose saving Grace eventually summons him back to the Grail Castle. From this chain of narrative events, it certainly seems as if Books X through XVI portray a gradually increasing level of "joy," which culminates in Parzival's dramatic meeting and combat with Feirefiz, his healing of the wounded Fisher-King Anfortas, and the revelation of his kinship with the entire Grail-family atop the allegorical "Mount of Salvation" on Pentecost Sunday (*rubedo*).

In contrast, Herman J. Wiegand's "spring-autumn-spring" pattern, examined in his little known 1938 article on the poem's time sequence, illuminated this interpretive problem by suggesting that Wolfram very likely intended his audience and readers to notice, perhaps even calculate, the actual years Parzival spends on his quest for the Grail and redemption. As discussed earlier in this chapter, Wolfram's audience would have been familiar with the rhythmic cadences of the Christian year as ordinary time ebbed and flowed through the festal times of the liturgical calendar. Seven years is the time span that hearers and readers of this tale notice from a first Pentecost when Parzival becomes a knight, to a seventh Pentecost when he becomes King of the Grail Castle. It is remarkable that it is almost always Pentecost when significant turning points occur in Parzival's life and journey, a feature of this story offering us a window into the pneumatological sensibilities of medieval men and women, for whom the 50-day Pentecost cycle of the Christian liturgical calendar was a time for both the regeneration of Nature with the onset of spring, as well as deep prayer and spiritual discernment in preparation for the annual commemoration of God's gracious outpouring of the Holy Spirit.

The most dramatic Pentecost moment in Wolfram's *Parzival* occurs near the story's conclusion when events transpire in such a way that Parzival meets the chivalric battle-champion from the Islamic Middle East, Feirefiz, for mortal combat on the afternoon of the evening before Pentecost. They charge at each other for hours in a jousting field set between two hills with the Arthurian fraternity of the Round Table perched on one hill to witness the contest and the Grail-family looking on from the other hill. As the two young knights dismount their horses and get set to face off in a sword fight, the narrative suggests they are gazing at each other as if recognizing something familiar about the other. As they begin their death match Parzival's sword miraculously breaks on the Muslim knight's helmet, and Feirefiz suddenly gains the upper hand. As this point the two combatants pause for a moment and begin speaking about each other's family for each one has a brother in a foreign land that he has never met before. Each one claims to be related to the French Royal House of Anjou, which Parzival cannot believe. They remove their helmets and realize that they are indeed brothers born of different mothers and fathered by the same man, Gahmuret the Angevin, who served bravely as knight in Europe under Christian lords, and then left to join the service of the Caliph of Baghdad. Thus, by the grace of God the two brothers are spared the sin of killing another kinsman. In Wolfram's words:

> With kisses Feirefiz and Parzival concluded their enmity, and friendship be-
> seemed them both better than heart's hatred against one another. Faith and love
> rendered that battle decision.[102]

The following day on Pentecost Sunday, the sorceress Cundrie rides forth from the Grail Castle and informs Parzival that his name has been revealed by the grace of God on the grail-stone as the next King of the Grail-family and that his brother Feirefiz has also been summoned to the service of the Grail-family. Here again a remarkable piece of information is revealed, the surname of the Grail family we learn is *"Mazadan,"* and this too was Gahmuret's family name. The father-quest motif is a well-known one in literature, but this is no ordinary example of two young warriors in search of their father's identity. Although King Arthur's family line descends from Uther Pendragon, Parzival and Feirefiz learn that they are descendants of the union between *Mazadan and the* fairy queen, *Terdelaschoye,* meaning "Land of Joy" (*Terre de Schoye*), and apparent-ly derived from the name of the mountain called *Feimurgân* or *Famorgan,* which was known to medieval Arthurian and Grail romance writers like Wol-fram as a sacred site associated with the water-fairy Morgan Le Fay, yet another bewildering mixture of pre-Christian elements with Pentecostal symbolism.[103] The name *Mazadan* renders the Middle High German phrase *"mâc Adam,"* liter-ally "son of Adam." Once again we pause and wonder by what authority this adventure steers: *What does this mean?* When combined with the fantastic motif of the matriarchal fairy, this allusion to the Biblical line of descent from Adam elevates the *Parzival's* kinship ties to both primal and cosmic proportions, and we realize that on this particular Pentecost the message is about a kinship of all believers capable of holding together pre-Christian beliefs alongside the theme of Muslims and Christians as descendants of Adam and children of the Most High.

In a dramatically creative way, Wolfram's *Parzival* reconstructs the story of Pentecost as the underlying structure and backdrop for an allegory of kinship and reconciliation among people of different faith traditions, who, during his lifetime, were constantly at war with each other over territory, material posses-sions, and religious differences. His epic story is one of the clearest examples of how the imaginative possibilities of Pentecost manifest in divergent and unex-pected ways throughout the long history of Christianity. Wolfram's story is also another curious example of the theological reconstruction of Christian tradition empowered by the Pentecost narrative from Acts 2 when aligned with social and individual spiritual reflection during the natural rhythms and ecclesial comme-morations of the seven-times-seven-days of the annual Pentecost cycle.

PENTECOST IN MALORY'S LE MORTE D'ARTHUR, CA. 1485

Although we have already discussed several aspects and features of Malory's famous late medieval version of the Arthurian saga, one unique aspect of his *Le*

Morte d'Arthur bears special discussion before concluding this chapter. Malory's version of the story provides a code of conduct for Christian warriors serving King Arthur. It is often referred to as the "Round Table Oath," but it is more commonly known as the "Pentecostal Oath" because the Knights of the Round Table were required to swear by this oath each year on the occasion of Pentecost Sunday. Let us examine the question of how this Pentecost Oath was related to the significance of Pentecost in a literary work about building a better society through the leadership of its king and an elite militaristic fraternity.

The text of Thomas Malory's Pentecost Oath, which is unique to his late fifteenth century version of the story, reads as follows:

> The king established all his knights, and gave them that were of lands not rich, he gave them lands, and charged them never to do outrageousity nor murder, and always to flee treason; also, by no mean to be cruel, but to give mercy unto him that asketh mercy, upon pain of forfeiture of their worship and lordship of King Arthur for evermore; and always to do ladies, damosels, and gentlewomen succour, upon pain of death. Also, that no man take no battles in a wrongful quarrel for no law, ne for no world's goods. Unto this were all the knights sworn of the Table Round, both old and young. And every year were they sworn at the high feast of Pentecost.[104]

Malory was predominantly concerned with the construction of a just and orderly society. He lived in the mid-1400s when the ideals and institutions of knighthood and chivalry had been largely compromised by changes in military strategy and the rise of nation-states like France who were building standing armies from urban mercenary factions and others like Spain for whom naval power was becoming the essential aspect of their armed forces. Hence, Malory's fictional King Arthur has much to say about moral integrity and political justice even as his beloved Camelot is disintegrating in a blaze of feudal instability, competitive envy, and chivalric quarreling.

Malory's combination of King Arthur's code of chivalry as expressed in the Pentecost Oath alongside the person of the Holy Spirit whose high feast was celebrated annually on Pentecost with the culmination of the fifty-day Whitsuntide cycle brings a few aspects of the social logic of this text into sharper focus. For one thing, the outpouring of the Holy Spirit on the first Pentecost, which gave birth to the church, was synonymous among medieval Christians with notions of the ideal Christian community, counsel and comfort, charity, and the gifts of the Holy Spirit. These were the characteristics of the Holy Spirit which empowered human beings to carry out the work of God for the people of God, and which propelled all things towards potential fullness. Thus, Malory's emphasis on moral integrity and political justice among the members of the Arthurian community he created seems all the more appropriate since Malory and his readers lived in the twilight years of chivalry and knight errantry that were accompanied by anxious social changes and turmoil across Europe.[105]

The association of Pentecost with King Arthur, or Pentecost alongside themes of chivalry and knighthood, was not new to Malory's contemporaries. For centuries before Malory's time, many younger and older men were knighted on Pentecost and counseled at their dubbing ceremonies to work faithfully as men-at-arms by promoting charity and humility in the service of the Church and maintaining steadfast loyalty to their secular Lord or Royal Sovereign. The chivalric honoring of the Holy Spirit and Pentecost was associated with giving and fullness and akin to an *imitatio Christi* in the ideals of knighthood. Fictional texts like Malory's Pentecost Oath underscored these positive ideals and served as social reminders of the vices to be avoided in the chivalric community, such as for example "envy" at court as the negative opposite of "charity." Treason as suggested in the oath was one of the worst sins that could be committed in the system of medieval chivalry based upon loyalty and trust in the feudal contract and the bonds of feudal kinship that characterized most European courts until the end of the fifteenth century. On the other hand, these codes of chivalric conduct whether real, as in the surviving chronicles by various knights, or imagined, as in Malory's Pentecostal Oath for the Knights of the Round Table, attest to the inherent instability and violence of medieval feudalism. Profaning the Feast of Pentecost was perceived as an offense against the Holy Spirit and the Theological Virtues of faith, hope, and charity. In this context, the Pentecostal legacy served a positive and hopeful function by curbing feudal violence and political instability while safeguarding the liberty of the Church from the medieval State, and by appealing to warriors' higher aspirations.

The great variety and multitude of Arthurian romances and Grail quest tales originating during the period, from Geoffrey of Monmouth's *History of the Kings of Britain* in 1138 to William Caxton's publication of Malory's *Le Morte d'Arthur* in 1485, is bewildering to both the medieval scholar and the educated layperson. Scholars and literary critics have known about the presence of Pentecostal imagery and allusions in Arthurian and Grail literature for a long time but most have ignored the historical and religious implications of this material for quite some time. My objective in this chapter was not to offer a comprehensive overview of information easily accessible in studies of medieval literature, but instead to map the contours of the literary and historical terrain in which so many allusions to Pentecost or Whitsuntide abound, yet remain relatively misunderstood or completely unexamined despite the passage of over two centuries of the modern academic enterprise. Perhaps Martin Shichtman and James Carley said it best in the introduction to their fine volume of edited essays on the social implications of the Arthurian and Grail legends:

> It is almost universally acknowledged by scholars that even if a king named Arthur did once exist, all efforts to portray either what he or his court were like have failed... To study the shifts in the Arthurian legend demands involvement in such diverse disciplines as literature, history, art, politics, economics, and gender study. To study the shifts in the Arthurian legend demands an understanding that the boundaries the academy routinely erects around these disciplines must be crossed, if not destroyed altogether... There remains yet much to be done in recognizing the significance of the legend's relationship to Western society.[106]

This chapter has dared to cross the boundaries erected by the academy that separate historiography from theology and literature, while also daring to combine materials across the illusory historical periodization schemes constructed by historians trained to avoid trans-local interpretations and narratives. By focusing on the seven week celebration of the Pentecostal season in terms of the gifts of the Holy Spirit, contemplative prayer and the liturgical calendar, Wolfram's attempt at a dialogue of mutual edification among Jews, Christians, and Muslims through a Grail saga spanning seven Pentecosts, and the legacies of the pagan past for medieval celebrations of Pentecost, we have drawn a historical picture of the season's rites, stories, and aspirations.

What role did the image of the Holy Spirit play in converting pagan rites of spring and spiritual transformation into the Christian cosmology and feast days of medieval society? I invite my colleagues in the history of Christianity and its cognate disciplines, along with concerned readers (and seekers) from other disciplines, to take up the quest for a deeper understanding about how and why our medieval forbears' conceptions of Pentecost and the Holy Spirit were so energetically and thoughtfully inflected through the legends of King Arthur and the Holy Grail. A religious movement such as Christianity with a totalizing moral discourse and an exclusivist cosmology based upon the trajectory of salvation history and the ideal of converting the whole world beckons us as scholars to focus on both local and *trans-local* expressions of Christian identity and culture. Given the geographic distribution of the Celts and Europe's other pre-Christian indigenous groups, a similar attention to both local and trans-local influences and vestiges of these once mighty peoples is also warranted by the variety of Arthurian and Grail sagas that were passed down to medieval Christian culture. Noting the presence of such Pentecostal references and symbols in this corpus of works and legends is by no means a novel observation, and yet I confess that these continuities and discontinuities from the pre-Christian past into the medieval Christian period are deeply perplexing. Perhaps as perplexing today as when Herman Weigand noted some of these Pentecost themes in the late 1930s,[107] or when Roger Sherman Loomis commented in the 1960s on the academy's continuing bewilderment over the origin and meaning of these stories after a century of scholarly investigations on King Arthur and the Grail.[108] We are reminded of the Pentecostal refrain from the book of Acts: *What does this mean?* Perhaps the answer lies somewhere in between the domain of the natural world and humanity's primordial experience of feeling embedded in the cycles and rhythms of *Natura*.

The relationship of medieval celebrations of Pentecost to pagan rites and traditions in the merrie month of May (and early June) points to a type of medieval syncretism to which the image of the Holy Spirit's presence in the natural world of flora and fauna seems particularly well suited. This syncretistic blending of pagan and Christian traditions around Pentecost were essentially at odds with each other, yet each tradition was convinced that in Nature's assorted acts of generation and rebirth, something ineffable about humanity's place in the order of creation was revealed for the greater good of all living creatures. In the next chapter, we will discuss what role the image of Holy Spirit played in the

What does this mean?

medieval social and political arenas by examining notions of ecclesiastical reformism and egalitarian liberty that emerged from Joachim of Fiore, the Spiritual Franciscans, and a few other spiritual movements in the High Middle Ages.

NOTES

1. Roger Sherman Loomis, *The Grail: From Celtic Myth to Christian Symbol* (New York: Columbia University Press, 1963), 1.
2. Delwin Brown, *Boundaries of Our Habitations*, 73-74.
3. For book length studies of the problem of God and Nature, the goddess *Natura*, and the Divine Feminine in medieval European history and discourse see the following: Barbara Newman, *God and the Goddesses: Vision, Poetry, and Belief in the Middle Ages.* (Philadelphia: University of Pennsylvania Press, 2003); Hugh White, *Nature, Sex, and Goodness in a Medieval Literary Tradition.* (Oxford: Oxford University Press, 2000); and George Economou, *The Goddess Natura in Medieval Literature.* (Cambridge, MA: Harvard University Press, 1972).
4. Bernardus Silvestris, *Cosmographia.* Peter Dronke, ed. (Leiden: Brill, 1978), 1-15; 29-50.
5. Alain of Lille, *Liber de planctu Naturae.* Nikolaus M. Haring, Ed. *Studi Medievali,* Third Series, 19 (1978): pp. 797-879.
6. Newman, *God and the Goddesses,* 52.
7. Ibid. 89.
8. Ibid. (See Ch. 2: "Natura (I): Nature and Nature's God," 51-89; Ch. 3: "Natura (II): Goddess of the Normative," 90-137).
9. Ibid. 54.
10. Richard Barber, *The Holy Grail: Imagination and Belief* (Cambridge: Harvard University Press, 2004), 3.
11. Bernadette Filotas, *Pagan Survivals, Superstitions and Popular Cultures in Early Medieval Pastoral Literature.* Studies and Texts, 151. (Toronto: Pontifical Institute of Medieval Studies, 2005).
12. Ibid. 120-152.
13. Ibid. 145.
14. Thomas O'Loughlin, *Celtic Theology: Humanity, World and God in Early Irish Writings.* (London: Continuum, 2000), 1.
15. Ibid. 1-2.
16. Ibid.
17. Ibid. 13.
18. Teresa Pérez-Higuera, *Medieval Calendars* (London: Weidenfeld and Nicholson, 1998), 17-64.
19. Ibid. 184-198.
20. Ibid. 194.
21. Ibid.
22. Ibid. 190.
23. Ibid.
24. O'Loughlin, *Celtic Theology,* 167.
25. Ibid.
26. For an excellent discussion of the encounter between pre-Christian paganism and early medieval Christian societies, with special emphasis on religious women in monaste-

ries, nunneries, and rural villages see Christina Harrington, *Women in a Celtic Church: 450-1150* (New York: Oxford University Press, 2002), 23-48; 59-110; 131-165.

27. Stephen C. McCluskey, *Astronomies and Cultures in Early Medieval Europe* (Cambridge University Press, 1998), 101-103.

28. Patricia M. Rumsey, *Sacred Time in Early Christian Ireland* (London: T & T Clark, 2007), 1-22.

29. Ibid. 69-104; 167-200.

30. See Eric Voegelin, *The Ecumenic Age* (Baton Rouge: Louisiana State University Press, 1974).

31. O'Loughlin, *Celtic Theology*, 184.

32. Ibid. 169.

33. Ibid. 183.

34. For Robert Graves' interpretation of these Celtic myths and historical possibilities see his highly contested and now largely discredited *The White Goddess: A Historical Grammar of Poetic Myth.* Amended and Enlarged Ed. (New York: Farrar, Straus, & Giroux, 1948; Rev. Ed., 1960), 27-48; 61-73; 165-222.

35. For a detailed analysis of the debunking of Robert Graves' history of the "Celtic Tree Calendar," see the following article by one of the world's most preeminent Celtic scholars, Peter Berresford Ellis, "The Fabrication of Celtic Astrology," *Astrological Journal* (Vol. 39, N. 4, 1997); For comprehensive overviews of Celtic history and cosmology see the following works by Peter Beresford Ellis: *Celtic Myths and Legends* (New York: Carroll & Graff Publishers, 2002;) *The Celtic Empire: The First Millennium of Celtic History, 1000 BC – AD 51* (New York: Carroll & Graff, 2001); and *A Brief History of the Druids* (London: Constable & Robinson, 2001).

36. Ellis in *Celtic Myths and Legends*, 26.

37. Anne Ross, "Ritual and the Druids," in Miranda Green, ed. *The Celtic World* (London: Routledge, 1995), 431-432.

38. David McManus, *A Guide to Ogam,* Maynooth Monographs 4 (An Sagart: Maynooth, 1991).

39. See Ellis' *Celtic Myths and Legends*, 25-28.

40. F. Kelly, *A Guide to Early Irish Law* (Dublin: Dublin Institute for Advanced Studies, 1988), 198; as cited in Anne Ross "Ritual and the Druids," 432.

41. Mark Redknap, "Early Christianity and Its Monuments," in M. Green, ed. *The Celtic World*, 765.

42. Justo González, *Acts: The Gospel of the Spirit* (New York: Orbis, 2001), 2-11.

43. See Jeremy Cohen, *"Be Fertile and Increase, Fill the Earth and Master It:"* The Ancient and Medieval Career of a Biblical Text (Ithaca: Cornell University Press, 1989), 3-7; 306-314.

44. Ibid. 6.

45. Ibid. 166-220.

46. For detailed discussion and information on the clearing of the forests in medieval and early modern Europe up to 1675 see the lengthy and well-documented volume by Michael Williams, *Deforesting the Earth: From Prehistory to Global Crisis* (Chicago: University of Chicago Press, 2003), 102-241; and Sing C. Chew, *World Ecological Degradation: Accumulation, Urbanization, and Deforestation, 3000 B.C. – A.D. 2000* (Lanham, MD: Altamira Press, 2001), 1-12; 117-130.

47. Lynn T. White, Jr., "The Historical Roots of Our Ecologic Crisis," *Science* 155 (1967): pp.1203-1207.

48. See Cohen's sixth chapter, "The Primordial Blessing and the Law of Nature," for an informative and useful overview of various medieval views of Nature and humanity's relation to the natural world, 271-305.

49. See H. Paul Santmire's *The Travail of Nature: The Ambiguous Ecological Promise of Christian Theology* (Philadelphia: Fortress Press, 1985), which was inspired by the ecological concerns of the late 1960s and 1970s, and by the impact of Lynn T. White's historic essay, is the finest and most thought-provoking work that I have yet come across in my research on this topic. Santmire's book, although a bit dated now more than two decades after publication, thoroughly surveys the Scriptural and Patristic foundations of Christianity's view of Nature and then pursues this line of inquiry through each of the subsequent major periods of Euro-Western, Christian history that culminates in his concluding chapter with a highly balanced account of the pros and cons for an ecologically balanced view of Nature deriving from the Old and New Testament, see especially pp.189-218.

50. Ibid. 23-27.

51. Ibid. 1-12.

52. For data on the origins, history, and traditions of the Romani Gypsies and their role in this region of France see the fine edited volume by Walter Weyrauch, ed. *Gypsy Law: Romani Legal Traditions and Culture* (Berkeley: University of California Press, 2001); or Isabel Fonseca's, *Bury Me Standing: The Gypsies and Their Journey* (New York: Knopf, 1996); and Bart McDowell, *Gypsies: Wanderers of the World* (Washington: National Geographic Society, 1970).

53. Before 1000 BCE the Ligurians were the indigenous people who occupied Provence and other portions of Southern France and they coexisted with the Celts for centuries. The Celtic-Ligurian period in this area extends from about 1000 BCE until 122 BCE when Roman military conquests ushered in the Gallo-Roman Period across most of present-day France (122 BCE – 500 CE), also known as the Romano-Celtic cultural era in Provence.

54. Joseph Goering, *The Virgin and the Grail: Origins of a Legend* (New Haven: Yale University Press, 2005).

55. Ibid. x-xii.

56. Ibid. 100-107.

57. Ibid. 138-137.

58. Barry Cunliffe, *The Celtic World* (New York: McGraw-Hill, 1979), 89.

59. See Miranda Green's chapter on the role of Celtic water-goddesses as "Healers and Mothers," in her edited volume *Celtic Goddesses: Warriors, Virgins, and Mothers* (New York: George Braziller, 1996), 116.

60. The most famous of the sacred wells associated with Coventina is located near the village of Carrawburgh along Hadrian's Wall in England. Since its discovery in the 1800s, the site has been extensively excavated and studied by several generations of archaeologists and historians. For a good overview of these findings and their relation to Celtic water-goddess traditions and rituals, see the fine essay by Lindsay Allason-Jones, "Coventina's Well," in Sandra Billington and Miranda Green, Eds. *The Concept of the Goddess* (London: Routledge, 1996), 107-119.

61. See Barbara Newman's essay "Did Goddesses Empower Women? The Case of Dame Nature." In *Gendering the Master Narrative: Women and Power in the Middle Ages.* (Ithaca: Cornell University Press, 2003), 135-155; and her groundbreaking and excellent study *God and the Goddesses: Vision, Poetry, and Belief in the Middle Ages.* (Philadelphia: University of Pennsylvania Press, 2003), 1-137; 291-327; and *From Virile*

Woman to WomanChrist: Studies in Medieval Religion and Literature (Philadelphia: University of Pennsylvania Press, 1995), 1-18; 182-248; see also Newman's chapter on the "Feminine Divine" in her book length study, *Sister of Wisdom: St. Hildegard's Theology of the Feminine* (Berkeley and Los Angeles: University of California Press, 1987), 42-88. For an overview of the changing view of women's power and social roles in the medieval world see also the introductory chapter by Erler and Kowaleski, "A New Economy of Power Relations: Female Agency in the Middle Ages." In Mary C. Erler and Maryanne Kowaleski, Eds. *Gendering the Master Narrative: Women and Power in the Middle Ages.* (Ithaca: Cornell University Press, 2003), 1-16.

62. Newman, *God and the Goddesses,* xii.

63. Ibid. 53.

64. Ibid.

65. Brown, *Authority and The Sacred: Aspects of the Christianisation of the Roman World.* (New York: Cambridge University Press, 1996), 59-74; and *The Cult of the Saints: Its Rise and Function in Latin Christianity* (University of Chicago Press, 1982); and "The Rise and Function of the Holy Man in Late Antiquity," *Journal of Roman Studies* 61 (1971): pp. 80-101.

66. Delwin Brown, 74.

67. Miranda Green, "The Gods and the Supernatural," in M. Green, Ed. *The Celtic World* (London: Routledge, 1995), 486.

68. Delwin Brown, 119.

69. R. Barber, *The Holy Grail,* 1.

70. Peter Hunter Blair, *An Introduction to Anglo-Saxon England.* Third Ed. (London: Cambridge University Press, 2003), 30.

71. Rodney Castleden, *King Arthur: The Truth Behind the Legend* (London: Routledge, 2000), 33.

72. Roger Sherman Loomis, *The Grail: From Celtic Myth to Christian Symbol* (New York: Columbia University Press, 1963), 1.

73. Ibid. See Loomis' second chapter on "The Origins and Growth of Arthurian Romance" (7-19), and his third chapter, "Celtic Myths: Their Mutations and Combinations" (20-27).

74. Queen Eleanor of Aquitaine (ca. 1122-1204) and her daughters from two royal marriages were the most influential supporters of the cult of courtly love in the late-1100s. Eleanor's grandfather, William IX of Aquitaine (1071-1126), was one of the first and most influential Troubadours of French literary history. Thus, she grew up in a noble household where creativity and learning were fostered, even for the women of the family, which is a far cry from the medieval courtly view of a noble lady's quiet comportment and submissiveness in a male dominated socio-political domain. After her father's untimely death, fifteen year old Eleanor married King Louis VII of France, who she divorced in 1152 after obtaining a papal annulment. Her controversial second marriage to a man eleven years her junior, King Henry II of England, oddly enough took place soon afterwards on Pentecost Sunday May 18, 1152. The Plantagenet and Capetian lines of descent that were born from Eleanor's two marriages exerted a powerful influence across Europe for the next three hundred years, which included the successful rule of the English King Richard the Lionheart (1157-1199), a son born from her second marriage to the King of England, and the successful artistic and literary patronage of Countess Marie de Champagne (1145-1198), the daughter born from her first marriage to the King of France. All of which underscores the fact that Chrétien de Troyes was in the service of an important royal family with a long history of artistic patronage and familiarity, with the

Anglo-Norman heritage portrayed in *Le Roman de Brut.* Countess Marie de France was also quite interested in all manner of mythic and legendary Breton adventures, known as *lais* or *lays*, of pre-Christian or Early Medieval Celtic folkloric origins, from which it is almost certain Chrétien derived some of his Arthurian material. For an insightful review of both Eleanor's influence on her daughter Marie and scholarly opinions about this relationship see: June Hall Martin McCash, "Marie de Champagne and Eleanor of Aquitaine: A Relationship Reexamined," *Speculum*, Vol. 54, No. 4 (Oct. 1979): pp.698-711.

75. For more comprehensive evaluations of Chrétien's role in European literary history, and within the genres of Arthurian literature and the Holy Grail tradition, see the following studies: Norris J. Lacy and Joan T. Grimbert, Eds. *A Companion to Chrétien de Troyes* (Cambridge: D. S. Brewer, 2005); Karl D. Uitti, *Chretien de Troyes Revisited* (Twayne Publishers, 1994); Norris J. Lacy, D. Kelly, and K. Busby, Eds. *The Legacy of Chrétien de Troyes*, Vols. I and II (Editions Rodopi, 1988); and the highly celebrated study by the twentieth century's leading French Arthurian scholar Jean Frappier, *Chretien de Troyes: The Man and His Work.* Raymond J. Cormier, Trans. (Athens: Ohio University Press, 1982).

76. From the original Old French version of *Lancelot, Le Chevalier de la Charrette*, also known as Chrétien's *Lancelot* (ca. 1170-1180), translated by W. W. Comfort, *Chretien de Troyes: Arthurian Romances* (London: Everyman's Library, 1914).

77. See Annie Combes, "The Continuations of the *Conte du Graal*," in *A Companion to Chrétien de Troyes*, 191-201.

78. Nigel Bryant, *The High Book of the Grail: A translation of the thirteenth-century romance of Perlesvaus* (Totowa: Farleigh, 1978), 19.

79. Since Wolfram scholars disagree on the exact dates of composition, the actual date thus ranges from as early as 1195 to as late as 1215, and despite Wolfram's comments about being merely the transmitter of this tale, it is certainly probable that he spent somewhere between ten and twenty years fine-tuning and polishing his masterpiece.

80. Although not central to my arguments concerning pneumatological themes, Wolfram indicated to his medieval audience and readers that he was "transmitting" this story in German verse as it was "told" to him in French by Kyot de Provence. Wolfram explains how Kyot learned this "true-story of the Grail" from its alleged author who was actually a Spanish Moor from Toledo named Flegetanis. Kyot then learned Arabic in order to read the story given to him by Flegetanis, whom we are also told was a descendant of King Solomon (see Bk. IX; sec. 453-454). I doubt very much that Wolfram's version of the tale is a mere transmission since its bears a certain resemblance to two other works of his, *Willehalm* and the unfinished *Titurel*. In any case, such questions of origins and authorship have remained a highly complex and persistently unsolvable problem during two centuries of academic studies on this medieval German literary classic.

81. Arthur Groos, *Romancing the Grail: Genre, Science, and Quest in Wolfram's 'Parzival'* (Ithaca: Cornell University Press, 1995).

82. See the two studies by Henry and Renée Kahane, *The Krater and The Grail: Hermetic Sources of the 'Parzival'* (1965 Urbana: University of Illinois Press, reprinted 1984); and "Wolframs Gral und Wolframs Kyot," *Zeitschrift für deutsches Altertum*, 89 (1958-59).

83. Albert Hernandez, *Islam and the Holy Grail: 'Convivencia,' Allegorical Transformation, and Ecumenical Visions in Wolfram von Eschenbach's "Parzival"* (Ann Arbor: UMI Dissertation Services, 2001).

84. For a concise yet highly detailed overview of these and many more speculative biographical details on Wolfram see: Henry Katz, *Wolfram von Eschenbach's 'Parzival:' An Attempt At A Total Evaluation* (Bern: Francke Verlag, 1973), 9-83.

85. Ibid. 9-11.

86. It is not certain at which point in his bardic career *Titurel* was undertaken, but it was surely after the completion of the romance about Parzival. Had Wolfram completed this work, it would most likely have had a different title, for the plot was conceived as a love story dealing with two of the characters from *Parzival*.

87. Zeydel observed that there were "at least five copies" of this Northern Renaissance folio volume in United States libraries when he published his partial translation of the work, and suspected that many more Renaissance editions were still available in European libraries and collections; in Edwin Zeydel's, *The 'Parzival' of Wolfram von Eschenbach* (Chapel Hill: University of North Carolina Press, 1951), 21.

88. This now classic study was grounded in a thorough analysis of the complete and fragmentary medieval manuscripts available to Lachmann in the early 1800s, and it was revised and updated twice in the twentieth century by Eduard Hartl. The Lachmann-Hartl edition is still regarded as the best primary source text among Wolfram specialists; see Karl Lachmann, Ed. *Wolfram von Eschenbach: 'Parzival'* Sixth Revised Edition. Edited by Eduard Hartl 1926, reprinted 1952 (Berlin: Walter de Gruyter, 1999).

89. Jacob Grimm, *"Rede auf Lachmann"* in *Kleinere Schriften Vol. I, 2* (Berlin: Auflage, 1879), 157.

90. K. Bartsch, *Wolfram von Eschenbach: Parzival und Titurel* (Leipzig: Auflage, 1875), 5.

91. In *The Complete Grimm's Fairy Tales.* P. Colum and J. Campbell, Eds. (New York: Pantheon Books, 1994), xiv.

92. Ethnogenesis constructions among German Romantic and nationalist intellectuals in the 1800s defined the *"Volk"* as the organic collectivity of individuals whose pure blood and noble souls bound them together as the primordial spirit of their race or *"Volksgeist."* This was a profoundly misguided attempt to construct the "ties that bind" along racialized mythical origins for the sake of national identity when Germany was just emerging as a new nation state in the nineteenth century. The resulting race protology, and its ideological amplification by the early 1900s, would have devastating consequences in the hands of the Nazis. Certainly not the sort of unifying and compassionate pneumatological vision communicated in Wolfram's *Parzival*, but from the late-1800s through the 1940s, Richard Wagner's recreation of this medieval saga into a very popular, *"volkish"* and nationalistic opera, *Parsifal*, offered Germany a new version of the story cleansed of Wolfram's medieval Pentecostal and Semitic motifs and received high praise from audiences all over Germany. As it turned out, *Parsifal* became Adolf Hitler's favorite opera.

93. For the most comprehensive and scholarly significant work ever published on the relation of Wolfram's to Chrétien de Troyes' treatment of the Grail story, see Jean Fourquet, *Wolfram d'Eschenbach et le 'Conte del Graal:' Les divergences de la tradition du 'Conte del Graal' el leur importance pour l'explicacion du texte du 'Parzival'* (Paris: Sorbonne, 1966).

94. From the prose translation by Helen M. Mustard and Charles E. Passage, *Parzival* (New York: Vintage, 1961), 430; For the Middle High German version of this passage see Karl Lachmann, *Wolfram von Eschenbach 'Parzival.'* Sixth Edition. (Berlin: Walter de Gruyter, 1999), 420, Buch XVI, sec. 827, lines 1-14. These two works will be

referenced respectively from this point forth in this study as the Mustard and Passage trans., and as the Lachmann 6th Edition.

95. The Kahanes maintained that the Grail accounts of both Chrétien de Troyes and Wolfram von Eschenbach were based upon an older, lost version of the legend, which they referred to as the "Urparzival." In their estimation, the enigmatic book Kyot obtained from Flegetanis in Toledo was the *Corpus Hermeticum*, a Hermetic treatise well-known in esoteric Christian circles about spiritual transformation and understanding the secrets of Nature whose origins can be traced back to Hellenistic Egypt, but also a work with clearly identifiable pneumatological possibilities; see Henry and Renée Kahane, *The Krater and the Grail*, 5.

96. Mustard and Passage trans., 4; Lachmann 6th Ed., 3.

97. Ibid., 78; Lachmann 6th Ed., 74.

98. Ibid., Lachmann.

99. Herman J. Weigand, "Die epischen Zeitverhältnisse in den Graldichtungen Chrestiens und Wolframs," *PMLA* 53 (1938). Reprinted in English as "Narrative Time in the Grail Poems of Chrétien de Troyes and Wolfram von Eschenbach," in H. J. Weigand, *Wolfram's 'Parzival:' Five Essays with an Introduction* (Ithaca: Cornell University Press, 1969), 18-75.

100. Mustard and Passage trans., Intro. *li.*

101. Adapted from Bk. VI, sec. 281 in Mustard and Passage trans., 153; or see Buch VI, 281.10-22 in Lachmann 6th Edition, 145.

102. Bk. XV, sec. 748 in Mustard and Passage trans., 390; or see Buch XV, 748.5-8 in Lachmann 6th Edition.

103. See the informative and insightful chapter, "Morgan Le Fée in Oral Tradition," in Roger Sherman Loomis, *Studies in Medieval Literature: A Memorial Collection of Essays* (New York: Burt Franklin, 1970), 3-34.

104. Sir Thomas Malory, *Le Morte D'Arthur, Volume I.* Janet Cowen, Ed. (New York: Penguin Classics, 1970), 115-116.

105. For more information on the social and political implications of Malory's interpretation of the Arthurian and Grail romance traditions see: Kenneth Hodges, *Forging Chivalric Communities in Malory's Le Morte Darthur* (New York: Palgrave MacMillan, 2005), 63-78; 109-128; Dorsey Armstrong, *Gender and the Chivalric Community in Malory's 'Morte d'Arthur* (Gainesville: University Press of Florida, 2003), 4-34; and Martin B. Shichtman and James P. Carley, Eds. *Culture and the King: The Social Implications of the Arthurian Legend* (Albany: SUNY Press, 1994), 4-14.

106. *Culture and the King*, 11.

107. Weigand, (1938).

108. Loomis, *The Grail: From Celtic Myth to Christian Symbol* (1963).

85 - Nature + Medieval ch'd
 earth song celebrate
 — New Poem —
   I think of Peirce as
   kind of clergy
  Ghost might

86 - Insist that HS assoc. w/ this
   world + time

87 - Time of P might to XX

88 - Joachim + Parzival
 ↓70   influence by East / Islam

90 - Joachim - apocalyst + pneumahlgd
   most   inspirit
   focus
       might →
        → inst
       Church of
        HS

92 - Age of HS - 1265
   Love in heart
   — no need for church hierarchy

95 - Practice of praying daily office
   + liturgical calendar reform
   grounded   JF interpreted of
   his vision

48 Breath of God
99 - Accepted by church + then not

102 - Francis
106 ~ Fraticelli - church reform
107 ~ convert by Haydu that had done good
   critism of church before

108' poverty of church controversy
110 - New Angelic pope + four new orders of
                           monks

CHAPTER 3
PENTECOST AND THE CHURCH OF THE HOLY SPIRIT

My breath is a fire that will consume you.

Isaiah 33:11

And it shall come to pass afterward, that I will pour out my Spirit on all flesh; your sons and your daughters shall prophesy, your old men shall dream dreams, and your young men shall see visions.

Joel 2:28

The Spirit of the Lord is upon me, because he has anointed me to preach good news to the poor. He has sent me to proclaim release to the captives. And recovering of sight to the blind, to set at liberty those who are oppressed, to proclaim the acceptable year of the Lord.

Luke 4:18-19

The past is the material of the future; the future is made from the past, constituted by what has gone before . . . the making of the future is always a remaking, a *reconstruction*, of what has gone before.

Delwin Brown, *Boundaries of Our Habitations*[1]

For most educated European Christians who lived during the High Middle Ages, the story of Pentecost was synonymous with the Third Person of the Trinity and with the birth of Christ's earthly church following the inspirational events of the first Pentecost. Since the Holy Spirit gave birth and voice to the church for transforming society, through centuries of biblical exegesis and theological amplification, *ecclesiology*, the doctrine of the Church, became synonymous with *pneumatology*. The complementarity between the Holy Spirit and the doctrine of the church (*ecclesia*) invariably led Christian clergy and laity to considerations of both service and leadership to the church, concerns which became particularly acute when either clergy or laity felt church leadership was deficient or corrupt. The works of the Church Fathers and of medieval Scholastic theologians are replete with references and explanations about the Spirit's bountiful presence in the church and in the lives of pious individual Christians. Throughout the Mid-

83

dle Ages, Augustine of Hippo's views on the Holy Spirit informed the official pneumatological beliefs and doctrines of the Latin Church in Western Europe. At times, pneumatology was interpreted through the monotheistic and metaphysical lens of Platonism, a feature of Christian theology that had been in use since Justin Martyr composed his apologetics in the second century CE. From Basil's *On the Holy Spirit* to Aquinas and Bonaventure's classic Roman Catholic pneumatological formulations in the 1200s, there is a steady line of doctrinal consistency and Scholastic amplification of ideas and traditions about the Third Person of the Trinity. However, no book length study has yet examined the history of pneumatology through the particular lens of visionary conceptions about Pentecost, although such ideas, and the personal religious experiences recorded by numerous Christian visionaries and writers, are highly significant for both medieval understandings of the Holy Spirit and for modern historical understandings of the scores of spiritual and mystical movements that flourished in the High Middle Ages. The Pentecostal visionaries surveyed in this chapter span the period from the late twelfth to the middle of the fourteenth century, and represent just a few examples of the diverse ways that medieval Christian writers and thinkers conceptualized the meaning of Pentecost and the empowering presence of the Holy Spirit in their personal lives and ministerial careers.

Contemporary society and ecclesiastical leadership often perceive talk of "subversion" as a negative sentiment or impetus aimed at overturning established forms of order and socio-political authority. But, what if in its concern for "the fullness of all things" under God's majesty, and in its relationship with human particularity as Christ's "Paraclete," the Third Person of the Trinity *kindles*, and, as needs arise across time and place, *re-kindles* a liberating *"subversive fire"* in the hearts and minds of the men and women who serve Christ's Church (*ecclesia*) on earth? In its classic and literal sense, "hierarchy" meant "Holy Order," and as a symbol of divine and cosmic harmony signified far more than the all too worldly politics of institutions like the medieval Church or the medieval feudal State. The pneumatological sensibility highlighted by the figures in this chapter is exemplified in St. Paul's exhortation to the Corinthians as ministers of the New Covenant: "Now the Lord is the Spirit, and where the Spirit of the Lord is, there is freedom" (2 Corinthians 3:17). Working against the disorder of an oppressive world which they believed lived in denial of human dignity and God's celestial harmony, and laboring against what they perceived as a betrayal and derailment of Christian ecclesiastical purpose and tradition, Abbot Joachim of Fiore, the Franciscan Spirituals, Guglielma of Milan's followers, and the Italian revolutionary Cola di Rienzo were inspired to become prophets and reformers through their experiences of the Holy Spirit and their contextual understandings of Pentecost.

As already demonstrated in Chapter Two, regional climate patterns and local traditions accounted for a wide range of differences as to how the Feast of Pentecost was actually commemorated or celebrated across Medieval Europe. Although the Christian liturgical calendar was superimposed on pre-Christian cosmologies and naturalistic tribal customs, reverence for Nature was an integral aspect of medieval monastic life. Evidence for the medieval association of Pentecost with the rebirth of flora and fauna, and with agricultural renewal each spring is well attested. Indeed, in some communities the practices and rituals attached to Pentecost were as important as those associated with Easter. Whether Easter arrived in late March or in the middle of April, much of medieval Europe still had late winter snow on the ground during Holy Week. To this day, spring arrives a little later in Continental Europe than in most of North America. Given the syncretism of pre-Christian beliefs and pagan practices alongside the Christian traditions discussed in the previous chapter, it is fair to say that more than a few of the pre-Christian fertility festivals celebrated in May and June intersected with the Christian Feast of Pentecost, sometimes occurring during the same month. The notion of the Holy Spirit "greening" (*viriditas*) people and things, and the symbolic references to the use of Pentecost "green" by some medieval writers and clergy, as opposed to the traditional "red" more commonly associated with Pentecost, are fine examples of the medieval association of the third Person of the Trinity with the particularity of Nature. Despite a general decline in the fascination and reverence for Pentecost among many Christian denominations during the last few centuries, some of these naturalistic practices are still evident in many of today's Christian communities around the world, especially among Christianized indigenous cultures across the Southern Hemisphere.

The Feast of Pentecost, arriving usually in the month of May, became synonymous with the onset of spring and spiritual rebirth through the descent of the Holy Spirit, a fact attested to in a wide range of medieval calendar illustrations, Pentecost sermons, and the popular literary works dealing with chivalry examined in the previous chapter. Throughout medieval Christendom, the seven-times-seven-days from Easter to Pentecost were dedicated to spiritual and theological reflection on the gifts of the Holy Spirit, and contemplative prayer through the seasons of the liturgical calendar and the Holy Hours, along with sporadic attempts at theological dialogue with other monotheistic, non-Christian communities like Jews and Muslims whose sacred books and sacred languages proffered a common denominator for pondering and discussing the mystery of how each one might hear the Word of God in his or her own tongue, just as they did at the first Pentecost.

Before proceeding, three observations of the figures and movements we are about to meet in this chapter need highlighting. First, the authors and figures examined in this chapter are grouped together because of similarities in the ways each envisioned the legacy and meaning of Pentecost. Some of them, like Abbot Joachim of Fiore and the Franciscan Spirituals, have been studied extensively for the content and influence of their apocalyptic visions. However, the protagonists in this chapter neither shared, nor promulgated, the same pneumatological or Pentecostal vision as earlier generations of Christian writers and theologians. Their pneumatological spirituality was more like an early form of Pentecostal liberation theology along the lines of Luke 12:49: "I came to cast fire upon the earth; and would that it were already kindled." This chapter focuses primarily on figures and movements which were born and flourished on the Italian Peninsula in the shadows of the Holy Roman Empire and the Papacy. As a result of this specific geographic location, this chapter should also be read with an eye on the specter of the historic struggle between the Latin Church of the West and the medieval State as represented by late feudalism, the German Empire, and the rise of nation-states like France and Spain in the 1300s. Since the coronation of Charlemagne by Pope Leo III in Rome on December 25, 800 his heirs, who ruled the Holy Roman Empire until its collapse during World War I, believed they had a very special and privileged relationship with all future Bishops of Rome. The Byzantine Empire's historic interests in southern Italy, and Constantinople's historic resentment over Pope Leo's designation of the Frankish King as *Imperator* and *Augustus* of Italy, also set the stage for centuries of Byzantine meddling in political and military affairs across Italy, as well as provoking strong Byzantine prejudices against the Holy Roman Empire, which many regarded as neither "holy," nor "Roman," nor an "empire." On the other hand, the Vicar of Christ in Rome usually had a very different perspective about the role of the Papacy in relation to the Holy Roman Empire, or about the liberty of Christ's Church amidst the political and territorial ambitions of this Germanized Empire. It is possible that the sharp and intense tone of the protagonists surveyed in this chapter resulted from a growing sense of frustration over the repeated derailment of ecclesiastical reform efforts, the ongoing effects of dealing with pro-German anti-popes, and the continued threats to the Papacy from the Holy Roman Empire throughout the 1100s and 1200s.

Second, the dates spanning the most significant and active part of Joachim of Fiore's career (ca. 1180-1202) coincide with the close of the Twelfth Century Renaissance, regarded by historians as the apex of medieval Christian civilization. In the twilight years of this Twelfth Century Renaissance, there was a curious parallelism between the theological creativity of Abbot Joachim, and the equally creative inventiveness of Wolfram von Eschenbach's *Parzival* epic. Whereas the conceptions of Pentecost discussed in the previous chapter focused mainly on Nature and the Christian literary imagination, the conception of Pentecost that emerges in this chapter centers on prophetic leadership and the struggle for ecclesiastical reform waged by so many forgotten Christian visionaries of the High Middle Ages, like the Franciscan Spirituals and Cola di Rienzo, whose religious imaginations were fired up by the Joachimist prophecy of the coming "Age of the Holy Spirit." From this point of view, the apocalyptic and millennialist connotations of the figures discussed in this chapter reveal a deep yearning to transform their "present" moment in history, rather than an obsession with the "future" transformation of society and the world. Their focus on questions of leadership and liberty come as no surprise because when Christians take time to contemplate the implications of the Holy Spirit for spiritual leadership and egalitarian empowerment, the results are usually dynamic, progressive, and often explosive to the point of unleashing a "*subversive fire*" that propels all things and all persons toward the fullness of being, an eruption of transformative flames that sometimes holds devastating consequences for Church and State.

Lastly, the reformist agendas of the figures and movements discussed in this chapter were primarily concerned with issues of accountability and integrity concerning the doctrine and mission of the Church in their time and in the *not-yet* of the future eschaton. This was about more than simply preaching the Good

News of Christ's heavenly kingdom to the poor! Joachim of Fiore's Pentecostal visions echoed the sentiment of Luke 4:18-19 as the liberation of those who were being oppressed by the growing power, wealth, and exploitation of both Church and State became paramount in the 1200s and 1300s. Perhaps pneumatology and ecclesiology had more in common then than in today's theological and academic circles. Inspired by the Holy Spirit and fully aware of the moral and creative resources of the Christian tradition, Abbot Joachim and the Franciscan Spirituals shared a liberating and deeply altruistic vision of what it meant to be a member of Christ's Church. Here again, the relevance and applicability of Delwin Brown's theory of tradition, across time and place, comes into high relief as we realize that the men and women discussed in this chapter applied "feeling and thought in interaction as the vehicle" of their beloved Christian "tradition's recovery and innovation."[2] Indeed, out of the resources of the Christian tradition, the Abbot of Fiore and the Spiritual Franciscans, along with Guglielma of Milan and Cola di Rienzo, offered bold and controversial *reconstructions* of ecclesiology and society by looking back in time to the empowering story of the first Pentecost when the third Person of the Trinity inspired the birth of Christ's earthly church, a Pentecostal subversion aimed at spiritual liberation and ecclesiastical revitalization.

ABBOT JOACHIM OF FIORE   1132 - 1202

The Calabrian Abbot, Joachim of Fiore, might be the most significant figure in this book because so many of the writers and movements of the Holy Spirit that we will meet in subsequent chapters were somehow indebted to his vision of Christianity's future. Due to the stimulation that later generations derived from the pneumatological and ecclesiastical implications of his prophetic writings, more than a few scholars over the past two centuries of the modern academic enterprise would rank Joachim among the top ten most creative, insightful, and influential thinkers of the entire Second Millennium of Christianity. His profound insights came to him on a fateful Pentecost Sunday in either 1183 or 1184 at the Abbey of Casamari, located in Lazio just south of Rome. The exact year is irrelevant, but Joachim of Fiore's case is yet another significant medieval example of the Christian tendency toward highly transformative, personal religious experiences during the seven-times-seven-days of Pentecost, an overlooked and commonplace occurrence in the social logic of medieval Christian identity whose recovery motivates this book's historical inquiry.

Very little is known about the details of the enigmatic monk's life. Most accounts agree that he was born about 1132 or 1135 in the Calabrian village of Celico, which was then part of the diocese of Cosenza.[3] His mother was Gemma and his father, Mauro, served as a notary at the court of King Roger II of Sicily. As was the customary expectation for first-born sons in those days, Joachim followed in his father's footsteps and entered the service of the Sicilian Court at Palermo as a clerk and notary. The twelfth century was one of the most exciting periods of medieval European history, and as the capital of the Norman Kingdom of Sicily, Palermo was perhaps the most sophisticated royal court in all of

Christendom! Muslim and Jewish learning thrived alongside the Greek, Latin, and Arab influences that filled the air. Palermo was a multicultural realm in the truest sense for its time and place, with genuine toleration for the place of Byzantine and Islamic learning in a Christian state. Despite these tantalizing possibilities, the kingdom was not without military or political strife as ongoing feuds between the Papal Court in Rome and the Byzantine Empire to the East often left the Sicilians feeling like the rope in a tug of war. During Joachim's life, the Normans and the Hohenstaufen rulers of the Holy Roman Empire often vied for control of Sicily and Naples, Apulia, and Calabria.

Sometime during the late 1160s, the young Joachim traveled to Constantinople as part of a diplomatic mission sent by King William I of Sicily to the Byzantine Emperor Manuel I Comnenus. The surviving biographical accounts and legendary narratives of his life are silent about the full details of his next move, but seeking to discern God's supernatural stirring of his heart and mind, Joachim left the king's service in Byzantium and headed south by himself toward the Holy Land. The peacefulness of the Palestine desert appealed to Joachim as he discovered a profound attraction to asceticism and the monastic life. According to the sources, while meditating on Mount Tabor during Lent, his spiritual experiences intensified and culminated on Easter when he felt called by God to the religious life. The exact date is unknown, but this was probably sometime during 1168 or 1169.

Joachim returned to Sicily, where he spent a few years living as a hermit in the region of Mount Etna, before returning to the mainland at Calabria and staying for a time at the Cistercian Monastery of Sambucina in Luzzi. His father, Mauro, soon learned of his resignation from the royal court and chastised him for abandoning the family's high hopes that he would bring them honor and wealth by faithfully serving the Sicilian King. Joachim responded by reminding his father that he now served "Heaven's King" and lamented that some parents unjustly obstruct their children's call to religious service.[4] Joachim later appealed to the local bishop for ordination and about 1171 became a monk and entered the service of the Benedictine Monastery of Corazzo. Although Joachim's personal life would be blessed with multiple outpourings of God's spiritual gifts, this was the major turning point of his professional life as a cleric. We might describe the trajectory of his career from this point forth as one focusing on biblical exegesis and prophetic leadership. About 1178, following the death of Abbot Colombano, the monks appointed Joachim as Abbot of Corazzo, a promotion attesting to the young monk's popularity among his religious leaders and monastic brothers.

Joachim's life spanned the most intriguing and theologically creative period of medieval Christian history, which also coincided with some of the most tumultuous political and military events of the European Middle Ages, such as the recapture of Jerusalem by Saladin, King Richard the Lion Heart's ill-fated Third Crusade, and the rise to power of Pope Innocent III. Whether legendary or factual, Joachim's extant biographical accounts suggest that both kings and popes sought him out for advice on spiritual and temporal issues, and that among these were such notables as England's Richard the Lion Heart, Pope Innocent III, and

King Henry VI and his consort Empress Constance of the Holy Roman Empire. His friend and biographer, Luke of Cosenza, reports that Joachim died when he was about sixty-seven years of age on March 30, 1202 while working on the establishment of a new monastic retreat center at San Martino di Giove. Just six years earlier, Pope Celestine III granted papal approval to the monastic rule he founded, the Order of St. John of Fiore. The new order, known as the Florensian Order, thrived for centuries after his death until the monks were reincorporated into the Cistercian Order sometime between 1570 and 1633. Joachim's body was returned to his beloved monastery of San Giovanni di Fiore in 1226, where it remains today in the abbey church rebuilt in the 1970s, that in 1982 became the official home of the International Center for Joachimist Studies.[5]

PENTECOST AND JOACHIM'S THEOLOGY OF THE SPIRIT

Bernard McGinn observed that "without the evidence of his written works, the abbot of Fiore would remain an obscure southern Italian monk who had made a powerful impression on his contemporaries," and noted how effectively Joachim's writings and commentaries "spread his ideas far and wide and guaranteed him a permanent place in the history of Western thought."[6] Even before modern researchers became interested in Abbot Joachim's works, our medieval forebears honored him with the title: *magnus propheta*. Joachim's *theology of history*, couched in the apocalyptic language and cosmological symbolism of the Middle Ages, accounts for a considerable portion of Western Europe's subsequent eight centuries of fascination with his life and work. Indeed, from Dante and the Franciscan Spirituals to Hegel and Marx; from the Protestant Reformers to the Radical Reformation; from Thomas Müntzer to German Pietism; from the Jesuit and Franciscan missionaries of colonial Latin America to modern intellectuals like Carl Jung, James Joyce, and D. H. Lawrence; from German nationalists like Oswald Spengler to courageous critics of the Nazis like Eric Voegelin, the list of Western thinkers and movements influenced by Abbot Joachim's ideas and prophecies is far longer than most students of church history can imagine.

What if Western Europe and Christianity's historic obsession with the Joachimist paradigm is not the product of our penchant for apocalyptic prophecy and millenarian movements, but the result of Christianity's predisposition towards pneumatological thinking and sensibility as engines of change, especially when oppression and injustice warrant subverting the ecclesiastical and socio-political status quo? What if Western Christianity's historic "pneumatological deficit," noted by Kärkkäinen and others,[7] merely obscured the medieval Pentecostal legacies at the heart of the Joachimist corpus? And, what if our modern and postmodern colleagues who recovered this significant body of work, with eyes fixed primarily on apocalyptic themes, overlooked crucial aspects of Joachim's spiritual message, especially those aspects dealing with Pentecost's liberative and imaginative possibilities? What if the long-awaited eschaton merely slumbers in the human heart, full of spiritual power in the promise of a "personal Pentecost," and not somewhere "out-there" in a post-apocalyptic world beyond a thousand imagined tomorrows that will never happen so long as so many hearts and minds remain closed to the "divine kiss" of the Holy Spirit, the same "divine kiss" which sparked Joachim's ecclesiastical and scholarly career?

Joachim's *theology of the Holy Spirit*, arising out of his Trinitarian and exegetical concerns, and fueled by his intense Pentecost visions at the Abbey of Casamari in either 1183 or 1184, has received scant attention from modern scholars for whom the apocalyptic and millenarian implications of his *theology of history* occupied center stage on their research agendas. In the early 1900s, Italy's Ernesto Buonaiuti and Germany's Herbert Grundmann reopened the Joachimist corpus for modern medievalists with a series of translations and bibliographic studies of the Calabrian Abbot's major and minor works.[8] Due to numerous interpretive errors dating back to the 1500s and 1600s, when admirers incorrectly attributed apocryphal writings and pseudo-Joachimist treatises among the Calabrian Abbot's major works, there was much intensive manuscript labor to be conducted and then sorted for accuracy. Scholarly interest in the abbot's major works, his view of history, and his apocalyptic visions expanded considerably as a reputable and prolific Joachimist bibliography emerged by the 1970s. Among these were seminal studies by the leading Joachimist scholars in Euro-American academic circles for several decades, such as Henri de Lubac, Henry Mottu, Delno West, Bernard McGinn, and the far-reaching works of Marjorie Reeves.[9] I will not challenge the legacy of such distinguished colleagues, whether living or deceased, but my reading of Joachim's works and influence suggests that almost everything written by modern scholars about the Calabrian Abbot has suffered from too great an emphasis upon his so-called *theology of history*, and not enough attention given to the implication of Joachim's pneumatological inspiration during his fateful Pentecost experiences at the Abbey of Casamari, which would require the academic community to reframe his life's work and central message as expounding a *theology of the Holy Spirit* that prophesied the advent of a *Church of the Holy Spirit*.

Historicism played a significant role in the self-understanding of nineteenth and twentieth century interpreters of Joachim's works. Indeed their own millennialist leanings and quasi-apocalyptic concerns probably found solace in the abbot's works from modern ideologies prophesying human or social perfectibility amidst modernity's faith in unlimited scientific and material progress.[10] This historicism was clearly part of the academic milieu in which most twentieth century readings of Abbot Joachim were conducted. One is reminded here of Fernand Braudel's dictum: "The past is about the present." Even Stanley Burgess' popular and informative multi-volume overview of the Holy Spirit in church history relegates Joachim to a brief section in a chapter dealing with "the heretic fringe" of the Middle Ages.[11] Such attitudes miss the undeniable significance, and bewildering persistence, throughout eight hundred years of Joachimism in Western thought, that Reeves and McGinn demonstrated so effectively in their outstanding studies of the Calabrian Abbot.

Although Joachim's *theology of history* appealed to the historicist sensibilities of modern researchers, Joachim's life and work must be examined in light of the two areas of expertise by which *his* twelfth century contemporaries judged the significance of his spiritual gifts: biblical exegesis and visionary prophecy. He was known in his day by several popes and powerful monarchs and among his monastic brothers as *magnus propheta*. Joachim's talents in these two areas were understood within the social logic of medieval Christianity as *pneumato-logical gifts*, which his fellow monks would have attributed to the empowering presence of the Holy Spirit acting in their brother's life through Divine Grace.

As a biblical exegete, Joachim was first and foremost concerned with the amplification of Trinitarian doctrine. In the sense of Anselm's famous dictum, "Faith seeking understanding" (*fides quaerens intellectum*), he sought a fuller comprehension (*plenitudo intellectus*) of the cosmic and existential reality of the three Persons of the Holy Trinity through meditative practice focused on the interpretation of the Scriptures. As a devout and pious interpreter of the *not-yet of the future*, Joachim was concerned with Christ's return and how this "Second Advent" would transform the church by inaugurating what he perceived as the *third status* of history or the "Age of the Holy Spirit." Our modern and postmodern academic fascination with Joachim's *theology of history*, while highly intriguing for the historicist leanings of the past two centuries, and highly significant in the context of medieval apocalypticism, has never quite succeeded at unveiling the deeper spirituality or pneumatological possibilities inherent in Joachim's *theology of the Spirit*. To be sure, it was the liberating possibilities of his pneumatological visions about the future of humanity and the Christian Church that the Spiritual Franciscans found so invigorating and, which later, Roman pontiffs and the ecclesial hierarchy found so naïve and worrisome.

During the days between Easter and Pentecost, in either 1183 or 1184, Abbott Joachim of Fiore had two profound visions at the Abbey of Casamari that ignited his career as a prophet and as a biblical exegete, a career whose influence reached far beyond the parameters of his own time and place. The first of these insights was an Easter vision about the harmony of the Old and the New Testaments that he later elaborated in two books: his *Liber de Concordiae novi et veteris testamenti* and the *Expositio in Apocalypsim*. Joachim had been working hard for several months on the Book of Revelation while petitioning the Cistercian order to incorporate his beloved monastery of Corazzo into the order, but Providence had other plans for his religious career. Unable to fathom the reasons for his bewilderment, Joachim had sunk into a mood of perplexity while working on an exegesis of Revelation 1:10-11: "I was in the Spirit on the Lord's day, and I heard behind me a loud voice like a trumpet saying, 'Write about what you see in a book and send it to the seven churches.'" Little did Joachim realize how much writing of his own would be forthcoming over the next ten years as a result of this revelation and his discernment process over the next forty-nine days. In the *Expositio*, Joachim described the Easter vision that came to him while wrestling with these verses from Revelation:

> Having gone through the preceding verses of the Apocalypse to this place [in the text], I experienced such great difficulty and mental constraint beyond the ordinary that it was like feeling the stone that closed the tomb [of Christ] opposed to me... Since I was involved in many things, forgetfulness led the matter far away. After a year, the feast of Easter came around. Awakened from sleep

about midnight, something happened to me as I was meditating on this book, something for which, relying on God's gift, I am made more bold to write. Since some of the mysteries were already understood, but the greater mysteries were still hidden, there was a kind of struggle going on in my mind . . . Then, on the above-mentioned night, something like this happened. About the middle of the night's silence, as I think, the hour when it is thought that our Lion of Judah rose from the dead, as I was meditating, suddenly something of the fullness of this book and of the entire harmony of the Old and New Testaments was perceived with clarity of understanding in my mind's eye. The revelation was made when I was not even mindful of the chapter mentioned above.[12]

The second, and much more intense, vision took place on Pentecost and consisted of an outpouring of the symbolic images, or *figurae,* subsequently depicted and described in his third major book, the allegorical *Psalterium decem chordarum,* or *Psaltery of the Ten Strings.*

In the meantime, when I had entered the church to pray to Almighty God before the holy altar, there came upon me an uncertainty concerning belief in the Trinity as though it were hard to understand or hold that all the Persons were one God and one God all the Persons. When that happened I prayed with all my might. I was very frightened and was moved to call on the Holy Spirit whose feast day it was to deign to show me the mystery of the holy mystery of the Trinity. The Lord has promised us that the whole understanding of truth is to be found in the Trinity. I repeated this and I began to pray the psalms to complete the number I had intended. At this moment without delay the shape of a ten-stringed psaltery appeared in my mind. The mystery of the Holy Trinity shone so brightly and clearly in it that I was at once impelled to cry out, 'What God is as great as our God.'[13]

This second vision convinced him that a new age of human possibility, or as he called it a *"plena Spiritus libertas,"* was approaching, and that it was the logical and progressive outcome of the sacred teachings and theological anthropology conveyed in the Old and New Testaments.

According to biographers who knew him well, Joachim began writing his three major exegetical and prophetic works, the *Liber de Concordiae, Expositio in Apocalypsim,* and the *Psaltery of the Ten Strings* at Casamari sometime between spring 1183 and the fall of 1184. Throughout these works he complains about abbatial duties, such as leading his fellow monks in their studies or managing the resources and affairs of the abbey, interrupting the progress of his biblical scholarship. Joachim probably finished all three of these works sometime before 1192, works that taken together foretold the coming of an "Age of the Holy Spirit" set to begin sometime during the approaching thirteenth century or in the centuries beyond. He tentatively proposed 1265 as the year to watch. He described the "new age" (*aetate nova*) as a time when humanity would transcend its religious quarrels, when Christ-like love and compassion would reign supreme in the hearts of men and women, and when Christians would outgrow the need for an institutionalized earthly Church governed by an authoritarian hierarchy.

As we will discuss later in this chapter, despite stimulating hope among Western Europe's downtrodden and oppressed, Joachim's vision of the future threatened the growing power structures and political alliances upon which the medieval Church and State were building a self-confident *Respublica Christiana*, aimed at consolidating the feudal and trans-local power arrangements that ironically fueled many of the territorial and military conflicts of the 1200s and early 1300s. While apocalyptic concerns played a significant role in the imagination and piety of European Christians at this time, it is also true that these new structural arrangements were understood as both local and trans-local means of ensuring peace and justice, which Rome's ecclesiastical elite and Europe's powerful expansionist royal families believed could be achieved without an apocalyptic intervention from heaven. Joachim's prophesied "Age of the Holy Spirit" must have sounded bizarre and foolishly idealistic to Church or State officials who believed the emerging *Respublica Christiana* would curb feudal violence, balance royal and ecclesiastical power across Europe, and mount an adequate line of defense against Muslim or Turkish expansion from the Eastern Mediterranean.

Joachim's *Liber de Concordiae* is the only one of his three major works completely finished. Designed as a detailed exposition on the "concordance" or harmony between the Old and the New Testaments, this book was undertaken following his Easter vision at Casamari. Some Joachimist scholars regard it as the abbot's most important work, a rationale based on the percentage of the book Joachim devoted to outlining his theory of prophetic exegesis. Here he also explains the parallels between the generations of Hebrew patriarchs and prophets cited in the Old Testament, and the generations of apostolic Christians cited in the New Testament, which were central to his prophetic understanding of Salvation history leading up to his own times in the twelfth century. In Book III of this work, Joachim looks at the meanings and correspondences of the seven seals from Revelation. He concludes his exposition by applying and explaining his method in the context of the Old Testament's historical books and their implications for the future trajectory of history as extended into New Testament times and beyond. From the exegetical analysis of these two texts, Joachim posited a numerological structure of two stages, or histories, comprising Salvation history. The first stage, or *status* as he later called these eras, was that of the Father and the Hebrew people in the Old Testament. The second stage, or *status*, was that of the Son and Christianity in the New Testament. The third element in this structural and eschatological view of cosmic time and human memory was the creative role of the Holy Spirit that was poured forth at Pentecost and gave birth to Christ's church on earth. The *Liber de Concordiae* focuses primarily on the first stage of Salvation history, namely that of the Father through the teachings revealed to the Hebrews and preserved in the Old Testament.

The relationship of the three Persons of the Trinity to human history became the structural basis for Joachim of Fiore's *theology of history* and informed his understanding, and redemptive hopes, for the future of both the Christian Church and the human race. In 1184, Joachim appeared before Pope Lucius III at Veroli, who was impressed with his gift for interpreting prophecies and commissioned him to write the *Liber Concordiae*. Joachim's application of the Trinity to the conceptualization of history would have a lasting effect on subsequent Western European figures like Dante, Christopher Columbus, Hegel and Marx and movements like the Protestant and Catholic Reformations, and the Rosicrucian Enlightenment discussed later in Chapter Five, as well as scores of other writers and visionaries beyond the scope of this book. Following his study of the Old Testament's prefiguring of the Incarnation and the Holy Spirit in the *Liber de Concordiae*, which, I reiterate, he identified as the *first status* or stage of Salvation history, Joachim began pondering the roles of the Son and the Holy Spirit in the past, present, and future of humanity.

The next major manuscript resulting from Joachim's personal religious experiences and biblical scholarship at the Abbey of Casamari was the *Expositio in Apocalypsim*. If the *Liber Concordiae* is the abbot's most important and foundational work, then surely the *Expositio in Apocalypsim* is the most thorough example of his prophetic method applied to the biblical text, in this case that of St. John's Revelation.[14] Divided into eight sections or books, along with a lengthy introduction, the *Expositio* offers a line-by-line analysis and interpretation of the book of the Apocalypse, with special emphasis on the eschatological and structural meanings of the number seven throughout the text. In keeping with earlier exegetical interpretations of Revelation by Rupert of Deutz or Anselm of Havelberg, Joachim suggests that the history of the world and the Church is divided into seven stages (*septem tempora specialia*), which correlate precisely with the seven stages of Revelation and the mystique of the number seven throughout the biblical text.

Readers of this exegetical manuscript on Revelation soon realize Joachim's writing of the *Expositio* was motivated by his struggle to comprehend the role of the Risen Christ, and the prophesied New Jerusalem, during the era of the *second status* or stage of Salvation history, in which Joachim believed he and his contemporaries were still living. But the divine disclosures set forth in the two testaments were juxtaposed in Joachim's theological imagination with the tripartite structure of God's providential self-disclosure through the successive generations of Jewish and Christian believers. Just as the Father and the Son had their appointed times, Joachim believed the Holy Spirit would have its own time:

> Hence, just as God the Father was openly seen at work in the first five ages, and in the sixth age the Son, it is necessary that he will also be at work in the seventh. Just as God is a Trinity, so too the works of the three times agree with the individual Persons of the Godhead by the signification of the mystery. They are seen to be distinct by their own limits and significations. These are the three times, which by reason of the true nature of their particular gifts we believe should be called the three *status* of the world.[15]

It is important to note that Joachim did not believe that yet another "new" or "third testament" would emerge from the third *status* of the Holy Spirit. Instead, he believed this model of the history of salvation accounted for the Trinitarian nature of the cosmos, while keeping open the doors of eschatological transformation for the *ecclesia* and the *mundus*. Hence, this temporal openness was for

Joachim a "gift" of divine grace sent forth (*missio*), or poured out as on Pentecost, through the intercessory power of Christ's Holy Spirit as the appointed intermediary between humanity and the first Person of the Trinity. Joachim did not believe that the ecclesial and the human dispositions characterizing the *second status* were going to last for all time. He understood these as intermediary stages in preparation for a time yet to come when God's Grace would shepherd humanity into the *third status* of the Holy Spirit, a view which led many of his readers and admirers in subsequent centuries to criticize the Church of their particular historical moment in favor of a more egalitarian, empowering, and reformed institution.

Joachim's cosmic schema, often portrayed as three concentric and overlapping circles, is more than a mere chronological reordering of salvation history into three neat divisions based on the Trinity. Here we detect the influence of medieval ideas about patriarchal and apostolic succession alongside that of royal genealogies and hagiographic schools, as he proceeds to calculate the generations from Abraham to Moses, from the Hebrew prophets to the Incarnation of Jesus, and then from Jesus to his late-twelfth century context. McGinn has described Joachim's theology of history as a "history of the *ecclesia*" with strong parallels to Augustine of Hippo's *De civitate Dei*, solidly grounded in seven centuries of medieval millenarian hermeneutics,[16] yet boldly breaking with tradition by peering into the coming seventh *aeta* or *third status* when, according to Joachim's pneumatological visions, peace and harmony and the *spiritualis intellectus* will be poured forth into the hearts and minds of all.

From Joachim's personal statements scattered throughout the *Liber Concordiae* and the *Expositio*, it is evident he was struggling to discern the voice of the Spirit speaking through the divine letter of the Old and New Testaments. He believed with deep conviction that the advent of the *third status* was at hand. While his certainty emerged from that defining Pentecostal experience at Casamari, his theological style and work ethic were grounded in praying the Daily Office and commemorating the feasts of the church year, and then augmented deeper still by years of meticulous biblical study and reflection as he wrote the works discussed herein. Joachim also illustrated his views of the Trinity in history by drawing "genealogical trees" adorned with flowers and showing abundant new growth, which were most likely influenced by depictions of Jesse Trees bearing the Seven Gifts of the Holy Spirit that he observed in various treatises, like the *Speculum Virginum*, available during his lifetime. Later he developed these *figurae* into a series of three trees representing each of the three epochs of the Trinity in sacred history for the Father, Son, and the Holy Spirit. Even eight centuries after his passing, we can detect how monastic religious practices, like those discussed in Chapter Two linking monastic spirituality with the liturgical calendar, nurtured his musings on Scripture and bore him the intellectual fruits for which he ardently prayed. The rhythmic cadences of daily prayer and ritual observance, while living within and through the seasons and festivals of the Christian liturgical calendar, placed Joachim in a contemplative, altered state as he read and pondered the meanings of the Holy Scriptures, all the while praying and attending daily Mass. He even tells us that in moments of exegetical frustration or spiritual aridity, he resorted to singing the Psalms, a meditative practice that always focused his mind and calmed his heart. He was blessed with an abundant surplus of *donum intellectus spiritualis*, but from a pneumatological standpoint his most important prophetic insight may have been the dynamic image of a ten-stringed psaltery he received at Casamari on that fateful Pentecost.

Pentecost holds an interesting and important role in the Christian tradition of prophetic utterance because the story of Pentecost reminds believers that the Word of the Lord is often spoken through a finite human being through whose interpretive agency the Word may be led astray or misinterpreted. Or, in the best of circumstances, the message of the Word may revitalize the church and the individuals who receive its message of faith, hope, and charity. Joachim divided the *Psalterium decem chordarum* into three sections, or books, whose overall focus is primarily the *intellectus spiritualis* of the third *status*. The *Psalterium* is not nearly as well planned as the *Liber de Concordiae*, nor as exegetical and expansive as the *Expositio in Apocalypsim,* but the *Psaltery of the Ten Strings* served a much more important role in the Joachimite corpus by allowing its author an allegorical vehicle for pondering and communicating the meaning of his theological insights. This book resulted from Joachim's integrative vision of a psaltery with ten strings received while studying and meditating at the Abbey of Casamari south of Rome on Pentecost Sunday around 1183 or 1184.[17] Considering our brief discussion in Chapter Two about this particular abbey as the possible twelfth century site where the magnificent "flower tapestries," known as *infiorata*, were first assembled each year after Pentecost during the Feast of Corpus Christi, then this would have been a particularly numinous abbatial setting for the Abbot of Fiore's discernment of the meaning of his spiritual visions while writing down his interpretations of the Son and the Holy Spirit's roles in salvation history. Considering the fondness for flowers (*floris, flora,* and *fiore*) in the Italian region where he spent his later years and founded the "Florensian Order," these are both tantalizing and plausible possibilities.

Given Joachim's intensive exegetical labors at the time, the vision of the ten-stringed psaltery or lyre seems to have served as a *concordatio oppositorum*, a harmony or synthesis of disparate but related elements whose prophetic dimensions he was still struggling to comprehend. These elements included the historicizing of the Trinity, the Gifts of the Holy Spirit, the seven ages (*aetates*) and the three epochs (*status*) of salvation history as inflected through the generations of the Old and New Testaments, all of which he concluded would culminate very soon in the "Age of the Holy Spirit." The new era would be characterized by spiritual freedom and universal love. The first section of the *Psalterium* offers a detailed study of the Trinity, while the second section examines possible mystical meanings for the number 150 as representative of the total number of Psalms in the Hebrew Scriptures. In this section, we realize Abbot Joachim derived his notion of the number of Psalms revealing a hidden numerological clue (*solemnes numeros*) by which he worked out a new and complicated prophetic pattern based on the numbers fifteen and ten, which, in turn, inspired the symbol of the ten-stringed psaltery (*decem chordae*).[18] The third section describes rules and practices for the contemplative recitation of the Psalms. Here Joachim also ponders the meaning and role of the three orders (*tres ordines*) of individuals serving Christ's earthly church: monks, clergy, and laity.[19] He then posits the coming of a new monastic order, which will arise and proliferate around 1260 or 1265, and whose revitalized Christian ideals will eventually characterize the Age of the Holy Spirit.

The figure of the ten-stringed psaltery becomes for Joachim the ideal representational model for the relational mystery among the members of the Trinity. He believed the image of a psaltery conveyed the fundamental unity of the Trinity while simultaneously conveying an understanding of the relational vitality among the Father, Son, and Holy Spirit.[20] Musical harmony and the harmonious functioning of the celestial realm were closely associated aesthetic and metaphysical themes in medieval religious thinking, especially within the ranks of educated monks or clergy like Abbot Joachim. This particular type of psaltery is shaped like an equilateral triangle with a blunted top, which represents the position of the Father in the cosmos and in the order of Creation. The left corner represents the Son and the right corner represents the Holy Spirit. There is a circular emblem, or *rose circle*, in the center of the figures. Joachim carefully explains how this lyre's resulting musical harmony exemplifies the mystery and equality of the Trinitarian relationship and the presence of the Three Persons in sacred history. The ten musical strings represent the Three Theological Virtues (faith, hope, and charity) and the Seven Gifts of the Holy Spirit. He suggests that the approaching *status*, or Age of the Holy Spirit, will be an epoch characterized by an outpouring of love and grace from the Trinity acting through the Holy Spirit, whose primary epochal feature (*proprietas*) will be the spiritual "liberation" and empowerment (*libertas; liberum*) generated by the manifestation of the Theological Virtues and the Gifts of the Holy Spirit in the hearts of both laity and clergy alike. Joachim's views on the power of the Spirit to teach and impart divine wisdom in the human heart, which is superior to mere "human wisdom," were clearly influenced by his exegesis of I Corinthians 2:3-16. He places great emphasis on the notion of the Father's sending forth (*missio*) of the Son through the Incarnation, and in the Son's sending forth (*missio*) of the Holy Spirit through the tongues of fire revealed at Pentecost, which set the stage for the long awaited reconciliation of humanity to the Father through the vehicle of the Imago Dei implanted in the human heart since the creation of Adam and Eve.

The figure of the triangular psaltery with the blunted top signified for Joachim both the eternity of the Father and the sending forth of the Son and the Holy Spirit represented by the sharp left and right angles of the triangular psaltery. The enigmatic circle, or rose, pictured in the center of the psaltery represents the heart of the Trinity beating in an eternal rhythmic cadence, always open to human understanding through the gift of the *spiritualis intellectus*. On the other hand, perhaps Joachim's penchant for the allegorical reading of Scripture's hidden truths intended this rose-like circle as an image of God's mouth from whose rhythmic, cosmic breathing issued the divine breath that created Adam into a "living spirit." And from God's breath flowed the very Word of God (*Logos*) in the Incarnation when Christ became the Second Adam and the prototype of future human spiritual unfolding. I am speculating here but given Joachim's explanations of the psaltery figure and its relation to the Trinity, one is left wondering if the manifestation of God's will in salvation history might manifest in this sort of rhythmic respiratory mystery which aligns so well with ideas and symbols about "the Breath of God" and the "Spirit of God" known to Christian exegesis of both the Old and the New Testaments. Given the unity of essence (*essentia*) and substance among the Three Persons, the Son's sending forth of the Holy Spirit at Pentecost further reconciled humanity's embodied nature to its heavenly origins and set Christ's temporal ecclesia on its missiological and eschatological path toward the third *status* of the Holy Spirit, when the promise of the New Testament would be fulfilled in an epoch of unprecedented love and spiritual liberation. This is the gist of Joachim's Pentecostal inspiration and ecclesiastical insights received at the Abbey of Casamari. It is doubtful whether Abbot Joachim realized the influence his allegorical and highly imaginative *Psaltery of the Ten Strings* would assume during the centuries that followed his prophetic and exegetical career.

THE JOACHIMIST LEGACY IN CHRISTIAN HISTORY

Abbot Joachim's spiritual visions at the Abbey of Casamari inspired his imaginative reconstruction of the Church's future from the traditioned resources of the Christian past preserved in the Hebrew Bible and in the New Testament. As a result of the Abbot's exegetical work on the Trinity's role in human history, many believed with conviction that the Holy Spirit had motivated his theological reconstruction, which, in turn, ignited the reformist ideas and "Pentecostal" sensibilities of countless Christian men and women after Joachim's passing in 1202. His conviction in the rise of a new monastic order of "spiritual men" (*viri spirituales*), who would help usher in the egalitarian "new age" of mutual love and human empowerment, gave rise to movements of the Holy Spirit throughout Western European Christianity whose founders often saw themselves as the prophesied transformative fraternity of the third *status*. Beyond these apocalyptic dreams and millenarian hopes, one could argue that Pentecostalism is not just a modern, twentieth century phenomenon, but rather there is a *Pentecostal tendency*, as well as a *Pentecostal tradition*, in Christian thought and practice that has been part of the story of Christianity since the beginning of the seven-times-seven days leading up to the first Pentecost recorded in the Book of Acts. This is true regardless of whether or not modern and postmodern scholarship have paid sufficient attention to these trajectories in church history. In this context, part of Joachim's legacy is that while firmly rooted in *lectio divina* and in the recitation and singing of the Psalms, as well as in the liturgical calendar cycles of Christian monasticism, he elaborated and disseminated a *theology of the Spirit* constellated around the Feast of Pentecost into a *theology of history* that Christian writers and visionaries later applied across a much wider spectrum of both religious and secular concerns, than if it had remained solely within the orbit of pneumatology and the language of medieval prophecy.

Despite the suspicions with which later Popes and Scholastic theologians regarded the Calabrian Abbott's view of salvation history for almost twenty years, from 1184 until his death in 1202, Joachim sought and obtained papal permission to write about his biblical insights and prophetic revelations. As already mentioned, Lucius III first gave him such approval in 1184, and then in 1186 Pope Urban III renewed this commitment. While visiting Rome during early summer 1188, Pope Clement III issued a papal bull authorizing him to complete the *Liber de Concordiae* and the *Expositio in Apocalypsim* and then submit these for theological discussion and papal approval. Finally, the recognition of the constitution and title of Joachim's new monastic order on April 25, 1196 by Pope Celestine III would suggest that, even at this late stage of his life and career, his exegetical and prophetic works were considered theologically sound and free from ecclesiastical repudiation by church officials. If this state of affairs is accurate and true, then one cannot avoid asking: "What went wrong with the reception of Joachim's prophecies?" In the next section, we will explore this question and examine the reception of Joachim's work by the Fraticelli, who were also known as the Spiritual Franciscans, and who believed that as the true protectors of St. Francis' Rule their branch of the Franciscan Order was destined to help bring about the Joachimist Age of the Holy Spirit.

THE SPIRITUAL FRANCISCANS

Joachim of Fiore (ca. 1132-1202) and Francis of Assisi (1182-1226) were contemporaries. Although the Florensian Order founded by the Calabrian Abbot played no part in his prophecies about the rise of a Church of the Holy Spirit, the Spiritual Franciscans, who saw themselves as the orthodox and true followers of St. Francis' Rule, developed a radical fondness for Joachim's egalitarian vision of the Holy Spirit's role in the transformation of humanity and Christian society. Among the Spiritual Franciscans, Abbot Joachim's pneumatological visions inspired an acute reformist fervor aimed first at the Franciscan Order, which some believed had been led astray by its worldly successes and dealings with the papacy, and later aimed at Christendom as the reform minded Spirituals took aim at the corruption, violence, and neglect of the poor they perceived plagued Europe and the Middle East in the thirteenth and fourteenth century. These convictions eventually cost some of the Franciscan adherents of Abbot Joachim's *plena spiritus libertas* their lives. Despite the fondness for Joachim's visionary exegesis of the Old and New Testaments among several Popes and reform minded clergy, the implications of his prophecies about the emergence of an egalitarian, decentered, and charismatic church around the year 1260 did not sit well with those occupying seats of power across the emerging *Respublica Christiana* of the High Middle Ages. In this section, we will briefly discuss those aspects of St. Francis' life and character, which the Spiritual Franciscans perceived as synonymous with the spiritual and charismatic virtues of Joachim of Fiore's prophesied Age of the Holy Spirit. We will then examine the broader spiritual motivations of these "Fraticelli" who challenged the power of both Church and State in their ill-fated theological controversy over the poverty of

Christ versus the growing worldliness and wealth of the Christian Church during the 1200s and 1300s.

Once ecclesiastical leaders became aware of the full implications of Joachim's eschatological predictions, whether in Rome or throughout medieval Christendom's powerful bishoprics, his ideas were received with alarm and garnered little support from the elite. The first sign of disfavor appeared in November 1215 at the Fourth Lateran Council where Pope Innocent III heard arguments on Joachim's Trinitarian views versus those of Peter Lombard (ca. 1100-1160) whose ideas and works were rapidly becoming important in the growing thirteenth century pedagogical and philosophical enterprise taking place in Europe's Christian universities. The subsequent condemnation of Abbot Joachim's understanding of the Trinity opened his exegetical and prophetic works to further critiques of his unique interpretation of the three *status*, or epochs, of salvation history being based upon the Trinitarian Persons. As friars in the Franciscan ranks became increasingly concerned about the Papacy's turbulent and expanding struggle with the Holy Roman Empire, and the Franciscan Order's growing power, wealth, and influence, some friars found in Joachim's works and prophecies about the future what they believed to be a prophecy of their own order's agency in the coming transformation of feudal society and the Church, which led to the second outpouring of disfavor concerning Joachimist prophecy and its sympathizers.

Such pronounced monastic discontent with existing ecclesiastical and secular power structures, mingled with a heightened mood of apocalyptic expectation, culminated in 1254 with the ardent rejection at the University of Paris of a treatise written by the Franciscan Joachimite friar, Gerard of Borgo San Donnino. Gerard's radical appropriation of the Calabrian Abbot's prophecies about the demise of the hierarchical *ecclesia* in his book on the "Eternal Gospel" (*Liber Introductoris in Evangelium aeternum*) probably would have been condemned by Joachim if he had been alive to read it. Gerard equated the prophecies of Joachim with the mention of an "eternal gospel" in Revelations 14:6, and then equated the mission of revitalizing the Church with the mission of the Franciscan Order. Pope Alexander IV condemned the book as heretical in October 1255. Gerard was arrested, his works outlawed and burned, and he eventually died in prison around 1276. There are no surviving copies of his infamous "Introduction to the Eternal Gospel," but the connections he posited between the Franciscan Order and Joachimist prophecy became an increasingly complex issue in the ecclesiastical and political affairs of Italy, France, Provence, and Naples until the late 1340s.

In other ways, however, the notion of devoted Franciscan friars responding positively to Joachim's theology of the Spirit, and contemplating his prophecies about the coming third *status* and its new monastic order of "spiritual teachers" who would bring about the Age of the Holy Spirit, is not surprising from our vantage point today. Nor were such sympathies unexpected among the Franciscans, for there are significant parallels between the Franciscan mission of radical humility and the Joachimist *missio* of the Holy Spirit's egalitarian role in both Church leadership and in the piety of individual monastic servants of Christ's

Church. These pneumatological sensibilities in the Joachimist and Franciscan movements paralleled each other despite their respective differences, and were clearly on a collision course with the growing political, economic, and military power of the Latin Church of the High Middle Ages. Francis had once emphatically suggested that the monastic Rule he drafted as the mission statement of the Friars Minor was aimed at promoting "the Spirit of the Lord and Its Holy activity."[21] Despite St. Francis' ecclesiastical loyalty and doctrinal correctness, there is an unmistakable affinity between the charismatic ideals of the Joachimist vision and the boldness of the Franciscan vision of humility, service, and human dignity, which each in their own way understood as an *imitatio Christi* through the power and presence of the Holy Spirit.

Saint Francis of Assisi is without question one of the most influential and beloved Christian figures of the Middle Ages. Numerous historical and legendary episodes from St. Francis' life story would figure prominently in a history of medieval pneumatology, or in a history of medieval Christian conceptions of Pentecost, especially since the saint himself held a special reverence for both the work of the Holy Spirit in the world and for the Feast of Pentecost in the church calendar. Even among some of Francis' most beloved early disciples who joined the Friars Minor, like Anthony of Padua, we find examples of profound pneumatological gifts. We have, for example, the famous accounts and images of Francis preaching to the birds, which in medieval iconography and symbolism were well-known markers of pneumatological presence and mystery. We also have accounts of his fascination with flowers, animals, food, the sun and the moon, and with Nature's beauty, which in the style of Saint Hildegard of Bingen also marked the spirituality of St. Francis as vitally open to the presence of the Holy Spirit in the natural world of flora and fauna. Roger Sorrell attributes this to Francis' "nature mysticism" as noted in *The Little Flowers of Saint Francis (Fioretti)*, Francis' *Canticle of Brother Sun,* Bonaventure's *Legenda maior,* and Thomas of Celano's *Treatise on the Miracles of Blessed Francis.*[22] Sorrell notes that the term, *Natura*, appears nowhere in Francis writings, but instead we find a very special emphasis in the saint's theology on the skies and the earth reminiscent of the Psalms, and a genuine love for "all creatures, which are under the heavens."[23]

We also have the story of Francis arriving in Egypt in 1219 during the Battle of Damietta, at the height of the Fifth Crusade, determined to evangelize the Sultan of Egypt, Malek al-Kamil. Their subsequent theological conversation and brief friendship stand out as one of medieval history's most impressive examples of mutual edification and toleration among the Children of Abraham. Here we encounter the story of the Holy Spirit's powerful presence in the saint's life in both the "trial by fire" before the Sultan and in the "divine fire" that burned ever more intensely in Francis' heart after his meeting with the Sultan, episodes embellished for generations in later medieval iconography and hagiography.

Finally, we have the fascinating stories of miraculous preaching and "tongues of fire" found in the medieval primary sources, and in the stories still being told and circulated today in Padua and the surrounding Italian villages, about one of the most famous and beloved Franciscans, Saint Anthony of Padua

(1195-1231). According to legends mentioned in sources like the *Legenda prima* and the *Annales minorum*, St. Anthony's "tongue" sometimes became "the pen of the Holy Ghost." Men and women listening to his sermons were reminded often of the Day of Pentecost as they reported miraculously hearing him preaching in their native, local languages. A fifteenth century painting of St. Anthony, by Benozzo Gozzoli, portrays the saint with a book in his left hand, and a brilliant flame in his raised and outstretched right hand. Thirty years after his death, while the citizens of Padua were building a new shrine to house his relics, Bonaventure, who, as Minister General of the Franciscan Order in the mid-1260s, was called upon to supervise the exhumation of Saint Anthony's body, reported finding that while the body had decayed to dust, the saint's tongue had not decomposed and still retained a vibrant red color. Pope Gregory IX canonized Anthony of Padua at the Cathedral of Spoleto, less than a year after his death, on May 30, 1232, and, not surprisingly, it was Pentecost Sunday.

Pneumatological sensibilities like those discussed above from the life of St. Francis, and Pentecostal legacies like these echoed in the life and legends of St. Anthony of Padua, remind us of the importance of both the Holy Spirit and the Feast of Pentecost in the lives, religious traditions, rites and worship practices of medieval European Christians. On the other hand, the significance of such sensibilities and legacies for questions of ecclesiology and mission (*missio*) also opened many Franciscan hearts and minds to the *intellectus spiritualis* articulated in the works of Abbot Joachim of Fiore. A brief overview of St. Francis' life story and the origins of the Franciscan Order will highlight the ideals and themes inherent in the Franciscan movement that predisposed many among the Friars Minor in favor of Joachim of Fiore's prophecies about a new monastic order that would lead the church into the Age of the Holy Spirit.

Francis was born in 1181 or 1182 at Assisi in Umbria where his father, Pietro Moriconi, was a very successful and wealthy cloth merchant. His father was also known as Pietro di Bernardone, after the nickname derived from his Tuscan grandfather meaning "big" or "fat" (Bernardo), and which apparently stuck as an additional surname for the family.[24] His mother, Pica, had him baptized "Giovanni," against his father's wishes, in honor of her reverence for John the Baptist, and with sincere hope that her infant son might one day become a devoted and pious servant of Christ. Resentful of his wife's decision while he was away on business, Pietro changed his son's name to "Francesco," in honor of his admiration for the rising feudal fortunes and sophisticated culture of France. Francis received a fine education in the cathedral school of Saint George's Church near the family's home in Assisi, where he excelled in Latin studies. Pietro Moriconi had big plans for his son's future as an important business leader in Assisi. Thus, Francis experienced the social, political, and military opportunities typical among upper class Umbrian males in those days. Tradition informs us that Francis exhibited a talent for leadership, and that his peers and the community of Assisi liked him very well. Thomas of Celano (ca. 1200-1255), the first of Francis' medieval biographers, observed that Francis was fond of revelry and the worldly pleasures afforded by his family's wealth.[25] Francis' medieval biographers also report he was quite a gifted poet, and that he fancied himself a troubadour writing lyric poetry while traveling through the countryside between Umbria and France.

The fanciful and varied trajectories of Francis' youth, however, were interrupted by his service as a knight in the war between Assisi and Perugia. In 1202, while fighting in the Battle of Collestrada, near Perugia, Francis was wounded, captured in battle, and imprisoned for about a year. During his time in prison, Francis became very ill with malaria, and, after being ransomed and released to his father, began the long process of discernment about peace, justice, and poverty that culminated in his vocation for religious service against his father's financial ambitions. Francis eventually healed from that illness and resumed his life of comfort in Assisi until his passion for knighthood and military service resurfaced in 1205 when he enlisted as a knight in the service of Count Walter III of Brienne. News of Count Walter's military victories in southern Italy on behalf of the Papacy's struggle against the Holy Roman Empire motivated Francis to resume his chivalric ambitions and again seek the honors of knighthood. On the way to Brienne, however, he learned of Count Walter's premature death in battle near Sarno against German forces, and Francis fell into a deep depression accompanied by another bout of malaria in Spoleto. One night in the midst of his physical and emotional agony, Francis heard a voice asking him: "Who do you think can best reward you, the Master or the servant?" Francis replied, "The Master," and he was convinced that it was the voice of God speaking to him about the vanity of a military career. He resumed contemplation and discernment about the next stages of his life. A few years later while riding through the woods he encountered a leper on the road, and, rather than tossing him a coin or two, Francis dismounted his horse, embraced the stranger, and kissed his deformed hand. Francis discovered that he felt a genuine concern for the welfare of the sick and the poor, which manifested in him a new and deeper appreciation for the liberty of the Gospel message and the promise of Christ's mission when contrasted with the poverty of worldly riches.[26] Years later on his deathbed he recalled this encounter with the leper as one of the most significant moments of his entire life, which helped him turn the corner away from a career in business or knighthood and contemplate a life of service and ministry for Christ.

The final and most decisive turning point in Francis' conversion process occurred in 1206 while walking outside the abandoned Church of San Damiano in Assisi when, according to Saint Bonaventure's *Life of Saint Francis* (*Legenda maior*), the Holy Spirit inspired him to go inside and pray. Francis heard the voice of Christ speaking to him from a Byzantine icon in the nearly ruined sanctuary in words retold and made famous by every biographer of the saint's life since the Middle Ages: "Francis, go and repair my house which, as you see, is falling completely into ruin."[27] The mysterious voice repeated these words three times, which left Francis both "amazed" and "trembling with fear" while "he received in his heart the power of the divine words."[28] Bonaventure suggests it was a few years before the young Francis of Assisi realized the voice was not indicating the repair of this physical building, nor of the several other ruined churches in nearby towns that Francis restored with his family's wealth, but that Christ's words on that fateful day had a broader meaning.

Returning finally to his senses, he prepared to obey, gathering himself together
to carry out the command of repairing the church materially, although the principal intention of the words referred to that Church which Christ purchased
with his own blood (Acts 20:28), as the Holy Spirit taught him and as he himself later disclosed to the friars.[29]

Here we have a clue as to the ecclesiastical mission of St. Francis and the
Franciscan Order who, in their dedication to the poor and the marginalized
across Christendom, also saw their task as one of reforming the Church's comportment with society by offering and demonstrating the example of radical
love, unselfish service, and egalitarianism in the tradition of the *imitatio paupere
Christi*, in imitation of the poverty of Christ.

Bonaventure's reference to the text of Acts 20:28 sheds light on St. Francis'
supernatural experiences that day in San Damiano, but also illuminates our appreciation for this moment's significance in the monastic career that unfolded
afterwards. This particular verse from Acts 20, and the following verses (Acts
20:29-38), allude dramatically to the powerful presence and empowerment of
the Holy Spirit by which followers of Christ are made "overseers, to care for the
church of God." This was one of the most important themes in the early Franciscan movement's labors for the revitalization of the Christian Church in medieval
society, and in the lives of individual believers who came in contact with the
teaching and example of Saint Francis. Through the words of St. Paul speaking
to the elders at Miletus and Ephesus, this passage was also important for the
Franciscan vow of poverty and the renunciation of worldly power to which St.
Francis became thoroughly committed after his ecstasy at San Damiano: "I co-
veted no one's silver or gold or apparel. You yourselves know that these hands
ministered to my necessities, and to those who were with me. In all things I have
shown you that by so toiling one must help the weak, remembering the words of
the Lord Jesus, how he said, 'It is more blessed to give than to receive.'" (Acts
20:33-35).

After rejecting his father's materialistic ambitions, renouncing his inheritance, and physically rebuilding several ruined churches, Francis found himself
surrounded by a growing circle of devoted disciples. Three years later, in 1209,
while working on the restoration of an old Benedictine shrine known as the
Church of Portiuncula, the Order of Friars Minor (*fratres minores*) was founded.
The meaning of the term "minor" (*minores*) was specifically intended by Francis
as a permanent reminder in the hearts and minds of these new friars of their
vows of poverty and humility to remain in a lowly station while avoiding the
arrogance of the learned and the pride of high-ranking church offices. By the
end of the year, the fledgling movement, known simply among the local populace as the Brothers of Penance, or as the Penitents of Assisi, was granted Papal
approval of the original rules Francis drafted. This emerging movement grew
rapidly into the Franciscan Order. In November of 1215 Francis attended the
Fourth Lateran Council in Rome where Pope Innocent III had assembled over
twelve hundred leaders and dignitaries from the Latin Church. There he met and
befriended Saint Dominic, who was still seeking final Papal approval for the

Dominican Order. In less than a decade, the Friars Minor extended their preaching and service to the poor across Italy, and was planning on opening permanent chapter houses in Spain, Germany, and England. By the time the First General Chapter of the Friars Minor convened on May 5, 1217, Pentecost Sunday, at the Church of the Portiuncula near Assisi, it was clear that the movement begun by Francis of Assisi was destined for a long and fruitful history serving Latin Christendom and the rest of the world. By the time of Francis' death at the Portiuncula on October 3, 1226, the Franciscan Order he founded, with the aid of his earliest companions dedicated to poverty and peace, had become one of the most respected and trusted of the medieval European mendicant orders.

As the Franciscan Order unfolded during the thirteenth century by opening more chapter houses, convents, and hermitages across Europe and the Middle East, the Friars Minor gained enormous influence along with church properties forming a vast network that transcended the Mediterranean world's feudal and imperial boundaries. The Franciscans gained the attention of feudal lords throughout Spain, England, France, and Italy, as well as the attention of the Holy Roman Empire, whose centuries-old pattern of meddling in the affairs of the Papacy and of the Roman nobility in Southern Italy positioned its rulers as major players in European ecclesiastical and secular events. Even before his death in 1226, Francis foresaw the mounting challenges of gaining too much success and political influence for the moral integrity of his beloved monastic rule, emphasizing the poverty and humility of Christ. It was for this reason that, shortly before his passing, he drafted a stronger version of the Franciscan Rule, known as his *Testamentum*, which looked back to the movement's early days when smaller numbers of friars serving local and regional communities had no need for the temptations of a larger movement serving within the trans-local power dynamics of European Christendom's bishoprics, warring feudal states, and growing imperial designs.[30] This worldly success and ecclesiastical fame proved to be too much for some of Saint Francis' most devout followers, who became known as the Fraticelli or the Franciscan Spirituals. The Fraticelli developed a fondness for Joachim of Fiore's prophecies about the rise of a new order of "spiritual" monks (*viri spiritualis*) around 1260 or 1265 that would help usher in the Church of the Holy Spirit (*ecclesia Spiritualis*).

Although largely forgotten by most contemporary Christians, the Spiritual Franciscans were known by various appellations, such as the Fraticelli or Zealots (*Zelanti*), or as the Fioretti, meaning the "little flowers" of St. Francis. The precise Latin term for the sect, identified from archival records by Decima Douie's pioneering work on the movement's origins is "Fraterculi."[31] Papal records and Inquisition accounts refer to two main sects: the Spiritual party identified as the "*Fraticelli de paupere vita*," and the followers of Michael of Cesena known as both the "Michaelists" and as the "*Fraticelli de opinione*." These sectarian distinctions were probably first articulated by Inquisitors who needed to differentiate between the common use of the term Fraticelli designating, the numerous monastic communities under the jurisdiction of local bishops, but not affiliated with any particular monastic order. Among modern researchers, the movement and the various regional factions are generally referred to as either the Fraticelli or as the Spiritual Franciscans.

In the late 1200s, and especially during the early 1300s, the Fraticelli believed themselves the true followers of Saint Francis' Rule and monastic legacy of poverty, humility, chastity and service. They maintained that the Holy Spirit had appointed them, through their beloved saint and founder Francis, as "overseers, to care for the church of God" (Acts 20:28) by working for the restoration of peace and justice among the people of God. This conviction trumped the juridical authority of popes and bishops in the church hierarchy, while uplifting the charismatic authority of Saint Francis and the Fraticelli, in ways that corresponded too closely with Joachim of Fiore's vision of the Church of Holy Spirit (*ecclesia Spiritualis*) detailed in the *Psaltery of the Ten Strings*. This is another example of the "*subversive fire*" contained in the story of Pentecost as read, told and retold, commemorated, and liturgically experienced among the early Franciscans and their brothers and sisters with Joachimist leanings. The implication of such pneumatological and charismatic sensibilities for the revitalization of the Church at large in the thirteenth and fourteenth centuries placed the Spiritual Franciscans on the frontier of ecclesiastical reformism.

The alleged origins of the Spiritual Franciscans during the years of transition and administrative realignment among the Friars Minor following the death of Saint Francis are not very clear, especially since it was not until the period from the mid-1250s through the 1270s that the group begins to appear as a problematic faction within the Franciscan Order and in certain regions of medieval Christendom. While David Burr sketched out the best narrative picture available of the so-called Proto-Spirituals and the rest of the Fraticelli through the 1300s, the assumption has persisted among both scholars and the general public that the Franciscan Order was divided from its earliest days between two factions, the Conventuals versus the Spirituals.[32] The Conventuals maintained that the order needed to change with the times, but preferred strict obedience to their Minister General and to their other leaders. The Spirituals, on the other hand, might best be described as the mavericks within the order whose charismatic style and visionary gifts led them into various disputes, like their strict adherence to the vow of poverty and rejection of worldliness, no matter how much society changed since the death of St. Francis. Burr believes the factionalism dates from a later period when the first generation of St. Francis' companions were passing away and a new generation of Franciscan friars were facing a new set of religious, social, and political concerns in the late 1200s.[33] Although he does not question the Joachimist leanings of the Spirituals, Burr observes that Saint Francis' vision of leadership and human agency was thoroughly "spiritual" and sought "no power to coerce" from the outset of his project of ecclesiastical revitalization.[34] Burr supports this observation by citing Francis' reply to several brothers complaining about the unwelcome attitude certain bishops showed with regard to the Friars Minor preaching in their churches or ministering in their dioceses,

> You do not comprehend the will of God and do not permit me to convert the whole world in the way God wills. For I wish to convert the prelates first through humility and reverence, and when they see our holy life and reverence

for them, they will ask you to preach and convert the people, and this will serve you better than the privileges you want, which will lead you to pride. If you are free from all avarice and persuade the people to render their dues to the churches, they will ask you to hear the confessions of their people, though you ought not to be concerned with this, as, if they have been converted, they can well find confessors. For myself, I wish to have this privilege from the Lord, that I have no privilege from man.[35]

Burr's research wisely reminds us that, despite the founder's nagging sense the Order declined from 1217 to 1224 due to its growth in monastic membership and trans-local prestige, Saint Francis' commitment to the ideal of Christ-like poverty, as well as radical love and service among the oppressed, predisposed many among the Franciscan ranks of the next one hundred years to hear and respond favorably to the liberative and egalitarian elements already articulated in the charismatic visions of Joachim of Fiore.

Both St. Francis of Assisi and Joachim of Fiore understood the pneumatological and ecclesiastical potential for a reconstruction of Christian tradition inherent in the story of Pentecost and in the New Testament's view of the Holy Spirit's abiding presence in Nature, in the heart of the individual believer, and in the broader arenas of Christ's earthly church and salvation history. However, as a monk with a reformist agenda, and founder of his own monastic rule known as the Florensian Order, Abbot Joachim consistently equated the rejection of poverty and humility with the influence of the Anti-Christ whose evil nature delights in undermining the Theological Virtues and the Gifts of the Holy Spirit articulated in works like the *Psaltery of the Ten Strings.* Among the radical and moderate movements of the Holy Spirit that proliferated across Latin Christendom throughout the High Middle Ages, we find the tendency to equate the worldliness and desire for wealth and prestige of the medieval Church and Papacy with the growing influence of evil in the cosmos as humanity moved closer to its appointment with the Apocalypse. John of Parma, who served as Minister General of the Franciscan Order from 1247 to 1257, was a considerate supporter of the Spirituals who was tried for heresy after he resigned from his generalship because of his alleged sympathetic teachings about Joachim of Fiore. Although he was later acquitted of the charges, there is some indication that his commitment to the "strict" interpretation of the Rule of St. Francis was another motivation for the charges brought against him. This period also witnessed the trial and imprisonment of the Franciscan friar, Gerard of Borgo San Donnino, for Joachimist ideas expressed in his treatise on "The Eternal Gospel." The climate of opinion in ecclesiastical affairs during the mid-1200s and early 1300s was such that radical groups like the Dolcinists or the Brethren of the Free Spirit sounded similar to the ideals of reformist factions like the Joachimists, Fraticelli, and Spiritual Franciscans. Eventually, some among the diverse radical factions even accused the Papacy of being a wolf disguised as a shepherd and the very embodiment of the Anti-Christ. For the medieval Church, after working so hard over the centuries to provide a number of basic services ranging from cathedral schools to orphanages, and while working equally hard at curbing the incessant cycles of feudal violence that often devastated towns and farmland, there was much more at stake than just a vision of the approaching Age of the Holy Spirit.

The *usus pauper* controversy over the poverty of the Church first erupted as a seriously contentious debate among a group of Franciscan friars from the Marches of Ancona in 1274, and then gradually extended its influence throughout Provence, Italy, and portions of northern France during the 1290s and early 1300s. The trigger point actually occurred at the Council of Lyons (1274) when Pope Gregory X suggested that he wanted all of the mendicant orders to hold property in common like the monastic orders of earlier centuries. It does not appear that Pope Gregory's intentions were malicious or intended to cause dissent, and in time it was revealed that much of the information being reported about this papal decree was false. Still, a group of friars from Ancona persisted in criticizing the Franciscan Order, defying papal oversight of the order's activities, and defending the literal observance of their vow of poverty among the Spiritual Franciscans. Michael Robson accurately and eloquently summarizes the traditional Franciscan position on evangelical poverty as depicted in chapter seven of Bonaventure's *Legenda maior,* Thomas of Celano's *Vita secunda,* and as taught by *Il poverello,* as St. Francis was known to his followers and the northern Italian public who knew of his good works:

> Francis placed his imitation of the poor Christ above everything else and subverted the values of society in order to pursue this virtue. The memory of the poverty experienced by Christ and his mother often reduced Francis to tears; he called poverty the queen of the virtues because it was so evident in the life of the king of kings and of the queen, his mother. Poverty was the special way of salvation and the source of humility. It was conceived as the root of all perfection and it was the treasure hidden in the field of the Gospel. In order to purchase it the friars were required to sell everything, and anything that cannot be sold should be abandoned for the love of it. The poverty of Christ and his mother provided the blueprint for the friars' perfection. It occupied a special place among the friars, whose emblem it became.[36]

These lovely and noble convictions became radicalized among the Fraticelli and Spirituals along with a number of other concerns the so-called *Zelanti* held about the growing wealth and influence of the once humble Friars Minor. David Burr, who has thoroughly researched the story of the Franciscan Spirituals, and written more extensively about the Fraticelli than any other historian of medieval Christianity, suggests that the episode at Ancona in 1274 is difficult to uncover and fully explain given the meager evidence.[37]

The compilation of stories about Francis and his earliest companions, known as the *Fioretti* or *Little Flowers of St. Francis,* has often been attributed to the influence of the proto-Spirituals, who preserved the oral teachings of their blessed founder, and indicates a strong Franciscan charismatic presence in Ancona: "The province of the Marches of Ancona was once full of holy men shining like lights from heaven. Their holy, resplendent example filled the skies as stars illuminate the world on a dark night."[38] Jon Sweeney surmises that there were also holy women in the growing Franciscan movement of the Ancona region.[39] These references are reminiscent of the holy men and holy women that Peter Brown identified as "*arbiters of the holy*" through their reliance on the power of the Holy Spirit in an era when the Greco-Roman past was giving way to the emergent Christian era of Late Antiquity.[40] References to the populace hearing the words of St. Anthony of Padua preaching sermons in their ancestral local dialects, which echoed the miracle of the first Pentecost, suggest from our vantage point that Christianization was still an ongoing process in the Italian countryside during the 1200s. St. Anthony and other Friars Minor would have been in a position to serve as "*arbiters of the holy*" amidst the syncretism of pre-Christian and Christian traditions that characterized the religious practices and beliefs of the rural Italian villages and small towns in these regions. Guarded by the seclusion of their forest hermitages and their monastic cells in local churches, the Spirituals of Ancona felt safe from the noisy cities and royal courts in which many of their brothers had been doing the work of the order and been tempted to consider a relaxation of their once highly cherished and inviolable vow of strict poverty and simplicity of living. Whether it was the spiritual liberation of the Holy Spirit, or whether it was their charismatic rejection of the second generation of Franciscan leader's authority, or a combination of both these attitudes, we will probably never know the complete story of the social, monastic, and pneumatological situation on the ground in the Marches of Ancona.

We know with certainty, however, that the Franciscan unrest in the Italian area of the Marches of Ancona led to the rise of Angelo Clareno, Ubertino of Casale, and Peter John Olivi as three of the leading dissident voices in the growing Spiritual Franciscan movement from the 1270s to the severe persecution of the faction during the pontificate of John XXII.[41] Each of these three Fraticelli seems to have been influenced by Joachimist prophecies of the Age of the Holy Spirit as explained in the *Psaltery of the Ten Strings,* and became radical voices in the apostolic and ecclesiastical poverty debate, a conflict that led to book burnings and declarations of heresy for some friars, while other friars and beguines were burned at the stake for their charismatic and reformist convictions over both the *usus pauper* controversy and the rising tide of Joacihmist fervor.

Angelo of Clareno (1247-1337) is regarded, by both medieval accounts and modern appraisals of his career, as one of the first Spiritual Franciscan leaders who emerged from the controversy in the Marches of Ancona following the Council of Lyons in 1274. Angelo was an outspoken critic of the corruption and worldliness of the Church in his day and of steady dilution of strict adherence to St. Francis' Rule and vow of poverty by both the Papacy and misguided Franciscan leaders.[42] He was reported to be a worker of miracles through the power of the Holy Spirit, and that he healed the sick as he made his way around various villages and towns. He is credited with recording the first wave of persecutions against the Spiritual Franciscans in his major work: *Historia septem tribulationum Ordinis Minorum* (ca. 1332-1336).[43] Reading the prophecies of Joachim of Fiore influenced him profoundly, and he began gathering disciples around himself with whom he shared both his Franciscan radicalism on the *usus pauper* controversy and his personal conviction in the coming of an *ecclesia spiritualis* that would transform the Christian community and the world. Angelo believed in the coming of an "Angelic Pope," who would found the new order of monks, the *viri spiritualis*, foretold by the Calabrian Abbot, a belief shared by many Joachimist sympathizers in those days.

Following the religious unrest they fomented in Ancona and its surrounding areas, Angelo and his closest companions in the new activist faction were sentenced to life in prison in the mid-1280s. But, they were miraculously released in 1290 by the new Minister General of the Franciscans, Raymond Geoffroi, who was sympathetic to Angelo's ideas and to the Spirituals faction. This kind of high ranking support, reminiscent of John of Parma's support for the Fraticelli three decades earlier, indicates that despite their alleged radicalism, the themes and ideas of the Spirituals were not isolated to the region of Ancona, nor limited to Angelo's small group of followers. He and his followers, known as the Clareni or as the Poor Hermits, then spent a number of years traveling through Greece and Armenia serving the needs of the people and communities they met in these regions, but without much pastoral success. Even in the Christian East their outspoken views on radical poverty and their rejection of various forms of authority in favor of the liberty of the Spirit and of the Gospel message caused trouble for them.

During the pontificate of Boniface VIII while the Roman curia was still based in Rome, the Papal Court charged Angelo again with heresy. In 1311, Angelo journeyed to Avignon to face his accusers during the pontificate of Clement V, and he was on the verge of having some of the charges dropped through the intervention of sympathetic cardinals when the new Pope, John XXII, had him excommunicated and returned to prison in 1317. Sometime the following year Angelo escaped from prison, fled from Avignon into hiding, and lived most of the remaining two decades of his life as an itinerant preacher and fugitive from the Inquisition. Orders for his arrest were issued several times during these years, but Angelo always managed to elude the grasp of papal envoys and secular authorities. When he died, he left behind a solid reputation as a worker of miracles among his Fraticelli brethren despite John XXII insisting that Angelo Clareno was nothing more than a "demented heretic." One of Pope John's primary concerns was ending the strife and division caused in the Franciscan Order between the Conventuals and the Spirituals. Popular wisdom paraphrased his words and credited him with the epithet: "Great is poverty, but greater is obedience." John was a strong leader who wanted to curtail the power of the Holy Roman Emperor, Louis of Bavaria. He was also a controversial pontiff who issued a decree against alchemy in 1317, although many among the clergy dating back to Albertus Magnus, had been practicing a form of "sacred magic" known as "Christian magical theology" (*theologia magica Christiana*). We will examine the relation of this esoteric tradition to pneumatological thinking at length in Chapter Five. Pope John also declared the famous German mystic, Meister Eckhart, a heretic after reviewing his works in 1329. Angelo's life story, and what little we can glean about his small group of followers, provides an example of the empowering vision the Spirituals noted in the Joachimist corpus, their deep conviction in the Franciscan mission of radical poverty and ecclesiastical revitalization, and in the abiding power of the Holy Spirit that they believed would lead all things to spiritual fullness and freedom. John XXII died in 1334 after nearly two decades of unsuccessfully trying to suppress the Spirituals movement. Church historians have interpreted Angelo's passing in 1337 as the waning moment of the Spiritual Franciscans in Italy as their substantial numbers of the 1200s and early 1300s gradually diminishes in theological discourses and historical records from the 1340s and beyond to the end of the fourteenth century.

Looking back to the origins of the Spirituals that coincided with the beginnings of the *usus pauper* controversy in the 1270s and 1280, there were other figures like Peter John Olivi and Ubertino of Casale who emerged as outspoken Franciscan activists with deep sympathies for the prophecies of Abbot Joachim of Fiore. When the Franciscan Spiritual theologian Peter John Olivi (ca. 1248-1298)[44] was asked by Pope Nicholas III in 1279 to write a short treatise commenting on the Franciscan ideal and rule of poverty, it led to his views being condemned as heresy at the Franciscan General Chapter of Strasburg in 1282.[45] Although most of Olivi's evangelical activities took place in Provence, Church officials and the Papacy perceived the reformist agenda suggested in his writings as thoroughly related to the Franciscan Spirituals faction from the Marches of Ancona. As a result, many of his works were condemned at the University of Paris, and some were burned, for his tough Franciscan stance on the "strict" poverty of the Church. Olivi held tenaciously to the *usus pauper* ideal as an essential clerical virtue versus the excessive power of the Papacy as a dangerous temptation and betrayal of ecclesiastical mission and purpose.

Despite stern papal condemnation of his Joachimist tendencies, in the example of Olivi's theological career, it is easy to see how his convictions about the Church, monastic rules, and clerical service to society found a theological and prophetic corollary in the Abbot of Fiore's liberative and egalitarian theology of the Spirit. These views are expressed in his *Commentary on the Apocalypse*.[46] The Joachimist paradigm offered Olivi a platform from which to reflect on the corruption and misguided leadership of the Church of his time and the role of strict adherence to clerical poverty as a means of combating such corruption. General chapter conclaves after his death repeatedly condemned his views and forbade the reading of his works, yet the faithful venerated his grave for decades after his death, while fellow friars regarded his words as inspired by the Holy Spirit, until Pope John XXII unwittingly gave permission for the destruction of his tomb. From the late 1400s through the 1700s, Olivi's life and works were reassessed by new generations of friars and popes who read his works in a different climate than that of the turbulent 1300s and who praised his scholarly acumen on a variety of subjects.[47] Although he died long before his fellow activist in those first struggles of the Marches of Ancona, Angelo Clareno, and before his outstanding pupil Ubertino da Casale, Olivi's Joachimist views and position on the *usus pauper* influenced their interpretations of both the relevance of Joachimism to the Spiritual Franciscan cause and the literal interpretation of the apostolic poverty dispute.

The most revered and theologically brilliant of the Spiritual Franciscans was the charismatic monk regarded by many as their finest leader, Ubertino of Casale (1259-ca.1330), who joined the Friars Minor in his native Genoa about 1273, and then studied and traveled with Peter Olivi from 1287 until his beloved master's death at age fifty in 1298.[48] Dante mentions Ubertino in Book Twelve of the *Paradiso* praising his knowledge of the Scriptures and his moral integrity. Ubertino was also featured as a character in Umberto Eco's novel, *The Name of the Rose* (1983), wherein he appears as an outspoken critic of the Church's political and economic power and as a controversial advocate for the observance of apostolic poverty among the Friars Minor. Ubertino of Casale's personal and ecclesiastical objectives centered on the revitalization of the Church and the Friars Minor against what he perceived as the mounting wealth and political temptation of Christ's Church by the forces of Anti-Christ, a theological reconstruction of the ecclesiastical and pneumatological traditions he and his fellow Fraticelli had inherited from the "past," while also dreaming dreams and seeing visions of a Joachimist influenced "future" Age of the Holy Spirit.

Despite his association with powerful members of the Papal Court like Cardinal Napoleone Orsini and Cardinal Giacomo Colonna, Ubertino was one of the staunchest critics of the popes who governed the Church during his lifetime, and a major critic of the Franciscan Order which he chastised for abandoning the original purity and poverty of the Rule of St. Francis. The Orsini and Colonna clans were members of the influential and contentious Roman nobility that played a significant role in disputes between the Papacy, the French Monarchy, and the Holy Roman Empire. The Colonna barons and their kinsmen were involved in events surrounding the arrest and death of Pope Boniface VIII in 1303, and both families emerged as combatants against the reformist government of the Roman Tribune and Pentecostal visionary, Cola di Rienzo. We will look at how these powerful families affected Roman and Papal politics during the mid-1300s in this chapter's discussion of Cola di Rienzo.

Against the Conventuals' more relaxed and pragmatic position on the practical observance of the order's rule, Ubertino argued strictly for the literal and narrow (*ad litteram*) observance of the Franciscan Rule. Around 1285, Ubertino traveled to the Hermitage of Greccio to meet with the famous Spiritual Franciscan and former Minister General of the Friars Minor, John of Parma. He reported learning much about the Fraticelli from this visit and receiving insightful wisdom from John about the future of the world. This was probably the first time that Ubertino learned about Joachimism since he reports that the elderly John "was still an ardent Joachimite" who "believed earnestly in the coming of a new age, when the present Church, which was not Jerusalem the bride of Christ but Babylon the harlot, would be destroyed."[49] Ubertino also had occasion to meet and be instructed by the great mystic and devotee of the Third Order Rule of St. Francis, Angela of Foligno. By the turn of the century, Ubertino had received an impressive education, had been mentored by some of the greatest names in Franciscan piety and mysticism, and had developed a deep disdain for the corruption and worldliness of the Church in those days, which seemed to many among the clergy and laity as the worst of times in church history. He taught for a few years at Paris and later dedicated his energies to preaching in various locations around Umbria, Tuscany, and Perugia before controversies over his outspoken views complicated his freedom of movement around northern Italy and he was exiled to the Convent of La Verna for prayerful rest and discernment. It was at La Verna that he wrote his most important and controversial treatise.

Ubertino of Casale's apocalyptic theories as set forth in his *Arbor vitae crucifixae Jesu Christi* (ca. 1305)[50] are a synthesis of Joachim's theories and those of his master Peter John Olivi, with whom Ubertino had studied for about a decade. This prose epic with its often exhausting allegorical, theological, polemical, and utopian elements was allegedly written by Ubertino in three months and seven days, which is either a misrepresentation of the truth, or an indication of the degree of pneumatological inspiration he somehow attained just prior to undertaking the composition of this monumental treatise. In the opening pages of the *Arbor Vitae,* one realizes the book is an extended meditation on the role of Christ and the Blessed Virgin Mary in salvation history as exemplars of loving God with all of one's heart and observing the rule of poverty in service to God and society. What makes this work so unusual in the catalog of medieval Christian allegories is that it crosses the boundaries of more than one genre because Ubertino's extended meditation on Jesus, the Virgin Mary, and the cross as the "tree of redemption," is juxtaposed with a commentary on the Apocalypse of St. John from a Joachimist and Spiritual Franciscan perspective. The poverty of Christ's birth, the simplicity of the Virgin Mary's life, and the renunciation of personal wealth by the Apostles, are all mentioned as proof of the apostolic and sacred mandate for the Church to observe the vow of poverty as strictly as possible, or at least as emphatically as taught by St. Francis of Assisi. The scene of the Crucifixion is read through the theme of poverty and self-sacrifice in juxtaposition with the power and wealth of Imperial Rome, which we must interpret as an allegorical cloaking device aimed at the Papacy with whom Ubertino had some very serious disagreements before, during, and long after he composed the *Arbor vitae.*

The book's central metaphorical image is a "Tree of Life," which seems intentionally analogous to the "Jesse Trees" of medieval iconography, and to the "historical trees" featured in Abbot Joachim's works and drawings. Ubertino's "Tree of Life" depicts the history of humanity from Creation to the Incarnation and Crucifixion of Jesus Christ with the fruits of this story being reflected in the lives and careers of the elect who served God, Church, and humanity with love, humility, and integrity.[51] Although Ubertino apparently borrowed this imagery from St. Bonaventura's *Lignum Vitae,* St. Francis is portrayed as the prototype of a new type of spiritual monk and teacher of righteousness alongside bizarre references to the prophesied "Angelic Pope" (*Papa Angelicus*) who will govern the Church in the approaching Age of the Holy Spirit. One wonders if Ubertino is implying that St. Francis is going to be reborn in person, or if the saint is going to return by other supernatural means. The seven ages of salvation history, typical of medieval apocalyptic literature, and the three *status* or dispensations of the Joachimist paradigm, are described in ways reminiscent of John of Parma's and Olivi's Joachimist interpretations of the future.

Ubertino of Casale's overall conception of the *Arbor vitae* follows the trajectory of most medieval allegories dealing with eschatological expectation. The book also contains many of the characteristic features identified by postmodern allegorical theorists like Edwin Honig, Angus Fletcher, and Maureen Quilligan.[52] Religious allegories, whether produced in the ancient, medieval, or modern context, deal with antecedent books or sacred texts, or what Quilligan refers to as the "pre-text" on which the allegorist has based his or her narrative.[53] Fletcher believed that allegory was "a human reconstitution of divinely inspired messages, a revealed transcendental language which tried to preserve the remoteness of a properly veiled godhead."[54] Ubertino's "divinely inspired messages" are the empowering legacy of Pentecost, the observance of poverty and humility, and the gifts of the Holy Spirit as read through the written works and living examples of those from whom he learned about spiritual liberation and power: Joachim of Fiore, John of Parma, Peter Olivi, Angela of Foligno, and his beloved founder of the Friars Minor, St. Francis. Texts like the *Arbor vitae* are "symbolic power struggles" whose dynamic text-context relationship rests on the author's "involvement with authoritarian conflict" and resistance to the "censorship of dissident thought."[55] Rejection of various forms of authority, and radical affirmation of the spiritual liberty of the Gospel message and the Holy Spirit, were central themes of both the Joachimist Age of the Holy Spirit and the missiological convictions of the Spiritual Franciscans. As Honig maintained, "the re-creation of authority necessitates a critical view of reality, a reexamination of the objective norms of human experience in the light of human ideality," which "includes the making of a new version of reality which the reality of the fiction proves."[56] Such was the pneumatological dissatisfaction of the Spiritual Franciscans with the social, political, and ecclesiastical status quo in the late 1200s and early 1300s that Ubertino's allegorical re-creation of authority served as both a commentary on the Book of Revelation and as a vision of hope for the future of Christendom.

On the other hand, reading through Ubertino's vehement hatred of the Papacy and the leaders of the Friars Minor sounds rather unbecoming of Franciscan humility and charity. He repeatedly chastises the Church and its ecclesiastical leadership for spending huge sums of money on lavish buildings and cathedrals that rob the poor and the sick of resources that could be applied directly to the alleviation of human suffering and serving the mission of Christ's Church. He compares several popes and cardinals to the beasts from the Book of Revelation and speaks of their chastisements in violent terms that sound harsh and incongruous with Christian discourse, and it was here that his angry discourse went over the top of the acceptable prophetic language and protest boundaries of his day. Throughout the lengthy Prologue, he repeatedly asserts that the Church has belittled the meaning of the Crucified Lord and undermined the mission that began on the first Pentecost as a "*super destructione Christi vite et adulterate ecclesie.*"[57] Ubertino's comments may sound harsh and disrespectful by modern standards, but his pneumatological sensibilities and determination to revitalize the Church and the Franciscan Order came together in the allegorical polemics of his *Arbor vitae* and burst forth as a "*subversive fire*" in the name of Christ and the Holy Spirit, and especially for the mission of his beloved St. Francis, who, in his own words, when "purified by the seraphic fire and consumed by the divine heat, inflamed the whole world."[58]

When four members of the Spiritual Franciscans were accused, tried, and convicted of heresy at Marseilles and then burned to death on May 7, 1318 during the heart of the seven-times-seven-days of the Pentecostal cycle, a period of the liturgical calendar held in such high esteem among partisans of both the Conventuals and Spirituals factions of the Franciscans, it became clear that Pope John XXII, and his secular allies in the French monarchy, were not going to tolerate defiance of Papal orders. For Ubertino, it signaled a turning point in Pope John's determination to crush the Spirituals and Fraticelli throughout Italy, Provence, and northern France. In September 1325, Ubertino was charged with heresy and most likely fled to Germany where the Holy Roman Emperor, Louis of Bavaria, was reputed to have been a supporter of the Spirituals and a rival of Pope John XXII. After 1329, Ubertino of Casale drops out of the historical record. Knowledge of his whereabouts after this date, or evidence of the final moments of his life, is completely uncertain. In the 1400s, unsubstantiated rumors surfaced among the Fraticelli that agents of Pope John XXII had killed Ubertino around 1330, but although the Church did its best to hunt down the radicals and ensure obedience within the ranks of the Friars Minor, such unsubstantiated claims must be read and interpreted with extreme caution.

The influence of the Spiritual Franciscans among the nobility was felt foremost among the rulers of Naples who, as the Counts Calabria, also controlled one of the geographic regions most associated with Joachimist influences. The Neapolitan dynasty arrived in Naples and Sicily, at the invitation of the Papacy for protection against the Holy Roman Empire around 1262, under the command of King Charles I of Anjou (1226-1285). In the early 1300s, these Neapolitan Angevin nobles allowed their kingdom to become a safe-haven for the Fraticelli. The General Chapter of Naples was held on May 31, 1316 under the support and patronage of the King and Queen of Naples, Robert of Anjou and his wife, Sancia of Majorca. Although archival records suggest the meeting was beset by low attendance, the chapter elected Michael of Cesena as the next Minister General of the Order. Michael became the leader of the Fraticelli faction known as the "Michaelists," and the following year saw the installation of Pope John XXII, whose personal convictions on clerical discipline and obedience motivated his persecution of the Spirituals. Through the queen's fondness for the works and piety of the Friars Minor, and through the recent canonization of Robert's brother, the Franciscan Saint Louis of Toulouse, King Robert and Queen Sancia of Naples were suspected of being discreet sympathizers with the spiritual ideals of the Fraticelli faction. In fact, there is a substantial body of evidence linking Robert the Wise to the Spirituals, first through contact with Peter John Olivi, while he and his brothers were being held captive by the King of Aragon in Catalonia, and later as a result of his personal piety and interest in radical and liberative religious issues.[59] The dynasty also founded a little acknowledged and mysterious chivalric fraternity called the Order of the Holy Spirit (*Ordo Sancti Spiritus*). This fraternity, which was also known as the "Order of the Knot," appears again later in the historical record in conjunction with Cola di Rienzo's vision of a revived Roman Republic out of his Pentecost inspired revolt in May 1347. Despite the intriguing nature of these connections, a full assessment of the mysterious trajectories and continuities linking the Neapolitan House of Anjou to the Spiritual Franciscans is beyond the scope of this study.

The pneumatological and reformist legacies of Joachim of Fiore and the Spiritual Franciscans ebbed and flowed through the remainder of the 1300s, and resurfaced periodically in succeeding centuries. The effects of the Black Death from 1347 to 1351, and the subsequent pandemics and famines of the late fourteenth century altered the nature of religious, social, and political organization in Europe, while apocalyptic visionaries hoped and prayed for the advent of their long awaited transformation of Church and State. Apocalypticism and millennialism received much scholarly attention during the twentieth century, but this was not the only motivation that fueled the eschatological and ecclesiastical dreams of reform-minded Christians from the High Middle Ages to the end of the 1300s. Christian liberation and pneumatological sensibility moved inversely proportional to Papal authority and the Church's worldliness. When popes like John XXII stood emphatically for ecclesiastical order and monastic obedience, visionaries like Angelo Clareno, Peter John Olivi, and Ubertino of Casale stood emphatically for spiritual liberation and personal piety. Ironically, both camps stood for reform as well as liberty. I believe, however, that the real source of inspiration behind these continuities and contradictions is found in the imaginative possibilities of the story of Pentecost, and in the empowering Gifts of the Holy Spirit, whose fiery nature offered a means of subverting misguided and oppressive structures of authority, while inspiring divergent reconstructions of ecclesiastical tradition from the cherished resources and exemplars of the Christian past.

PENTECOST AND GUGLIELMA OF MILAN, CA. 1260-1300

A fascinating example of what appears to be yet another late thirteenth century Joachimist inspired pneumatological movement centered on a female lay minister known as Guglielma of Milan.[60] Her followers believed she was the incarnation of the Holy Spirit who would usher in the long awaited *renovatio* of the *ecclesia spiritualis*. For a long time modern scholars doubted whether she had been an actual historical person, or a fictional lay nun whose imaginary life in Lombardy became a convergent site for Joachimist expectations of the third *status* of the Holy Spirit. Guglielma's sudden appearance in Milan around 1260 coincided with the general mood of Joachimist fervor surrounding the decade of the 1260s as the period to watch for the rise of the charismatic Church of the Holy Spirit. During the tumultuous decades of the late 1200s, Guglielma's story as a prophetess also became a convergent site for the millenarian hope that European Christendom might soon triumph over the mounting threats coming from the Islamic and Byzantine powers of the Eastern Mediterranean. Her devotees, not surprisingly, claimed that she would convert the Jews, Muslims, and all of the remaining pagans after rising from the dead and ascending to heaven as the Holy Spirit. Princess Guglielma, or Guglielma of Bohemia as she was also known after her arrival in Milan, was the alleged daughter of the King of Bohemia. It is reported by her Milanese disciples that she arrived there in 1260, as a widow with her first-born son, whom we must assume was already an adult from contemporary accounts stating that Guglielma herself was middle aged at the time of her arrival. In other accounts she is referred to as Guglielma of Brunate, after the mountain village near Lake Como where she is venerated to this day as a beloved local saint. Although the Roman Catholic Church has never granted her official hagiographic approval, she is still referred to as Saint Guglielma. Commenting on the spread of innovative research about medieval women's piety in the past thirty years, Barbara Newman observes that such notions of female agency and the Holy Spirit were "activated not only by the ferment of Joachite thought, with its typological vision of a coming 'Age of the Holy Spirit,' but also by a new ideal of gender complementarity rooted in the changing relationships of holy women and their male devotees" during the 1200s.[61] Scholasticism's overtly patriarchal tone and theological "consensus that excluded female language and imagery for the Holy Spirit had the probably unintended consequence of marginalizing the Third Person entirely."[62] In this context, the historical example of Guglielma and her followers sheds light on medieval conceptions of the Holy Spirit, and on the story of Pentecost as both a repository of Christian wisdom and a liberative trope in Christian discourse.

It seems that Guglielma's royal pedigree, which surely enhanced her stature as a saintly and trustworthy religious woman, was indeed true. Newman reports recent studies by Jaroslav Polc confirming Guglielma's Bohemian identity as Princess Blažena Vilemína, who was the daughter of King Ottokar I of Bohemia and Queen Constance of Hungary.[63] Her family tree of Bohemian, Hungarian, and Polish royalty was blessed with an abundance of well-known religious women such as her younger sister Saint Agnes of Bohemia, who was canonized in 1989 by Pope John Paul II. And, through her mother's lineage, Guglielma was a cousin of Saint Elizabeth of Hungary (ca. 1207-1231), one of the most famous and revered female saints of the High Middle Ages, who was also known as St. Elizabeth of Thuringia. Pope Gregory IX canonized her at Perugia on Pentecost Sunday, May 28, 1235. Elizabeth was also an ardent admirer of the teachings of St. Francis of Assisi, and a steadfast supporter of the Friars Minor in Germany during the 1220s. Throughout her relatively short life, she desired to follow St. Francis' rule of poverty and give herself in service to the poor. Guglielma's awareness of these cultic linkages might account for her devotion to poverty, works of charity, and simplicity of living as a *pinzochera*, a lay religious woman serving church and society from her own home. On the other hand, these saintly and dynastic connections offer us another window for comprehending the fascination with which her story was accepted and disseminated among the populace during the two decades of her lay ministry in Milan and Lombardy before her death around 1281.

Guglielma's alleged kinship ties with St. Elizabeth of Hungary opens some intriguing possibilities with the Angevin dynastic branch that became the rulers of Naples and Sicily in the 1260s and that developed strong ties with the Franciscan Order and the Spiritual Franciscans until the mid-1300s. This Angevin dynasty, led by Charles I of Anjou (1226-1285), whose powerful and famous brother, Saint Louis IX, was King of France, were invited by Pope Clement VI on May 23, 1265 to become the rulers of Naples and Sicily in the sincere hope that this new line of Norman power in Italy and the Mediterranean might safeguard the Papacy from the House of Hohenstaufen's interference in the Italian peninsula. In 1270, when the future Angevin King of Naples, Charles II of Anjou, married Maria Árpád of Hungary (1257-1323), the House of Anjou became linked with the legacy of St. Elizabeth of Hungary and the Franciscan Order because the barely twelve-year-old Maria was a great-niece of St. Elizabeth of Hungary. In addition to their struggles against the Holy Roman Empire and Spain's House of Aragon, the Angevin rulers of Naples were major supporters of the Franciscan Spirituals from about 1280 to the death of King Robert "The Wise" in 1343. Some of Charles' successors also fancied themselves heirs to the title "Dukes of Calabria," the region where Joachim of Fiore had been born and raised. As attested by iconographic evidence found on a sidewall of the choir in the Neapolitan Church of Santa Maria Donna Regina, the Angevin rulers of Naples held a special reverence in their lives for both their famous ancestor, St. Elizabeth of Hungary, and for the Feast of Pentecost. On the other hand, while historically fascinating and spiritually alluring to modern readers, these *beata stirps* as tales of such saintly origins are called, offered valuable political and religious advantages to lesser dynastic lines like these Neapolitan Angevins seeking elevation to the rank of their more prominent and powerful Capetian cousins of the French Monarchy, or similar to the status of the Angevin-Plantagenet line that ruled England for several generations in the 1100s. Medieval dynasties often enlisted the cult of royal saints to gain legitimacy in both the secular and ecclesiastical realms.[64] When Robert of Anjou (1277-1343) married Sancia of Majorca (1286-1345) as his second wife in July 1304, the Capetian-Angevin line of Naples was overjoyed by the spiritual legitimacy this union conferred on the family because Robert and Sancia were both descended from St. Elizabeth of Hungary.[65] Thus, the more royal blood one had mingled with saintly blood in his or her family tree, the greater the secular and ecclesiastical legitimacy one could hope to claim and use with diplomatic and symbolic savvy.

We lack hard evidence connecting Guglielma to the Spiritual Franciscans and some of the evidence I suggested above is merely circumstantial. Nonetheless, these tantalizing connections with the Franciscan Order on the maternal side of Guglielma's family line, and that particular Hungarian dynastic line's kinship ties with the Angevin dynasty of Naples, whose protective support for the Franciscan Spirituals was well known by 1310,[66] should be taken into account as part of the bigger picture informing our continually developing views of Guglielma's life and context before moving to Milan.

According to the enigmatic stories and beatific legends circulated about her, Guglielma was born on Pentecost Sunday as a Bohemian princess. After arriving in Milan, she desired to devote herself to contemplation and service to the poor, lived a very simple life, and apparently bore the stigmata on her body, invisibly, on more than one occasion. She later became associated as a laywoman with the Cistercian Abbey of Chiaravalle, to which she left her possessions and wealth along with instructions for her burial at the abbey. Stories of her simple but courageous acts of charity, miraculous healings, deep piety, and gift of prophecy abound to this day in Lombardy. As admiration and respect for her grew, Guglielma eventually attracted both men and women disciples from Milan and the surrounding territories that venerated her with respect for her sanctity, and for their growing conviction in her embodiment as the pneumatological presence and power of the Third Person of the Trinity on earth. It seems that her message and example of pious living struck a chord of sympathy among the populace for her followers represented a cross section of society's different classes and ranks. Among her devotees were members of the feuding factions of Milan's most powerful families, like the Torriani and Visconti clans, a feature that increased her mystique as a reconciler and teacher of peace in the minds and hearts of the people. We have no reason to think that Guglielma approved of the fantastic claims being made about her identity and spiritual powers. Historical records suggest that she denied most of these claims. According to Felice Tocco's account of the inquisitorial proceedings that came upon her followers in 1300, Guglielma emphatically stated on more than one occasion: "I am not God."[67] After her death, which scholars have dated between 1279 and 1281, Guglielma's followers collected her relics, circulated stories of her spiritual gifts and healings, and began building a case for her canonization. This process culminated in the exhumation and transfer of her remains from a temporary resting place in Milan to the abbatial crypt at Chiaravalle, where she and her followers had originally requested that her bones be buried upon her death.

In the years from about 1281 or 1282 to their infamous eschatological Easter Mass of 1300, the cult of the Guglielmites steadily grew under the joint leadership of an influential Milanese businessman, Andreas Saramita, and Guglielma's closest disciple, the Humiliata nun Mayfreda da Pirovano. Rumors and reactions to Mayfreda's unauthorized Eucharistic celebration on Easter in 1300 finally brought the radical sect of the Guglielmites to the attention of Dominican inquisitors in Milan. The key source of their serious troubles with the Christian orthodoxy of their time was that Saramita and Mayfreda believed their beloved Saint Guglielma would soon resurrect from her tomb and ascend to heaven as a divine being, and the world would finally know her true identity as the incarnation of the Holy Spirit. This would result in an outpouring of divine gifts and favors on the church through the mission of the Guglielmites, and precipitate Mayfreda's ascension in Rome as the first ever female Pope, (*la Papesse*), who would elevate the role of women in church leadership by ordaining female cardinals and bishops in the name of the Holy Spirit as part of the new dispensation brought on by Saint Guglielma's ascension. Saramita suggested and commissioned new literary and poetic texts. Just as the New Testament had vindicated and superseded the Old Testament, now a *third gospel*, accompanied by new hymns and an entirely new canon, would set forth a new covenant with God and

Christ as a further revelation of God's egalitarian and charismatic plans for humanity in the Age of the Holy Spirit.

Despite the Joachimist radicalism of Andrea Saramita's position, it is perhaps historiographically prudent to distinguish between Guglielma's life and lay ministry, which on the surface seem quite sound and balanced, and what became of her life's story and purpose in the hands of the Guglielmites led by Saramita. Although Guglielma preferred a life of simplicity and renunciation, it is clear that Saramita reached out to a rather wealthy and influential cross section of Milan's citizenry, an issue that must have disturbed Mayfreda's admiration and commitment to Christ-like poverty. Muraro and Newman both suggest that even the pious Humiliata, Mayfreda, might have been an unwitting pawn of Saramita's Joachimist exuberance,[68] in which case Mayfreda's deep adoration and respect for her beloved female teacher and exemplar could have blinded her to Saramita's social and apocalyptic ambitions. Although our scanty evidence on these matters relies on the proceedings of a Dominican inquisitorial tribunal at Milan, which took place from late July to December 1300, and which most certainly used torture to extract statements and confessions from some of the three dozen Guglielmites interrogated for heresy, it seems that Mayfreda's connections to the powerful Visconti family also worked against her in these proceedings. We are not sure how many of the Guglielmites were burned at the stake before the end of that year. Having succeeded in connecting her name with radicalism and heresy, the inquisitors exhumed Guglielma's body, destroyed her tomb and her relics, wiped out images of her story that decorated several churches in the region, and burned the books that her followers compiled about her life. Guglielma's bones were ritually burned, for she was now a heretic, and her ashes scattered to avoid any lingering sectarianism or new cultic activity on her behalf in Lombardy. Saramita and Sister Mayfreda must have been sentenced to the stake for their leadership roles in this sectarian controversy, which from our vantage point seems to have been as much about resistance to female leadership inspired by the Holy Spirit as it was about the Joachimist prophesy of a new world order.

In conclusion, Barbara Newman, who has written more about Guglielma of Milan than any other contemporary medievalist writing in the English language, observes that: "In the later middle ages a pervasive apocalyptic mood, combined with the disrepute of the papacy and the prestige some men accorded to women mystics, created a particularly favorable breeding ground for this type of religiosity."[69] While Newman interprets the story of Guglielma of Milan and the Guglielmites "as a particular manifestation of a perennial underground current within the Church," whose "esoteric motif of a feminine Holy Spirit facilitates a critique of the establishment Church and the elaboration of millennial hopes pinned on charismatic women,"[70] I interpret these episodes as manifestations of that tendency toward *theological reconstruction* that Christian tradition perpetually engages as needs continually arise to remake the present, and the future, from the resources of the Christian past. Newman is fully aware of these tendencies and trajectories in Christian history, and comes quite close to my theme of *"subversive fire"* when she states, "To reclaim the personality of the Spirit meant, in at least some cases, to reclaim the fluidity of leadership."[71] Transformative leadership in church and society is what these visions about a "Church of the Holy Spirit" were all about, especially since it was in the domain of ecclesiastical leadership that the pneumatological visionaries and reformers surveyed throughout this book, whether male or female, lay minister or fully ordained clergy, and whether priest or nun, worked out the content and implications of profound revelatory insights involving such a divergent range of conceptions and experiences of Pentecost and the gifts of the Holy Spirit. Given the pneumatological and Pentecostal sensibilities echoed in the Joachimist and Guglielmite ideas that converged with the life story of this obscure thirteenth century religious woman, and alleged cousin of St. Elizabeth of Hungary, the imaginative possibilities of the Pentecost story, and the empowering role of the Holy Spirit in the history of the Church, must be taken into consideration alongside Newman's important contributions to our understanding of female agency and the goddess traditions in the High Middle Ages. Transformative leadership, pneumatological liberation, and power over the Classical and Christian "past" were also significant aspects of the revolutionary agenda of Cola di Rienzo, to whose story we turn next.

PENTECOST AND COLA DI RIENZO, CA. 1347-1354

One of the most stunning medieval examples of the commingling of pneumatological and Joachimist sentiments is Cola di Rienzo's extraordinary Pentecost Sunday revolution on May 20, 1347. Seven centuries after his rising from humble origins to the power and prestige of restoring the Roman Republic against the recalcitrant barons and nobles of his day, this man's story endures as a testament to both the vitality of the Pentecostal legacies surveyed throughout this book and the people's sincere hopes for a less violent and more prosperous future in late medieval Italy. The city had been dealing for decades with a series of setbacks involving corrupt local Barons, the meddling of the Holy Roman Empire in its affairs, and the recent departure of the Papacy to Avignon. Although the main objectives of Cola's insurrection and his controversial leadership style were colossal failures, the revolution that erupted on that now forgotten Pentecost morning was unlike any political upheaval the city had witnessed since the days of ancient Rome. Out of the fractured "eternal city," where St. Peter and St. Paul rested alongside the ruins of the Roman Senate and the eroded statues of long dead Roman Emperors and Tribunes, Cola planned to build the "Good Estate" (*Buono Stato*) of the medieval eschatological imagination by combining the glories of ancient Rome with the liberative potential of Pentecost and the abounding power of the Holy Spirit.

On Saturday May 19, the day before Pentecost, Cola sat through an estimated thirty masses dedicated to the Holy Spirit and sent trumpeters and heralds all over Rome announcing that there would be an assembly of its citizens late Sunday morning at the Church of Sant'Angelo in the Pescheria district. Cola made sure that the populace knew of his nightlong vigil and of his solemn prayers for peace, liberty, and prosperity on behalf of Rome and its citizenry. After emerging from the church in full armor, and accompanied by a contingent of armed men, he made his way to the Palazzo del Campidoglio and claimed a new age of prosperity, justice, and the restoration of the Roman Republic under the protective aegis of the Holy Spirit. Cola immediately took the title: "Liberator of the Republic," which was only the first of many fulsome titles he would either grant himself or demand from the municipal council governing Rome in the absence of the local barons and the papal administration. Unfortunately, while Cola proved quite skillful at staging and carrying out his revolt, his inconsistent methods, and poor diplomatic savvy, and violent tactics led to the downfall of his regime and his excommunication by Pope Clement VI by the end of December 1347. Cola's idealistic dream of a restored capital and a unified Italy relied upon the glorious memory of Republican Rome, and on the egalitarian promise of Joachim of Fiore's "Age of the Holy Spirit," as the civic and spiritual cement with which he planned on binding the citadel's disparate factions into a new and improved *Respublica Romana Christiana*.

Countless scholars and popular biographers of this heroic Italianate life have observed over the centuries that Cola di Rienzo was a master of theatrical oratory and employed the visual arts for propaganda, a feature of his persona and career that made him a favorite subject of study among tyrants, dictators, and Fascists during the past two centuries. He created flags to personify and popularize issues he wanted to bring to the people's attention. He commissioned paintings that today would be considered either "public service announcements" or brilliantly astute public propaganda that almost always succeeded in communicating his message and intentions to Rome's populace and civic officials. Even at the end of his life when all was lost and an angry mob stood ready to tear him and his broken rebellion to pieces, his enemies knew that if they allowed him to speak or address the crowd he would have probably changed their minds and persuaded the multitude to let him go. The historical record clearly demonstrates Cola's shrewd ability to command both secular and religious symbol systems, skills which allowed him to gain power over the past and project his vision of the future in ways that captivated members from all of the major social classes and political factions of mid-fourteenth century Rome.

Ironically, Cola's skills in the domains of theatricality and propaganda also account for the resurgence of Romantic interest in his life and career among nineteenth and early twentieth century Italian and German devotees of heroic individualism, like Richard Wagner, who dedicated an entire opera, *Rienzi*, to the short-lived political career of the enigmatic Italian. The Italian dictator, Benito Mussolini, knew Cola's story well and emulated some of its heroic aspects and longing for the glories of ancient Rome. For the Fascists, however, it was not the egalitarianism of Republican Rome, but the absolute power and political mastery of Imperial Rome they found so alluring and utilitarian. Adolf Hitler also fancied himself an admirer of Cola di Reinzo's heroic leadership, which reminds us of the misguided interest that twentieth century German and Italian Fascism took in some of Cola's skills, like his mastery of symbols, his invention and construction of flags for a multitude of purposes, his intoxicating public speaking skills, and his uncanny ability to motivate the people into joining revolutionary causes against seemingly impossible odds. Cola's excesses and horrific downfall, however, reveal as much about the people and culture of his times in the middle of the fourteenth century as it does about his diplomatic and moral shortcomings.

However, there may be other reasons why modern or postmodern scholars have only recently begun paying serious attention to Cola's religious ideals and familiarity with Joachimist visions of a future *renovatio* of Church and State. Although Renaissance Humanism was in full swing before Cola's dramatic emergence from the Church of Sant'Angelo on Pentecost in 1347, early twentieth century historical scholarship, with its training in logical positivism and suspicion of "enthusiast" revolutionary factions, tended to view Cola's deeply religious motivations with suspicion, and, in the end, did not really know how to handle the Pentecostal and pneumatological elements contained in his life story. Hence, by discounting the value of his ideas about the Holy Spirit and his Joachimist tendencies, Cola was not taken seriously enough by the majority of writers and scholars examining the history of European revolutionary movements, or surveying the Trecento phase of the Italian Renaissance, an interpretive obstacle that remained in place even while many admitted their fascination with reading about Cola's fantastic life and leadership skills.[72] In the following pages we will review his life story and examine his pneumatological sensibilities as a dramatic example of the grand possibilities, and unrestrained behavior, to which human nature is prone when the *"subversive fire"* of Pentecost as liberative trope and as agent of Christian revitalization gets mingled with the misguided desire for absolute power over others, fiscal excess, personal greed and hubris, and the instability of fourteenth century local and international power conflicts.

Many of the details that would provide a more complete picture of Cola's birth and childhood are not available to us, a situation for which Cola, in his desire to cover up his lowly family origins, probably bears some responsibility. His real name was Nicola Gabrini, which was later shortened to "Cola." Other accounts list him as Nicola di Lorenzo, meaning "Nicola, Lorenzo's son," which was shortened to "di Rienzo" or "di Rienzi" as Cola is sometimes also known among the many biographers and writers who have delighted in telling and retelling his fantastic story. His father, Lorenzo Gabrini, was an innkeeper, who apparently earned a modest living working out of his family owned and operated house tavern in Rome's Regola district on the Tiber River among the mills near the Church of Saint Thomas. But we do not know any other significant information about Lorenzo Gabrini's background or lineage. As for his mother, apart from her name, Matalena, and that she "earned her living by washing clothes and carrying water" not much more is known about her life or her family origins.[73] The anonymous fourteenth century biography, *The Life of Cola di Rienzi,* informs us that he had other siblings, but we are not certain of their names, or of how many brothers or sisters he actually had.

Cola often stated that he was the illegitimate son of Holy Roman Emperor Henry VII who, while his army laid siege to Rome in May of 1312, crossed the barricades and hid in his parent's tavern for about two weeks pretending to be sick to avoid capture by the Guelph troops of Robert the Wise, King of Naples, and his brother John of Gravina, whose forces had been summoned by the pope to repel Henry's insistence on being crowned in the ancient capital like his ancestor Charlemagne. In a letter written by Cola from prison in July 1350 to the Holy Roman Emperor, Charles IV of Prague, he explained how his mother laid with Henry during his days in hiding at the tavern ensconced in Rome's mill district, and how he was conceived in adultery, which given Cola's desire to upgrade his political ties and kinship pedigree on par with the lineage of the Holy Roman Emperors, was the least of his concerns at that moment of incarceration. Whether or not the events recounted in the letter are true, is perhaps not that important since Cola had a penchant for fantastic tales and historians sifting through his biographical data are accustomed to sorting fact from fiction. His letter goes on to explain that it was for this reason, and "on account of his wife's infirmity," that his father, Lorenzo, sent him away to Anagni to be raised by relatives until his mother revealed the truth to a priest on her deathbed, who, in turn, informed Cola of the details.[74]

Cola's early education, and his family life after returning to Rome around the age of twenty, is also obscured from our view by the sheer lack of information about his formative years, and about his personal and professional life before his rise to prominence around 1342. Cola was raised in the rural vicinity of Anagni in Lazio, which was then part of the diocese of Rome despite being about sixty miles from the Holy See. He developed a voracious appetite for reading and studying the Latin classics of Livy, Seneca, Cicero, Valerius Maximus, and Boethius, as well as the histories of Julius Caesar. After Cola's ascendancy as Tribune of Rome, he self-consciously celebrated the memory and political accomplishments of Caesar's nephew, Octavian Augustus Caesar, and the Emperors Vespasian and Constantine the Great as builders and restorers of Roman power and glory. He reasoned that just as these three men had led Rome through difficult transitions, he too, would one day have a chance to lead his countrymen through transition and restoration. His grammatical and rhetorical skills earned him the respectability of the type of classical and literary education that eluded him as a result of his family's lower class status. We have no idea who Cola's teachers were, but his mastery of the Latin classics, and his passion for the history of ancient Rome and the Greek sages, suggests rather forcibly that he had access to either an educational center, like a cathedral school, or to an accomplished private tutor of the *ars grammatica.* In the fourteenth century, this type of education consisted of a grammatically based "liberal arts" curriculum (*artes liberales*), which in the next century would be replaced by the *studia humanitatis* of the Florentine Renaissance. Based upon documentary and archival evidence of potential lifetime earnings among late medieval innkeepers and tavern owners in a city like Rome, which was well known for attracting antiquarian travelers and religious pilgrims, Musto suggests that perhaps Cola's father, Lorenzo, might have had the means to pay for either a formal education or private tutors.[75] Unfortunately, we will never know the complete story of how Cola acquired his mastery of Latin grammar and his abiding love for the ancient classics, which he recited with such remarkable ease and eloquence that even professional scholars, like Petrarch, with far more literary training than he possessed, were certainly impressed.

Cola's anonymous biography recounts how he returned to Rome when he was about twenty years old, presumably on account of his father's death, and became a professional notary. This was probably sometime between 1332 and 1334. As a notary he performed various economic, legal, and civic services for which he charged and collected fees. Cola earned a fair and decent living wage, regardless of whether he worked for a notary firm, or whether he worked independently at keeping fiscal record books and processing documents for different clients.[76] In the ensuing thirteen or so years leading up to the 1347 Pentecost revolution, Cola married a woman named Livia Mancini (or Martini), about whom we know very few details beyond his being captivated by her beauty and that she came from a family of successful Roman notaries. In addition, Cola and Livia may have had as many as four children during these years. Cola served as Notary of the Camera Urbis from 1344 to 1347, an important fiscal position handling all of Rome's civic revenues and municipal budgets, which significantly changed Cola's professional fortunes and exposed him to Rome's most influential citizens and civic employees. Amanda Collins astutely observes "the *publica fides* with which the notary was invested also lent itself to a personal authority that could be wielded across all of society."[77] His position as Notary of the Chamber, together with Livia's support and dowry from her wealthy parents, could have sustained a family of six quite comfortably at that time in Rome. While his diplomatic skills and political cunning served him well in his plot to restore the Roman Republic against the abuses and corruption of the Roman nobility, it was the prestige Cola gained from being one of Rome's municipal notaries, which, according to Collins, also signified and circumscribed Cola's professional image "as repository and representative of the statutory authority of the city and its antimagnatial polity," which "could be readily depicted as the natural enemy of the lawless, 'suburban' tyrant, the baron."[78] Ironically, as she further explains, "the barons were also the successful notary's best customers,"[79] a social reality of Trecento Italian culture that explains Cola's incredible rise to power in only three years from his municipal appointment in 1344 to his Pentecost Sunday insurrection and seizure of power in 1347.

Cola was no stranger to sharp disagreements and impassioned clashes with Rome's baronial families. In 1342, there was a brief revolt by the Roman people against the barons and the enduring nepotism of their control over Rome's civic and ecclesiastical affairs. This was the insurrection known as the "Government of the Thirteen Good Men," which ended in failure despite the departure of many among the ranks of Rome's barons to their countryside estates. Some of the nobles, intent on spending time away from Rome's troubles, served as part of a delegation formed to visit the Papal Court at Avignon in hope that it might soon return to Rome. We will return to Cola's role in this delegation, and its subsequent impact on his personal disdain and mistrust for Rome's barons, after a brief overview of why Rome's barons sought influence over the Papal Court and how this relationship developed into open conflict with the Papacy.

The feudal nobility and powerful clans that controlled the fiefdoms, towns, castles and fortresses, and large estates in the territorial vicinity of Rome were locked in a seemingly endless dispute with the Holy Roman Empire and its vassals over the question of their mutual and individual relations with the Papacy and the Papal Court. The debate over which of these factions should exercise more influence or control over papal succession and church administration dated back to the ninth century and the feudal warfare that consumed the Holy Roman Empire for a generation following Charlemagne's death. His descendants and imperial heirs maintained that the appointment of pope and imperial bishops was an aspect of ecclesiastical authority in which the Holy Roman Emperor had the right to exercise a certain temporal authority going back to Charlemagne's historic relationship with the Papacy. These dynamics were at the root of the political, ecclesiastical, and military conflicts that had pitted the pro-papal Guelph party against the pro-German Ghibelline faction for centuries before Cola's lifetime. Rome's barons and feudal nobility disagreed with both factions and maintained that their local authority and geographic proximity to the Holy See put them in a special relationship with the Bishop of Rome. The most powerful among fourteenth century Rome's noble families were the Colonna and the Orsini clans. During the 1290s, the Colonna's became embroiled in a major family dispute over feudal lands and territories surrounding their fortress at Palestrina, which threatened the feudal stability of the entire region. The Colonna were also keenly interested in strengthening their ties with the House of Valois, who by 1300 controlled the French Monarchy and were well-known advocates of expanding and centralizing European secular authority against the trans-local authority of the Papacy and the Holy Roman Empire. When Pope Boniface VIII intervened for the good of all the parties in the Colonna's regional dispute, the situation only worsened as Colonna family members became enraged over the pope's interference amidst threats of excommunication and the dissolution of their feudal contracts with various Colonna vassals.

On the other hand, during the late 1200s and early 1300s, the Papacy came under the increasing influence of the French Monarchy as a means of protection and autonomy from the Holy Roman Empire, who opportunistically claimed a special relationship with the Vicar of Christ dating back to Charlemagne and his successors in the ninth century. By the reign of King Philip IV, this protective pact between the Capetian-Angevin royal houses, and the various pro-Guelph Italian factions, collided with the designs of Rome's powerful Colonna barons and cardinals to control the Papacy and increase their family's feudal lands and vassals across Italy. The tragic death of Pope Boniface VIII (Pontificate: 1294-1303) at Anagni in 1303 may have resulted from his violent incarceration and beating while in the custody of the French royal minister, Guillaume de Nogaret, who wanted the pope arrested and arraigned for trial for standing up to King Philip, and Sciarra Colonna, who had vowed to kill the pope if he ever saw him again for meddling in his family's feudal disputes. King Philip's overtures to the Colonna faction through his chief minister, Nogaret, and the subsequent death of Pope Boniface VIII from injuries received while in their custody, muddied the process of papal succession and jeopardized the autonomy of the Church by increasing the trans-local authority of nation states like France. The French monarchy's strategic aims also included minimizing the adverse effects of the lingering feuds and regional ambitions of clans like the Colonna and Orsini barons of Rome. With the election of Pope Clement V in 1305, the Papacy and the Roman Curia were completely transferred four years later from their traditional home in Rome to their new center of French power in Avignon by March 1309. This dramatic move, which lasted until January 1377, came to be known in the history of the Papacy as the "Babylonian Captivity." The reformist factions among the clergy perceived at the time that removing the Papal Court from the reach of Rome's barons and the Holy Roman Empire would safeguard the liberty of the Church, but this faction naively underestimated the French Monarchy's potential for manipulation of the Church by an increasingly unified polity developing into one of Europe's first nation-states.

Although Cola was not yet born at the beginning of these thorny and contested events, the specter of how Boniface VIII died at Anagni must have been part of the aura of complexity and remorse that haunted the people of the town in which Cola spent the first two decades of his formative years. The budding esteem for Cola's oratory and rhetorical skills among representatives of the insurrectionist "Government of the Thirteen Good Men" led to his being selected in 1342 as an ambassador from the city of Rome to Pope Clement VI (Pontificate: 1342-1352). The delegation was charged with persuading the newly elected Pontiff to return to the Papacy's historic and traditional home in the Eternal City and declare a Year of Jubilee in 1350. The first part of the embassy's mission, of course, failed completely, but the second objective was approved and granted by Pope Clement. Cola's speeches and letters on behalf of the Roman cause made him an instant sensation. According to the anonymous *vita*, Cola's inspirational speech at Avignon was a great success and moved Pope Clement so deeply that he developed an instant admiration for this bold young man from Rome. The chronicler informs us that, Clement and Cola spent many days together in conversation, and that Cola eventually brought the city's troubles to his attention by informing the Holy See of the nobles' complicity in the decline of the ancient capital of Christendom:

> Then Cola spoke to him at length, saying that the barons of Rome were highway robbers; they allowed homicides, robberies, adulteries, and every sort of crime; they were responsible for their city's ravaged condition. On hearing these things the Pope became angry at the nobles. But then at the petition of Cardinal Janni Della Colonna, Cola fell into such disgrace, such poverty, such infirmity, that he might as well have been a pauper at a hospital. With his little coat on his back he stood in the sun like a snake.[80]

Janni Della Colonna later rectified the situation by enlisting the aid of Petrarch, who was profoundly impressed by Cola's erudition and public speaking skills, and Cola was brought back before the Pope and "restored to favor."[81] In an apparent attempt to make up for publicly humiliating an ambassador of the Roman people, Cola was appointed Notary of the Camera Urbis, the providential post he occupied until 1347 that began his meteoric rise to prominence in the fiscal and municipal affairs of Rome. The damage to Cola's self esteem, however, was not so easily restored. As indicated by the anonymous chronicler, his disdain for the Colonna family would linger in his heart as a wound that never healed: "He returned to Rome very quickly, muttering threats between his teeth."[82]

In four years Cola would transform his shame into decisive political action and a pneumatological vision of a revitalized Rome, freed from the exploitation of barons and nobles like the Colonna family. Nonetheless, for this barely thirty-year old man, born among the working class mills and taverns of Rome's Regola neighborhood on the musty shores of the Tiber River, and then sent away to be raised by relatives due to his mother's alleged adultery with a German monarch that resulted in his illegitimate birth, any additional shame or dishonor must have been painfully alienating, especially since he had worked so hard to become educated and rise to his present rank as both ambassador to the Papal Court at Avignon and chief notary of Rome's municipal government. However, not long after his return to Rome in 1343, Cola roused the members of the Roman Assembly by criticizing their cowardice in standing up to "the cruelty and injustice of the nobles" and "for neglecting the *buono stato* of Rome. "[83] The chronicler reports that a member of the Assembly, Andreuozzo Normanno, who was also a kinsman of the Colonna, approached Cola and slapped him on the face for showing such disrespect to the officials and rulers of Rome, while another member of the Senate made obscene gestures at him in front of everyone. This second public shaming for his commitment to justice and good citizenship only hardened Cola's resolve to act as an agent of change in Rome. Unfortunately, the incident also hardened his contempt and vengefulness toward the Colonna and their allies, with whom, out of necessity and political expediency, he patiently worked and collaborated during the next four years, while enduring their public ridicule of his speeches and mockery of his reformist aims.

At this point in the young Cola's civic career, two political concepts and propagandistic techniques that characterized his leadership style began to emerge. First is the concept of the Good Estate, or *Buono Stato*, which became a distinctive feature of his government after the 1347 Pentecost uprising. Cola used this concept in conjunction with elaborate speeches, eloquent letters, sensational flags, and artistic images filled with allusions to the nobility of character and moral integrity of the ancient Roman senators, tribunes, and good emperors who exemplified the ideals of Republican Rome. Never mind that the ancient "republic" of Rome endured centuries of conflict and civil war, and finally gave way to an "empire" that marginalized many of its citizens and subjects, and persecuted the Christian sect. Cola focused his romanticized vision of the past and rhetoric of restoration on his favorite benevolent rulers like Octavian Augustus Caesar, Vespasian, Marcus Aurelius, and Constantine the Great. As Cola's rhetoric of renewal and reform captivated the imaginations of Rome's officials and citizenry, he gained power over the past while promising a better future for Rome, and for all of Italy, which he referred to as "the garden of Rome." In speech after speech he encouraged the people and the nobles into joining together against the barons in the construction of the Good Estate, which projected a vision of the future akin to the prophesied Joachimist renovation of the Church in the *third status* of salvation history.

Secondly, the anonymous *Life of Cola di Rienzo* describes in detail how Cola began using large painted images embellished with allegorical figures and representations from Classical civilization and, occasionally, interspersed these with Christian symbols like the dove of peace or the flames of the Holy Spirit. Since these images were often painted, or hung, on the walls of the Piazza del Campidoglio, or on the walls of certain buildings lining the Capitoline Hill area, Senators and other dignitaries of the Roman Assembly believed these images were intended for them to ponder and digest. But, like the Roman statesmen of antiquity, who knew the masses were the key to securing power in the capital, Cola had a much broader and larger audience in mind. He anticipated the use of these images and paintings would inform the Roman people of his agenda, and motivate them to reevaluate the sad state of affairs in Rome and its surrounding territories as a result of the barons' abusiveness and inability to marshal their vast wealth and resources for the "public good."

Since the death of Boniface VIII in 1303, and the removal of the Papal Court and Cardinals to Avignon after 1305, economic conditions in Rome and its adjacent territories had plummeted. Not only had the flow of religious pilgrims and travelers with antiquarian interests declined substantially by the 1340s, but the departure of large numbers of support staff employed by the papal bureaucracy consisting of clerical assistants, secretaries, archivists, etc., also caused the population of the city to decline to some of its lowest levels of the medieval period. With their secure wealth and feudal land holdings, in the court of public opinion, Rome's barons and nobles must have seemed immune to this economic downturn in the region's fortunes. The anonymous author of Cola's vita Romana repeatedly chastises the barons for not being present in Rome to exercise leadership and serve the needs of its citizenry, especially in the domains of the rule of law and civic order. Describing the situation on the eve of Cola's rebellion, the chronicler writes:

> Meanwhile the city of Rome was in agony. It had no rulers; men fought every day; robbers were everywhere; nuns were insulted; there was no refuge; little girls were assaulted and led away to dishonor; wives were taken from their husbands in their very beds; farmhands going out to work were robbed, and where? —in the very gates of Rome; pilgrims, who had come to the holy churches for the good of their souls, were not protected, but were murdered and robbed; even the priests were criminals. Everywhere lust, everywhere evil, no justice, no law; there was no longer any escape; everyone was dying; the man who was strongest with the sword was most in the right. A person's only hope was to defend himself with the help of his relatives and friends; every day groups of armed men were formed.[84]

This was the deplorable and desperate situation of Rome and her people in 1347, and, if this is true, the chronicler's tone also explains the city's loss of municipal revenue and its citizen's confidence in its economic viability. Cola di Rienzo capitalized on this state of affairs with his ingenious use of images about Rome's former civic glory, and by blaming the upper classes for their repeated failures of leadership. He chastised the nobility for their sins of civic and egalitarian omission that precipitated the departure of the Pope and his court, the Cardinals, and the various agents and wards of the Holy Roman Empire from the once proud and economically viable ancient city.

The chronicler then recounts the chain of events that led to the bloodless revolution on May 20, 1347 by Cola and his fellow conspirators, who would soon be hailed as "liberators" and "reformers" of the new Roman Republic. For some time before Cola's insurrection the myth had surfaced that the restoration of the Roman Republic would serve as a model of justice and prosperity for the whole world, a regime sanctioned by the Holy Spirit and worthy of the best ideals and virtues taught by Jesus Christ and his Apostles.

> The nobles and barons were not in Rome. Messer Stefano Della Colonna had gone with the militia to Corneto for grain; this was at the end of the month of April. Then Cola di Rienzi, on the first day, [Saturday May 19th] sent out a trumpeter with a proclamation asking every man to come unarmed to the Good Estate at the sound of the bell. The following day, after midnight, he heard thirty Masses of the Holy Ghost in the church of Sant'Angelo in Pescheria.[85]

In the morning he emerged from the church fully armed, apart from his head, which he left exposed so that there would be no doubt concerning his identity. He was accompanied by about one hundred men-at-arms recruited from the city's various social classes and by the papal representative to the Roman populace, the Pope's Vicar, Raymond de Chameyrac, and Bishop of Orvietto. Once the procession of rebels reached the Campidoglio, Cola ascended the speakers' platform and delivered an impassioned address to the crowd of onlookers in which he emphatically stated: "that he was exposing his person to danger for the love of the Pope and the salvation of the people of Rome."[86] The presence of the Papal Vicar at his side, and the resplendent unfurled flags blowing in the wind on that Pentecost morning, conferred an aura of legitimacy on these events in the hearts and minds of the crowd. The banners depicted symbolic images of St. Peter, St. Paul and St. George, and of their beloved city personified in glory as *Roma* flanked by majestic lions and palms. He then asked an assistant to read the Ordinances of the Good Estate, which although fifteen clauses from the document are cited in the anonymous vita, probably numbered many more items and proscriptions for the public good and for limiting the rights and authority of the barons and nobles who formerly governed the city.[87]

Within a few days Cola and his supporters entered the Christian imagination as the providentially empowered agents of the coming "Age of the Holy Spirit." Here we encounter again the academic blind spot, discussed in other sections of this book, concerning the liberative and empowering role of the Pentecost story and its power to inspire pneumatological movements throughout the history of

Christianity. This is attested to by the common assumption in both the secondary and popular literature available on Cola's life and career in which he is almost always stereotypically described as a "popular leader who tried to restore the greatness of ancient Rome," or as the misguided rebel who "tried to create a state based on the ancient Roman republic." Cola's revolution has been read, examined, and historically narrated for over two centuries of the modern and postmodern academic enterprise without much attention given to understanding the power of its Pentecostal overtones, and without much attention to the role of pneumatological sensibilities in Cola's reformist agenda. It is worth noting that the Pentecost story not only held special significance and traditional power for Cola, but the pneumatological tone of Cola's insurrection was already mirrored in the hearts and minds of the people and officials who supported his cause through their own traditional familiarity and spiritual affinity with the story of Pentecost. Given the emphatic ways Pentecost shows up in Christian visionary movements and theological works across time and place, Cola's reliance on the Pentecost trope and the tradition of ecclesiastical liberation and personal empowerment associated with the Gifts of the Holy Spirit, found its corollary in the hearts and minds of his supporters. From this particular perspective, it must have appeared to more than a few who were present at the Campidoglio Palace that day, and to others across Italy, France, and Germany who heard the news of Cola's unbelievable coup, that, indeed, something of significant eschatological and pneumatological importance had transpired in Rome on Pentecost Sunday, 20 May 1347. Where else might such an important revelation from God and his Son, sent through the third Person of the Holy Trinity, pour forth its liberative and *"subversive fire,"* if not in the ancient citadel where the Roman Caesars and the successors of St. Peter once vied for the soul and future of the world?

Not long following Pentecost, Cola had a serious argument at the Campidoglio with Stefano Della Colonna, who vowed not to follow the dictates of the Good Estate and refused to swear allegiance to Cola and his new government. Cola confronted and addressed him in full battle armor, and then sounded the alarm bells at the Campidoglio summoning troops and the masses to the palace, the sheer numbers of which must have intimidated Stefano since the chronicler reports he rode off to seek the aid of his kinsmen and vassals. The bloodless coup of a few days earlier then turned violent as the chronicler reports that Cola began ordering numerous arrests and torturing of prisoners, while some opponents were hanged and others were beheaded.[88] Cola then issued an edict ordering the barons to leave Rome and retire to their castles and country estates. In a style reminiscent of the ancient historical figures that Cola adored and emulated, Cola and the Papal Vicar were named *Liberator rei publicae* and *Tribunus populus Romanus*, respectively meaning "Liberators of the People" and "Tribunes of the Roman People." As the weeks passed and spring became summer, Rome's barons and their local vassals agreed to abide by some of Cola's precepts for restoring the rule of law, protecting grain supplies, and promoting the public good. Privately, however, the barons and nobles looked forward to the day when Cola would be removed from power and secretly plotted to overthrow his regime.

Pope Clement VI at first supported Cola's government, especially since, in the short term, law and order were restored throughout the city, its adjacent districts, and for the people of Rome. Given the place of honor Cola reserved in the *Buono Stato* for the pope's vicar, Bishop Raymund of Orvietto, the pope could not disapprove publicly of the new regime, and Cola effectively used this diplomatic maneuver to considerable advantage for a few months. The Colonna Cardinals and their allies at the Papal Court disapproved of Cola's revolt from the start. Pope Clement was suspicious of Cola's long term intentions and inexperience as a high-ranking leader, concerns confirmed for the Pontiff when Cola dismissed Bishop Raymund as his co-leader less than three months after taking over Rome. Clement and the Papal Court also disapproved of Cola's ostentatious displays of personal and civic glory. Cola's title was later changed, at his insistence, to *Tribunus Augustus* of the Roman people, which recalled the title of one of his favorite ancient heroes, Octavian "Augustus" Caesar. This unusual request must have generated suspicion about his alleged imperial ambitions and dictatorial aims for many in the ranks of the nobility and papal clergy, civic employees, and the general citizenry. This was only the beginning of a series of egotistical maneuvers that in a few months would bring Cola's pneumatological and Joachimist leanings to the forefront and reveal the misguided hubris and authoritarianism that slumbered in his heart and mind.

In July and August of 1347, Cola di Rienzo staged a series of expensive knighting and coronation ceremonies for himself, which, we can only guess, were intended to elevate his authority and stature among the people of Rome. He asked the Senate to confer additional titles on him. First he was declared *candidatus dello Spiritus Santo*, meaning "Candidate of the Holy Spirit," which, when juxtaposed with his increasing references to the *renovatio* of the Roman Republic through the Good Estate he had inaugurated a few months earlier on Pentecost, conjured up all sorts of historical and eschatological images. The whole scene was reminiscent of Joachim of Fiore's prophecies dismissed as heresy by several popes, and of the Fraticelli factions of the Franciscan Order who were still at odds with the Papacy in 1347. Then he staged an elaborate knighting ceremony in which he ritually bathed in a baptismal font attributed to the Emperor Constantine, and finally he was dubbed "Knight of the Holy Spirit" (*Cavaliere dello Spirito Santo*), brandishing and swirling his ceremonial sword in the air three times as if claiming the protection of the Holy Spirit and the Holy Trinity for the Good Estate. In the meantime, Cola wrote letters, sent emissaries and ambassadors abroad to European rulers, and planned for the reunification of Italy by extending the ideals of the Good Estate beyond the administrative districts and territories of Rome. Other elements of these highly structured ceremonies, completed by August 15 1347, recalled traditional symbols and rituals reserved for the coronations of Popes or Holy Roman Emperors at Old St. Peter's.[89] Such grandiose schemes must have bewildered many of Cola's loyal supporters and unnerved many of his detractors and enemies, who were merely tolerating and enduring his command until they or someone else deposed him, dissolved the Good Estate, and restored the rule of the barons and nobles.

During the fall of 1347, the demise of Cola's short lived regime accelerated as he squandered Rome's treasury to pay for military campaigns and battles against the Colonna and Orsini factions who were more determined than ever to depose the former notary from his self-glorifying position as Tribune of Rome. Cola became unhinged by his declining fortunes, and ever more repressive and unpredictable. He dealt harshly with his opponents by making frequent use of torture and executions, and stifled the open dialogue about peace and justice that had characterized the beginning of his reign. Many began to think of Cola as a dangerous madman and religious charlatan who thought only of his own glory and prestige and was turning out to be just another traitor to civic justice like the barons he criticized before becoming Tribune. None of these developments and events escaped the attention of Pope Clement VI and the Papal Court in Avignon. The Angevin rulers of Naples to the south and the rulers of the Holy Roman Empire to the north also took note of these strange proceedings in Rome and carefully weighed their political and military options as Cola dreamed of uniting Italy under the banner of a revitalized Roman Republic that each day acted more tyrannical and less egalitarian. When news of Cola's expansionist agenda began circulating around the royal courts of France and Germany, and among northern Italy's powerful and affluent city-states who valued their independence highly, a growing alliance of anti-Cola factions, kingdoms, and states emerged across the region.

Cola's fatal mistake was inviting the barons and nobles to come to Rome for an important meeting that autumn and imprisoning them overnight, while mockingly informing them of their impending executions at sunrise, an order which his closest advisors and other officials of the city persuaded him not to carry out. Among the prisoners were the male elders and sons of both the Colonna and Orsini families, who wasted no time in plotting for war against the Roman Tribune after being released. If any of these powerful men ever had any respect for Cola di Rienzo, this incident cost him whatever deference and forbearance they had left for him and his style of governance. The nobles fortified their castles and fortresses, and began dispatching armed bands on forays to test Rome's defenses and scout the roads and bridges leading into the city. Meanwhile, the Papal Legate sent by Clement VI tried to calm the situation by calling for dialogue and diplomacy, but Cola dismissed his efforts, refused to listen to the pope's messages, and then imprisoned the legate. The night before the final battle, Cola delivered one of his rousing speeches, in which he alluded to avenging the death of Pope Boniface VIII and purging Rome of "the enemies of God" like the Colonna and their allies. The citizen volunteers and paid soldiers who made up the rank and file of Cola's forces probably reacted to his vengeful rhetoric of the Colonna barons as Rome's scapegoats, especially since the populace disdained the baron's abuse of power and tight control over economic opportunities in the city and its districts. He then announced the "watchword" for the guards and the rallying-cry for the next day's battle as "Knights of the Holy Ghost,"[90] which would have stunned Abbot Joachim and the Spiritual Franciscans who believed earnestly in the promise of justice and human flourishing that would characterize the coming "Age of the Holy Spirit."

On November 20, 1347, a ferocious battle was fought by the gates of San Lorenzo, in which scores of barons and nobles were killed, including some of the Orsini clan, and three of the leading members of the Colonna family. This was interpreted then, and over the centuries by admirers of Cola's story and scholars studying his life and times, as sheer luck on Cola's part, or as poor military planning by the Colonna and their invasion force. The Roman mob, which accompanied the knights and other men-at-arms defending the barricades, went into a rage at the sight of the fallen Colonna leaders and repeatedly wounded and desecrated their bodies in the course of the battle. When the widows and families of the fallen barons, nobles, and former Senators of Rome came to the Campidoglio to request the honor of burying their loved ones with Christian dignity, Cola belittled them, denied them the right to mourn and recover the bodies, and sent them away in humiliation. He was out of control and publicly praised the vicious deaths of his Colonna opponents, which would cost him the respect of his captains and soldiers.

Instead of consolidating his victory at the Gate of San Lorenzo on behalf of Rome and its citizens, and crushing his opponents by pursuing them to the Orsini castle at Marino, over the next three to four weeks Cola wallowed in arrogance and disrespectful revelry, raised taxes and various municipal fees on the beleaguered Roman people, and lost the loyalty and respect of the knights and citizens who had supported him in battle against the barons. It is possible Cola secretly developed an opportune alliance, based on a mutual interest in authority and survival, with the Orsini and their allies by playing them against the Colonna in the sequence of events leading to the outbreak of hostilities on November 20, but we cannot know for certain from the surviving fragmentary evidence. The Papal Legate publicly declared him a heretic and pledged his support for the Colonna clan and other nobles, like the exiled Neapolitan Count Janni Pipino, who stirred the people into another rebellion so that he might succeed Cola as the next "Liberator of the People." When Cola's remaining troops could not hold the count's militia from breaching the barricades in December, the anonymous biographer reports, Cola became paralyzed by fear, locked himself up in the Castel Sant'Angelo with several Orsini allies, and wept at the thought that he would soon die: "Now in the seventh month I descend from my dominion."[91] Perhaps the Tribune of Rome, who began his revolutionary government with such lofty promises of peace and justice, but brought the city and its people to the edge of anarchy in seven months, was emotionally spent and demoralized by the failure of his envisioned Good Estate. Finally in late December 1347, Pope Clement VI excommunicated Cola and ordered his immediate arrest. Cola responded by fleeing Rome with his wife, going into hiding, and living as a fugitive and prisoner for most of the next six years.

The following year witnessed the outbreak of the Black Death across Europe and the Mediterranean region, which further devastated Rome's fortunes as an estimated one-third of Europe's population perished in this pestilence. Unlike other intermittent epidemic outbreaks that medieval Europeans had previously witnessed, this particular disease could not be contained effectively. Hence, the plague did not discriminate among the social ranks of its victims as nobles and clergy, citizens and lower class workers, servants and serfs perished. Among Cola's enemies and supporters back in Rome, and elsewhere in the regions and kingdoms that had dealt with the former Tribune, there were numerous deaths from the plague. The state of emergency generated across Europe for the next several years by the spread of the plague, worked temporarily in Cola's favor by first slowing down the individuals and forces that wanted him tried for heresy and treason, and then claiming the lives of people who knew his story and still wanted him apprehended for various personal or legal reasons.

As for Cola's whereabouts from January 1348 to July 1350, no one in those days or since has provided satisfactory information. He simply vanished from the historical record. Scholarly attempts to trace his wanderings, or reconstruct his life during these two years, must be read with caution because such accounts have tended to rely on "connecting-the-dots" and "filling-in-the-blanks" from statements expressed in Cola's letters from 1350 to 1354.[92] Amanda Collins has done research on Cola's history a great service with her insightful description and analysis of the sources and figures by which Cola increased his awareness of the apocalyptic language and paradigms of Joachim of Fiore and the Fraticelli faction during his years of wandering from 1348 to 1350, and how he came to view himself as one of the prophesied agents of the coming renovation of the world.[93] Cola finally turns up again in Prague at the court of the new Holy Roman Emperor, Charles of Bohemia, apparently disguising himself while seeking the emperor's favor and warning the imperial court that the plague and recent earthquakes are signs of the impending transformation of the world in the approaching Joachimist "Age of the Holy Spirit." Emperor Charles IV, whom Cola maintained was really his nephew through his mother's adulterous affair with Emperor Henry VII, eventually discovered the strange man's identity and imprisoned him immediately. Charles later informed Pope Clement VI in Avignon about the identity of the wanderer who had shown up at his court in Prague ranting about the Holy Spirit, and comparing his restoration of the Roman Republic in 1347 to the reformist mission of St. Francis of Assisi a century earlier.

While the tone of Cola's rhetoric and personal claims in his letters to Charles IV sound like the words of either a shrewd political manipulator, or like those of a religious madman, the emperor and others at court engaged him in an epistolary dialogue. The fact that Charles and imperial theologians, like the Archbishop of Prague, Ernst von Pardubitz, actually listened to the deposed Roman Tribune, who was now a fugitive from justice and an accused heretic, reveals their own curious mood of apocalyptic expectation following the devastation of the plague. These episodes also indicate the lasting impression of himself that Cola created abroad among other European courts during his governance of Rome from May to December 1347. Cola's powers of persuasion and his propagandistic rhetoric had not been diminished by either living on the run or living in prison. In a letter to the emperor preserved in the Vatican archives, and described by Amanda Collins, Cola "urged Charles to reconsider the prospect of an Italy united and loyal to him by Pentecost, the Feast of the Holy Spirit, 1351, and pictured him entering Rome in triumph alongside the twin consort of 'widowed' Rome, the pope."[94] The master of theatricality had not given up on his pneumatological visions. Cola then compared the Papal Court at Avignon to the corrupt and worldly church that St. Francis and his truest disciples had sought to reform, which reminds us again of the ongoing dispute between the Fraticelli and the Avignon Papacy, and the Church's stern handling of the Spiritual Franciscan faction in Italy. The Archbishop of Prague investigated Cola's heretical comments and accusations, and Charles IV remained content to leave Cola in prison until he retracted and lessened some of his accusations of the pope and the Avignon clergy. Whether Charles and the Archbishop of Prague cared at all about Cola's fantastic claims and apocalyptic babble, or whether Charles was just using Cola as another pawn in the Holy Roman Empire's international chess game with the Papal Court at Avignon and the French Monarchy at Paris, cannot be determined with complete certainty from Cola's surviving letters, nor from the replies he received from these two high ranking leaders. But, Cola's usefulness to Charles IV eventually ran its course when the emperor consented to Pope Clement's request that Cola be transferred to Avignon.

Cola arrived in France by the end of summer 1351, and, although Clement VI immediately threw him in prison, by July 1354 Cola would be on his way back to Rome with the support of Clement's successor, Pope Innocent VI, intent on regaining complete control of Rome. Cola disliked being in jail and the conditions under which he was kept in Avignon, but he was fortunate not to have been executed. The chronicler reports that he used this time to read and feed his mind on the wisdom of the ancient histories and Latin authors he admired. He read the Bible, studied the Classics, and ate well to regain his strength.[95] Clement VI died in 1352. During the new pope's first year in office, Cola petitioned Innocent VI to reopen the case concerning the charges of heresy and the order of excommunication issued against him five years earlier. Astonishingly, in September of 1353, Cola was released from prison with a full papal pardon and overtures from Innocent VI about serving alongside the current Papal Legate to Rome, Cardinal Alvarez Carillo Gil de Albornoz, a Castilian priest of royal ancestry who was also an accomplished expert in warfare and a hero of the Spanish Reconquest. Cola agreed to the invitation and the pope named him a Senator of Rome. Cardinal Gil de Albornoz was dispatched to Rome to quell the latest uprising by the barons and nobles against the pope's administrative and military representatives, and Cola both served and assisted in the leadership of this papal militia. The cardinal did not trust Cola, but during the spring and summer of 1354 Cola defeated several of Rome's nobles, raised extra funds to finance incursions further south into Rome's territories, and paved the way for an assault on Rome designed to restore the rule of law.

On August 1, 1354, Cola di Rienzo delivered another one of his signature speeches to the people and leaders of Rome. Comparing himself to the exiled King Nebuchadnezzar, Cola told the crowd that by the power of God he had returned as the Pope's vassal to reform the government of Rome.[96] The people granted Cola another opportunity to lead them into a better future, but the Colonna and other baronial families had not forgotten his humiliating arrogance or violent excesses in the deaths of their kinsmen seven years earlier. After Cola's triumphal entry into Rome and reinstatement ceremony at the Palace of the

Campidoglio, he summoned all the barons to an assembly and dictated the terms of justice and obedience he expected of them for the public good. Stefaniello Della Colonna, who had been just a young boy seven years ago when his father and brother were killed in battle at the Gates of San Lorenzo, led the opposition to Cola's return to power, and refused to be summoned by Cola from his family's fortress palace at Palestrina. Cola exhausted the people and resources of Rome and its surrounding districts as he became obsessed with devastating Palestrina and wiping out the Colonna.[97] He increased taxes on wine and salt, ordered the execution of popular and respected citizens whom he feared, and fell behind schedule on regular payments to his soldiers. It is worth noting that if the surviving accounts of these events are accurate, Cola's cavalry and infantry pursued the Colonna all over Romagna from the middle of August through the end of September 1354, which means that Cola's exorbitant tax increases, and other sudden fiscal measures to pay for the army, were imposed on Rome's citizenry in a very short span of time. Given the mission of restoring order for the public good in the struggling citadel and its districts, which had been entrusted to Cola as the pope's newly appointed Senator of Rome, and to Cardinal Gil de Albornoz, as the newly appointed Papal Legate to Rome, it is not surprising that Rome's nobles, cd commoners rejected Cola's harsh policies and tax increases.

The Roman people's patience with Cola ran out on October 8, 1354 when an angry mob marched on the Campidoglio looking for him. The armed crowd, in its rage, shouted different slogans. "Long live the people!" "Death to the one who made the tax!" And, "Death to the traitor, Cola di Rienzi!"[98] Cola summoned his soldiers and the city's militia by sounding the alarm bells, but none came to his aid. He tried to address the populace from a balcony, but the crowd threw stones at him and set fire to the historic Campidoglio Palace. As the situation got out of control Cola panicked, disguised himself as a commoner, and attempted to escape from Rome one more time until he was recognized not far from the gates by one of the rioters. Cola was surrounded by a multitude of men with weapons, then stabbed and pierced repeatedly as his body was torn to pieces and desecrated before being burned. In this horrific way ended the life of the man who served as Tribune of Rome in 1347, and who emerged from prison and the ruins of his shattered career to be named Senator of Rome by Pope Innocent VI less than eight weeks before his final demise. Cola passed into the pages of history as one of the most amazing examples in Italian history of a leader who rose from humble origins to the pinnacle of power, then fell hard from grace, and resurrected his image and career against seemingly impossible odds to momentarily regain some of his former glory before fading into legend.[99]

In conclusion, Cola di Rienzo's use of pneumatological imagery, prophetic language, and key aspects from the story of Pentecost, alert us to the power and longevity of these Christian images and traditions especially when issues of justice, liberty, or ecclesiastical mission were at stake. Cola was a charismatic orator and highly manipulative leader whose governance of late medieval Rome in both 1347 and 1354 must be judged as colossal failures. Many have questioned the integrity of his political motivations, while some have questioned his sanity. In Cola's lifetime there was much talk about "Good Government" among Italian leaders and clergy, as exemplified at the time by Pietro Lorenzetti's frescoes on *Good and Bad Government* (ca. 1340) in Siena's Palazzo Publicco. The rising tide of humanist scholarship, and the growing autonomy of northern Italy's fiercely independent city-states, created an atmosphere in which discourse about virtuous secular government coexisted alongside the discursive tradition concerning ecclesiastical leadership and reform. Amanda Collins expressed it best when she referred to Cola's strange mixture of prophetic language and personal apotheosis as a "secularized *imitatio Christi*."[100] Cola's bizarre desires for titles like "Candidate of the Holy Spirit, or "Knight of the Holy Spirit," appears arrogant and misguided by modern theological standards. However, in the tradition of the Pentecost story, surveyed throughout this volume, as both liberative trope and repository of Christian charismatic wisdom, on matters ranging from personal piety to ecclesiastical purpose and reform, he was on solid ground. Despite Cola's penchant for theatricality and the propagandistic use of religious symbolism, the extant historical accounts suggest the people of Rome responded positively to his May 20, 1347 Pentecost Sunday insurrection. Armed with his rhetoric of justice, liberty, and civic virtue, and calling upon the power of the Holy Spirit, he sought power over the barons and nobles while also gaining power over the Classical Roman "past." It was this desire for power over the past that fueled his hope of building a brighter and more glorious "future" for Rome, and for himself as head of the newly restored Roman Republic. Hence, despite unmistakable echoes of Joachimist and Spiritual Franciscan influences in his life and political career, the ancient Roman past and the ancient Pentecostal legacy of liberation and reconstruction served Cola as alternatives to the failed missions and promises of the Papal Court in Avignon and of the Holy Roman Emperors. Cola's fantastic and tragic story is a complex and thought-provoking example of the divergent ways Pentecost manifests in the history of Christianity as a *revitalizing* and *subversive fire*, which can burn out of control if one is not cautious about the Holy Spirit's transformative power.

SUMMATION: THE CHURCH OF THE HOLY SPIRIT

This chapter has focused primarily on pneumatological movements involving Italy, Provence, northern France, and the Holy Roman Empire from the active lifetime of the Calabrian Abbot Joachim of Fiore (ca. 1180) to the demise of the Roman Tribune Cola di Rienzo (ca. 1347-1354). For the sake of time and space constraints, there is much that I intentionally left out of the long story of so-called movements of the Holy Spirit during the High Middle Ages. Nonetheless, it is possible to learn more than a few cursory things about medieval conceptions of Pentecost and the Holy Spirit from the individual vignettes and selected texts surveyed in this chapter.

Although they were men of very different temperament, Abbot Joachim and Cola di Rienzo were deeply affected and moved by the possibilities of the story of Pentecost and the role of the Third Person of the Trinity in the Church and society, and the world at large. The Spiritual Franciscans of the 1200s and 1300s stood somewhere in between the visionary piety of Abbot Joachim and the misguided excesses of Cola's tragic life. The stories of St. Francis and St. Anthony of Padua remind us of the role of pneumatological ideas in the liturgical and monastic practices of the medieval period, and of the abiding power of the story of Pentecost as a reminder of the egalitarian ideals and liberative mission of Christ's Church on earth. The followers of Guglielma of Milan remind us of the voice of the Divine Feminine as contrasted with the masculine terminology for the godhead expressed in three Persons of the Holy Trinity and the male dominated Church hierarchy of the Middle Ages. Finally the fantastic and sad life of Cola di Rienzo reminds us of why the Church historically cautioned its members against "enthusiast" political visionaries and rebel factions promising quick solutions to social evils and universal prosperity. Cola's violent excesses and demand for absolute power shows us in dramatic fashion that sometimes the distance between a beatific vision and a murderous dictatorship is only a few short steps removed from seeing the presence and love of Christ in one's fellow citizens. At the end of this trajectory stands the specter of the Plague and its devastating aftermath, which cannot be ignored as the great engine of social, political, economic, and religious change for European Christendom. The Church of the Holy Spirit that Joachimist sympathizers eagerly awaited during the High Middle Ages did not arrive as anticipated, but instead got pushed ahead into the *not-yet* of the future as successive generations of Christian reformers and visionaries read the Calabrian Abbot's works and pondered its meaning for their particular time and place in salvation history. By the time the Florentine Renaissance of the 1400s was in full swing, new visions of social organization and human agency were beginning to affect how Christians understood the makeup and leadership of both church and state, but, as we shall examine in Chapters Four and Five, these "new visions" of the Renaissance, Reformation, and Scientific Revolutions were motivated by a number of pneumatological ideas and sensibilities that spoke to human liberation and empowerment. In the next chapter, we will examine the persistence of pneumatological ideas and the story of Pentecost in the imaginative transformations of Church and State that developed during the Protestant and Roman Catholic Reformations, and their mutual mistrust of the *"subversive fire"* inherent in revolutionary movements of the Holy Spirit.

NOTES

1. Delwin Brown, *Boundaries of Our Habitations: Tradition and Theological Construction* (Albany: SUNY, 1994), 113.
2. Ibid. 118-119.
3. For more detailed accounts of Joachim's biography see Morton Bloomfield, "Joachim of Flora: A Critical Survey of his Canon, Teachings, Sources, Biography, and Influence," *Traditio* 13 (1957) 249-311; and G. La Piana, "Joachim of Flora: A Critical Survey," in Delno C. West, ed. *Joachim of Fiore in Christian Thought: Essays on the Influence of the Calabrian Abbot, 2 Volumes* (New York: Burt Franklin, 1975), V. I: 3-28.
4. From the Anonymous *Vita beati Joachimi abbatis* discussed in Herbert Grundmann's *Studien über Joachim von Fiore*, 2nd ed. (Darmstadt, 1966), 530-31; as cited in B. McGinn, *The Calabrian Abbot* (New York: Macmillan, 1985), 19; fn. 40-41.

5. For more information on the center's programs, academic resources, and intellectual leadership of Joachimist studies, see the useful website of the CISG at www.centrostudigioachimiti.it/index2.asp

6. Bernard McGinn, *The Calabrian Abbot: Joachim of Fiore in the History of Western Thought* (New York: Macmillan, 1985), 30.

7. Kärkkäinen, *Pneumatology*, 16-19.

8. See E. Buonaiuti, *Gioacchino da Fiore* (Rome: Collezione meridionale editrice, 1931); H. Grundmann, *Studien über Joachim von Floris* (Leipzig: Truebner, 1927) and *Neue Forschungen über Joachim von Floris* (Marburg: Simons, 1950).

9. See Henri de Lubac, *La postérité spirituelle de Joachim de Flore* (Paris: Lethielleux, Two Volumes, 1979 and 1981, respectively); Henry Mottu, *La manifestation de l'Esprit selon Joachim de Fiore* (Paris: Delachaux and Niestle, 1977); and the two-volume compilation of essays by Delno West, ed. *Joachim of Fiore in Christian Thought* (New York: Burt Franklin, 1975); for studies by Marjorie Reeves see *Prophecy in the Later Middle Ages* (Oxford: Clarendon Press, 1969), *Joachim of Fiore and the Prophetic Future* (London: SPCK, 1976), and her study and translation with Beatrice Hirsch-Reich, *The Figurae of Joachim of Fiore* (Oxford: Clarendon Press, 1972); for Bernard McGinn see *Visions of the End* (New York: Columbia University Press, 1969) and *The Calabrian Abbot: Joachim of Fiore in the History of Western Thought* (New York: Macmillan, 1985).

10. For the best overview of Joachim's influence from the 1700s to the early 1900s see the masterful and erudite study by Marjorie Reeves and Warwick Gould, *Joachim of Fiore and the Myth of the Eternal Evangel in the Nineteenth Century* (Oxford: Clarendon Press, 1987); see also Henri de Lubac, *La postérité spirituelle de Joachim de Flore*, Volumes I and II.

11. Stanley M. Burgess, *The Holy Spirit: Medieval, Roman Catholic and Reformation Traditions* (Hendrickson Publishers, 1997), 125-140.

12. Adapted from the Latin text of Joachim's *Expositio in Apocalypsim* (Venice 1527), folio 39r-v; as cited and translated by Bernard McGinn in *The Calabrian Abbot: Joachim of Fiore in the History of Western Thought* (New York: Macmillan, 1985), 22, fn. 42.

13. From the Preface to the *Psalterium decem chordarum* (folio 227r-v; Venice, 1527) as cited and translated by Bernard McGinn, *Apocalyptic Spirituality* (Mahwah: Paulist Press, 1979), 99.

14. For a concise and useful discussion of the structure and meaning of Joachim's *Expositio in Apocalypsim*, see Chapter Five in Bernard McGinn, *The Calabrian Abbot*, 145-160.

15. Ibid. 156, fn. 160, McGinn's translation as adapted from the Latin text of the *Expositio in Apocalypsim* (Venice, 1527) folio 37va.

16. Ibid. 154-157.

17. The most reliable extant Latin text of the *Psalterium decem chordarum* remains the 1527 Venice Edition (Frankfurt, Germany: reprint edition 1965). See also the recent edition sponsored by the International Center for Joachimist Studies: Gioacchino da Fiore, *Il salterio a dieci corde*. Trans. by F. Troncarelli. (Rome: Viella, 2004).

18. See Marjorie Reeves and Beatrice Hirsch-Reich, *The 'Figurae' of Joachim of Fiore* (London: Oxford University Press, 1972), 16-19.

19. For more on the history of medieval Christian society and the structure of the various medieval monastic orders see Christopher Brooke, *The Age of the Cloister: The Story of Monastic Life in the Middle Ages* (Mahwah: Hidden Spring/Paulist Press, 2003);

Guy Bedouelle, *The History of the Church* (New York: Continuum, 2003), 59-81; C. H. Lawrence, *Medieval Monasticism: Forms of Religious Life in Western Europe in the Middle Ages*, Third Ed. (Longman, 2000); and Georges Duby, *The Three Orders: Feudal Society Imagined*. Trans. A. Goldhammer (Chicago: University of Chicago, 1982).

20. For a concise discussion of Joachim's views on the Trinity in history and the role of Christ in history see Delno C. West and Sandra Zimdars-Swartz, *Joachim of Fiore: A Study in Spiritual Perception and History* (Bloomington: Indiana University Press, 1983), 41-68; 78-98.

21. Francis of Assisi, *Later Rule X, 8* as cited in *Francis of Assisi: Early Documents; Volume II: The Founder* (New York: New City Press, 2000), 20, fn. 42.

22. Roger D. Sorrell, *St. Francis of Assisi and Nature: Tradition and Innovation in Western Christian Attitudes toward the Environment* (New York: Oxford University Press, 1988), 6-8; for an excellent analysis of medieval Christian understandings of Nature and Creation versus Francis' traditional and innovative approach to these themes in his *Canticle of Brother Sun*; see also Sorrell's three chapter long discussion on these topics, 98-137.

23. Ibid. 7, from Francis' *Office of the Passion* as cited by Sorrell, who also identifies Genesis 1 and 2, Psalm 148, and Daniel 3 as the primary Biblical sources for Francis' understanding of the relation between humanity and Nature; see fn. 31, 161 in Sorrell.

24. See Ivan Gobry, *Saint Francis of Assisi: A Biography* (San Francisco: Ignatius Press, 2006), 24.

25. Ibid. 26-28.

26. Ibid. 39-41.

27. Saint Bonaventure, *The Life of Saint Francis (Legenda Maior)* in *Bonaventure: The Soul's Journey Into God, The Tree of Life; The Life of Saint Francis*. Ewert Cousins, Trans. (Mahwah: Paulist Press, 1978), 191.

28. Ibid.

29. Ibid. 191-192.

30. David Burr opens his magnificently accessible and comprehensive volume on the story of the entire Spiritual Franciscan movement during the 1200s and the 1300s with a chapter entitled "The Franciscan Dilemma," discussing the dichotomy of Saint Francis' rule versus the incredible success and growth of the Franciscan Order by 1260, in *The Spiritual Franciscans: From Protest to Persecution in the Century After Saint Francis*. (University Park: Pennsylvania State University Press, 2001), 1-10.

31. Decima Douie, *The Nature and the Effect of the Heresy of the Fraticelli.* (UK: Manchester University Press, 1932), 210.

32. For a useful and concise summary of the Spirituals and Conventuals from 1291 to about 1378, see John Moorman, *A History of the Franciscan Order: From Its Origins to the Year 1517* (Chicago: Franciscan Herald Press, 1968), 188-204; 307-338.

33. Douie. 11-41.

34. Ibid. 19.

35. From Section 115 of *Scripta Leonis* in Rosalnid Brooke, *Scripta Leonis, Rufini et Angeli Sociorum S. Francisci* (Oxford: Clarendon Press, 1970), as quoted in Burr's *The Spiritual Franciscans*, 19-20, fn. 33.

36. Michael Robson, *The Franciscans in the Middle Ages.* (Woodbridge: Boydell Press, 2006), 89-90.

37. Burr, *The Spiritual Franciscans*, 43-46.

38. From the opening lines of Chapter 42 as cited in Jon M. Sweeney, *Light in the Dark Ages: The Friendship of Francis and Clare of Assisi.* (Brewster: Paraclete Press, 2007), 154, fn. 127.

39. Ibid. 154-155.

40. *Authority and The Sacred*, 60.

41. Since this chapter's central focus is the influence of Joachim's pneumatology and Pentecostal visions about the approaching "Age of the Holy Spirit" on the various thirteenth and fourteenth century movements of the Holy Spirit, I have intentionally avoided an exhaustive analysis of the official policies, papal bulls, or personal concerns of Pope John XXII against the Franciscan Spirituals. For a concise and careful treatment of Pope John's dealings with the Spirituals see Michael Robson, *The Franciscans in the Middle* Ages, 130-140.

42. For a useful, although dated, summary of Angelo's life and works, see Douie's *The Nature and the Effect of the Heresy of the Fraticelli,* 49-80; for a more recent assessment see Michael Robson, *The Franciscans in the Middle Ages,* 124-129.

43. Angelo Clareno, *A Chronicle or History of the Seven Tribulations of the Order of Brothers Minor.* Translated by David Burr and E. Randolph Daniel. (New York: St. Bonaventure University and Franciscan Institute Publications, 2005).

44. For an overview of Olivi's life and major written works see, Decima Douie, 81-119.

45. For a discussion of Olivi's censure in 1283 and its consequences up to his death in 1298, see David Burr, *Olivi and Franciscan Poverty: The Origins of the Usus Pauper Controversy.* (Philadelphia: University of Pennsylvania Press, 1989), 88-158.

46. See David Burr, *Olivi's Peaceable Kingdom: A Reading of the Apocalypse Commentary* (Philadelphia: University of Pennsylvania Press, 1993).

47. As chronicled and assessed by the Franciscan historian Luke Wadding, *Annales Minorum* (Rome, 1732), 381-393.

48. For an overview of Ubertino's life and major written works see Douie, 120-152; or Robson, 119-124.

49. From the *Arbor Vitae* as cited in Douie, 123, fn. 3.

50. I have relied for this discussion on the modern reprint edition of the 1485 Venice edition of Ubertino of Casale, *Arbor vitae crucifixae Jesu* (Turin: Bottega d'Erasmo, 1961).

51. *Arbor vitae*, Prologue, 4.

52. See the pioneering works on allegorical theory and its postmodern recovery as a mode of discourse and symbolic knowledge by Edwin Honig, *Dark Conceit: The Making of Allegory* (Cambridge: Walker/De Berry, 1960); Angus Fletcher, *Allegory: The Theory of A Symbolic Mode* (Ithaca: Cornell University Press, 1964); and Maureen Quilligan, *The Language of Allegory: Defining the Genre* (Ithaca: Cornell University Press, 1987).

53. Quilligan, 97-98.

54. Fletcher, *Allegory*, 21.

55. Ibid. 22-23.

56. Honig, 109-110.

57. *Arbor vitae, 3.*

58. From the *Arbor vitae* (L. V. cap. iii,. F. I, r.) as cited in Douie, 142, fn. 2.

59. For more on Robert of Anjou's personal piety, relations with the Fraticelli, and role in the anti-Spirituals conflict with Pope John XXII see Samantha Kelly, *The New Solomon: Robert of Naples (1309-1343) and Fourteenth Century Kingship.* (Leiden and Boston: Brill, 2003), 73-79.

60. For more expansive studies of this virtually unknown female religious leader of the High Middle Ages see: Marina Benedetti, *Io non somo Dio: Guglielma di Milano e i Figli dello Spiritu Santo.* (Milan: Edizioni Biblioteca Francescana, 1998); Barbara Newman, *From Virile Woman to Woman Christ: Studies in Medieval Religion and Literature.* (Philadelphia: University of Pennsylvania Press, 1995), 182-223; and Luisa Muraro, *Guglielma e Maifreda: Storia di un'eresia femminista* (Milan: La Tartaruga, 1985).

61. Newman, *From Virile Woman to Woman Christ,* 184-185.

62. Barbara Newman, *God and the Goddesses: Vision, Poetry, and Belief in the Middle Ages.* (Philadelphia: University of Pennsylvania Press, 2003), 249.

63. Newman, *From Virile Woman to Woman Christ,* 185, fn 13, 296.

64. For more on the political agendas arising from the use and misuse of this saintly ancestry by these Angevin and Hungarian dynastic lines, see the excellent study by Gábor Klaniczay, *Holy Rulers and Blessed Princesses: Dynastic Cults in Medieval Central Europe.* Eva Pálmai, Trans. (Cambridge University Press, 2002), 195-242; 295-394.

65. Sancia of Majorca, was the daughter of King James II of Majorca and Queen Esclaramunda of Foix, but her paternal grandparents were James I of Aragon and Violant of Hungary (ca. 1216-1253), and Queen Sancia often used her saintly lineage for persuasion and influence as in this example of a letter she wrote to a Franciscan Chapter gathering in Naples around 1316: "Know, fathers, that God caused me to be descended from such a lineage and family tree...to be a descendant of blessed Elizabeth, who was such a true and devoted daughter of blessed Francis and mother of his order. She was the blood sister of the lady mother of my father, Lord James, well remembered king of Majorca." Translation of letter by Ronald G. Musto, "Queen Sancia of Naples (1286-1345) and The Spiritual Franciscans," pp. 179-214. In *Women of the Medieval World: Essays in Honor of J.H. Mundy.* Julius Kirschner and Suzanne Wemple, eds. (New York: Oxford University Press, 1986), 208.

66. See the two studies on the support of the Spiritual Franciscans during the Neapolitan reign of King Robert the Wise and Queen Sancia of Majorca by Ronald G. Musto, "Franciscan Joachimism at the Court of Naples, 1309-1345: A New Appraisal," *Archivum Franciscanum Histroicum* 90 (1997): pp. 419-486; and "Queen Sancia of Naples (1286-1345) and The Spiritual Franciscans," in *Women of the Medieval World,* pp.179-214.

67. Felice Tocco, ed., "Il Processo dei Guglielmiti," *Rendiconti Della Reale Accademia dei Lincei: Classe di Scienze Morali, Storiche e Filologiche,* ser. 5, Vol. 8 (Rome 1899), 334.

68. Muraro, 145-150; Newman, *From Virile Woman to Woman Christ,* 187-189.

69. Newman, *From Virile Woman to Woman Christ,* 184.

70. Ibid.

71. Newman, *God and the Goddesses,* 249.

72. For a concise and accessible account of the changing nature of European and American scholarship on Cola di Rienzo from the Enlightenment to the present, see the fine introductory chapter in Ronald G. Musto, *Apocalypse in Rome: Cola di Rienzo and the Politics of the New Age.* (Berkeley and Los Angeles: University of California Press, 2003), 1-21.

73. From the anonymous vita Romana written during the fourteenth century available in a definitive English version as *The Life of Cola di Rienzo.* Medieval Sources in Translation, No. 18. John Wright, Trans. (Toronto: Pontifical Institute of Medieval Studies, 1975), 31.

74. Musto, *Apocalypse in Rome,* 25-27.

75. Ibid. 29-30; 34-37.

76. *Life of Cola di Rienzo*, 31.

77. Amanda Collins, *Greater than Emperor: Cola di Rienzo (ca. 1313-54) and the World of Fourteenth Century Rome*. (Ann Arbor: University of Michigan Press, 2002), 206.

78. Ibid.

79. Ibid.

80. *Life of Cola di Rienzo*, 32.

81. Ibid.

82. Ibid.

83. Ibid. 33.

84. Ibid. 40.

85. Ibid.

86. Ibid. 41.

87. Ibid. 41-43.

88. Ibid. 44.

89. Ibid. 69-74.

90. Ibid. 81-82.

91. Ibid. 93.

92. The main source of compilation and information on Cola's correspondence is Annibale Gabrielli, ed. *Epistolaria di Cola di Rienzo* (Rome: Forzani, 1890).

93. See the excellent second chapter, *"Plus Quam Imperator:* King of Kings, Lord of Lords?" In Collins, *Greater than Emperor*, 60-100.

94. Ibid. 23.

95. *Life of Cola di Rienzo*, 128.

96. Ibid. 135.

97. Ibid. 137-142.

98. Ibid. 147-148.

99. I must confess to being influenced, in this concluding statement, by the tone of Luigi Barzini's fascinating chapter, "Cola di Rienzo or the Obsession of Antiquity," (117-132). In Barzini's popular post-World War II book intended as a travel guide for English-speaking tourists seeking native Italianate opinions about Italy's history and different cultural regions, *The Italians*. (London: Hamish Hamilton, 1964).

100. *Greater than Emperor*, 100.

CHAPTER 4:
THE SPIRIT OF PENTECOST
IN THE REFORMATION

But if we hope for what we do not see, we wait for it with patience. Likewise the Spirit helps us in our weakness; for we do not know how to pray as we ought, but the Spirit himself intercedes for us with sighs too deep for words. And he who searches the hearts of men, knows what is the mind of the Spirit, because the Spirit intercedes for the saints according to the will of God.

Luthe

Romans 8: 25-27

I believe that I cannot by my own reason or strength believe in Jesus Christ, my Lord, or come to Him, but the Holy Spirit has called me by the Gospel, enlightened me with His gifts, sanctified and kept me in the true faith; even as He calls, gathers, enlightens, and sanctifies the whole Christian Church on earth, and keeps it with Jesus Christ in the one true faith; in which Christian Church, He daily and richly forgives all sins to me and all believers, and will at the Last Day raise up me and all the dead, and give unto me and all believers in Christ eternal life. This is most certainly true.

Martin Luther
Small Catechism, Third Article

The meaning of a tradition changes as it makes its way through history. For this reason, no single interpretation of a tradition is 'correct in itself.' A tradition is many things, some of them good and others bad, some to be judged true and others false. The variety of things that a tradition is, that is, the multitude of possibilities that it harbors, become known as these potentials are actualized in history.

Delwin Brown
Boundaries of Our Habitations[1]

As surveyed in the preceding chapters, imaginative visions of Pentecost and the Holy Spirit were common in the private and public lives of European Christians during the twelfth, thirteenth, and fourteenth centuries. Despite the trouble caused by radical Christian factions claiming special liberative dispensations through the Holy Spirit, like the French Cathars or the Brethren of the Free Spirit, and despite the emergence of the "new philosophy" (*via Moderna*) advocated by Italian and Northern Humanism, the divergent pneumatological trajectories of the Christian Church continued generating prophetic leaders and spiritual seekers during the fifteenth and sixteenth centuries. By the end of the 1400s, political and military power in Europe had shifted away from the Holy Roman Empire and the Italian peninsula towards the rapidly growing nation-states of Spain, France, and England. Hence, in contrast with the Italianate preoccupation of the previous chapter, the socio-political landscape inhabited by the protagonists who appear in the following pages is set amidst the religious and international turmoil that pitted the growing power of the Spanish Empire against the declining fortunes of the Holy Roman Empire. At the time the empire was dealing with the German nobility, who supported the Lutheran Reformation, while simultaneously opposing Spain's global ambitions and attempted manipulation of the Papacy. The verse from Romans cited above was one of Luther's favorite Bible passages. As an Augustinian monk, Martin Luther (1483-1546) understood the implications of the "new philosophy" of Humanism for his times as well as the need to revitalize the Church of his day by looking backwards to the origins of Christianity (*ad fontes*) in yet another theological reconstruction of the Christian tradition. Luther's emphasis on *sola Scriptura* as the basis for Christian ecclesiastical, theological, and pedagogical renewal was shared by most of the reformers of the 1500s and early 1600s. He was also not alone in his conviction that there were lessons yet to be learned or unearthed in the New Testament origins of the Church, in the Christian Humanism of Augustine, and in the egalitarian Spirit of the early Christian movement.

The period of the Protestant Reformation, and the Catholic Reformation that surfaced in response to the former, serves as a model case study of the theory of tradition articulated by theologian Delwin Brown in *Boundaries of Our Habitations*. Each of these reformation movements, together with the often misunderstood Radical Reformation, understood pneumatology and the Holy Spirit in very different ways than interpreted by modern and postmodern scholarship on the history of Christianity. Indeed, we have not done a very effective job of either analyzing or fully comprehending what historian Peter Matheson, identifies as "the imaginative world of the Reformation,"[2] in a book of the same title which we will have occasion to discuss later in this chapter. In this case our collective aporia stems from an excessive emphasis on the history of doctrine and Christian thought when writing and rewriting the history of the Protestant Reformation from the late 1800s throughout much of the twentieth century. There was a time when one could simply trace the discursive trajectories of a "doctrine" or theological idea and call this "church history" or offer it up to one's students and colleagues, and ministerial readers as a typical "chapter" in the history of Christianity. What was missing from this approach was an emphasis on the "social logic" from which all Christian doctrines and theological ideas emerged; an understanding of the social and cultural history that rendered all such "ideas" and "doctrines" as texts constructed by specific persons who inhabited a particular place and time. This is not to say, that Christian ideas and doctrines possess no objective validity or that such concepts did not represent a major trajectory in the intellectual history of the Medieval European world.

However, there is another well-established trajectory in the history of Christianity represented by the ebb and flow of medieval "revivals of learning" that alternated with the variety of attempts at "ecclesiastical reform." These twin strands in medieval Christianity were exemplified in the context of those times by the related principles of *renovatio* and *reforma*, potent ideals that were then bequeathed to the Renaissance and Reformation movements. Hence the Italian Renaissance, in its fifteenth century Florentine phase, set in motion a "revival of learning" aimed at renewing Greek and Latin grammatical studies across Europe as the basis for the study of the ancient Classics and the New Testament, which eventually influenced the ecclesiastical reformism and vernacular literacy that Protestantism undertook in the early sixteenth century. The rallying cry of Renaissance Humanism, *ad fontes*, meaning "To the Sources," found its corollary in Protestant notions about an ecclesiastical "Return to Origins" and the primacy of Scripture as the guiding light for the faithful. These ideals were later summed up by John Calvin (1509-1564) and his followers in the dictum: "*Eccelsia reformata, semper reformanda secundum verbi Dei.*" These twin characteristics of medieval civilization, *renovatio* and *reforma*, were exposed by Steven Ozment, in *The Age of Reform,* as continuations of different yet interrelated social, political, and religious assumptions about "reforming" the Church and "reviving" Antiquity.[3] Ozment's articulate analysis of how the Reformation and Renaissance agendas of transformation denote identifiable and persistent tendencies in the intellectual and religious history of medieval and early modern Christendom parallels nicely with this volume's application of Delwin Brown's theory of tradition as perpetually constructing and reconstructing religious identity and traditions from the resources of the past.

For this reason Delwin Brown's theory of religious tradition, *constructive historicism*, with its awareness of the flow of religious history across time and place as ever recurring and divergent reconstructions of liturgy and ritual, text and canon, or symbol and institution, resonates so effectively with the imaginative role that pneumatological ideas and sensibilities have played among Christian visionaries and reformers, especially in the various reform movements and figures surveyed in this chapter. As Brown observes:

The conceptual reconstruction of a tradition's past is inextricably tied to the affective life of that tradition. If history cannot live without creativity and creativity without history, neither can they live long apart from the affections, for feeling and thought in interaction serve as the vehicle of a tradition's recovery and innovation. This does not necessarily mean that every effective theologian must be a believer; quite obviously the sensitive observer, too, can contribute to the reconstruction of a tradition's inherited symbols. But it does mean that the ongoing task of theological construction will falter unless it somehow has vital roots in practicing religious communities that allow it both to draw upon and contribute to the imaginative play within the tradition. Whether or not he or she is a believer, the theologian is an artist as well as a critic of tradition, seeking to discern the varied conceptual possibilities apparent within the lived realities of a tradition, formulating and elaborating these potentialities, evaluating them in terms of the needs of the community and the broader arenas of critical discourse, thus advocating some variants over others and, finally, serving in ways appropriate to the individual theologian's circumstance the integration of these reconstructions back into the felt practices of the community from which they originated.[4]

The agendas of the Protestant Reformation and of the Catholic Reformation, programs of *renovatio* and *reforma,* as well as discourses about *restauratio* (restoration) were each, in their own local and trans-local contexts, "processes of creating, sustaining, and recreating viable individual and communal identities."[5] Indeed, as Brown noted in an essay published about a decade after *Boundaries of Our Habitations*: "Effective change . . . requires the reconstruction of inheritance."[6] While the effectiveness of the Protestant and Catholic Reformations is not a central concern of this study, each movement's focus on the role of pneumatological ideas and sensibilities in opening up European Christendom's theological imagination for ecclesiastical and pedagogical reform speaks to the "persistent power of the past in the formation of the present," a quality that also characterized the pneumatological aspects of Renaissance thought and culture.

Although Steven Ozment's *The Age of Reform* (1980) and Bard Thompson's monumental study, *Humanists and Reformers* (1996)[7] convinced me years ago that the Renaissance and the Reformation are undeniably intertwined as regards root causes and historical effects, the influence of pneumatological ideas and sensibilities about Nature, stemming from late medieval Christian magical theology (*theologia magica Christiana*), on the rise of scientific thought and experimentation in the seventeenth century warrants discussion in a separate chapter. Hence, the role of pneumatological ideas and visions of Pentecost in fifteenth century Humanism and the Florentine Renaissance, and among the precursors and founders of the Scientific Revolution will be treated separately in Chapter Five.

My understanding of the complementary trajectories of ecclesiastical reform and pedagogical revival in the history of Christianity includes recognizing the reality of the other element so often ignored or left out of the picture by modern and postmodern scholarship. Namely, the historicized continuities and discontinuities by which medieval and early modern discourses of *renovatio* or *reforma* were accompanied by pneumatological ideas and sensibilities calling for the restoration (*restauratio*) of Christ's Church to a state akin to the Spirit of the first Pentecost. In the 1500s and early 1600s, this vision was closely related to the heart of what the Protestant Reformation, and the so-called Radical Reformation, understood when each, in different ways, argued for a "Return to Origins," or when reformers like Martin Luther argued for the primacy of *sola Scriptura*. In other words, although Luther did not present himself as a pneumatological visionary, and persistently warned his followers against the excesses of pietistic radicals and spiritual "enthusiasts," by invoking questions of Christian origins and *sola Scriptura* he rekindled the "*subversive fire*" that lays dormant in the story of Pentecost and in the broader outlines of Christian tradition. By the time Luther pinned his *95 Theses* to the door of Wittenberg Cathedral on October 31, 1517, this pneumatological tradition was firmly anchored in centuries of Christian discursive understandings about the cycles of the liturgical calendar, prophetic leadership, human flourishing, and ecclesiastical revitalization through the intercessory agency of the Holy Spirit.

This chapter examines the role of Pentecost and the Holy Spirit in the theological reconstructions and ecclesiastical agendas of the Protestant and Roman Catholic Reformation movements of the 1500s and early 1600s. After briefly discussing the comingling of suspicion and reverence for the role of pneumatology in the theological beliefs and socio-political agendas of the major Protestant reformers, Martin Luther and John Calvin, the present chapter's attention turns to the lives and careers of two radical reformers whose dramatic clashes with their mainline Protestant colleagues led to some of the most intriguing and violently contested early modern examples of Christianity's Pentecostal legacy: Thomas Müntzer (1490-1525) and Michael Servetus (ca. 1511-1553). Although Thomas Müntzer and Martin Luther shared a mutual interest in the teachings of the fourteenth century Dominican monk, Johann Tauler (ca. 1300-1361), they eventually became bitter rivals over questions of social justice and church reform rooted in their different understandings of pneumatology, religious authority, and the plight of the German peasants. Michael Servetus clashed so severely with John Calvin over questions of spiritual liberation and Trinitarian doctrine that in 1553 Servetus was tried and executed for heresy at Geneva.

Furthermore, in the mid-1500s and early 1600s the Latin Church of Western Europe responded to both, its unfinished reformist agenda and the perceived challenges of Protestantism, by launching its own religious and pedagogical revitalization project known as the Catholic Reformation. In the second half of this chapter, the conversation shifts to the role of pneumatological modes of thought and piety in the lives and careers of Roman Catholic reformers from Spain such as Ignatius of Loyola, Teresa of Avila and John of the Cross. As Roman Catholic leaders, religious visionaries, and educational pioneers each of these Spaniards exerted a profound influence on the future of Christendom. While earlier medieval reform efforts centered on Joachimite pneumatological inspiration, or mystical visions of Pentecost, and represented identifiable and persistent trajectories in Christian tradition, the Protestant and the Roman Catholic Reformation movements, and their splinter movements, sparked a series of theological reconstructions and innovations whose effects are still part of global Christianity today. This is especially true in the domain of modern Roman Catholic piety and pedagogy which has been profoundly influenced by the dissemination of works by Teresa of Avila and John of the Cross, which for decades have been popular among both general readers and scholars in fields like church history, religious studies, and the academic study of spirituality. The same is true of the widespread influence of Jesuit education, social service programs, and Ignatian piety as fostered through the publication, dissemination, and practice of *The Spiritual Exercises*.

TAULER'S INFLUENCE ON THE REFORMATION

Although the name of the fourteenth century Dominican monk, Johannes Tauler (ca. 1300-1361), is relatively unknown today outside of academic and theological circles, his ideas about Pentecost and the Holy Spirit exerted a significant influence on subsequent European Christian piety and on the spirituality of the Protestant Reformation. One could even build a case with sufficient evidence arguing that Tauler's influence even reached Spanish mystics of the Catholic Reformation like John of the Cross,[8] and perhaps Spanish Protestant writers like Juan de Valdes.[9] As Protestantism moved further and further away from Roman Catholicism in the late sixteenth and early seventeenth centuries, Protestantism's historical emphasis on Tauler's sermons and mystical ideas functioning as a sort of late medieval precursory theology of its own reformist piety, drove his works and influence from popular Roman Catholic memory in Germany and other parts of early modern Europe. The collaborative censorship of Pope Paul IV and Bishop Fernando de Valdés of the Spanish Inquisition led to the infamous Valdes Index of 1559 that banned Tauler's works, along with those of other German mystics, by mistakenly associating his pneumatological ideas with charges of Lutheranism then widespread in both Spain and Italy. Ironically, Tauler's name and devotional piety had been well-known among Italian and Spanish readers of Latin before these repressive measures took effect.

Tauler is regarded as one of the three most important medieval German mystics, a position he shares with Meister Eckhart (ca. 1260-1328) and Heinrich Suso (ca. 1295-1366).[10] Tauler probably first met Eckhart around 1315 when he enrolled in the Dominican novitiate at Strasbourg. His education was also influenced by extensive readings of St. Thomas Aquina's *Summa theologiae*, classical Neoplatonism, and the works of St. Augustine. About a decade later, however, Eckhart taught and mentored both Tauler and Suso while the two young men were enrolled in the *studium generale* at Cologne. Some of the surviving historical accounts suggest that Tauler was more popular than his teacher, Eckhart. Unfortunately Tauler's mentor was accused of heresy in 1327 by Pope John XXII. Eckhart died the following year.

Eckhart's troubles with the Inquisition began with Dominican leaders at Cologne who were concerned about his growing popularity among the uneducated German laity for whom he allegedly preached in the vernacular, and for whom he occasionally translated sermons from Latin into Middle High German so that they might fully receive and understand the Lord's message through this service. Indeed it was a fellow Dominican and Bishop of Cologne, Henry of Virneburg, who convened the inquisitorial commission that brought the initial charges of heresy against Eckhart's teachings. For the remainder of their earthly lives, Suso and Tauler were haunted and disturbed in different ways by the memory of their beloved teacher's heartbreaking demise at the hands of Christian leaders, a deep sadness and lamentation that might have led each of them to profound disillusionment with religious and secular authorities. This is a theme that scholars have noted more so among Suso's emotional and abstract writings than among Tauler's more emotionally balanced and highly popular sermons.

However, the historical evidence portrays a picture of Tauler as an outstanding and extremely popular preacher for whom spiritual humility and profound faith in the power of the Holy Spirit to transform human anxiety and suffering into the joys of a soul aligned with God's love and mercy were the driving convictions of his ministerial career. Perhaps his even temperament and pastoral position as a spiritual director prevented an over fixation on the growing corruption and worldliness of the Church, or perhaps his teacher's tragic end convinced him to avoid the intellectual and Scholastic world of the universities in favor of serving as a local minister and inspiring preacher among the German laity and among his Dominican brothers and sisters in the towns of Strasbourg, Cologne, and Basel, where he spent most of his life. Tauler seems to have been preaching and writing in the German vernacular long before other German scholars and theologians of his times began moving away from disseminating their ideas and teachings strictly in Latin. Following Ferdinand Vetter's 1910 critical edition of Tauler's sermons and minor works, a sizeable portion of works previously attributed to him were shown to be the work of others who knew him well, or of other writers who regarded themselves as followers of his teachings about the Holy Spirit and about personal spiritual development. Ironically, the humble simplicity of Tauler's ideas, and his abidingly strong pneumatological counsel, led many Reformation era readers in the 1500s to interpret him as a late medieval Roman Catholic precursor of their Protestant ideals and piety.

Setting aside this contested pseudo-Taulerian corpus as a source of evidence about Tauler's conception of Pentecost and the Spirit is not a major problem because his surviving sermons offer a wealth of mystical concepts and spiritual advice penned for his hearers who were wondering about their relationship to the Word through the Holy Spirit. At first Tauler's sermons were disseminated in handwritten form across the Rhine region and other areas of Germany from notes taken possibly by persons who sat in the pews while he preached at Strasbourg, Cologne, or Basel during his lifetime. His sermons became available to the Renaissance and Reformation eras first through an edition printed at Leipzig in 1498, which was followed by a reprint of the same text at Augsburg in 1505. It was the Latin version of his sermons, however, that won the late Dominican preacher a widespread following across Europe in the sixteenth, seventeenth, and eighteenth centuries.

Tauler's pedagogical approach and spiritual counsel in these sermons is fascinating because, unlike Eckhart's more poetic and intellectually abstract approach, Tauler emphasizes practical approaches and methods for attaining what he sometimes called: "The Birth of God as Word in the Soul." His sermons are filled with references to the soul of the believer as the "Ground" that needed to be readied to receive the "Spark of the Soul" through the Holy Spirit following long periods of silence and stillness along with concentrated prayer practices. Hearing these teachings in German must have been a very empowering experience for the laity and the lower clergy who frequently attended his sermons in large numbers. He also made sure to keep the heavenly realm of God separate from the terrestrial realm of the human creature, an approach which kept the

Inquisition and Papal authorities from hearing Tauler's message as either prone to mystical hubris or heretical.

Nonetheless, the central message about Christian piety and duty conveyed in Tauler's sermons is about the transformation of the believer through the power of the Word and the Holy Spirit for the fulfillment of Christ's redemptive and liberating mission through the Church. Evelyn Underhill once described Tauler's sermons as "trumpet calls to heroic action on spiritual levels,"[11] while Alois Haas observed in the preface to the Paulist Press edition of Tauler's sermons that his "impact on the whole of Europe has not yet found the expression commensurate with its rank."[12] Reading through Tauler's sermons, one is stuck by how closely his pastoral themes parallel the stages and seasons of the liturgical calendar, and by his special fondness for the presence of the Holy Spirit in both the Christian life and the natural world. He believed with deep fervor that the Holy Spirit would come into the human soul, just as it had been poured out on all flesh and filled the entire house on the day of Pentecost. This Tauler maintained would come to pass so long as the individual believer prepared himself or herself through prayer, silence and stillness, and by turning away from the anxieties and greed of the material world. Tauler's sermons written for the weeks from Ascension through Pentecost demonstrate a gradually increasing emphasis on preparing one's self to receive the Holy Spirit in commemoration of the event that began the Christian Church on Pentecost Sunday. Then, as this infusion of the Spirit remains ever-open to all true believers, Tauler encouraged both laity and clergy to begin their soul's journey of transformation by successively receiving each of the seven gifts of the Holy Spirit. Here we have further proof of how the seven-times-seven days of Whitsuntide served as a season for both festal remembrance and encouraging prayerful reflection and deep piety among the laity.

This style of preaching also served as a bridge between the doctrinal teaching roles of local clergy and the formation of lay piety with an emphasis on religious practice and spiritual experience that few laypersons could access outside the walls of monastic communities. Tauler advocated "an absolute surrender to God" and a "true poverty of spirit according to the will of God" in the hearts and minds of the faithful as "true witnesses" who "are firmly anchored in Him."[13] One gets the impression from these sermons that Tauler genuinely believed mystical states of awareness and loving union with God were not just reserved for saints, monks, and cloistered nuns, but were the inheritance of all true Christians who practiced silence and stillness while waiting patiently with open hearts and minds for a personal Pentecost.

Tauler's Sermon 24 for the Monday before Pentecost, based on a passage from the Epistle of Peter (1 Peter 4: 8), demonstrates Tauler's sense of how the Holy Spirit empties the individual's soul even as it infuses each soul with the joy and power of the Spirit's fullness through God's grace. This particular sermon, with its rich naturalistic imagery, is also a fine example why his preaching style was recorded by chroniclers as being very popular among both the laity and the clergy. It also reminds us of the medieval meditative practice of preparing yourself, imaginatively and prayerfully, to receive the outpouring of the Holy Spirit each year as one's religious life journeyed in rhythmic observance through the seasons and feast days of the liturgical calendar, which in this instance represented the approaching culmination of the seven-times-seven days of Whitsuntide nine days after Ascension Sunday. Tauler cites the Latin text of the New Testament: *"estote prudentes et vigilate in orationibus,"* which is a call to live wisely as one gathers the senses together in deep prayer. Tauler states:

> And since we are now approaching the lovely feast of the Holy Spirit, we should prepare ourselves with all our strength to receive Him with a heart abounding in holy desire. As we said yesterday, we must search,   in a spirit of discernment, whether there is perhaps anything in our actions and in our lives that is not of God. We mentioned that this   preparation falls into four parts: detachment, abandonment, inwardness, and single-mindedness. Furthermore, it is necessary that the outer man be at peace with them and well versed in the natural virtues, the lower faculties governed by the moral virtues, after which the Holy Spirit will adorn the higher faculties with infused virtues. All this must, of course, be ordered and directed by true discernment and applied to our lives by the light of reason. Let everyone examine, first, whether his life is wholly directed toward God, and should he discover anything in his actions that is not, let him correct it.[14]

Having explained the urgency of this attitude of mind and spirit as the Feast of Pentecost approaches, Tauler then calls upon an agricultural metaphor, which is as interesting to modern readers for its naturalistic symbolism as it must have been at that time to its medieval listeners for its pneumatological spring-time significance. He urges the congregation to proceed in these spiritual, inner tasks "like a farmer who in March sets out to prepare his ground; when he sees the sun climbing higher, he trims his trees, he pulls up the weeds, and turn over the ground, digging diligently. In the same manner we should work deeply into our ground, examine it, and turn it over thoroughly."[15] Hence each year as the annual commemoration of Eastertide in March or April comes and then gives way to the annual cycle of Whitsuntide in May or early June, the individual follower of Christ needs to prune his or her trees and pull up the weeds that interfere with the fertile ground into which Christ's Holy Spirit soon shall be infused on Pentecost. "Now is the time for the divine sun to shine upon the well-prepared ground . . . a downright may-blossoming is about to unfold. The gracious, eternal God permits the spirit to green and bloom and bring forth the most marvelous fruit, surpassing anything a tongue can express and a heart can conceive. Such is the rapture that arises within the spirit."[16] In language reminiscent of our earlier discussions in Chapter Two about Pentecost, the "greening" of the Spirit, and the "merrie month of May," Tauler explains that this "ecstasy the Holy Spirit so richly and generously bestows as a gift on the well-prepared soul" as he blends naturalistic and pneumatological imagery before exclaiming: "May has arrived and stands in full bloom."[17]

Tauler's exposition about this type of religious or spiritual experience then takes a turn and offers a warning about the effects of this high-voltage incident on one's affective and cognitive state. He cautions that human nature is all too prone towards either immersing one's self in this altered state, or prefers falling

asleep in it and becoming intoxicated by the ecstasy and empowerment that being filled by the Spirit offers our finite nature. This tendency, he emphatically
suggests, must be resisted for the Holy Spirit can neither be contained nor possessed in this self-centered way. Tauler then refers to the even more serious
problem of allowing the senses and the mind to be tricked into falsely believing
that one has been infused with a special spiritual freedom that sets one apart
from the norms of society or from the will of God. This, he suggests, is what
Saint Peter meant when he advised us to live wisely and keep our senses awake
so that the Christian believer might prepare himself or herself to receive the
Seven Gifts of the Holy Spirit just as the disciples were all filled with the Spirit's presence and power on the day of Pentecost.[18]

In this, and several other sermons about Pentecost, Tauler communicated a
consistent message that the abyss of the human soul when encased in the body
and governed by the senses is very deep, a chasm of nothingness, made all the
worse, by the moral and physical temptation of the Seven Deadly Sins. However, the Holy Spirit's propensity towards making all things full, and towards connecting the human and the divine realms of being, transforms the human heart
and mind in such a way that the abyss is filled by divine love and mercy so that
the soul reflects the light of God and embodies the piety and righteousness of
Jesus Christ. Given the popularity of his mystical preaching, and the widespread
appeal of his ideas about the Holy Spirit, it is ironic that Tauler's cautionary
message about the need for being grounded in humility and prudence when
working on one's inner life was not heeded by more of the pneumatological visionaries, theological reformers, and religious leaders we will meet later in this
chapter.

AUTHORITY AND SPIRIT IN THE REFORMATION

Protestantism found in the Holy Scriptures, what it believed was an impregnable
rampart against the powerful institution of the Roman Pontiffs and the steadfast
hierarchy of the Papal Court. However, the innovations and theological reconstructions of Christian tradition advocated by the Protestant Reformation, the
vast majority of which were rooted in visions of Pentecost, or in the liberating
power of the Holy Spirit, also had the effect of sparking the Christian imagination in ways that Europe's entrenched social, economic, and political power
structures were incapable of handling. The repeated failures of the Papacy and
Conciliarism to effectively restructure the Roman Church's leadership and educational structures, and mitigate their dubious relations with the growing economic and military power of late medieval nation-states, like France and Spain,
paved the way for the rise of revolutionary Christian movements like the Protestant Reformation that erupted in Germany. The Roman Catholic Reformation
also surfaced in Spain under reformers like Ignatius of Loyola, Teresa of Avila,
and John of the Cross. Given the empowering legacy of the story of Pentecost in
the personal and ecclesiastical lives of Christian believers, and considering the
strife that emerged among Martin Luther, John Calvin, and Ulrich Zwingli, it is
not surprising that the Reformation era also witnessed the spread of the Spirit of

Pentecost's *"subversive fire"* through radical visionaries like Thomas Müntzer, the Anabaptists, and Michael Servetus. Far from wishing to purify both church and state in a wildfire of the Spirit, these figures and movements sincerely hoped for the emergence of a church and state capable of finally living into the liberating and egalitarian promises of the Gospel story. Since one of the common images for the Spirit is that of "fire," we could interpret the dark side of the Reformation's outpouring of spiritual insight and ecclesiastical discontent through the phrase: "Too hot to handle." But the historical realities that derailed Protestantism's promises of reform, liberation, and combating evil were infinitely more complex than this. In the end the old attitudes and prejudices about institutional unity, cultural homogeneity, and doctrinal conformity reasserted themselves in the new structures of ecclesiastical authority and social cohesion that Protestant and Roman Catholic reformation communities developed after 1520.

In *The Imaginative World of the Reformation*, historian Peter Matheson revisits the stories and legacies of the Protestant era, by "seeing it less as a doctrinal shift or structural upheaval, though it was both of these, than as an event in the imagination."[19] This landmark study's novel approach resonates with the creative possibilities I contend are always contained in and transmitted across time and place through the story of Pentecost. It also indirectly serves as a reminder of the transformative power believers ascribe to the Holy Spirit, and which we see reflected in both the private and public lives of Christian laity and clergy throughout the history of Christianity. As observed in Brown's theory of tradition: "The conceptual reconstruction of a tradition's past is *inextricably tied to the affective life of that tradition*. If history cannot live without creativity and creativity without history, neither can live long apart from the affections, for feeling and thought in interaction serve as the vehicle of a tradition's recovery and innovation," (emphasis added).[20] Although not familiar with Brown's theological work, Matheson, nonetheless, is aware of how the Enlightenment and nineteenth century Romanticism generated an interpretive modification of the Reformation heritage, and cites Jaroslav Pelikan's *The Vindication of Tradition* (1984) on the question of traditions that are alive and vibrant versus the ideological and stultifying nature of "traditionalism."[21] Matheson contends that the heightened role of *imagination* in the different Reformation discourses of change and revolt indicates a dramatic sixteenth-century "shift in the basic paradigms through which people perceived their world,"[22] a shift which he traces through the art and literature, popular songs, apocalyptic expectations, and rhetoric about the future recorded in extant letters and diaries, and in some of the colloquial phrases of the period such as "stirring the brew" or "joining the dance." Coming to terms with this paradigmatic shift is for Matheson a necessary step for any postmodern historian intent on getting "closer to" the "deeper level" of the mental and affective world that underlay "The Spirituality of the Reformation," which is also the title of the concluding chapter of his highly original and thought provoking exploration of the period.[23]

Throughout the research and writing of this book, I have been deeply intrigued, on the one hand, by the interplay of the personal and the collective aspects of religious imagination with the pneumatological inspiration generated by the story of Pentecost. On the other hand, I have also been deeply disturbed by the persistent tendency toward doctrinal intolerance and religious violence among the ecclesiastical and secular authorities whose sense of duty and fear of change were obviously stirred into over reaction by the dreams of the pneumatological visionaries under investigation. The Reformation era offers us many examples of such adverse reactions and socio-political dysfunction. Matheson is acutely aware of the dark side of the Reformation and emphatically suggests that,

> There may perhaps be no access to the heritage of the Reformation until we come to terms with its nightmarish dimensions, its divisiveness and destructive polemic, for example. It is not acceptable that central issues such as the witch-hunt or the drift into confessional warfare tend to be left to historians of culture and kept outside the purview of the church historian. Some 30,000 witches, the great majority women, died in the witch-craze. Religious intolerance was manifested in fierce disputes about doctrine and sharp controls on publishing and freedom of speech. Religious massacres and religious wars became the order of the day for more than a hundred years. Why did the great hopes for *besserung*, liberation from evil, death and sin, appear to have ended like this?[24]

The German word *"besserung"* literally means "improvement." Despite the tragedies of the sixteenth century Reformation, during the late 1400s and early 1500s reform minded Christians throughout the German principalities of the Holy Roman Empire used it as an expression of their hopeful expectations for the future against the painfully real memories of recurrent plagues and costly feudal wars that punctuated their memories of the recent past.

The oppression and bloodshed spawned by religious intolerance, is one of the most bewildering aspects of the Reformation, which we will discuss and ponder later in this chapter through the case studies of Luther versus his colleague Thomas Müntzer, and Calvin versus the medical doctor turned radical reformer Michael Servetus. Matheson reminds us that, as fervor for reform and renewal increased and spread across Christendom, the tension between liberative leadership and reactionary authority clashed with the conflicting alliances that characterized late medieval society and the "whole batteries of competing Utopias" jostling for adherents and sovereignty alongside each other "as the battle for the mind and the battle for power were joined."[25] Commenting on this confused state of affairs, he asks: "The poets, artists, thinkers and dreamers who relied on the power of the imagination may have trusted in its creativity, but what happened when their advocacy of justice, freedom, light, covenantal values and the living Word of God subverted the academy, encouraged insubordinate attitudes to the magistrate or magisterium, urged the obsolescence of private property and questioned gender roles?[26]" Matheson concludes his discussion of the Reformation's "nightmarish dimensions"[27] by wisely stating that: "As historians we have a duty to honour the memory of the dreamers, to note that the dreams of some become the nightmares of others, and to take care that we do not perpetuate injustice by adopting uncritically the terminology of the oppressor."[28] Sobered by Matheson's wise counsel, we next turn our attention to the Radical

Reformers whose religious imaginations and political agendas were thoroughly imbued with the *subversive fire* of the Spirit of Pentecost.

THE CASE OF THOMAS MÜNTZER, (CA. 1490-1525)

Not far from the same area in Thuringia where the German poet-knight, Wolfram von Eschenbach, wrote his famous Grail romances and served local royal patrons, lays the village of Stohlberg in the Harz Mountains. Although not much about his biographical details is certain, Thomas Müntzer always claimed his family was from Stohlberg, where he was born sometime before 1491, and which, ironically, was located just several miles from, Eisleben, where Martin Luther had been born less than ten years before him. Very little is known concerning his parent's background, his childhood and family life, or about his early educational instruction and religious formation. We know that he attended the University of Leipzig for a short time, and he seems to have been well versed in the study of Hebrew, Greek, and Latin. We also know that he developed a special fondness for the theological and pneumatological ideas of Tauler, whose views on the freedom of the Spirit and the transformation of the world would play a decisive role in his radical break with the Lutheran Reformation.[29] Müntzer appears in the historical record most clearly when he became a student at the University of Frankfurt an der Oder in 1512. He was later ordained into the Catholic priesthood in 1513 and served as chaplain, confessor, and itinerant preacher until about 1518 or 1519 before his first major appointment at Zwickau in Saxony. His personality has been described as fiery, courageous, dynamic, and ambiguous. Thomas Müntzer probably met Martin Luther while preaching in Wittenberg, and by all accounts was an early admirer and supporter of Luther's ideas and reforms until their tragic disagreements led to both civil war and execution.

Recovering a clear picture of this sixteenth century German Catholic priest turned radical reformer is not an easy task. The changing and contested picture of Thomas Müntzer among historians and theologians, or socialist and communist revolutionaries, has not made the recovery and interpretation of his romanticized life and writings an easy task. All of these competing discourses about his life and work have been raging since his death in 1525. He was for a long time carefully studied by a wide range of socialist revolutionaries and communist theorists ranging from the former East German Republic to the former State of Czechoslovakia, and simultaneously vilified by generations of Protestant and Roman Catholic theologians for waging a utopian inspired war against the clergy and nobility as a "minister of Christ" during the Peasant's War of 1525. The romanticizing of Müntzer's political activism dates back to Karl Marx and Friedrich Engels who in the 1880s began the Marxist discursive tradition of interpreting his career as an early bourgeois revolution championing the needs of the common people in Reformation Germany, an interpretive model that was later expanded by scholars and propagandists in the German Democratic Republic of East Germany. Studies of Müntzer have the effect of polarizing both scholarly and ministerial opinions.[30] Indeed, as observed by Hans-Jürgen Goertz on the

five hundredth anniversary of Müntzer's birth: "Responses to Müntzer are characterized by fascination and repulsion,"[31] which suggests that given the widely
divergent socio-political and religious uses to which his legacy of "revolution
and revelation" has been subjected over the centuries, the recovery and interpretation of his story suffered a fate similar to that of the fourteenth century Italian
pneumatological revolutionary, Cola di Rienzo. Some readers of Müntzer's legacy have hailed him as the founder of evangelical Anabaptism,[32] while others
have resisted this claim since he was nearly dead and gone from the religio-
political scene when Anabaptism gained momentum among the Reformation's
more radical strains of non-conformists and activists whom Luther tried to dis-
credit by branding them mystical fanatics (*Schwärmer*) or spiritual "enthusiasts."

Despite the controversial images of Thomas Müntzer that have come down
to us over the past five centuries, images of a militant apocalyptic minister of the
Holy Spirit juxtaposed with images of early modern Europe's first socialist revolutionary, he fits the description of the type of pneumatological visionary articulated in this book's opening chapter. And, from that perspective, I offer this
reading of Müntzer's life and work as a reformist visionary who looked back to
the first Pentecost as a repository of Christian ecclesiastical and spiritual tradition from which the Church might be renewed (*renovatio*) in his times, and from
which the imagination of Pentecost as a liberative trope might offer the raw material for a reconstruction of Christian theology, social justice, and communal
living.

Müntzer's disagreements with Luther over a wide range of theological and
pietistic concerns led both men to major disagreements over the anticipated
reform of the church and society in Germany. Tauler's notion of individual
agency based on the liberative power of the Spirit within the human heart, propelled Müntzer towards an acutely revolutionary reformism comingled with
visions of the apocalyptic role he believed God had ordained for him in the coming transformation of the world. In addition, Luther and Müntzer disagreed on
infant baptism, on the extent of the social and religious reforms needed in Germany, and on the principle of *sola Scriptura,* which for the latter rested on the
equally important conviction that the authority of Scripture was second to God's
acts of direct revelation through the Holy Spirit to the chosen servants and
prophets among the elect. As discussed in this book's earlier chapters, this
pneumatological viewpoint had a history of generating stern resistance from the
Papacy and Roman Catholic authorities throughout the medieval period, and
would eventually ignite Martin Luther's and John Calvin's worst fears about the
euphoric hubris that mystical visionaries and apocalyptic reformers might un-
leash upon society and the churches if their preaching and writings were not
somehow censured by more rational and magisterial reformers like themselves.

In May 1520, during that year's commemoration of the seven-times-seven
days of Pentecost, Müntzer took on a preaching appointment at Saint Mary's
Cathedral in the town of Zwickau, a move which historians have long suspected
was encouraged and approved by his friend and fellow Wittenberg reformer,
Martin Luther. However, Müntzer was dismissed from this position in less than

a year on April 16, 1521 for disturbing the peace through his incendiary preaching against the Franciscans on allegations of church corruption and about state oppression against the local nobility. In his sermons he also praised the power of the Spirit within the ordinary person of humble means over against the hubris of the educated and wealthy clergy. His conviction in the power of the Holy Spirit to grant Christians direct revelation from God through dreams, pneumatic visions, or by speaking directly to the elect in deep prayer and contemplation, disturbed local clergy as well as Luther's growing concerns back in Wittenberg about the dangerous influence of such radical, "enthusiast" factions that were surfacing throughout the German countryside and among some of the larger cities and towns of Saxony.

Müntzer aligned himself with a group of local radicals known as the Zwickau Prophets who were led by Nicolaus Storch. He became increasingly interested in an ecclesiology based on the idea of the Early Church as an egalitarian, pneumatological community that issued forth from the fist Pentecost. This was further complicated by Müntzer's radical departure from Luther's views on the primacy of Scripture in favor of the Zwickau Prophet's insistence on the Holy Spirit's power to transmit direct revelation from God to individual Christian believers, even when these revelations appeared to contradict central tenets of the faith or traditional passages in the Old and New Testaments. From May 1521 to the spring of 1522, Müntzer's preaching inflamed the lower nobility and the poor into the nagging realization that despite all the optimistic chatter in the air about *"besserung"* and *"reforma,"* the power elites across greater Germany, with their dynastic ties to both the expanding Spanish Empire and the aging Holy Roman Empire, were not at all interested in civic or ecclesial actions promoting the liberative gifts of the Holy Spirit.

Scholarly opinion is uncertain of the specific Joachimist texts, Müntzer had access to. He seems to have become familiar, at least, with a portion of the Joachimist corpus while studying at either Leipzig or Frankfurt. His own Joachimist sympathies and mystical sensibilities played a role in his growing conviction that the time of the apocalypse was upon European Christendom. Burgess reports that Müntzer read and studied Joachim of Fiore's "commentary on Jeremiah, from which he came to think of himself as a chosen instrument of God."[33] The three hundred year old Joachimist vision of the approaching *plena Spiritus libertas*, and the equally long-standing debate over the Franciscan Order's role in the transformation of the church and society at large, might also account for Müntzer's vehement preaching against the Franciscans. Indeed, his fervent willingness to replace their traditional role serving the poor with his radicalized ministry among the German peasantry in the areas of Stohlberg and Zwickau, and throughout the rural region of the Harz mountains, is fairly representative of his belief that the Friars Minor had not lived up to their divinely ordained mission.

After the debacle at Zwickau, Müntzer moved to Prague where he continued preaching against oppression and published his "Prague Protestation," also known as the famous *Prague Manifesto,* or as *The Prague Protest.* The city of Prague had made attempts for allowing the existence of a reformed church after the tragic execution of Jan Hus in July 1415 that precipitated the Hussite Wars (ca. 1420-1434). This progressive image of Prague was perhaps also the reason for the general impression that the Kingdom of Bohemia's liberal religious climate surely influenced Müntzer's decision to move there. Müntzer was perhaps also thinking of the symbolic implications of issuing his manifesto from Prague since the very first line references his location as "the city of the precious and holy fighter Jan Hus."[34] Although this short position paper, dated November 25, 1521, was not officially published by Müntzer in his lifetime, manuscript copies of the document addressed to the people of Prague, the capital of the principality of Bohemia, were circulated widely. He refers to the clergy as "thieves," "murderers," "diarrhea-makers," and "a damned people" before identifying them all as "villainous traitors" for undermining the liberative message of the Gospel and the compassionate mission of Christ. The clergy he claims are mute, deaf, and blind to the presence of the Holy Spirit and the vital role that will be entrusted to the elect in the coming apocalypse of the Ant-Christ. The text's accusing, and occasionally vulgar, tone exasperated not only Roman Catholic authorities who sought to curb the spread of Protestantism, but also infuriated the growing center of the Protestant Reformation constellating at Wittenberg around the ministry and leadership of Martin Luther.

Müntzer opens his *Manifesto* with the observation that Prague is a city "filled with the new praise of the Holy Spirit" and claims that "Christ and all of the elect who have known me from my youth on confirm" the reformist project he is about the articulate.[35] He then demonstrates his indebtedness to both late medieval German mysticism and Tauler's pneumatological ideas in these emphatic words aimed at chastising the clergy of his day,

> The clergy have never been able to discover, nor will they ever, the beneficial tribulations and useful abyss that the providential spirit meets as it empties itself. The spirit of the fear of God has never possessed the clergy, but the elect firmly cling to this spirit as their only goal. The elect are submerged and drowned in an outpouring of this spirit (which the world cannot tolerate). In brief, each person must receive the Holy Spirit in a sevenfold way, otherwise he neither hears nor understands the living God.[36]

The fourteenth century Dominican preacher, and student of Meister Eckhart, Johannes Tauler had preached edifying Pentecost sermons and taught that after following a program of spiritual practice and coping with life's suffering the grace of God granted true Christians the sevenfold gifts of the Holy Spirit. Tauler believed these gifts sanctified the soul and equipped the human heart and mind for a life of deep piety, compassion, or leadership serving the spiritual sustenance needs of one's fellow pilgrims. Müntzer in this passage accuses ecclesiastical leaders of not being true Christians for presumably caring little for the pneumatic interiority and social humility that he regards as one of the fruits of being infused with the presence and power of the Holy Spirit. Ironically, Tauler did not believe that such infusions of divine ecstasy or supernatural communication through the Person of the Holy Spirit necessarily led to euphoria, exaltation or sorrow, religious anxiety or apocalyptic frenzy. Instead, when such excesses manifested in the aftermath of pneumatological experiences Tauler believed it indicated the presence of the Devil or demonic influences hovering over the believer's soul and mind.[37] Tauler's spiritual optimism, however, did not know the Reformation from our vantage point, nor would he have understood historian Peter Matheson's perspective about the Reformation's "nightmarish dimensions." Nonetheless for Müntzer and his followers the attainment of divine illumination by the elect through suffering, purification, and revolutionary social and political tribulation was the hallmark of an authentic Christian faith empowered through the gifts of the Holy Spirit.

Müntzer's primary reason for his vehement criticisms of the clergy is that they masquerade as parsons and ministers of Christ while silencing the liberative message of the Pentecost story and the sanctification of the seven gifts of the Holy Spirit. He accuses those priests and parsons whose faith he criticizes as not being "authentic" for being "*geticht*" about their faith, meaning "false" or "counterfeit." In Müntzer's pneumatological conceptions of Scripture and the nature of God, the Holy Spirit and the Word of God are one and the same. Indeed just as the tongues of fire that poured forth at the first Pentecost were the fulfillment of Jesus' promise that he would soon send forth his Holy Ghost so too are Christ and the Father also one and the same. The notion of "knowledge of the heart" was paramount in this radical reformer's theological anthropology for as he read and paraphrased the Scriptures, it convinced him beyond any doubt that: "There is no more certain testimony, as the Bible verifies, than the living speech of God, when the Father speaks to the Son in the hearts of people."[38] From this perspective then, one does not need the church hierarchy, or the machinery of institutional leadership that stretched from Germany and the court of the Holy Roman Empire all the way back to Rome and the Papal Court. It is the clergy's steadfast clinging to worldly pride and wealth along with their apathy for the plight of the poor that Müntzer ardently maintained, prevents so many among their ranks from genuinely hearing the Word of God and authentically knowing the presence of the Holy Spirit in their hearts and minds. This sad state of affairs, presided over by the Devil as the true "father of the clergy" necessitated the coming transformation of the world through the power of the Holy Spirit inspiring the elect who will emerge as the "true shepherds" of Christianity. This kind of rhetoric would lead eventually to violence and civil war.

Müntzer wanted to promote and build a community in which the Word of God was unhindered. By announcing and communicating itself to all true believers of Christ's message, such persons would not have to fear for their well being or safety whenever anyone claimed pneumatological inspiration. He also hoped this reformed community would be one devoid of ecclesiastical corruption, abuses of clerical privilege and power, and secular support for both the elect and for society's disenfranchised members like the peasants and the urban poor whose numbers had been growing in the early 1500s. He concludes his religio-political revolutionary program of revitalization and reform in the *Prague Manifesto* with this fiery and provocative passage:

In order that I may do this properly, I have come into your country, my most beloved Bohemians. I desire from you only that which your diligence should demand, you should study the living word of God out of God's own mouth. Through this you will see, hear, and grasp how the whole world has been seduced by deaf parsons. Help me, for the sake of Christ's blood, to fight against such high enemies of the faith. In the spirit of Elias, I want to ruin them in your eyes. For the new apostolic church will arise first in your land, and afterward, everywhere. I want to be prepared if in church people question me in the pulpit, to do enough to satisfy each and every one. If I cannot demonstrate such a skillful mastery of the truth, then may I be a child of both temporal and eternal death. I have no greater pledge.[39]

Müntzer's prophetic warnings about a coming conflagration and the reign of Anti-Christ across European Christendom eventually erupted as Protestant and Roman Catholics factions clashed in a series of wars and struggles between Northern Europe and Southern Europe whose flames did not subside until the end of the Thirty Years War in 1648.

Müntzer did not remain in Bohemia for too long after November 1521 because by the following year he appears to have been on the move yet again. From the spring of 1523 until about the autumn of 1524, we find him serving as a preacher and parson at Saint John's Church in Allstedt. This was perhaps the most productive and creative period of his ministerial career. As suggested by Michael Baylor and Carl Hinrichs, at Allstedt Müntzer "attempted to construct a 'counter-Wittenberg,' a model of a reformed church diametrically opposed to that being developed in Wittenberg by Luther and his associates."[40] One need only recall that this so-called Wittenberg model was university based and favored an agenda of ecclesiastical *reforma* and the *renovatio* of the Gospel message taught and filtered to the laity by theologically trained clergy who would later minister among congregations with strong ties to secular authorities like the German princes, etc. This for Müntzer was an intolerable betrayal of the ideals of *reforma* and *renovatio*. His counter-model developed among the small community of Allstedt was based on the "formation of religious community in which the Holy Spirit would be awakened in the minds of the laity directly. The community as whole, or at least the elect within it, would become the recipient of divine revelations, and the community would decide which of these revelations were authentic and which were spurious."[41] At the heart of his new egalitarian model of a pneumatological church was his notion of a covenantal "League of the Elect," charged with leading the "mass of the commoners" as well as dealing with external threats to the community's safety and eventual expansion in the coming transformation of Christian society.

In the spring and summer of 1524, Müntzer went over the edge when he and his closest associates in the League of the Elect attempted, what for lack of a better term could be called a rebellion aimed at hastening the transformative tribulations they believed were imminent. First, they burned a Cistercian chapel at Mallerbach in late March, and then in July he began preaching and publishing ever more provocative tirades against the local Saxon princes and the Holy Roman Empire. He was accused of being a Joachimite rebel, a charge he repeatedly denied, but one, which we should not ignore given the increasing apocalyptic tone of Müntzer's reformist program. At first he discouraged the use of violence in carrying out the goals and concerns that he and the League of the Elect had set for their "counter-Wittenberg" circle in Allstedt. However, as their concern for the plight of the commoners and peasants increased alongside growing suspicions of the Allstedt circle's aims among secular authorities, Müntzer found himself being demonized by Luther and his circle of followers as a dangerous and violent insurrectionist, which is actually the direction in which his thoughts about a rebellion inspired by the liberative power of the Holy Spirit were moving anyway by October 1524. That same month an urban revolt at Mühlhausen paved the way for one of the Reformation's most nightmarish episodes, the Peasant's War of 1525, known then as the Thuringian Revolt, and an uprising for which Luther and his fellow Wittenberg reformers never forgave Müntzer and his "enthusiast" supporters from Allstedt.

In the spring of the following year as rebellion gave way to regional war Müntzer and his followers formed the Eternal League of God at Mühlhausen, and by the end of April were actively recruiting commoners and peasants from as many towns and villages across Thuringia as possible to join the insurrection against the clergy, the Dukes of Saxony, and the Holy Roman Empire. Müntzer and the peasant forces were defeated on May 15 at the decisive Battle of Frankenhausen by a combined army led by, Philip of Hesse, who served as the Landgrave of Thuringia, Duke George of Saxony, and Count Ernst von Mansfeld.

It is a profound historical irony that Müntzer's pneumatological rebellion was defeated during that year's cycle of seven-times-seven days of Pentecost. He was captured at the battle, his papers and letters seized for information on other conspirators in the area, then tried and tortured along with fellow leaders of the Eternal League of God, and finally executed outside the walls of Mühlhausen on May 27, 1525.

Luther and the Wittenberg reformers wasted no time condemning Müntzer's cause and cautioning all reform-minded laity and clergy throughout Germany to view his demise as proof that excessive "enthusiasm" and spiritually inspired rebellions breed evil by allowing uncontrolled euphoria to overcome reason, charity, and restraint. Luther published a defamatory tract entitled, *A Terrible History and the Judgment of God upon Thomas Müntzer, in which God openly punishes and condemns a Lying Spirit* (1525). As noted by Hans-Jürgen Goertz, Luther could not interpret these outcomes otherwise for Müntzer's "shameful end was the refutation of a theology which had falsely claimed the support of the Holy Spirit."[42] If as Brown's theory of traditions and theological reconstruction maintains, "the effective reconstruction of inheritance, the kind of re-imagining that can make a lasting difference, is affective and actional as well as intellectual or cognitive," then the fate of Thomas Müntzer when contrasted with Martin Luther's persistent cautions about the power of pneumatological ideas and sensibilities indicates that a middle way between the affective and cognitive domains of theological discourse and religious experience is a necessity when the *subversive fire* of the Pentecost story is reactivated as either a liberative theological trope or as a repository of Christian ecclesiastical tradition.

THE CASE OF MICHAEL SERVETUS, (CA. 1511-53)

Next we examine the extraordinary case of a Spaniard who served in the entourage of the Holy Roman and Spanish Emperor Charles V and then left to join the growing Protestant Reformation in places like Basel, Strasburg, and Geneva. Michael Servetus was born around 1509 or 1511 in Villanueva de Sijena, about sixty miles north of Zaragossa in the powerful kingdom of Aragon. When he was about fourteen years old he entered the service of Juan de Quintana, a Franciscan monk educated at the University of Paris and a member of the Aragonese *Cortes*, who was also one of the preeminent theological scholars of his day. Quintana sent Servetus to the University of Toulouse in 1528, and, although we cannot completely trace the range and breadth of the young man's education, he must have been exposed to some remarkable teachers and Humanistic influences for he eventually came to be regarded, even by his opponents and detractors, as a man of vast erudition and scholarly curiosity. In an age of extraordinary virtuosos during the High Renaissance and Reformation periods in which he lived, the range of Servetus' intellectual pursuits was highly dynamic and impressive. He had been influenced by the Humanist ideals of the period, and he could easily discuss law, speculative philosophy, theology and biblical criticism, astrology and mathematics, and medicine. As a boy he wondered if the Doctrine of the Trinity was an accurate description of the nature of God, and as a Spaniard concerned for the evangelization of the Jews and Arabs he regarded the Trinity as an obstacle to their eventual conversion. Servetus' anti-Trinitarian views, which contained its own unique pneumatology and conceptualization of the story of Pentecost from the New Testament, were articulated in his *De Trinitatis erroribus* (1531) and then reaffirmed with the publication, near the end of his life, of his infamous treatise *Christianismi Restitutio* (1553).

Servetus chastised both the Roman Catholic and Protestant clergy of his day for abandoning as well as not knowing "the true faith of Christ." He firmly contends that the reform movements of Martin Luther and John Calvin did not proceed far enough towards the "restoration" of true Christianity aligned with the more practical concerns of the Spirit. He saw the division of Christianity into warring sects capable of being completely manipulated by secular and temporal powers as the work of Satan and the Ant-Christ. And, he believed with deep conviction that it was his destiny to alert humanity to the impending apocalyptic tribulations as well as to help save Christianity from the rule of Satan and the Ant-Christ. His system provides an odd mingling of the ideal of *reforma* and *renovatio* with that of *restauratio*, which became a main feature of the Radical Reformation dreams and objectives of "restoring" the sixteenth century church and European society to a moral and pneumatological state akin to that of the early church at the time of the first Pentecost. In *Christianismi Restitutio* he lays out his program for the restoration of Christianity by writing,

The purpose toward which we aim is as sublime in its greatness as it is easy to understand and demonstrate with certainty. There is nothing greater, reader, than to know God manifested in substance and his proper divine nature communicated. ...We shall explain clearly the true modes through which God manifested himself to us; externally in a visible way as the Word; internally in a perceptible way as the Spirit. Both are a great mystery in order that man might know and possess God.[43]

Particularly noteworthy for our purposes in the present study is Servetus' emphasis on the simultaneity of God's "external" manifestation in the world as the Word and God's "internal" manifestation in the hearts and minds of human beings as the Spirit, which links the cosmic event of Jesus' Incarnation as the Word of God with the outpouring of Jesus' Holy Spirit at the first Pentecost. Hence, the presumed historicity of a supernatural event like that of the first Pentecost gave birth to Christ's earthly church, as an institution empowered and sustained by the Spirit of the risen Lord in the hearts and minds of individual believers, until the prophesied defeat of the Anti-Christ and the restoration of humanity to God through the return of the Paraclete at the time of the apocalypse.

Servetus relied on a tripartite conception of Salvation history that reads and sounds much like the prophecies of Joachim of Fiore (ca. 1202) that we discussed in Chapter Three. Servetus believed that the Spirit of Christ manifested three times in the history of Christianity. First at the Creation as the Spirit of God moved over the face of the waters and the darkness. Second, at Pentecost with the outpouring of the Holy Spirit, and that the Spirit would come yet again at a future time to restore (*restauratio*) all of God's true children and chosen servants to the deity of Christ. As a cutting-edge humanist scholar, he possessed a growing sense of the vastness and complexity of church history. This might explain why he was so critical of what he regarded as a lingering legacy of the corruption of the true Christian faith and its ecclesiastical mission under the influence of both the Roman Emperor Constantine's opportunistic meddling in the affairs of the church (ca. 305-337 CE) and the error-laden decisions of the Council of Nicea (325 CE) presided over by the emperor who called himself the "Bishop of bishops." Servetus equated the rule of Satan with the power of the Roman Church, the Papacy, and the Papal Court, and with the derailment of the reformation's agenda in the hands of misguided leaders like Luther and Calvin. It is worth noting that in the middle of the sixteenth century such negative sentiments and critical opinions were not uncommon among European Christians across most social classes, especially when one considers that Christians of this generation were like the scattered debris of centuries of promised yet repeatedly failed ecclesiastical reforms. These disruptive and recurring cycles of the struggle between the state and the church for supremacy over each other led many young intellectuals like Servetus to question the entire transit from the medieval *scholastic* past to the so-called *via moderna* of his times as one long series of failed educational and religious reforms.

Servetus' theological anthropology is inseparable from his pneumatology. He firmly believed that since human beings became partakers of the divine na-

ture through the Incarnation of the Word in Christ, then so too could human
flesh be infused with the power of the Word through the Holy Spirit. Here we
arrive at Servetus' fascination with the power of the Spirit to render a pneumatic
transformation of the human heart, mind, and body to a state akin to the miraculous communication and empowerment that manifested on the day of Pentecost for as he explained: "As the spirit of Christ has the essential breath of incorruptibility, so when it is communicated to us our own spirit is returned inward to
its incorruptibility."[44] Elsewhere in the text Servetus adds that: "God is generally
in all things, and the Holy Spirit is said to be a special breath for the sanctification of our human spirit, divine breeze, divine impulse, divine impression, perceptible within and substantially subsistent in our soul."[45] And finally in what
might be Servetus' interpretation of the ancient Judeo-Christian concept of the
Imago Dei combined with an almost alchemical idea like that voiced by Renaissance Humanists arguing for the "divinity of Man," he emphatically states:
"Truly the Holy Spirit is life, soul, and Christ's impact. The Spirit of Christ is
within us, from the innermost recesses of his substance and the innermost recesses of his heart, given to us from the great love . . . so that we might be transformed into his image."[46] Marian Hillar's study and translations of his *Christianismi Restitutio* succinctly summarizes Servetus' dynamic treatment of the Holy
Spirit:

> The vehicle for this transmission of divinity from God to man is the Holy Spirit
> as the agency of God's activity of communication . . . The Spirit is considered
> as a 'second hand of God.' A divine message, a mental impulse in man, and is
> manifested under a variety of forms. This function of the Spirit accounts for the
> strict differentiation by Servetus between 'manifestation' and 'communication,'
> the two functions of the two hands of God.[47]

In Servetus' *Christianismi Restitutio* we encounter several of the characteristics that Christian believers historically ascribed to manifestations of the Holy
Spirit, features like miraculous communication, ecstatic visions, spiritual intimacy with God or Christ, and uncanny manifestations in both the physical and
ethereal realms of being. However, Servetus' pneumatological view of human
nature, and of humanity's relationship with God through the Spirit, also predisposed his system of thought and reformist agenda in favor of the liberative aspects of the story of Pentecost and the empowering presence of the Holy Sprit.
His personal life and scholarly career also attest to the function of the story of
Pentecost as a repository of Christian ecclesiastical tradition, which, once he
tapped into its limitless storehouse of power, he could no longer ignore the oppression, corruption, and intolerance of the world in which he lived. Thus, the
making of this radical reformer's life and story was more about justice and human flourishing than about the euphoria and enthusiasm triggered by an unworthy seeker's chance encounter with the *subversive fire* of Pentecost and the Holy
Spirit.

As the printing of his *magnum opus* was completed on January 3, 1553 both
the Roman Catholic Inquisition at Vienne and Protestant leaders in Germany
and Switzerland became increasingly interested in arresting him and censoring

his publications. The first edition of the *Restitutio* included about thirty printed copies of Servetus' letters to John Calvin concerning various doctrinal disputes. His old theological and doctrinal rival, John Calvin, soon exposed Servetus to Catholic authorities in Vienne, which led to his interrogation and imprisonment in the spring. Servetus escaped from Vienne in April, but his luck ran out in August when his identity was uncovered by authorities in Geneva. The Council of Geneva, under pressure from Calvin to make an example of this highly sought heretical teacher and scholar, condemned him to death for heresy. Michael Servetus was burned at the stake on October 27, 1553 along with as many copies of *Christianismi Restitutio* as the authorities could get their hands on to fuel the flames of this ghastly execution.

Trinitarian and infant Baptism controversies aside, the world of sixteenth century European Christendom was not yet ready for some of his progressive ideas, and his execution by the Calvinist wing of the Protestant Reformation echoes Peter Matheson's critical lament about the Reformation's "nightmarish dimensions." Only three copies of this brilliant, reformist pneumatological manifesto survived the flames and the censors, but three copies was all that posterity needed to remember Servetus' creative reinterpretation of the story of Pentecost along with his convictions about the empowering presence of the Holy Spirit that steadfastly manifest in the human heart and mind.

THE CATHOLIC REFORMATION IN SPAIN

Modern readers forget the role that Spain played in the contentious events leading up to the Protestant Reformation and its aftermath. The mere mention that, at the time he began his reformist endeavors at Wittenberg Martin Luther was a subject of the Spanish Empire generates puzzled looks from both undergraduate and graduate history students as they are either informed for the first time, or perhaps simply reminded, that the throne of the Holy Roman Empire, which included Germany, Austria, Hungary, and Italy, was then ruled simultaneously by the same man and dynastic line who also occupied the Spanish throne. Hence Charles I of Spain was also known as Charles V of the Holy Roman Empire. Germany did not yet exist in the 1500s for it was but one more territory among Spain's vast imperial domains, the largest and the wealthiest in European history since the Roman Empire's zenith in the late Second Century CE. Before discussing a few of the reformers and visionaries of the Catholic Reformation in Spain, a brief summary of the military and political events that influenced religious thought and personal piety on the Iberian Peninsula before the advent of the Protestant and Catholic Reformation movements will provide a contextual backdrop for the unique pneumatological sensibilities shared by the Spanish saints and mystics we will meet in this section.

The political climate on the Iberian Peninsula during the fifteenth century cannot be understood apart from the intermittent wars against foreign Islamic adversaries, known as *La Reconquista* (Reconquest). This long, drawn-out conflict was fought among Spain's medieval Christian kingdoms and the region's diverse Islamic principalities and caliphates, which endured on European soil for nearly eight centuries until the spectacular events of 1492 changed the course of European political and religious history. In 711 Berber and Arab invaders from Morocco overthrew the Visigothic kingdoms of the early medieval Iberian Peninsula. It was an unusual invasion since due to Visigothic feudal excesses and cruelty some Christians and Jews welcomed the alleged Islamic "invaders" as "liberators" preaching a message about the one, true God of Abraham along with ideas about human dignity, peace and justice, and education for all members of the community. Then around 756, a surviving prince of the massacred Umayyad dynasty of Arabia, Abd al-Rahman I, crossed from North Africa into Spain and after a series of local battles declared himself Caliph and set up his capital at Cordoba. This began a "Golden Age" of Islamic civilization in southern Europe as the new Cordovan state fostered economic prosperity, established law and order, promoted literacy, and extended full rights of citizenship to tax-paying Christians and Jews across the Caliphate.

As the Abrahamic "People of the Book," Jews and Christians were seen as theological kin. This was the land the Arabs called *al-Andalus*, and which the Spaniards called *Andalucía*. The Spaniards and Portuguese retreated to the northernmost corners of the peninsula and from there launched the Reconquest, which over the centuries would take on mythic dimensions, as these intermittent wars became an extension of the medieval European "crusades" against Islam. The knights, mercenaries, and crusaders who fought in this conflict were known as the "Conquistadors." It is hard to follow the ebb and flow of these conflicts spanning almost eight centuries, but suffice it to say that by the year 1000 there were clearly distinct Islamic and Christian territories across Iberia while other embattled frontier regions changed hands frequently.

The first turning point in the Reconquest came in 1085 when the Christian forces of King Alfonso VI of Leon-Castile retook Toledo from its Arab and Muslim rulers and hastened the demise of Cordoba. A few more Muslim kingdoms and states would rise and fall in the ensuing centuries along with considerable feudalistic warring among the Spanish kingdoms themselves. Then in 1212, a major military and political turning point occurred when the Christian army of Alfonso VIII of Castile joined forces with the kingdoms of Navarre, Aragon, and Portugal and overwhelmed a sizable Muslim army at the battle of Las Navas de Tolosa. His son, Ferdinand III, then re-united Leon and Castile and by 1236 concentrated his military efforts on three of the remaining major Islamic centers of power: Cordoba, Valencia, and Seville. Over the next eight years, all three cities fell to the crusading Spanish-Christian armies. As in the Crusades to the Holy Land, divide and conquer tactics played a decisive role in weakening resistance among the Hispano-Muslim cities and kingdoms. For their loyalty and military support, Muslim emirs and commanders, who fought for the Spanish kings, were rewarded by being granted the right to retain and govern the southernmost Islamic region of Iberia, known as the Caliphate of Granada. From a historiographic standpoint, we could argue that the Reconquest had reached its apex and a kinder, gentler political situation should have ensued across the Iberian Peninsula following the decisive military victories and treaties negotiated by 1250 between the Spanish and Islamic kingdoms.

However, it was not long before the House of Aragon superseded the supremacy of the other Spanish kingdoms by embarking on an aggressive expansionist agenda, both at home and abroad, which revived the Reconquest as a struggle for national unity as well as for the eventual expulsion of the Jews and Muslims from Iberia. In their view, Aragon was carrying out the "Will of God," and, in the apocalyptic views and expectations of an increasing number of Castilian and Aragonese clergy, Spain was providentially ordained as the agent of a great transformation across Christendom that would lead to the final conversion of the Jews and the Muslims as well as usher in the "New Age" and the return of Christ. In the growing cities of Spain, and throughout the Andalusian and Galician countryside, talk of the apocalypse flourished alongside millennial visions of Iberian glory and prophetic readings of both the Hebrew and Christian Scriptures. Indeed, church astronomers and prophetic visionaries during the fifteenth century astrologically perceived the approaching year 1500 as a cosmic marker of enormous apocalyptic importance and spiritual power.

The high ranking clergy in Castile-Leon and Aragon worried about the potential political and social dangers that all of this religious fervor and millennialist euphoria might pose for the nascent nation-state of Spain whose glorious birth many considered as originating with the marriage in 1469 of the royal cousins Ferdinand II of Aragon (1452-1516) to Isabel I of Castile (1451-1504). It was even suggested that Queen Isabel's personal confessor, Cardinal Francisco Jimenez de Cisneros, who, as Archbishop of Toledo was widely considered the third most powerful leader on the Iberian Peninsula, might be the person chosen by the Lord to usher in the New Age.

None of these notions are especially surprising when we consider that one of the most popular European Renaissance books, *De septem secundeis*, examined the role of the powerful Archangels and planetary spirits who many believed propelled both transformative and cataclysmic events on earth, by the grace and will of God, from the time of Noah and the Flood through the fateful and much anticipated year 2000, which allegedly marked the beginning of the seventh millennium since Creation.[48] Written shortly after the turn of the century between 1500 and 1508, and also known as the *Chronologia mystica*, this book profoundly influenced visionaries and reformist thinkers during the late Renaissance and early Reformation eras who by reading the skies and stars sought to understand God's will as a bewildering amalgamation of political and ecclesiastical events accompanied by the far-reaching social changes that swept across European Christendom from 1492 through the end of the sixteenth century. It was written by the mysterious and controversial Abbot Trithemius of Sponheim (1462-1516) whose life's work and pneumatological views are examined in Chapter Five of this volume. On a different but related note, during his final voyage to the so-called *Nuevo Mundo*, which he and the *Adelantados* and *Conquistadores* who followed him merely stumbled upon while exploring the Western Hemisphere, Christopher Columbus entertained the notion that, because of the significance of his conquests for the Spanish Crown, he might be the agent of change and unveiling destined to open the door of the long-awaited millennialist *renovatio*. Such was the psychological state of affairs among European

Christians whose anxieties about social and political upheavals intensified both their collective and individual sense of apocalyptic expectation in the years just before and after the Protestant and Roman Catholic Reformations.

The mythic conflict of the Reconquest did not only define the political and ecclesiastical consciousness of medieval and early modern Spain and Portugal, but also the long drawn out series of engagements eventually had adverse effects on the Spanish perception, treatment, and persecution of religious minorities. Desiring to bring an end to the Reconquest and assimilate Granada into the Christian ethos, a pattern of ecclesiastical uniformity was imposed by the Crown across early modern Spain. Hence when the Spanish Monarchs woke up on the morning of January 2, 1492, they found themselves as the masters of the most religiously and racially diverse society in all of Europe.[49] Rather than embracing these differences through a dialogue of mutual edification, or ensuring legal protections for each community as Christian and Muslim leaders had done centuries earlier following the conquest of Toledo in 1085 by King Alfonso VI of Castile-Leon, or as had been carried out after the capture of Seville in 1248 by King Ferdinand III of Castile, the young monarchy of King Ferdinand of Aragon and Queen Isabel of Castile enlisted the assistance of the Roman Catholic Church in a program of religious uniformity and Spanish national identity formation that would have dire consequences for both church and state. The conclusion of this cosmic battle in the same year as Christopher Columbus sailed off into the Atlantic in the name of these same Spanish Monarchs was proof enough for Spain and her leaders that this was "God's Will" for their new nation. Suffice it to say, that this sentiment among dominant groups or regimes, whereby one religious or ethnic group takes over and seeks to silence the traditions and practices of other groups has a long and tragic history among both imperial systems and modern nation-states.

However, the pneumatological traditions and the dynamic imagination of Pentecost also had a long history of fostering theological reconstructions of inherited symbols and doctrines, practices and rituals, and the elements of Christian canon. It is important for academic specialists and general readers of this historical narrative not to scapegoat the past by heaping excessive blame on the Roman Catholic Church. In the case of early modern Spain and the Catholic Reformation, the real peace and justice issues center on the excessively close association that emerged between the national will to power and misguided claims about the will of God favoring Spain among all other European nations. This late fifteenth and early sixteenth century national messianic myth, which was later reinterpreted by Spain's European rivals for their own nationalistic and imperialist objectives, also affected what could and could not be spoken or preached about, or taught, written, and published about the Holy Spirit in the Iberian Peninsula and the Spanish colonies. As the sixteenth century opened, local reform efforts and fledgling movements of the Spirit began manifesting throughout the cities and countryside of Andalucía in yet another manifestation of the liberative function of pneumatological ideas and sensibilities, which throughout this volume's chapters I have been referring to as *subversive fire*.

When juxtaposed with the Lutheran and Calvinist reform movements spreading on the empire's northern frontier, Spanish political and ecclesiastical authorities became acutely alarmed at the potential for dissent and disruption posed by so many new religious movements and local visionaries. Such persons and movements were perceived as a serious threat to the unity of both the new nation-state and its rapidly expanding messianic empire. The triangulation of a series of meaningful events of epic proportions, such those cited above during the "Miraculous Year" of 1492 alongside popular and Scholastic apocalyptic expectations, had convinced people from nearly all strata of Castilian and Aragonese society that the fateful year of 1500 was the event horizon separating the troubled past from the millennialist dreams of Spain's glorious future. In the view of many persons among Spain's royal and ecclesiastical elites, the "Will of God" had ordained the union of Castile and Aragon and their new nation was to be the agent of a great transformation across Christendom and spreading to the entire world. Perhaps this also explains why decentered pneumatological movements like the Illuminists (*Alumbrados*) of Toledo, or empowering theological anthropologies like that articulated in the writings of the lay theologian Juan de Valdés (ca. 1509-1541), were particularly intolerable to the Crown and the Holy Office of the Inquisition.[50]

One of the results of Spain's remarkable transformation and dramatic increase of power and wealth during the sixteenth century was the program of educational reforms and national identity construction that unfolded back home as well as throughout its colonies. During these years books on Castilian grammar began appearing everywhere in Spain, and were used as instruments of national and religious acculturation under the promise of education and literacy for the uneducated populace. Local religious communities and their liturgical traditions, such as Toledo's Hispano Mozarabic community, were not immune to these trends and initiatives as so-called "*abecedarios de la vida espiritual*" began appearing from the pen of reform minded clergy and humanistic scholars. These short instructional pamphlets, which were literally about learning the "ABCs of the spiritual life," were intended to teach the laity about the prayers and doctrines associated with the Roman rite.[51] This further reminds us that back in the 1500s for the then recently formed modern nation-state of Spain, a close association between national identity and religious identity was an integral part of the agenda the ruling Castilian and Aragonese elites had set for their new country. As chronicled and discussed by Raúl Gómez-Ruiz, the Hispano-Mozarabic community of Toledo responded to the changing social and political fortunes of that era by attaching even greater importance to their local traditions and practices of venerating the Cross, which, in turn, helped preserve their ethnic and cultural identities through their communal devotion to Christ.[52] This exemplifies one of the most enriching and persistent trajectories in the long history of Christianity that, despite the occasional imposition of trans-local doctrines and practices, local expressions of liturgical practice, commemorative feast days, and sacred processions have almost always managed to survive and serve as a bridge between the ancestral past of specific peoples and places, such as the Mozarabs of Toledo, and the sometimes misguided dreams of building a more theologically unified or politically centralized Christian future. Ironically, Toledo's Alcazar Palace also served as the home of Spain's Royal Court until 1561 when Philip II moved the court seventy miles away to his new capital city at Madrid. The ancient Mozarabic enclave knew enough to be careful that their pneumatological ideas did not run up against the new ideas of national identity being preached and taught from their Toledoan home on the Tagus River.

Similarly, the Spanish reform movement, known as the *Alumbrados* (Illuminists), was affected by the growing climate of suspicion towards minority religious groups living among the newly formed early modern nation state of Spain. Mystical piety and intense devotional practices had been a popular trend in Spain during the last decades of the fifteenth century, and most of these had some type of pneumatological component that manifested in varying degrees of meditative practices. However, as the nationalistic and religious fervor of the post-1492 era gripped Spain's populace and leadership, the rising tide of social suspicion and Inquisitorial persecutions of crypto-Jews or crypto-Moors made it increasingly difficult for religious movements like the *Alumbrados* to pursue their alternative spiritual views, rituals, and worship practices. In September 1525 Spain's Inquisitor General, Fr. Alonso Manrique, who also held the position of Archbishop of Seville, issued an Edict of Faith ordering the arrest and interrogation of the *Alumbrados*. For the next hundred years scores of men and women, laity and clergy, Jews and Moors, were accused of *alumbradismo* (illuminism) by Spanish ecclesiastical authorities as well as by disgruntled enemies seeking to settle a score or just vent their anger at religious minorities, pious women, or recent converts from Judaism and Islam. Some members of the sect operating in Seville as late as the 1620s claimed to be the "heirs of the Holy Spirit" (*herederos del Espiritu Santo*). Ironically, since the Holy Office of the Inquisition functioned as an instrument of the Spanish Crown for the sake of national unity and for rooting out heresy, alleged cases of *alumbradismo* were often much more about government and ecclesiastical fears of disunity through the infiltration and spread of Lutherans, or Anabaptists, or Calvinists across the Iberian Peninsula.

Considering Protestantism's provocative role in Greater Germany and the territories of the Holy Roman Empire, collective fear or political suspicion about religious dissenters is not surprising given, that, from the early 1500s to the late 1600s, Spain was Europe's most powerful and expansionist nation-state with dynastic ties and territorial claims in Italy, Austria, Germany, the Netherlands, and in the eastern European portions of the Holy Roman Empire. Nonetheless the Iberian cultural and mystical phenomenon of Illuminism was clearly a movement of the Spirit that disturbed both secular and religious authorities to the point of mobilizing the machinery of state persecution in an effort to protect Spain and its territories from radical religious ideas and enthusiast sensibilities. Instead of preaching or writing too much about the power and gifts of the Holy Spirit to inspire prophetic leaders, reformers and teachers, and interpreters of sacred Scripture; it was far safer to emphasize the power and presence of Jesus Christ or the Virgin Mary while downplaying the liberative power of the Pentecost story and the Holy Spirit. Movements of the Spirit, like the *Alumbrados*, and reform-minded visionaries whose hearts and minds were open to the empowering presence and communicative vitality of the Spirit of God, like Teresa of Avila, John of the Cross, or Ignatius of Loyola walked a fine line between their reformist agendas and the autocratic long-arm of the Spanish Inquisition. It is worth noting that recognizing such challenges and dangers is not the result of some latent anti-Catholic prejudice or stereotype. On the contrary, including an overview in this volume of the lives and works of these three highly influential Catholic Reformation figures is an example of the sort of dialogues of mutual edification required to honor the broad range of Christian pneumatology and interreligious possibilities that Word of God as received and heard in the story of Pentecost harbors across the centuries.

TERESA OF AVILA ON THE HOLY SPIRIT

Saint Teresa (1515-1582) was born in Avila to Don Alonso Sanchez de Cepeda and Doña Beatriz Davila y Ahumada. Her mother died when she was fourteen years old, and shortly after this tragic loss her father sent her to an Augustinian nunnery to complete her education. Illness and her father's aversion to seeing his daughter become a nun cut her time there short, but Teresa's steadfast desire for the religious life eventually led her to join the Carmelite Convent of the Incarnation at Avila against her father's wishes in 1535. Illness and emotional distress punctuated her life for many years until, in her late thirties, she began experiencing spiritual visions that led her to write about the mystical aspects of religious formation and the discipline required to navigate one's discernment process from the initiatory level to the lofty heights of mystical union. She described these visions as being perceived not through the eyes of the body, but through the "eyes of the soul" (*ojos del alma*). Her visions along with the influence of Saint Augustine's works and Francisco de Osuna's *Tercer Abecedario Espiritual (Third Spiritual Alphabet,* ca. 1527)[53] became the basis for many of the religious practices and spiritual exercises she later elaborated in such classic works as *The Way of Perfection* (ca. 1567) and the *Interior Castle* (ca. 1577).[54] Osuna was an advocate of a series of contemplative exercises and practices known as *recogimiento* (recollection), which was also known among the persecuted Alumbrados of Toledo. Although her books were intended for new Carmelite nuns preparing to take their solemn vows, since the wider publication of her books in the late 1600s, Teresa's works have been read by millions of readers interested in the practice of deep prayer and the mystical journey.

Teresa's ministerial career also included her work as one of the three major religious reformers and leaders of the Catholic Reformation in Spain. Her transformative work with the Carmelite Order also influenced the education of Roman Catholic clergy in Europe and the Americas for centuries. In August 1562, Teresa founded the Convent of Discalced Carmelite Nuns of the Primitive Rule of Saint Joseph at Avila, which was soon approved by the Father General of the Carmelite Order, who also approved of her strategy and plans for reforming the rules and educational expectations of the nuns entrusted to her leadership. Teresa often alluded to the piercing yet comforting presence of Christ in her heart through the mystery of the Holy Spirit, a confession that made some of her male confessors suspicious of her visionary piety for two reasons that both disturb and offend our postmodern worldview. First, for the simple fact that she was a woman, a member of the "weaker sex" (*infirmitas sexus*) going back to Eve's actions in the Garden of Eden, and everyone back then was certain that females were easily prone to demonic and Satanic influences. And, secondly, because her emphasis on literacy, deep piety, and the gifts of the Holy Spirit made her sound a lot like the Illuminists and other undesirable radical or religious factions.

During the last twenty years of her life she was able to combine the fruits of her personal piety with an attitude of "faith in action" that expanded the activities of the Carmelites and made it possible for the Order to open other convents throughout Spain for nuns, as well as other houses and monasteries for monks with the help of her Carmelite colleague and fellow mystic, Saint John of the Cross (1542-1591). We will discuss John's life and ministry, and his dynamic spiritual journey, in the next subsection after Teresa of Avila. It was also during these two decades later in life that her writing attained the momentum and acceptance she lacked in the early years of her ministerial career.

Saint Teresa's family lineage is significant because historical evidence unearthed in the late 1940s revealed that Teresa's grandfather, Juan Sanchez de Cepeda, had been summoned by the Inquisition on charges of being a Marrano, or "secret Jew."[55] Juan responded to the Inquisition's harassment by moving from his native Toledo to Avila, and then slightly changing his name to disappear into the mainstream of Spanish Christian society. The long term effects of such trauma on Teresa and her family can only be speculated, but it would be incorrect to assume that any family can pass through such an ordeal while their religious identity and public persona remained unaffected. Given the multireligious social conditions of medieval Spain in both Muslim and Christian controlled territories, this is not surprising since not only sixteenth century Spaniards but also modern day citizens of Spain and Latin American countries, as

well as Hispanic and Latino/a families living in the Southwestern United States have documented their *converso* origins from either Hispano-Jewish or Hispano-Arabic family ancestors. *Converso,* meaning "New Christians," was the legal term used in Spain from the 1300s to the early 1800s to signify recent converts to Christianity from either Judaism or Islam. Some of Teresa's works contain rather harsh statements about Jews, or about their negative role in Spanish society, which leaves modern readers wondering about her sense of toleration in the context of the general mood of religious persecution and opposition to the spread of Lutheranism that permeated Spanish political, social, and religious affairs during the sixteenth century. In Teresa of Avila's case one can only wonder, from a more positive angle, about how such a family secret concerning her grandfather, along with the textual and pietistic traditions such an identity implies, might have influenced her deep convictions about literacy, the importance of reading the Holy Scriptures as a meditative practice, and the deep prayer and personal piety she believed was not just the special praxis of the clergy, monks and nuns, and others serving in the various religious orders, but a genuine gift (*dones*) of God's mercy and grace for all believers through the presence of Jesus Christ and his Holy Spirit.

As word spread of Teresa's visions and locutions, both the local clergy and the laity of Avila began wondering about the authenticity of her revelations as well as about the discernment of beneficent versus evil spirits communicating with this sickly and restless nun. Local suspicions about the activities of the Il-luminists, and allegations of guilt by association with Illuminism, were not only in the air but heresy trials against Alumbrados were still an issue in several areas of Spain in the mid-1500s. Hence, Teresa had to be very careful about how she described the presence of the Holy Spirit in her mystical experiences, or about the types of meditative exercises she taught her Carmelite novices, and even more cautious when making any claims about individual agency or spiritual em-powerment by the Spirit as a result of her inner work and desire for union with God. In addition, because she was a female, and because the late medieval and early modern ministerial profession was dominated by men of power and rank who had been taught that women were especially weak and prone to possession by evil spirits and Satan, Teresa was assigned series of confessors who eva-luated the Christian validity of her message before authorizing her to begin writ-ing her now famous works of piety and mystical transformation. Although there are very few direct references to Pentecost, or about the Holy Spirit's liberative and creative power, in most of her works, she became quite adept at playing the game of self-deprecation as a lowly and sickly female while remaining firm with her male confessors and detractors about the essential message the grace of God compelled her to communicate through her written works.

In 1559, when Spain's Inquisitor General, Francisco de Valdés, issued the Index of Forbidden Books with over 250 titles that included numerous works of personal piety and spiritual practices, including texts read and approved of by Cardinal Francisco Jimenez de Cisneros at the beginning of the century, Teresa mourned the loss of these works as pedagogical and spiritual treasures. Not one to be easily subdued or deterred from her mission, Edward Howells reports that "This was precisely the kind of religious material used by women, who could not generally read Latin," and Teresa "describes its loss as a major reason for her decision to write on paper" as she then needed urgently "to provide a re-placement for teaching her nuns."[56] It is not necessary to recount the entire story of Teresa's persistence and courage to become a female religious author in an era of intense inquisitorial scrutiny and intellectual repression. Portions of the Teresian corpus echo ideas and themes expressed among the *Alumbrados*, who had been nearly wiped out, or forced underground, by the 1560s when she began disseminating her works among the Carmelite nuns and friars whose spiritual instruction became the major focus of her later years.

Hence Teresa's major works like *The Interior Castle* and *The Way of Per-fection* were written for a ministerial audience consisting of novices and mature clergy who needed instructional manuals in Castilian on contemplative prayer and the discernment process or stage of the mystical journey. It was her firm conviction that such inner, personal work was essential before commencing a program or career of pastoral work in the world at large. In other words, one has to cleanse and polish his or her internal spiritual nature before venturing forth to serve God in the external realm of church and society. Her emphasis on interiority touched upon numerous concepts and practices that modern readers would regard as pertaining to the disciplines of psychology or psychoanalytic theory. For example, she encourages both male and female Carmelite novices to share insights from their reading and reflection of the Holy Scriptures as well as insight derived from deep prayer and contemplation in settings we would refer to as "group dynamics." She also cautions her novices against sharing the special favors or gifts (*dones*) the Lord bestows on them through religious experiences in these group settings because our individual human nature is so prone to wonder why the Lord grants one person a certain gift of the Holy Spirit while holding back such a gift from another. She warns against the dangerous hubris that comes from Satan's temptations to assume that the loftiest heights of mystical experience come from the contemplative efforts of the individual self and not as a gift of God's divine grace. She was acutely aware of both the positive and negative side effects of the emotional cleansing or emptying that occurs as a by-product of taking up the mystical path of spiritual unfolding and deep prayer. She also warned her fellow sisters and Carmelite novices of how this process sometimes generates melancholy or depression in the religious seeker as he or she confronts more and more of the character and affective obstacles blocking one from realizing the power of the human soul to love God beyond all other earthly persons or things.

Finally, although Teresa and her sixteenth century religious contemporaries always had to be careful not to sound too much like the outlawed and persecuted Illuminists with whom they indeed shared some commonalities about contemplative prayer and the power of the Holy Spirit, her pneumatological sensibilities were solidly rooted in the Augustinian idea that the Spirit serves as the bond of intimacy and communication among the three Persons of the Holy Trinity. In the nineteenth chapter of *The Way of Perfection* Teresa addresses the enigmatic manifestations of the water and fire as an allegorical example of the presence of the Spirit in the life of prayer among those who seek understanding and perfection:

> So, as I say, the water, which springs from the earth, has no power over this fire. Its flames rise high and its source is in nothing so base as the earth. There are other fires of love for God, small ones, which may be quenched by the least little thing. But this fire will most certainly not be so quenched. Even should a whole sea of temptations assail it, they will not keep it from burning or prevent it from gaining mastery over them.
>
> Water which comes down as rain from Heaven will quench the flames even less, for in that case the fire and the water are not contraries, but have the same origin. Do not fear that one element may harm the other; each helps the other and they produce the same effect. For the water of genuine tears, that is, tears which come from true prayer, is a good gift from the King of Heaven; it fans the flames and keeps them alight, while the fire helps to cool the water. God bless me! What a beautiful and wonderful thing it is that fire should cool water! But it does; and it even freezes all worldly affections, when it is combined with the living water that comes from Heaven, the source of the above mentioned

tears, which are given us, and not acquired by our diligence. Certainly, then, nothing worldly has warmth left in it to induce us to cling to it unless it is something which increases this fire, the nature of which is not to be easily satisfied, but, if possible, to enkindle the entire world.[57]

The enigmatic quality of Teresa's Castilian prose and the paradoxical interplay of these images of water and fire, which seem to defy the ways we normally experience water and fire through the senses, reminds us that we are in the realm of the ineffable mystery of the Holy Spirit. It might be objected, that I am pushing the envelope regarding Teresa of Avila's cautionary use of pneumatological references and symbols. But, for a female Christian reformer, writer, and leader living and ministering in the patriarchal and intolerant culture of sixteenth century Spain, what one said or wrote about personal piety, spiritual perfection, and the empowering agency of the Holy Spirit could land one at the doorstep of the Inquisition with a lot of questions and a lot of explaining to do.

JOHN OF THE CROSS ON THE HOLY SPIRIT

Saint Teresa's close friend and fellow founder of the Order of Discalced Carmelites, John of the Cross was born on June 24, 1542 in the small village of Fontiveros near Avila. His father, Gonzalo de Yepes, had been disinherited by his own family of wealthy Toledoan silk merchants for marrying, Catalina Alvarez, a poor weaver of low social rank. Gonzalo and Catalina had three sons, but the couple struggled very hard to earn a meager living as cloth weavers. John's father died when he was about two years old, and then his brother Luis died a few years later. Rejected by her husband's family, even after asking them for financial assistance following his death, Catalina moved to Medina del Campo with her two surviving boys and resumed working as a weaver. In those days, Medina del Campo was a rapidly growing and economically vibrant commercial center in the Castilian heart of the expanding Spanish Empire. John's mother enrolled him in a grammar school serving the local poor where he received a basic education in Christian doctrine, and some training in trade skills for which he showed little interest. John's compassion for the sick caught the attention of Don Alonso de Alvarez, who headed a hospital serving the poor in Medina. John served the ailing and the needy at Medina as both a nurse and an alms-collector on behalf of the hospital until about age seventeen when Don Alonso, who admired his spiritual and intellectual gifts, helped him enroll in a local Jesuit academy. Don Alonso's generous mentorship of this young man's pastoral formation would bear significant fruit in the future as John of the Cross is now regarded as one of the foremost mystics of the Christian tradition, and one with a very special reverence and personal relation to the Holy Spirit.

The Jesuits were still a relatively new religious order, but their reputation for education and intellectual rigor was already becoming known among each of sixteenth century Spain's social classes. John thrived at Medina's Jesuit school from 1559 to 1563. He received an excellent academic foundation in the Greek and Latin classics as well as in literature, composition, and the humanities. He also maintained his service to the hospital while studying with the Jesuits, who would have been delighted had he petitioned to join their order. As Kieran Kavanaugh describes in his introduction to the official Carmelite Order's modern translation of Saint John's collected works: "These years of hospital work and study, tasks that called for responsibility and diligence complemented John's early experiences of poverty."[58] Indeed Don Alonso would have been delighted if John became the official chaplain at the hospital after ordination just as the Jesuits would have accepted him without reservations into their novitiate training program.[59]

However, the contemplative practices and special devotion to the Virgin Mary among Medina's Carmelite monks appealed in a very significant way to the twenty year old John. He entered the order's novitiate around 1563, and he was ordained in 1567 after completing theological studies at the prestigious University of Salamanca. He studied the Carmelite Rule carefully and read several medieval treatises expounding on the characteristics of the order's spiritual traditions and prayer practices. He was known to his superiors and fellow novices as Brother John of Saint Matthias. As European Christendom passed through the final stages of the High Renaissance and the dissemination of humanistic educational reforms, John spent three years studying theology and philosophy among the highly talented and renowned faculty of Salamanca as part of his required Carmelite studies. In Spain the tendency was to combine key aspects of Italian Humanism related to Augustinian and Thomistic theology while downplaying the Renaissance's fondness for pre-Christian philosophy and pagan mythological figures in the arts and literature.[60]

The surviving student records and anecdotal evidence from those who knew his spiritual sensibilities well, like Teresa of Avila, suggest that, although John excelled in his university studies, he yearned for solitude and spiritual detachment from the realm of the senses and from the distractions of the social arena. The wonders of the heart as reflected in deep prayer and contemplation on the Holy Trinity led John in search of ever more intimate experiences of God. Union with God and knowledge of the Trinity, which he believed was encrypted in the soul like the concept of the *Imago Dei*, was among John's primary goals as a monastic priest and Christian mystic seeking intimacy with God. Putting his faith into action as a religious reformer while in the service of the Carmelite Order was simply the natural outgrowth of his deep experience of God's boundless mercy and love for all creation. John's Christian altruism contrasts with his concern over humanity's tendency to fall away from God and drift into worldly pursuits, pride, and sinfulness. When juxtaposed against the plight of the poor and the sick he tended to at the hospital in Medina, John's university studies must have seemed insignificant. Given the suffering of so many to whom he could offer comfort and healing through the inspiration of the Holy Spirit and the example of Christ's ministry serving those who were suffering in the cities and towns of Andalucía without a worldly advocate or divine comforter took precedence in his discernment process over an academic career.

In a number of John's contemplative works one detects a certain disdain for the intellectual subtleties of Scholasticism and for the pride associated with the academic titles and honors that often accompany a university career. While we cannot presume to speak for him, these issues most likely had something to do with the "vocational crisis" that modern researchers and biographers often highlighted as a major concern of John's around 1567 while completing his studies at Salamanca. John's paradoxical notion of "unknowing knowing" or "knowing without knowing," (*no saber sabiendo*) expressively composed in his poem entitled, *Deep Rapture* suggests that he experienced a profound mystical awareness that trumped all Scholastic and rational categories of Christian thought. Hence, his next line in this poem about "transcending all science" (*toda sciencia tracendiendo*).[61]

Sentiments like those just mentioned are not mere sixteenth century examples of Spanish anti-clericalism or anti-intellectualism, but reveal popular prejudices against the ivory tower lifestyles and elitist scholarly pursuits projected on the high ranking clergy by the laity, the lesser nobility, and the poor. It also reveals the growing disdain for outdated medieval Scholastic titles and abstract theological discourses or treatises divorced from deep prayer and personal piety among both popular and ecclesiastical Spanish circles during this period. This is reminiscent of the sixteenth century lay theologian, Juan de Valdes (ca. 1490-1541), whose active career as an expatriate Spanish religious writer and preacher formerly accused of Lutheranism passed away just as John's life was beginning. Valdes often stated that: "The business of Christianity is not about *science* but *experience*," which reminds us that by referencing "science" Valdes was taking aim at Scholasticism, clerical corruption, and the intellectual abstractions that sometimes mistakenly passed for the genuinely compassionate piety of Jesus Christ or the empowering presence of the Holy Spirit. But in the Valdesian corpus we hear similar ideas like John's "unknowing knowing," from the pen of a lay theologian whom the Inquisition accused of heresy and Lutheranism before fleeing Spain and living the rest of his life as an exile in Naples, Italy. Thus, we should not to assume that John's poetic eloquence in the paradoxical notion of "unknowing knowing," so beautifully expressed in *Deep Rapture* is not only about contemplative perceptions beyond language and rationalism, but has its cultural and existential corollary in the juxtaposition of John's severely impoverished childhood against his humanistic and Jesuit studies at Medina del Campo. Life with all of it joys and suffering is about facing reality with passion and compassion. Faith is lived out in action, and not as an abstract, intellectual idea.

As the future saint quietly discerned whether or not to pursue a possible career in the ministry of teaching at the university level, another future saint, Teresa of Avila, was taking notice of the twenty-five year old Carmelite monk's special giftedness for personal piety, spiritual instruction, and compassionate service. Their friendship and collaboration on behalf of the Carmelite reform became one of the legendary pairings of female and male Catholic clergy in the service of the church and society. Jesus once stated that he had come to cast fire on the earth, and he added how very much he wished that it were already kindled and blazing (Luke 12:49). Likewise, the reformist endeavors that brought John of the Cross and Teresa of Avila into such close association with each other was the natural outgrowth of their respective experiences of the Holy Spirit's empowering gifts (*dones*), and the Carmelite mission to serve the poor. Indeed,

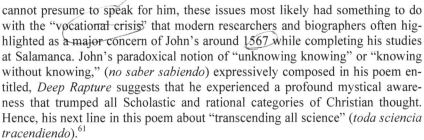

Teresa taught John that when one is so sweetly and blessedly called to the service of Mount Carmel, among the first fruits of the Spirit is the need to save souls from the bondage of poverty, hunger, and despair. This is what Teresa and John meant when each in their separate and unique ways referred to God's "touches" and the "wounds of love," inflicted on the soul as God reaches out to the spiritual seeker transforming one's earthly "wounds" into a healing power capable of turning poison into medicine and sinfulness into salvation.

Although John of the Cross wrote almost nothing about Pentecost in any of his mystical works or poems, he taught and wrote much about the vital role the Holy Spirit plays in communication between the human person and the other two persons of the Holy Trinity, the Father and the Son. This relational and communicative role of the Holy Spirit keeps humanity connected to the divine realm even when an individual believer assumes he or she is disconnected from the divine source of being. The Spirit is responsible for keeping the individual believer moving towards the fulfillment of his or her life of faith, which for some people, either by the grace of God or as a byproduct of their taking up the mystical journey, also leads one to pass through the purgative stages John identifies as the "dark night of sense" and the "dark night of spirit." In John's *Living Flame of Love* the Holy Spirit is both literally and figuratively "the living flame of love" between the Father and the Son, which also extends to the relationship of the human soul in union with the three Persons of the Trinity. Unlike other pneumatological visionaries and writers surveyed throughout this book, John, to an even greater degree than Teresa, maintained that the image and likeness of the Trinity was embedded in the human soul like the *Imago Dei* concept expressed in the opening sections of Genesis (1: 26-27) when the Father created Adam. Referencing the gospel of John (14:23), John of the Cross interprets God's words in a manner reminiscent of Tauler's deep piety and faith in the power of the Trinity by stating: "For He declared that the Father, Son, and the Hoy Spirit would take up their abode in those who love him by making them live the life of God and dwell in the Father, the Son, and the Holy Spirit."[62] The infusion of divine favor, or "enkindling" as the saint calls it in this text, touches the deepest centers of the soul, and reminds the soul of both its supernatural origins and of its supernatural end "every time it flares up" and "bathes the soul in glory."[63]

As for the infusions of divine grace and favor the soul receives from the Trinity through the intercession of the Holy Spirit, it is important to clarify what John meant by "recollection" and "locution," which throughout the corpus of his works is almost identical with Teresa of Avila's position on the meaning of these terms. Recollection, or *recogimiento*, is both a method of meditation and an attitude of detachment from the external world of the senses and withdrawing inward to the realms of the heart and the soul. A *locution*, also known as "interior locutions" and "external locutions," refers to the reception of spiritual insights or ideas in a revelatory state of mind. The trouble with locutions, and certain types of recollection, is that the individual soul can become prone to hubris and sin if the heart and mind of the recipient becomes inflated with selfish emotions and thoughts of his or her own importance in the eyes of God. Others, intoxicated by the high voltage of divine infusions, wallow in possessive thoughts and desires wishing to replicate the joyful experience of the divine flame. Some will even pray for repeated infusions of the divine presence in hopes of over- coming their melancholy or boredom. John steadfastly reminds his readers, that humility, charity, poverty of Spirit, holy simplicity, and compassion are out- wardly visible characteristics of God's genuinely beneficent locutions and recol- lections.[64]

John's pneumatology is closely aligned with his theological anthropology and his understanding of human spiritual transformation. His views are suc- cinctly expressed in Chapter 29 of *The Ascent of Mount Carmel*, where he writes about the process of how a person's heart and mind are prepared for the locu- tions the Spirit enkindles through recollection:

> Since their intellect is recollected and united with the truth, which is the subject of their thought, and the Holy Spirit is also united with them in that truth, for he is in every truth, it results that, while their intellect is thus communing with the divine Spirit by means of that truth, it simultaneously forms interiorly and suc- cessively other truths about its subject while the Holy Spirit, the Teacher, leads the way and gives light. This is one of the Holy Spirit's methods of teaching.[65]

The passage demonstrates John's awareness of the Spirit's power to guide and intercede on behalf of the individual Christian believer, or in the prayer practices and spiritual exercises expected of persons entering the Carmelite novitiate. He is also acutely aware of the dangers posed by those who would take up the mys- tical journey and succumb to the vanities "of those who will commit serious blunders if they do not practice great restraint."[66] This reminds us of the dangers inherent in all theological reconstructions claiming a spiritual mandate from God through the Holy Spirit. Perhaps this is the situation exemplified by the failed Pentecost revolutionary visions of Cola di Reinzo in the mid-1300s, and as ex- emplified by Thomas Müntzer's pneumatologically inspired Peasant's War in Germany, which for John's era was still a recent historical event.

Another key passage in the same text summarizes John's interconnected under- standing of how the loftiest religious experiences lead the intellect to humble- ness of faith, charity, and wisdom:

> If you ask me why the intellect must be deprived of those truths since the Spirit of God illumines it through them and thus are not bad, I answer: The Holy Spirit illumines the recollected intellect, and illumines it according to the mode of its recollection; the intellect can find no better recollection than in faith, and thus the Holy Spirit will not illumine it in any other recollection more than in faith. The purer and more refined a soul is in faith, the more infused charity it has. And the more charity it has the more the Holy Spirit illumines it and communicates his gifts because charity is the means by which they are communicated. Although in that illumination of truths the Holy Spirit does communicate some light to the soul, the light given in faith, in which there is no clear understanding, is qualita- tively as different from the other as is the purest gold from the basest metal, and quantitatively as is the sea from a drop of water. In the first kind of illumination, wisdom concerning one, two, or three truths is communicated; in the second

kind, all of God's Wisdom is communicated in general, that is, the Son of God, who communicates himself to the soul in faith.[67]

Hence, John's view of the human person ties faith and charity to the illumination that the Holy Spirit fosters in the soul just as the image of the "living flame of love" and the quest for knowledge of God is the hallmark of the image of the Trinity embedded in the souls of men and women.

Embarking on the path of spiritual transformation was nothing new in late sixteenth century Spain for such was the character of the Catholic Reformation in Spain which, from the time of Cardinal Cisneros' rise in the late 1400s, had emphasized a return to simpler forms of piety and worship focusing on personal interiority. Indeed, it could be said with historical accuracy that long before Luther's Wittenberg circle of reform minded clergy began attracting the attention of the German nobility and laity, reform minded Spanish Franciscans like the famous Cardinal Cisneros and Francisco de Osuna had fostered much of the preparatory changes enacted from the 1490s through the 1530s that created a religious climate sufficiently open to the visionary work of figures like Teresa of Avila, John of the Cross, and Ignatius of Loyola. Their ministerial careers and written works, set within the parameters of the Roman Catholic Reformation, offer an intriguing example of yet another theological reconstruction of Christian tradition from the juxtaposition of the dynamic repository of the Pentecostal story with the empowering infusion of pneumatological inspiration throughout the history of Christianity.

PENTECOST AND IGNATIUS OF LOYOLA

On September 27, 1540, amidst an unprecedented era of rapidly expanding Spanish political, economic, and military power that spanned several continents, Pope Paul III officially approved the founding of the Society of Jesus. At the time, European Christendom was torn between the spread of Protestantism across Northern Europe, and the steadfast Roman Catholic efforts to halt its spread into Southern Europe led by Spain and its allies. Like the founding of the Franciscan Order in the early 1200s, the Society of Jesus, known more popularly as the Jesuit Order, also grew dramatically during its first twenty years. Although the founder of the Jesuits, Ignatius of Loyola, was older than Teresa of Avila and John of the Cross, and his active ministry preceded theirs by almost half a century, I left him for last in this overview of the Catholic Reformation in Spain because the influence of the Jesuits as educational reformers and champions of the oppressed would eventually extended far beyond Spain and surpass the influence of the Carmelite's even in Ignatius' lifetime. In the next chapter Francis Bacon will praise the Jesuits for their willingness to reform Christian learning and for their contributions to scientific reasoning.

By the time the founder of the Jesuits died in 1556, his beloved "society numbered approximately one thousand members" who "resided in more than a hundred houses or colleges" in Spain, Portugal, France, Italy and Sicily, as well as Upper and Lower Germany.[68] Foreign missions, in Brazil and India, had already started before Ignatius' passing. In the nearly five centuries since the founding of the Jesuit Order, much has been written and praised about its positive role in education, while much has been criticized and vilified about the Order's role in the political affairs of the Spanish and French colonial empires. The Jesuits were on the vanguard of change and reform in both Europe and the colonial territories of European nation-states. Intense controversies and weird conspiracy theories followed them nearly everywhere the order was active until the late 1700s. However, Ignatius of Loyola's spiritual life was blessed with a series of extraordinary visions concerning the piety of Jesus Christ, the Holy Trinity, and the presence of the Holy Spirit in the experiential life of the individual Christian that most readers of his life and work often overlook. For this founder of *La Compañia de Jesus"* (the Society of Jesus) between 1536 and 1540, and author of *The Spiritual Exercises,* the main themes and practices of Ignatian spirituality emerged following a near fatal injury in battle during Pentecost.

Ignacio Lopez de Loyola was born in 1491 at the majestic castle of Loyola in Guipúzcoa, located in northwestern Spain's Basque country. His parents Don Beltran, Lord of Oñaz and Loyola, and Doña Marina Saenz were descendants of high ranking local nobility who had supported the kings of Castile since the beginning of the thirteenth century. They had twelve other children besides Ignacio, who was their youngest child. He was christened Iñigo and was known by that name among family and friends. His mother died when he was just seven years old, and his father died when he was about sixteen years old. Before his death, Don Beltran entrusted his son's upbringing and education to a relative, Don Juan Velázquez de Cuéllar from Arévalo in Castile, with an emphasis on the profession of arms and the political life of the royal court. As Treasurer of the Spanish Court, Velázquez de Cuellar was a wealthy and highly influential friend of King Ferdinand of Aragon and Queen Isabel of Castile. Serving as a royal page among courtiers and nobles at such a young age, Ignatius developed a considerable fondness for chivalry, fine clothing, horses, and weapons. In his spare time he read chivalric tales about champion knights, like Amadis of Gaul, while pursuing romance with the young ladies at the Spanish court. In the early 1500s, none of these frivolous pursuits or military training was out of the norm for a young man of his noble lineage. This was also considered an era of unprecedented Spanish power and glory as the young nation-state believed itself to be the agent of a great worldly transformation following the events of 1492.

After Velázquez de Cuellar's death in 1517, Ignatius entered the military service of the Duke of Nájera and Viceroy of Navarre. His quest for honor and glory was as strong as that of the heroic characters in the stories he loved reading, and he soon emerged as a commander in the viceroy's army. In the spring of 1521, the French army invaded Navarre and surrounded its capital city of Pamplona where Ignatius and his garrison were stationed. As the siege dragged on the French forces launched a massive artillery bombardment of the city during which Ignatius was seriously wounded on Tuesday May 20, 1521. His legs were nearly severed from his body by a canon ball. The garrison surrendered when they saw their captain had fallen, but he was not held prisoner for long by the French. He was soon allowed to return to Loyola, where relatives could help care for him while recovering, and where he began a long period of slow and painful recuperation that also triggered his spiritual conversion. He was probably also suffering from infection. By late June of 1521, about the time of the Solemnity of Saints Peter and Paul, his fever subsided and his condition began improving. Doctors did their best to set his broken leg bones without anesthesia, but Ignatius limped and felt occasional pain from these wounds for the rest of his life. His military career, and the chivalric honors, for which he had trained and dreamed of achieving for so many years, was now basically over.

Although historians have paid scarce attention to the festal date of Ignatius' fall in battle, it was ironically Tuesday of Pentecost week when circumstances humbled the would-be warrior and when the Holy Spirit began opening the doors of spiritual perception and experience for the now thirty year old former knight. He wanted to read in hope of distracting his mind from the pain, and allegedly asked for books about knight errantry and chivalric novels during his convalescence at Loyola, which unfolded throughout the remainder of that year's Pentecostal cycle of days. Since the castle library did not have the novels he requested, he was brought instead copies of Ludolph of Saxony's *De Vita Christi* and *The Golden Legend* of Jacobus de Voragine, also known as the *Lives of the Saints*. Visions of the various stages of Jesus' earthly life and of the Lord's personal piety in relation to the Father and the Holy Spirit permeated his prayers and reflections on Ludolph's *Life of Christ* during these months. The *Golden Legend's* emphasis on liberation from worldly passion and human sinfulness through the empowering presence of the Holy Spirit, whose outpouring at Pentecost reconciled the members of the Church to the Trinitarian Persons following Christ's Ascension, must have left an impression on his conscience that further inspired his process of discernment and repentance.

During his convalescence, Ignatius was also profoundly influenced by images and visions of the Virgin Mary in heavenly majesty with Jesus. Ignatius' physical recuperation from the severe leg wounds suffered at Pamplona turned into a spiritual *renovatio* that revealed the *prima materia* of his future ministerial career. Ironically, just a few years later he was accused of being an *Alumbrado* or Illuminist because of his independent, fiery spirit and due to the contemplative exercises he practiced and taught others who yearned for spiritual rigor and divine wisdom.

Before the end of 1522, Ignatius eventually left his relatives at Loyola and began his new life of service and ministry with dispatch. He decided to embark on a pilgrimage to Jerusalem from the port city of Barcelona, but not before stopping in Catalonia at the famous monastery of Montserrat, which also housed a Benedictine shrine dedicated to Our Lady. He subjected himself to three days of self-examination and penance before dressing himself in sackcloth and sandals, giving his wealth and fine clothing away to the poor, and symbolically leaving his sword and dagger at the altar of the Virgin at Montserrat. Form our contemporary psychoanalytic perspective, modern readers and interpreters of this story detect a curious psychological compensation in the transference of chivalric language about serving the state as a knight (*caballero* or *hombre gentil*) being transformed into the pastoral language about serving the church as a soldier, or as a spiritual knight, sworn to the service of Christ and Our Lady, as the Mother of Christ. He then resumed his journey towards Barcelona with the aim of reaching Jerusalem before winter.

While en route to Barcelona, Ignatius stopped at Manresa in Catalonia and stayed for about ten months, from the spring of 1522 to February 1523. During this stay, he perfected his religious practices and experienced some of the most significant mystical visions of his life. He had heard from a local woman about a series of caves just outside the town which were well suited to the ascetical and penitential exercises he sought to practice. Here the spirit of his former worldly desires continued to wrestle with the transformational work the Holy Spirit was still trying to fulfill in his heart and mind. Although Ignatius chose not to explain or write about his most important vision, which he received one day while praying by the banks of the Rio Cardoner outside Manresa, I believe that the contents of these religious experiences and integrative visions were most likely a combination of pneumatological and Trinitarian revelations.[69] Given the theological integration of his pneumatological sensibilities with his Trinitarian views concerning the indwelling and perichoresis of the Three Persons in equal majesty, and in relation with the human realm through the Holy Spirit, I believe this is entirely possible. If he was working out the details and instructions of the spiritual exercises that eventually became the basis of his book, as some scholars and the Jesuit Order have maintained throughout the ensuing five centuries, then Ignatius may have chosen to keep the contents of this particular vision between himself and his Savior.

Such a prudent decision is entirely in keeping with Ignatius' naturally cautious outlook later in life following the frequent accusations of being an Illuminist (Alumbrado) that he had endured as a result of his pneumatological insights, theological views, and religious practices. Little wonder then that *The Spiritual Exercises* concludes just as Jesus Christ disappears into the clouds during the miracle of the Ascension. We hear about the coming of the Holy Spirit as Jesus tells his disciples not to leave Jerusalem for they all "shall be baptized by the Holy Spirit not many days hence (Acts 1: 1-11).[70] The miracle of Pentecost, as the birth of the Church, belonged to the ecclesiastical domain and perhaps harbored too much high voltage for Ignatius' objective of writing a guidebook for discerning the will of God in one's spiritual and public life. John O'Malley describes that "He and the early Jesuits had to spend much time and effort trying to clarify how they differed from the *alumbrados*."[71] At one point Ignatius and his companions spent forty-two days in prison for being suspected of Iluminism and were warned by the authorities upon release to be very careful not to teach certain ideas or religious practices until their ministerial studies had progressed for several more years.[72] O'Malley's historical narrative of the first years of the Jesuit Order provides a masterful account of how the dynamic presence of the Holy Spirit guided the efforts and work of Ignatius and his early successors.[73]

POSTSCRIPT: THE JESUIT LEGACY

Considering the discussion of late medieval notions of *renovatio, reforma,* and *restauratio* with which this chapter's exposition of Protestant and Roman Catholic figures opened, Ignatius of Loyola and his Society of Jesus may have succeeded further than any of his Protestant or Catholic contemporaries with similar reformist objectives. It is a huge testament to this wounded Spanish knight's theological foresight and political savvy that in the early 1600s despite Francis Bacon's anti-Catholic biases and ardent English Protestantism following the Spanish Armada's attempted invasion and conquest of Britain, he praised Ignatius and his Jesuit Order for their sincere efforts at revitalizing Christian education and scientific learning. Indeed, inspired by Ignatian teachings and the power of the Holy Spirit, it was a Jesuit priest, Athanasius Kircher, who in the 1600s earned the title of "the last man who knew everything." Inspired and guided by the Holy Spirit, the first few generations of Jesuits who succeeded Ignatius of Loyola led the Society of Jesus to assume a very prominent role in the church and culture of the sixteenth and seventeenth centuries.

Athanasius Kircher's (1602-1680) birth in the picturesque little town of Geisa, located on the banks of the Upper Rhone River, occurred on May 2, 1602 in the heart of that year's Pentecostal cycle of days. His highly versatile curiosity and fascinating career knew no boundaries in the study if Nature and the cosmos. He was as comfortable in the study of volcanoes, magnetism, or mathematics as in the contemplation of astronomical bodies and alchemical principles. He has been called "the last true Renaissance man." His fascination with alchemy and its elusive mercurial spirit was synonymous with his pneumatological ideas and sensibilities. The esoteric tradition of Christian magical theology (*theologia magica Christiana*), from Albertus Magnus and Roger Bacon to Marsilio Ficino and Abbot Trithemius of Sponheim had long maintained that the Holy Spirit acted upon matter and energy, by the power and Grace of God, to effect the transformation of Nature's secrets contained in the material realm.

It might be objected that this tangent is at odds with the theologically rich Jesuit treatises and commentaries addressing the Holy Spirit or the Holy Trinity, and penned by devout followers of Saint Ignatius of Loyola and the Society of Jesus during the first two hundred years of the order's existence, etc. However, given the Hermetic and alchemical trajectories which we will pursue in the next chapter, Kircher's insatiable curiosity for knowledge of the natural world, as well as his role in the reformation and expansion of Christian learning at a crucial point in the early modern period when the commingling of new perspectives among scientific experimentation, religious knowledge, and spiritual wonder was still possible, has recently become the subject of an intensive scholarly reassessment of his life and work.[74]

The seventeenth century was an age of scientific wonders and far-reaching socio-political transformations that spawned the era that we came to know and understand as "modernity," and which we now inhabit. However, it was also a century whose experiences of prolonged international war, excessive bloodshed, and military devastation of the natural environment would not be equaled until the two World Wars of the twentieth century. The Thirty Years War, pitted northern European Protestantism against southern European Roman Catholicism, and eventually engulfed the entire continent while giving rise to a new world order in which *scientific rationalism* offered itself as the antidote to the unverifiable subjectivities of pneumatology and the medieval world view; a new world order in which *political rationalism* offered itself as the antidote for the failed *Respublica Christiana* of the Middle Ages and its legions of visionaries, prophets, and reformers claiming special revelations from the *subversive fire* of the Holy Spirit and the story of Pentecost.

Ironically, both the promised emancipation of knowledge and learning through the Scientific Revolution of the 1600s, and the ideal of forging a Republic of Reason in the 1700s, had inextricable ties to late medieval pneumatological ideas and sensibilities that stretch across the history of Christianity. The story of Pentecost and the role of the Holy Spirit in late medieval and early modern European culture served as repositories of religious tradition for theological reconstruction and spiritual revitalization. The next chapter surveys the broader story of the Holy Spirit as connected with the medieval fascination over Christian magical theology, miracles, medicine and alchemy, and the subsequent popularization of these esoteric currents among scientists, theologians, and medical doctors during the Italian Renaissance. This new generation of reformers and visionaries, many of whom can be classified as Humanists, wanted "to read the Book of Nature" or "to decipher the secrets of Nature" for the noble purposes of alleviating human suffering and expanding the boundaries of human industry. To that complex, and largely forgotten, pneumatological story we now turn for this volume's final chapter.

NOTES

1. Delwin Brown, *Boundaries of Our Habitations: Tradition and Theological Construction* (Albany: SUNY Press, 1994) 39.

2. Peter Matheson, *The Imaginative World of the Reformation.* (Minneapolis: Fortress Press, 2001).

3. See Steven Ozment, *The Age of Reform, 1250-1550: An Intellectual and Religious History of Late Medieval and Reformation Europe.* (New Haven: Yale University Press, 1980) 1-21; 290-317; 434-439.

4. Brown, *Boundaries of Our Habitations,* 119.

5. Delwin Brown, "Limitation and Ingenuity: Radical Historicism and the Nature of Tradition," *American Journal of Theology and Philosophy.* Vol. 24 No. 3 (Sept 2003): 201.

6. Ibid. 200.

7. Bard Thompson, *Humanists and Reformers: A History of the Renaissance and Reformation.* (Eerdmans Publishing, 1996).

8. John of the Cross' familiarity with Tauler's mystical ideas has been suggested by a number of researchers since the early 1900s. A 1548 Latin translation of Tauler's works by Surius made the Rhineland mystic's ideas available to a growing number of educated laity and clergy across Spain, but it was not until 1551 and then not again until 1669, that Spanish translations of Tauler's Latin *Institutio* were available in Spain. For recent ideas on John of the Cross' possible awareness of Tauler's mystical ideas see: R. A. Herrera,

Silent Music: The Life, Work, and Thoughts of St. John of the Cross. (Grand Rapid, MI: Eerdmans, 2004) 38, 80; and Edward Howells, *John of the Cross and Teresa of Avila: Mystical Knowing and Selfhood* (New York: Crossroad Publishing, 2002) 17, 62, 64.

9. Being influenced by Tauler's ideas about mystical piety and the Holy Spirit might be much harder to prove in the case of Juan de Valdes because he died seven years before Surius' Latin translation of Tauler's work was disseminated across Spain. On the other hand, Valdes still might have accessed Tauler's works and influence in Latin by way of other trajectories from Northern Humanism or perhaps during his exile and lay ministry in Naples, Italy.

10. For an overview of Tauler's significance in late medieval German theology and a concise summary of his major ideas see Bernard McGinn, *The Harvest of Mysticism in Medieval Germany, 1300-1500.* (New York: Crossroad Publishing, 2005) 240-296.

11. As cited in *Dictionary of the Middle Ages,* Volume 11. (New York: Charles Scribner's, 1988) 602.

12. In *Johannes Tauler: Sermons.* (Mahwah, NJ: Paulist Press, 1985) xiii.

13. Ibid. 76.

14. Ibid. 85.

15. Ibid. 85-86.

16. Ibid. 86.

17. Ibid.

18. Ibid. 86 and 88.

19. Matheson, *The Imaginative World of the Reformation,* 119.

20. Brown, *Boundaries of Our Habitations,* 118-119.

21. Matheson, *The Imaginative World of the Reformation,* 7-10; 119-120.

22. Ibid. 119.

23. Ibid.

24. Ibid. 78.

25. Ibid.

26. Ibid.

27. Ibid. 77.

28. Ibid. 100.

29. For an assessment of Johannes Tauler's influence on Müntzer and Luther see the excellent study by Abraham Friesen, *Thomas Muentzer, a Destroyer of the Godless: The Making of a Sixteenth Century Religious Revolutionary* (Berkeley and Los Angeles: University of California Press, 1990) 10-32.

30. Among the more balanced English language book-length studies that have appeared about this enigmatic voice of the Radical Reformation are the following works: Andrew Bradstock, *Faith in the Revolution: The Political Theologies of Müntzer and Winstanley* (London: SPCK, 1997); Michael G. Baylor, Ed. and Trans. *Revelation and Revolution: Basic Writings of Thomas Müntzer* (Bethlehem, PA: Lehigh University Press, 1993); Hans-Jürgen Goertz, *Thomas Muntzer: Apocalyptic Mystic and Revolutionary.* Translsted by Jocelyn Jaquiery and edited by Peter Matheson. (Edinburgh, Scotland: T & T Clark, 1993); Tom Scott, *Theology and Revolution in the German Reformation* (New York: St. Martin's Press, 1989); Eric W. Gritsch, *Reformer Without A Church: The Life and Thought of Thomas Müntzer* (Philadelphia: Fortress Press, 1967).

31. Hans-Jürgen Goertz, *Thomas Muntzer: Apocalyptic Mystic and Revolutionary.* Trans. by Jocelyn Jaquiery and edited by Peter Matheson. (Edinburgh: T & T Clark, 1993) xiii.

32. For an informative volume of edited essays on these connections see, James M. Stayer and Werner O. Packull, Eds. *The Anabaptists and Thomas Müntzer* (Dubuque, IA: Kendall-Hunt Publishing, 1980).

33. Stanley M. Burgess, *The Holy Spirit: Medieval, Roman Catholic, and Reformation Traditions* (Peabody, MA: Hendrickson Publishers, 1997) 203.

34. From Müntzer's "Prague Protest" as translated by Michael G. Baylor in *Revelation and Revolution: The Basic Writings of Thomas Müntzer* (Bethlehem: Lehigh University Press, 1993) 53.

35. Ibid.

36. Ibid.

37. See Susannah Winkworth, *The History and the Life of the Reverend Doctor John Tauler with Twnety-five of His Sermons.* (London: Allenson, 1905) 159-161.

38. From Müntzer's "Prague Protest" in *Revelation and Revolution*, 55.

39. Ibid. 59.

40. Ibid. 20.

41. Ibid.

42. Hans-Jürgen Goertz, *Thomas Muntzer: Apocalyptic Mystic and Revolutionary*, 9.

43. *Christianismi Restitutio* (Vienne: Dauphine, 1553) 3, as cited and translated in Marian Hillar and Clair S. Allen, *Michael Servetus: Intellectual Giant, Humanist, and Martyr* (Lanham, Maryland: University Press of America, 2002), v.

44. Ibid. 227.

45. Ibid. 705-706.

46. Ibid. 196.

47. M. Hillar and Clair S. Allen, *Michael Servetus: Intellectual Giant, Humanist, and Martyr* (Lanham, Maryland: University Press of America, 2002) 105-106.

48. Johannes Trithemius, *De septem secundeis intelligentiis sive spiritibus orbes post deum moventibus.* From *Opera Historica, quotquot hactensus reperiri potuerunt omnia* (Frankfurt: Typis Wechelianis, 1601).

49. María Rosa Menocal, *The Ornament of the World: How Muslims, Jews, and Christians Created a Culture of Tolerance in Medieval Spain.* (New York: Little, Brown, & Company, 2002) 244-247.

50. José C. Nieto, Ed. *Valdes' Two Catechisms:* The *Dialogue on Christian Doctrine* and The *Christian Instruction for Children*, By Juan de Valdes (d. 1541). (Lawrence, KS: Coronado Press, 1981) 53-165.

51. Alastair Hamilton, *Heresy and Mysticism in Sixteenth Century Spain: The Alumbrados.* (Toronto and Buffalo: University of Toronto Press, 1992) 12-23.

52. See Raúl Gómez-Ruiz, *Mozarabs, Hispanics, and the Cross* (Orbis, 2007)

53. See Francisco de Osuna, *Third Spiritual Alphabet.* Classics of Western Spirituality. Mary E. Giles, Trans. (Mahwah, NJ: Paulist Press, 1981).

54. See Teresa of Avila, *The Way of Perfection.* E. Allison Peers, Trans. (New York: Image Books/Doubleday Publishing, 1964); and *Interior Castle.* E. Allison Peers, Trans. (New York: Image Books/Doubleday, 1989).

55. Catherine Swietlicki, *Spanish Christian Cabala: The Works of Luis de Leon, Santa Teresa de Jesus, and San Juan de la Cruz* (University of Missouri, 1986) 49-51.

56. Edward Howells, *John of the Cross and Teresa of Avila: Mystical Knowing and Selfhood* (New York: Crossroad Publishing, 2002) 62.

57. Teresa of Avila, *The Way of Perfection.* E. Allsion Peers, Trans. (New York: Image Books/Doubleday, 1964) 137-138.

58. Kieran Kavanaugh and Otilio Rodriguez, Trans. *The Collected Works of St. John of the Cross.* Rev. Ed. (Washington, D.C.: Institute of Carmelite Studies Publications, 1991) 10.

59. Ibid. 9-12.

60. See Ibid, 11-12 for a short but informative summary of the possible range of courses and philosophical themes to which John was exposed during his student years at the University of Salamanca.

61. See *The Poems of St. John of the Cross.* Third Edition. J. F. Nims, Trans. (Chicago: University of Chicago Press, 1979) 24-29.

62. *The Collected Works of St. John of the Cross*, 639.

63. Ibid. 641.

64. Ibid. 257.

65. Ibid. 256.

66. Ibid. 257.

67. Ibid. 257-258.

68. See George E. Ganss, ed. *Ignatius of Loyola: The Spiritual Exercises and Selected Works.* (Mahwah, NJ: Paulist Press, 1991) 46.

69. Ibid. 81.

70. Ignatius of Loyola, *The Spiritual Exercises of St. Ignatius.* (New York: Image Books/Doubleday, 1989) 126; 198-200.

71. John W. O'Malley, *The First Jesuits.* (Cambridge: Harvard University Press, 1993) 27-28.

72. Ibid. 27.

73. Ibid. 264-271.

74. See Paula Findlen, *Athanasius Kircher: The Last Man Who Knew Everything.* (New York: Routledge, 2004); Joscelyn Godwin, *Athanasius Kircher's Theatre of the World: The Life and Work of the Last Man to Search for Universal Knowledge.* (New York: Inner Traditions, 2009).

[Handwritten notes:]

194 - God is present in Nature + humans

Spirit in bodies

Key 196 - first
def - different way of knowing

201 - transmute base → precious
mercy / gold
human → soul (soul)

magic = power inherent in nature

202 fire is key

204 - word play + allegory - many meanings
discernment when read Bible
or right to nature

CHAPTER 5
"THOSE PONDERABLE FIRE PARTICLES..."
DECIPHERING NATURE'S SECRETS IN THE SCIENTIFIC REVOLUTION

Truly, truly, I say to you, he who believes in me will also do the works that I do; and greater works than these will he do, because I go to the Father.

John 14:12

For that nothing parcel of the world, is denied to Mans enquirie and invention: hee doth in another place rule over; when hee sayth, 'The Spirite of Man is as the Lampe of God, wherewith hee searcheth the inwardnesse of all secrets.'

Francis Bacon, *The Advancement of Learning*[1]

There are, of course, particular events that we call experiments, in which the operation of these laws is most clearly manifested, just as there are focused moments of encounter with the divine . . . The difference is that experiments can be contrived but moments of intense religious experience are given . . . Yet, just as we can be aware of natural laws outside the laboratory . . . so God is not confined to the realm of the conventionally sacred.

John Polkinghorne[2]

Traditional symbols can have revolutionary consequences . . . Symbols can invert as well as reinforce social values . . . Old symbols can acquire new meanings, and these new meanings might suggest a new society.

Caroline Walker Bynum[3]

In the opening pages of *The Story of Christianity*, Justo González suggests that the Acts of the Apostles in the New Testament is really "not so much" about "the deeds of the apostles as the deeds of the Holy Spirit through the apostles and others."[4] While his bold perspective is not typical among historians trained in modern positivism or postmodern critical theory, it does raise significant questions about reason and faith, as well as of continuity and discontinuity in the long sundry story of Christian pneumatological traditions. The period surveyed in this chapter might be described as *the fulcrum* of the epochal break between the medieval religious worldview and the modernist enterprise of scientific empiricism, an era characterized by a gradually increasing Euro-Western individualism that led to many of the achievements of scientists, inventors, scholars and artists over the last five centuries. The writers and movements examined in the following pages began their investigation of Nature and uttered their burning pleas for the reform of Christian learning with a deep sense of wonder about God's role in Creation and about humanity's place in the universe. If González' insight about the history of Christianity as "a history of the deeds of the Spirit in and through the men and women who have gone before in the faith"[5] resonates with believers everywhere, then the protagonists we are about to meet in this chapter pondered the meaning and mystery of the Holy Spirit no less faithfully than their ancient and medieval predecessors. Each protagonist considered himself a devout and pious Christian, even while church leaders and contemporaries accused some of sorcery or heresy. In their vigorous pursuit of knowledge about the natural world, of Nature's causes and effects, they, too, uttered the age-old Pentecostal inquiry: *What does this mean?* Their fascination with chemical operations, spiritual energy, and force fields grew out of a profound respect and curiosity about the Spirit's relationship to matter, described by scientific pioneers like Jan Baptiste van Helmont and Robert Boyle as "*those ponderable fire particles.*" Van Helmont lived at a time when alchemy was giving way to modern chemistry, and once, when feeling at a loss for words about his new profession and research agenda, identified himself as a *philosophus per ignem*, literally as a "philosopher of fire."[6]

This chapter examines the intersection of Christian _pneumatology_ and conceptions of Pentecost with the early modern emphasis on _scientific knowledge_ about the natural world. This was a convergence that, from the Florentine Renaissance in the late 1400s to the founding of the Royal Society of London in 1660, generated dramatic reformulations of European life and thought along with the eventual reordering of Christian tradition, theology, and pedagogy that produced a "new society" by the eighteenth century, which as quoted above from Bynum's study of symbolism and tradition reminds us that: "traditional symbols can have revolutionary consequences."

MEDIEVAL SCIENCE: MAGIC AND THE HOLY SPIRIT

The history of both Christianity and experimental science can be better understood by studying the pneumatological convictions _of early modern_ esoteric movements whose founding figures and writers were among the earliest precursors and pioneers of experimental science. In her landmark study on the Rosicrucian Renaissance, Frances Amelia Yates suggested that, given the particular historical circumstances and intellectual innovation of the sixteenth and seventeenth centuries, any early-modern European nation that "did not over-persecute for magic would therefore be a country in which science would develop fairly freely."[7] Magic, especially in its manifestation as philosophical and practical _alchemy_, served since the 1200s as the proto-experimental repository of a steadily growing scientific rationalism focused on decoding, understanding, and finally employing the "secrets of Nature" (*secretum Natura*). In the hands of devout Christian priests and theologians, its aim was both the alleviation of human suffering (*medicina chimica*) and the promotion of human flourishing (*Beatitudo*). Yates firmly believed "such a country was Elizabethan England," but also noted these tendencies in early modern Germany, Bohemia, France, and the Netherlands. As observed by B. J. Gibbons: "The securing of health and long life was one of the traditional goals of alchemy; this, after all is the purpose of the elixir of life."[8] This notion of the healing arts, found in both medieval Christianity and the various esoteric mystical traditions, was quite fond of the medical epithet: *Natura naturam curat*. In the late 1920s, Lynn Thorndike began writing his masterful eight-volume *History of Magic and Experimental Science* by explaining "that magic and experimental science have been connected in their development; that magicians were perhaps the first to experiment; and that the history of both magic and experimental science can be better understood by studying them together."[9] Most historians of science and European intellectual history today accept these connections as foundational to the rationalist enterprise of the 1500s and 1600s, but few of us working on the history of Christianity have paid careful attention to the role of pneumatological ideas and sensibilities in this most definitive permutation of Christian tradition at the dawn of modernity. This reformulation of traditional Western and Christian symbols exerted a vast influence on modernity despite the great divide which later opened up between that which science classified as empirically unverifiable or ontologically unknowable, and that which Christians, by then identifying each other as Roman Catholics or Protestants, still regarded as the verifiable and knowable mystery of God's loving presence in Nature and in the human heart through the Holy Spirit.

Although unbeknownst to many devout Christians today, and though neglected by most contemporary historians of Christianity, pneumatology and the rise of science intersected among the esoteric, spiritual pathways of magic, alchemy, Hermeticism, Cabala, and mysticism. This was the point at which religious experience and curiosity about natural phenomena coalesced from about 1470 through 1670 before going their separate ways. The medieval and early modern Christian discourse on magic was replete with warnings about conjuring demons and malevolent spirits (*black magic*), while its nearly forgotten counter-discourse known as *theologia magica* (or *white magic*) was conducted under the protective aura of the Holy Spirit. In other words, concern about daemonic spirits preying on human frailty and hubris rendered the magician's *magnum opus* suspect and prone to charges of heresy or sorcery often leading to imprisonment. In contrast, acknowledging the sanctifying and empowering presence of the Holy Ghost with reverence and humility, while reminding one's colleagues or readers of Scholastic authorities and Christian saints, like Albertus Magnus, who also dabbled in this miraculous realm, rendered the magician's attempt to command the powers of Nature theologically and morally acceptable as a *magnum miraculum Christianum*.

During early modern times, Pentecost and the Holy Spirit was imagined by esoteric Christian movements such as the Rosicrucians in Germany, and the Freemasons in England and Scotland, as providing the *pneumatological influx* or motivational cause for the transformation of both individual and society. Even the English founder of the Scientific Revolution, Francis Bacon, envisioned a "Second Pentecost" based upon the gifts of scientific reasoning in his novella *The New Atlantis* (1627). Modern science, indeed, flowed out of this early-modern fascination with the inexplicable interaction of Spirit (*Sancti Spiritus*) and primary matter (*materia prima*) in the physical world. With this chapter, the book's historical narrative concludes in the same domain that our exploration began in Chapter Two, in the imaginal space where Nature's chemical secrets and rhythmic cycles intersect with the mystery of the Holy Spirit.

A BRIEF HISTORY OF ESOTERIC CHRISTIANITY

Several years ago, I was asked by the faculty review board, at the theological school where I teach, why my syllabus included a brief overview of Christian alchemy in a survey course on medieval church history designed for Master of Divinity students. Their inquiry was allegedly motivated by a concern for how much material a professor could adequately cover during a ten week introductory survey class, a legitimate concern in graduate theological education as well as in survey courses across all sectors of higher education. I sensed the inquiry was more about my colleagues' lack of familiarity with the topic in question than about "how much material to include in a survey class." I responded cordially by reminding them how medieval alchemy represented a stage in Western religious and intellectual history at which the pre-modern fascination with matter and Spirit led to a deeper interest in mechanical and chemical operations aimed at gaining mastery over Nature, and that the fruits of such labors issued directly through Italian Humanism's recovery of magical theology and into the Scientific Revolution and Rosicrucian Enlightenment of the 1600s. In the hands of devout medieval Christians, the use of magic and alchemy sought increased understanding of natural causes and effects for curing the sick and serving society. Indeed, as observed by William Newman and Walter Principe,

> It is clear that there did exist a strong experimental tradition in the alchemy of Western Europe from the High Middle Ages through the seventeenth century. Not only did alchemy involve considerable laboratory experience and practice. But many alchemists were even deeply concerned with testing; some employed a kind of quantitative method that is both akin to the later traditions of chemistry and quite alien to the image of alchemists as primarily seekers of an *unio mystica*.[10]

Furthermore, the notion of God's miraculous, living presence in Nature and matter is also at the heart of the Doctrine of Transubstantiation, the traditional Roman Catholic belief whereby the Communion Host is mystically transformed into the actual Body and Blood of the Lord Jesus Christ. Such ideas of God's immanence in the physical world also explain Hildegard of Bingen's numerous statements about the mystifying presence of the Holy Spirit in Nature as a manifestation of God's grace and love. St. Francis of Assisi's attitude of deep reverence for animals, birds, trees, and food is another fine example of the medieval concern for the harmony of humans with the community of all God's creatures. In time, these concerns would engender a curiosity about the hidden essence and vitality behind Nature's veil.

Basic knowledge of esoteric Christian traditions, and their vocabularies of human potential and mastery over Nature, has not been widely known among scholars or laypersons since the late 1700s. In an effort to facilitate readers' understanding of how this early modern enthrallment with Nature's secrets, and the puzzling operations of the Holy Spirit, motivated some of the earliest scientific investigations, I offer this brief overview of the little known and often misunderstood history of Esoteric Christianity.[11]

Despite all of our postmodern academic jargon about "culture," "textuality" and "contextual location," or about our status as embodied beings, postmodern discourse offers surprisingly few avenues for reclaiming the presence of Spirit in Nature or in actual physical bodies, either human or animal. Contextual and naturalistic pneumatology has been ignored or dismissed by the majority of leading theologians as a topic on the "fringe" of reputable scholarship. Among our medieval and early modern forbearers, the Christian life, on the other hand, was about the experiential transformation of the individual's heart and mind in relation to God through Jesus Christ (*imitatio Christi*). Faith was imbedded in traditioned practices and the sacraments as mediated through the Holy Spirit in the community of the Church. These aspects of life were, in turn, reflected in both the concerns of natural philosophy (*philosophia naturalis*) and in the Christian liturgical calendar. Transubstantiation offers us a wonderful example of the ancient and medieval Christian understanding of the dynamic spiritual potentialities (*potentia spiritualis*) contained in the physical realm where the grace of God operated, and of the miraculous possibilities that ensued when an individual believer's "heart" (*cardiognosis*) was fully open to the Holy Ghost's "divine kiss." Even Martin Luther, despite his own eventual reinterpretation of Transubstantiation, commented on how he enjoyed reading alchemical allegories in his spare time, as these often helped him ponder "how God plays hide and seek with us in Nature." If effective historical and literary analysis rests, first and foremost, upon our scholarly ability to understand the distant past or a premodern text from the perspective of the public for whom it was intended, then the primary sources examined in this chapter suggest that modernism and postmodernism have overlooked the influence of Esoteric Christianity's conception of the Holy Spirit on the rise of early modern science and its quasi-religious concerns.

What matters most in the historical reappraisal of these spiritual currents is how much the magical and mystical dimensions of reality mattered to the pioneers of experimental science. The historical and literary record is replete with examples of this creative influence, but the discussion that follows in this chapter, and the materials examined herein, represent only a small fraction of that record. The same holds true for the influence of logical positivism on theology and the humanities that rendered the subject matter of pneumatology an "unverifiable subjectivity" from the mid-1800s throughout most of the 1900s.

Definitions of Western Esotericism, or of Esoteric Christianity, have varied in modern times as these terms gradually reappeared in academic discourse toward the end of the 1990s. Most experts in the field would argue that magical ideas and practices are inseparable from the various philosophical and religious strands that characterized these traditions since its beginnings in ancient Egypt and the Hellenistic world. In the words of Antoine Faivre:

Magia, understood as a search for the unity of Man with Nature, teaches us an active manner of being and having, rather than a method of manipulation. What one calls tradition is not a sort of immutable depository, an invariable doctrinal body, but a perpetual rebirth. The tragedy of a culture occurs when everything is perceived in the form of an empty and abstract concept. This could well be our tragedy.[12]

Faivre, in his book on theoretical and methodological approaches to the study of Western Esoteric traditions and movements, defines *esotericism as "a form* of thought, the nature of which we have to try to capture on the basis of the currents which exemplify it." He also encourages researchers to look beyond long-standing stereotypes of "something secret" or "initiatory" behind these currents of European intellectual history. Faivre explains that the role of hermeneutic interpretation in the esoteric domain "serves to designate a type of knowledge, emanating from a spiritual center to be attained after transcending the prescribed ways and techniques" of one's spiritual development. He cautions that the details of these traditions are "quite diverse considering the schools or currents that can lead to it."[13] This way of thinking about esoteric, mystical traditions has been used since the nineteenth century, but its roots stretch from the ancient world through the Renaissance and early modern period. Esoteric Christianity thus includes "currents" or domains like Christian Neo-Platonism, Pythagorean mysticism, magic, alchemy and Hermetic philosophy, Christian Cabala, theosophy, and certain forms of mystical theology, devotion, and practice. As for the domain of mystical theology, we should note that although this is a vast and well-established tradition within Latin and Byzantine Christianity, more than a few of its proponents over the centuries have dabbled in one or more of the esoteric fields just listed. Thus, we have Hildegard of Bingen's enthrallment with the Holy Spirit's manifestations in the realm of *Natura* and her deep knowledge of medieval German folk-magic and the healing arts; Thomas Aquinas' alleged authorship of the alchemistic *Aurora Consurgens* while his beloved teacher, Albertus Magnus, wrote a number of works on the mystical powers of stones; and the Franciscan Roger Bacon's fascination with the promise of alchemy, all of which attest to the historical reality of these currents of thought and practice both inside and outside mainline Christian orthodoxy.

    The various traditions and movements identified as "Esoteric Christianity" might be more accurately described as a different *way of knowing* reality, or as *divergent modes of relating* Nature and humanity to the perceived order of Creation. Those currents of Christian thought termed "esoteric" have long espoused that human beings are not just the passive recipients of invisible powers, but can also serve as spiritual co-creators with God through the empowerment of the Holy Spirit. Whether the Spirit manifests as fire or water, or as a mighty wind, it cannot be prevented from liberating and revitalizing those who see, feel, or hear its vitalizing presence. With its capstone in the mystical tradition known as *theōsis,* Eastern Christianity has long espoused a more accessible and dynamic pneumatology whose objective was the "deification" or "divinization" of the individual follower of Christ through the power of the Holy Spirit.[14] Like the pneumatological protagonists in this volume's earlier chapters, the Spirit's empowering presence will lead many of this chapter's main figures to the subversion of dominant paradigms, while calling for a dramatic reform of Christian thought and pedagogy as the new scientific paradigm of the early modern era arrived "under Jehovah's wings."

The association of these currents of Western philosophical and religious thought with "occult elitism" or with "secret societies" aimed at subverting dominant ecclesiastical structures over the past five hundred years led many Roman Catholics and Protestants to reject or downplay their role in shaping modern history. But as B. J. Gibbons observes, secret societies did not only serve to perpetuate and propagate occult doctrine. They also functioned as powerful organizations for mutual aid and the promotion of various political and social programmes, and these functions may have become more important as the Masonic movement evolved from its occultist roots."[15] Esoteric quasi-Christian movements proceeding from these underground currents should not be ignored; fraternal currents like English and Scottish Freemasonry played a significant role in the emergence of modern representative, democratic government, and fraternities like the German Rosicrucians played a decisive role in shaping the rise of modern science. Indeed, a free and independent United States of America might never have existed without the brave network of Freemasons (and Rosicrucians) who fought and died in the cause of liberty during the American Revolution, and who later donated considerable sums of money for public library buildings, hospitals, and educational programs across North America. Gibbons maintains,

> The occult philosophy flourished in early modern Europe among an increasingly assertive sector of the population which nevertheless experienced life as precarious: the middling sort who, unlike the poor, were not absolved from social responsibility, and, unlike the nobles, were not compensated for their role in society by power and prestige . . . the occult sciences can be regarded as an abstraction of the conceptual framework of sorcery, a phenomenon which originates in *'resistance to society's pressure.'* It is a means of strengthening the individual against the given social consensus. Occultism continues this function of providing a magical armoury for those who are breaking free of social norms. This is why it became an important part of the world-view of some of those who were challenging the aristocratic order.[16] (Emphasis added)

However, what is missing from such contemporary historiographic models of esoteric and occultist study is an acknowledgement of the subversive and liberative role of pneumatological ideas and sensibilities that early modern advocates of these currents brought with them from their familiarity with Christian tradition and Scripture to both inspire and inform their reformist and revolutionary endeavors. Popular movies, like Disney's *National Treasure* films, remind us of the mystique that esoteric fraternities like the Freemasons, once commanded in the social arenas and nationalist mythologies of the early modern era.

Furthermore, the contemporary academic study of religion and historiography is suspicious of any approaches or persons proposing overarching, essentialist explanations that echo the old perennialist (*philosophia perennis*) assumptions of early twentieth century thinkers like Titus Burckhardt, Carl Jung, Henri Corbin, and Joseph Campbell. For contemporary scholars untrained in the linguistic maze of Western Esotericism, the teleological assumptions among these currents and movements raise a few red flags that postmodern scholars have been taught to regard with suspicion and careful scrutiny. Despite the philosophical sophistication of late medieval magicians and the intellectual openness of early modern Rosicrucians and Freemasons, the universalizing elements in their respective paradigms generated a dismissive attitude towards the study of esotericism among modern and postmodern researchers, another "blind-spot" which bequeathed most twentieth and twenty-first century intellectuals an incomplete picture of the philosophical and quasi-theological motivations of the founders of the modern world.

On the other hand, Kärkkäinen's observation about Western Christianity's long-standing *pneumatological deficit* has its counterpart in the unexamined assumptions by which modernist and postmodernist scholars in various fields passed judgment over that which was deemed either worthy or unworthy of serious academic investigation. The intellectual currents generally listed under "Western Esotericism" or "Esoteric Christianity" has been neglected by the majority of researchers in the history of Christianity precisely because of such unexamined assumptions about academic legitimacy and rational inquiry. If we are to recover and understand the *pneumatological sensibilities* of the esoteric currents whose fascination with the Holy Spirit and the material world inspired the rise of science at the dawn of modernity, then we need to look deeper into this eerie and unfamiliar story.

The history of the alchemical and Hermetic strains of Western Esotericism that formed the basis of the *theologia magica* espoused among medieval and early modern Christians begins in the Hellenistic world of the ancient Mediterranean basin. From its earliest beginnings, this tradition emphasized the fusion of Egyptian and Greek principles concerning astronomy, mathematics, medicine, and literary interpretation. For the ancient Egyptians, the tradition was equated with the Ibis-headed god Thoth, whom we are told gave humanity these four disciplines as gifts by which to improve human life and learn the secrets of reading signs in nature and in the heavens, divine secrets that humanity might then use for communicating with the gods in the celestial and unseen realms. For the ancient Greeks, the tradition became equated with Hermes, whom we are told was the son of Zeus and the mountain nymph Maia. Hermes served as the "messenger" of the Olympian gods. He was also known among the Greeks as the protector of tradesmen and travelers and as the guide of souls in both their sleeping hours and in their journey from the world of the living to the afterlife.

Clues to the etymology of his name may be derived from the words *hermaion* and *hermen*, which respectively signified a "pile of stones," erected to guide travelers on ancient Greek roads, and the "stone-pillars" erected in front of ancient Greek homes as dwelling places for the protective spirit of Hermes.[17] The Greeks also referred to Hermes as *kriophoros*, meaning "ram-bearer," an epithet designating his role and manifestation as "The Good Shepherd." The prevalence of this epithet led many early Christians to equate Hermes with Jesus Christ as

"The Good Shepherd." Thus, a bewildering association of myths and symbols about Hermes came to be represented among Christian proponents of *theologia magica* under the terms magic, alchemy, and Hermeticism, each term of which, in turn, represents long-standing spiritual practices and belief systems predating Christianity.

Among the ancient Romans, the figure of Thoth-Hermes was equated with the Roman deity, Mercurius, who functioned as the god of tradesmen and merchants, as well as the patron lord of thieves. But in his role as divine mediator and messenger of the gods, Mercury would be equated among early and medieval Christians with the inspiring and comforting presence of the Holy Spirit. One of his Latin epithets was *medius currens*, literally "running in the middle" or "mediator" between the human and divine realms. In the medieval Christian calendar, as in Roman times, Wednesday (*dies Mercurri*) was the day of the week honoring Mercury. Hence Hermes, as the Roman Mercurius, continued to exert a profound influence upon the Western imagination as an intermediary figure capable of bridging the gap between human existence and the Word of God and between matter and Spirit. This is well attested to by the persistent popularity of Martianus Capella's *The Marriage of Mercury and Philology* from the moment of its appearance in the late fourth century to the late seventeenth century. As one of the most widely translated, copied, and disseminated books of the Latin Middle Ages, *De nuptis Mercurii et Philologiae* joined Saint Augustine's *De doctrina Christiana* as forming the basis of a medieval Christian education in the humanities (*studia humanitatis*) and the liberal arts (*artes liberales*).

However, the syncretistic blending of traits shared by Hermes and Christ went even further. While the apologists and Church Fathers were busy appropriating and accommodating pagan wisdom, Hermes' association with sacred stones and scriptural references to Jesus as the "cornerstone, chosen and precious," yet rejected by the builders of the temple (1 Peter 2:4-10), attracted much attention in early Christian *herme*-neutical interpretation. The Egypto-Greek *Corpus Hermeticum*, or "Books of Hermes," for example, describes the Hermes-Thoth procession as that of a supernatural being that incarnated three times.[18] Thus, Thoth begat the first Hermes known as *Agathodaimon* or the "Good Spirit" (*agathon* = "good"); who then begat Hermes Trismegistus, who was the father of the third Hermes known as Tat, the son.[19] Hermes' appellation among Hellenistic sages as "Trismegistus" derived from the epithet "Thrice-Greatest" and would later influence esoteric Christian currents such as magic and alchemy. Hence, the idea among the Church Fathers was that Hermes was both herald of the one, true God and the founder of Trinitarian theology among the pagan religions and philosophers.

Another significant conception about Hermes-Thoth circulating among ancient and medieval Christians was the legend echoed in Saint Augustine's *The City of God*, that Hermes-Thoth had been the Egyptian sage who, by the Grace of God, taught Moses how to command the powers of Nature. This is a legend that was still alive and well in the High Middle Ages, and the Cathedral of Siena has a large fresco below the entrance featuring Moses receiving the "Books of

Hermes" (*Corpus Hermeticum*) from Hermes Trismegistus, which later became the foundational manual for the sacred science of alchemy.

Zosimos of Panopolis, who taught in ancient Alexandria around 300 CE, was the first sage to discuss the processes of transmutation and describe the goals of the alchemical work. The esoteric current, later known as *alchemy*, derived its emphasis on the transmutation of matter and spirit from the scientific context of Hellenistic Alexandria. Practices and techniques from ancient goldsmithing and metallurgy became intertwined with astrological and cosmological beliefs about human potential and the awesome powers concealed in Nature. It was about this same time in Hellenistic Egypt (ca. 200 BCE to ca. 200 CE) that the cosmological correspondences and uncanny associations described above most likely coalesced into the *Corpus Hermeticum*, perhaps aided by Zosimos of Panopolis.

Although many of the early Church Fathers dismissed the Egyptian deity, Thoth, as nothing more than a pagan demon, the rich legends and pastoral epithets about the Greek deity Hermes, and the Roman deity Mercury, helped preserve their status among the emerging Christian cosmology and beliefs of Late Antiquity. Hence their stories and symbols were preserved as beneficent pagan myths that signified anonymous aspects of Christ revealed in their fullness only after the Incarnation of the Word and the Resurrection of Christ. It should come as no surprise that a curious affinity developed among educated Christians and learned pagans with respect to those scholarly disciplines dealing with esoteric communication and the interpretation of God's will under the protective aura of Hermes: astronomy, mathematics, medicine, and biblical or literary interpretation. This accounts for the close association of this material with the humanities and the liberal arts traditions, as well as with metaphysical speculations about matter and Spirit, throughout the history of medieval Christianity.

Derived from the Arabic word for "transformation," *al-Kimiya*, the cognate English word "alchemy" refers to the pre-scientific practices associated with the transmutation of base metals, first into silver (*quicksilver* = mercury), and then into gold after the experiment was perfected. After the fall of the Western Roman Empire in 476 CE, the Arabs conquered Alexandria by 642 CE and inherited the great wealth of mathematical, astronomical, and philosophical wisdom represented in these esoteric traditions. By 800 CE the greatest figure in alchemical magic and Hermetic thought was the Arab-Muslim philosopher, Jābir ibn-Hayyān. Jābir was known among medieval and early modern European scholars by his Latinized name as Geber.[20] He was reputed to have authored hundreds of books on the transmutation of matter and energy, and some accounts credited him with composing the famous *Tabula Smaragdina*, also known as the *Emerald Tablet of Hermes*[21] (ca. 650-833 CE). Unfortunately, it was at the expense of Jābir's legacy that European rationalist and religious prejudices dubbed his works as "gibberish," presumably due to the incomprehensibility of his cosmic correspondences and alchemical formulae. Nonetheless, the Arab, Jewish, and Muslim scholars who collaborated on these works, and many other translations of Hellenistic-Alexandrian alchemical texts, helped preserve the wisdom contained in these esoteric currents until they reentered Latin Christianity through the so-called "Renaissance of the Twelfth Century" when European Christendom was ripe for a re-evaluation of their meaning and application.

The paradigm of Hermetic and alchemical magic was organized around a system of symbolic correspondences designed to alert both neophyte and magus alike to the unseen, spiritual properties and energies concealed in matter. These correspondences were based upon the dictum derived from the *Emerald Tablet*: "As Above, So Below," and also upon the mystical meanings of the number 7 as related to the seven base metals of alchemy and to the seven planets of ancient and medieval cosmology. Even the seven vowels were linked to the music of the seven planetary spheres.[22] Given the significance of the number seven in Greek, Roman, Jewish, Christian, and Muslim numerological symbolism, a multiplicity of cosmological and spiritual correspondences was possible with this number. Hence, the association of the alchemical work (*opus alchimicum*) with the seven days works of Creation; the seven last words of Christ on the cross; the Seven Liberal Arts; or with the seven-times-seven-weeks of the Pentecostal season of the liturgical calendar. In the early 1200s, Alexander Neckham explained how "the planetary gods correspond to the Seven Gifts of the Holy Spirit" and that Hermes-Mercury was "the dispenser of the *donum pietatis*" or "gift of piety."[23]

At the heart of any alchemical engraving, Hermetic icon, or magical treatise from the Middle Ages or early modern era, we find the idea of transmuting humanity's earthly and material nature (base metals) into the higher spiritual nature (gold) of human potentiality. In other words, the physical body represents matter, while the human soul represents the great secret or "golden treasure" trapped therein, the attainment of which was the primary objective among practitioners of this ancient mystical art. The end product of this process was usually personified in concrete form as the "Philosopher's Stone" (*Lapis philosophorum*). Some early modern scientific pioneers, like Robert Boyle and Isaac Newton, who regarded themselves as devout Christians, had well-stocked alchemical laboratories in which they conducted numerous operations and experiments aimed at producing the "Philosopher's Stone," which was usually described as a mysterious "red powder." Both men believed the elusive and enigmatic "Philosopher's Stone" facilitated communication with spirits and angels, and that it possessed amazing medical and healing properties.[24] Sometimes it was also referred to as the "Golden Child" (*filius philosophorum*) or as the "Elixir of Life" (*Elixir vitae*). The attainment of these mysterious spiritual goals conferred upon the magus extraordinary powers of healing and immortality, and mastery over the "Secrets of Nature." Thus, when medieval Christian writers, like Roger Bacon or Albertus Magnus, referred to *theologia magica*, they were referring to an esoteric wisdom tradition with a dynamic corollary in ancient and medieval views of the powers inherent in Nature, and an equally rich corresponding tradition for accessing this power in the domains of alchemy and Hermetic philosophy, which medieval theologians had spent centuries Christianizing despite orthodox taboos and prohibitions against magical operations.

According to the Medieval Latin text of the *Emerald Tablet* when a seeker motivated by a pure and chaste interest in *scientia* combines curiosity about the wonders and powers concealed in matter with the operations of heat and fire,he or she will discover that:

> From this come many wondrous Applications, because this is the Pattern. Therefore am I called Thrice Greatest Hermes, having all three parts of the Wisdom of the whole World.[25]

For some medieval Christian scholars, like Roger Bacon or Albertus Magnus, God's divine grace operating through the Holy Spirit would lead the pious and humble seeker to this perfect knowledge of the operation of the earthly elements and matter with the celestial mysteries and spiritual powers suggested in the *Emerald Tablet.* Esoteric texts like this one, which probably originated in twelfth century Spain, were as much about individual transformation as about deciphering the secrets of Nature, a mystery sometimes referred to in the primary sources as the *Secretum Secretorum*. Later scientific pioneers, like Francis Bacon and Jan Baptiste van Helmont, or like the Jesuit priest Athanasius Kircher and the Lutheran university professor Johann Valentin Andreae, or like Robert Boyle and Isaac Newton, would argue for the reformation of Christian learning and pedagogy through the expansion of scientific investigation based on the legacies of this esoteric wisdom tradition.

As the medieval Christian imagination found itself increasingly attracted to alchemical applications, the theory of mystical correspondences among Egyptian, Greek, Roman, Hebrew, and Arabian esoteric traditions led scholars and theologians to capitalize on the Bible's allegorical potential for justifying their growing curiosity about Nature and *Magia.* In this way, Christian devotees of alchemistic magic found the *prima materia* for their allegorical pursuits by drawing upon scriptural references to sacred stones as well as from key incidents in Jesus' life. For example, John 3:4-12 became a favorite passage among medieval Christian advocates of *theologia magica.* Perplexed by Jesus' miraculous ability to heal and move people's hearts and minds, the Pharisee Nicodemus comes to Jesus "by night" and remarks, "Rabbi, we know that you are a teacher come from God; for no one can do these signs that you do, unless God is with him." Jesus then replies: "Truly, truly I say to you, unless one is born anew (*anathon*; meaning "from above"), he cannot see the kingdom of God." Nicodemus is bewildered by this statement and hears the words literally and at surface level as he inquires: "How can a man be born when he is old? Can he enter a second time into his mother's womb?" Jesus then compels him to look deeper by emphasizing the *sensus spiritualis* of his message:

> Truly, truly, I say to you, unless one is born of water and the Spirit, he cannot enter the kingdom of God. That which is born of the flesh is flesh, and that which is born of the Spirit is spirit. Do not marvel that I said to you, 'You must be born anew.' The wind blows where it wills, and you hear the sound of it, but you do not know whence it comes or whither it goes; so it is with everyone who is born of the Spirit (3:5-8).

While Nicodemus' perplexity persisted, Jesus' next reply suggests an esoteric Hebrew spiritual tradition similar to that later claimed and amplified by medieval Jewish and Christian Cabalists: "Are you a teacher of Israel, and yet you do not understand this?"

Another example of the blending of Judeo-Christian wisdom with magic was the appearance around 1330 in Italy of a manuscript that was to become one of the most important alchemical allegories ever written in medieval Europe, *La Pretiosa margarita novella.* Known to English readers as *The New Pearl of Great Price,* its title was obviously intended to conjure allusions to the fabled "Philosopher's Stone" of Arabian and Latin alchemy.[26] The treatise contains a synthesis of Hermetic, alchemical, and Christian beliefs about the "Art of Transmutation." Its author was listed as Petrus Bonus of Ferrara, a name that not surprisingly means "Good Stone." Even the alleged author's name might be just another allegorical cloaking device intended to conceal the author's true identity. No one has ever succeeded in figuring out who was the real author of the *New Pearl.* The work opens in an apologetic tone as if the writer was trying to gain acceptance and respectability for this "Royal Art:"

> Hermes, in the beginning of his 'Book of Mysteries,' calls Alchemy a most true and certain Art, shewing that what is above is like that which is beneath, and that which is beneath is like that which is above, etc., etc. Again, our Art is more noble and precious than any other science, Art, or system with the single exception of the glorious doctrine of Redemption through our Savior Jesus Christ. It must be studied, not like other Arts, for gain, but for its own sake . . .[27]

Throughout the text, the writer repeatedly emphasizes the scriptural rightness and redemptive truth of alchemy while expounding on some of the wonders made possible through the Art of Transmutation, which he repeats several times "is more noble and precious than any other science, Art, or system with the single exception of the glorious doctrine" of Christianity.

Communication between the human and divine realms, literary interpretation, and the decipherment of a cosmic and religious code also figured prominently in *La Pretiosa margarita novella.* In an eighteenth century translation of the *New Pearl,* we are introduced to this cryptographic maze of esoteric communication and interpretation:

> And in those stories and fables they inserted this Art in a mystical way, with linguistic ornaments as their principal and hidden subject, but in such a way that their secret object could only reveal itself to those who have the intelligence of it. Because, as we have already stated, this science, with all the things [concerning it] that can be done or said, is mystical.[28]

Petrus Bonus informs his readers and fellow adepts that such truths lay hidden in fables and myths, religious literature and art, and among the great poetry of the ancient Greeks and Romans for "in truth every poem and every figure cover a plurality of significations. That is why it has pleased some to hide and to reveal this secret in stories and fables, others in tales concerning the gods."[29] Literary theorist, Maureen Quilligan, in her study of the linguistic challenges of allegorical texts, describes the interpretive difficulties posed by such texts by "the often problematical process of meaning multiple things simultaneously with one word."[30] This *herme*-neutical play of language and symbol was often described in the middle ages, and among early modern devotees of Esoteric Christianity, as the "Golden Game of Alchemy." Its objective was unearthing the allegorized, spiritual treasures contained in the Bible, in ancient wisdom and poetic works, and in the letters of alphabets like Hebrew, Greek, Latin, and Arabic deemed sacred by pious and devout visionaries who upheld that within the many names (*gematria*) used by different faiths to signify the highest divinity, lay the face and signature of the one God: "As Above, so Below."

Another curious example of esotericism's cryptographic and allegorical tendencies is one derived from the mockeries committed against the crucified Christ when the Roman soldiers nailed the sign to the cross reading: I. N. R. I. These initials render the Latin phrase: "*Iesus Nazarenus Rex Iudeorum*," which renders the English phrase, "Jesus of Nazareth, King of the Jews." However, Christian alchemists, magicians, and Hermetic sages alike interpreted these same initials as signifying the phrase: "*Igne Natura Renovatur Integra*." Translating the phrase into English, we uncover an alchemical stew with a certain pneumatological sensibility that echoes the *Emerald Tablet*: "By Fire, Nature is renewed Whole." What are the characteristics of this "Fire?" Does the acrostic refer to the "Fire" of the Holy Spirit, or does it merely signify the heat of a laboratory experiment? Is this elusive use of "Fire" a symbol for the creative energy of intense intellectual and affective contemplation of one's object of study? Or are all of these questions equally relevant in such a synchronicity of earthly elements and spiritual energies? This sort of biblically based wordplay was typical of alchemical treatises produced by medieval and early modern advocates of *theologia magica*, and required careful attention to the *sensus spiritualis* when reading and contemplating the Word of God in the Scriptures or when reading and contemplating the presence of the Holy Spirit in the Book of Nature (*Librum Naturae*).

RECOVERING ESOTERIC WISDOM IN RENAISSANCE FLORENCE

The Florentine phase of the Italian Renaissance, which began about 1400 in Tuscany, inspired European Christian intellectuals and visionaries to undertake a more vigorous recovery and revitalization of the ancient wisdom traditions (*prisca theologia*). When Italian Humanism returned to the origins of Western and Christian learning, it was making a statement and passing judgment on the inadequacy of the old university based Scholastic curriculum, which in their view had lost or diluted the real meaning of the liberal arts tradition. Christian pedagogy and philosophy seemed ripe for a creative revitalization of its theological roots, and "to the sources" (*ad fontes*) became the rallying cry of the Humanists. In Florence, the generous patronage of the Medici family assured a steady supply of wealth for the acquisition of ancient manuscripts and leisure enough to undertake lengthy translation projects. As observed by Stephen

McKnight, when Italian Humanism "first recovered what they believed to be a pristine revelation by God to the great wisemen of the Ancient Near East and Mediterranean" world, "this material was believed to be the key to establishing a universal theology that could reconcile Christian belief with the essential core of philosophy and religion."[31] In addition to Neoplatonism and Pythagorean mysticism this material included the esoteric currents of Christian thought described in this chapter's preceding section: alchemy; Hermeticism; magical theology; and Cabala. Given the focus on natural philosophy and reading the Book of Nature (*Librum Naturae*) inherent in each of these traditions, the idea of gaining mastery over Nature for the improvement of human life emerged as an early Humanist objective. However, revolutionary ideas about the fulfillment of humanity's spiritual potential, were about to be planted and nurtured in some very fertile Italian soil through the careers and written works of Marsilio Ficino and Pico Della Mirandola.

The fall of Constantinople to the Ottoman Turks in 1453 brought Byzantine monks with rare Greek manuscripts to Italy, a trend which greatly stimulated New Testament and Greek studies across Northern Italy and throughout Europe. The arrival of a complete Greek manuscript copy of the *Corpus Hermeticum* in Florence sometime between 1453 and 1463 revitalized the study of these ancient esoteric currents and, in time, welded them together with the emerging scientific theories of the 1500s and 1600s.

In 1463, the aging Cosimo de Medici asked Marsilio Ficino (1433-1499) to set aside his translation projects on Plato and Plotinus in order to begin translating the *Corpus Hermeticum* into Latin. Cosimo was nearly seventy years old and wanted to read the "Books of Hermes" in Latin before passing away. The entire constellation of earthly and heavenly correspondences accumulated in the traditions of what I have been referring to as *theologia magica* or Esoteric Christianity was about to be given a bold and respectable new platform from which to speak to the learned among European Christendom. Stephen McKnight contends that Marsilio Ficino was the most significant threshold figure in the "epochal break from the Middle Ages,"

> Ficino reintroduces the Hermetic conception of man as a terrestrial god and restores magic as the God-given knowledge that permits man to operate on the natural world and improve the human condition . . . Ficino's restoration of Hermetic magic is based on a cosmology that is closely connected to developments in science in the sixteenth, seventeenth, and eighteenth centuries.[32]

Thus, a growing discourse on the "Divinity of the Human Person" facilitated the reintroduction and reintegration of magic, alchemy, and Hermeticism in the late 1400s, while simultaneously moving these traditions from underground "esoteric" modes of praxis and expression to a more open, academic, and theologically progressive discourse. Renaissance scholars set this discourse within the parameters of the new Humanist pedagogy (*studia humanitatis*) and a revitalized emphasis on the Seven Liberal Arts (*artes liberales*) which were given ample expression at the Platonic Academy, financed by Ficino's Medici patrons, and housed at the Villa Careggi just outside the Tuscan capital.

The theological reconstruction of Greco-Roman and Christian beliefs advocated in Ficino's *Theologia Platonica* set forth, according to McKnight, "the epistemological foundation for a new image of man as the master of the natural world and the shaper of his own destiny," which resulted in the "description of man as a terrestrial god," and the "fundamental reconceptualization of God, the world and society."[33] Ficino boldly wrote about this and taught his pupils at the Florentine Platonic Academy that: "The entire striving of our soul is that it becomes God. Such striving is no less natural to men than the effort of flight is to birds."[34] He placed great emphasis on the human capacity for creativity and for the achievement of miraculous works through the manipulation and command of Nature's elements. In his own optimistic words:

> Here we marvel that the souls of men dedicated to God rule the elements, call upon the winds, force the clouds to rain, chase away fogs, cure the diseases of the human body and the rest. These plainly were done in certain ages among various peoples, as poets sing, historians narrate, and those who are the most excellent of philosophers, especially the Platonists, do not deny, the ancient theologians testify, above all Hermes and Orpheus, and the later theologians also prove by word and deed.[35]

Ficino was inspired by the view of human agency he learned from sources such as: Plato and the *Corpus Hermeticum;* the Imago Dei concept from Genesis 1:26-27; and the Three Theological Virtues of faith, hope, and charity advocated by Christ. In Ficino's Humanist understanding with its optimistic view of human potential and agency, it was the infusion of God's divine breath, through the Holy Spirit, that sparked and empowered the genius of human beings as co-creators alongside God and the angels.

In this Humanist reformulation of Christianity's inherited symbols and attitudes towards the pagan past, we have yet another fine historical example to which we can apply Delwin Brown's theory of tradition (*constructive historicism*) for: "Its principle claim is that the past creatively appropriated, imaginatively reconstructed, is the material out of which the future is effectively made."[36] This is precisely what Ficino, and other Humanists like Pico Della Mirandola and Francesco Patrizi, (1413-1494), believed and hoped would be the outcome of wedding their love for the *via antiqua* (Way of the Ancients) with the *via moderna* of late Scholasticism and Florentine Humanism. Although modern scholarship has paid little or no attention to the pneumatological and spiritual dimensions of their theological anthropology, these Humanist visionaries played a central role in the Renaissance reordering of European religious and moral philosophy that eventually exposed Christianity's inheritance from the ancient and medieval sources of *theologia magica* over the epistemological and ethical barriers Scholasticism had erected, with increasingly empirical and process oriented methodological perspectives in the study of Nature and the Cosmos.

Giovanni Pico Della Mirandola's (1463-1494) *Oration on the Dignity of Man* typified the attitudes and sensibilities of the age and has been regarded by scholars for over a century as "*the manifesto*" of the Italian Renaissance.[37] Pico was born into a very wealthy and powerful aristocratic Tuscan family, and even for his times, he was regarded as a child prodigy. Indeed, Pico enrolled in canon law studies at the University of Bologna at only fourteen and graduated a year later. He then traveled around Europe, as his abundant financial resources permitted, studying philosophy and theology at four more universities before stopping first in Rome and later settling in Florence. Pico was about sixteen when he met Marsilio Ficino and spent almost a year at the Platonic Academy. Although Pico was thirty years younger than Ficino, the two men eventually joined ranks as the leaders of the growing Florentine Humanist movement.

Pico composed the *Oration* in December 1486 as the Preface to a staggering document known as *The 900 Theses* in which he proposed arguing with anyone in Christendom about the fundamental congruence of Egyptian, Persian, Greco-Roman, Hebrew, Arabian, and Christian wisdom. He was already fluent in Latin, Greek, and Hebrew and apparently had begun learning Arabic and Aramaic. One of his noble titles was "Count of Concord," a term based on his family's feudal possessions at Concordia, and a title which he prudently explained as a sign of divine blessing favoring his goal of harmonizing the long-standing discord among Scholastic university factions. Pico abhorred the intellectual "warring" whereby Platonists argued the truth of their ideological commitments against those of the Aristotelians, or the Realists versus the Nominalists, or, as was the trend in his day, Scholasticism versus Humanism. The flamboyant Count of Concord even wrote a now lost colossal volume entitled: *The Concord of Plato and Aristotle.*

Pico's deep conviction in the fundamental unity of the great religious systems of his day stemmed, in large measure, from the rediscovery of the *Corpus Hermeticum* during his lifetime. Although one cannot ignore the role of Platonic theology, and Pico's very fruitful study of Jewish Cabala in shaping his idealism, it was the Hermetic view of the human person as an agent of personal, social, and cosmic transformation through the decipherment and mastery of Nature's secrets that propelled him over the top of the theological anthropology of his times. The *Corpus Hermeticum* exposed him to alchemy, which, in turn, led him and so many of his humanist minded contemporaries to the realm of *theologia magica.* As demonstrated in the preceding sections, magical theology was not a novel development among Western Christendom, for Albert the Great, Thomas Aquinas, Petrus Bonus, Roger Bacon, and many others had already expressed their fascination with "the secret of secrets" (*secretum Secretorum)* contained in the Book of Nature. And, after all, the *Emerald Tablet* had been well known to many of Ficino's and Pico's predecessors. However, the individualistic temperament of Northern Italian intellectual life, and the climate of progressive and syncretistic speculation, advocated among the Medici circle and at Ficino's Florentine Academy, when joined with the *Corpus Hermeticum's* faith in human potential, its theory of cosmic correspondences, and the fundamental oneness of all things and all Wisdom, led Pico to proclaim, *"nova afferre velle philosophiam,"* a new era in philosophy and history. As he stated: "I wish to bring forward a new philosophy. Let him praise it, if it is defended, or damn it if it is refuted."[38]

Pico's *Oration* invited all who were interested to debate his massive compilation of the *900 Theses* in Rome, before the Pope and the "most esteemed Fathers" of the Apostolic Senate, on or about the Feast of Epiphany in 1487. The debate never took place because Pope Innocent VIII suspended it and appointed a Papal Commission to investigate the work's congruence with Christian doctrine and tradition. Pico's exaggerated optimism and syncretistic enthusiasm led him into direct conflict with the Pope and leading theologians of his day. Charges of heresy and accusations of hubris soon followed. His preface opened by quoting Hermes Trismegistus and Asclepius on humanity's miraculous abilities: "What a great miracle is man!" Pico pointed out that:

> Man is the intermediary of creatures, that he is the familiar of the gods above him as he is lord of the beings beneath him; that, by the acuteness of his senses, the inquiry of his reason and the light of his intelligence, he is the interpreter of Nature, set midway between the timeless unchanging and flux of time; the living union (as the Persians say), the very marriage hymn of the world, and, by David's testimony but little lower than the angels."[39]

Pico's allusion to King David's rejoicing at the wonders of God's creation in the heavens as on the earth from Psalm 8: 4-6 is quite an interesting reference here at the outset of his project. "What is man that thou art mindful of him, and the son of man that thou dost care for him? Yet thou hast made him little less than God, and dost crown him with glory and honor. Thou hast given him dominion over the works of thy hands; thou hast put all things under his feet." These verses had been a favorite among Christian magicians and alchemists in ages before Pico and would continue to be a favorite among apologists for the Rosicrucian proto-scientific agenda in the centuries after Pico. This was especially true of the psalmist's points about the human agent being "little less than God" and having been "given dominion over the works" of God's hands. The wordplay here is reminiscent of the Cabalistic association of God's finger with God's sacred Word, or of God's holy tongue as synonymous with the Spirit of God. As the originator and interpreter of much of what came to be known as Christian Cabala, and as an accomplished philologist himself, Pico would have been aware of these linguistic symbols and etymological connections.

In the opening section of Pico's *Oration*, he explains the important roles of moral philosophy and natural philosophy in the project he is about to unveil. The aptly titled "Count of Concordia" argues passionately for peace to win out over rampant discord among the various factions and schools of thought across Christendom, and calls for the development of "an inviolable compact of peace between the flesh and the Spirit."[40] He eloquently cautions: "To bestow such peace is rather the privilege and office of the queen of the sciences, most holy theology."[41] Just before beginning his exposition on magic and natural philosophy, in an apparent paraphrase of John 14:26-27, Pico reminds his intended audience, the Pope, Cardinals and high ranking Fathers of the Latin Church whom he hoped would convene at Rome in January 1487, about Christ's promises of peace in the sending forth of the Holy Spirit as the Counselor to restore all who are spent and troubled: "Come to me you who are spent in labor and I will restore you; come to me and I will give you the peace which the world and Nature cannot give."[42] In one of the most moving passages of *The Oration*, Pico then offers further clues to the scope and trajectory of his 900 theological propositions:

> Summoned in such consoling tones and invited with such kindness, like earthly Mercuries, we shall fly on winged feet to embrace the most blessed mother and there enjoy the peace we have longed for: that most holy peace, that indivisible union, that seamless friendship through which all souls will not only be at one in that one mind which is above every mind, but, in a manner which passes expression, will really be one, in the most profound depths of being . . .
> This is the peace which God established in the high places of heaven and which angels, descending to earth, announced to men of good will, so that men, ascending through this peace to heaven, might become angels. This is the peace, which we would wish for our friends, for our age, for every house into which we enter and for our own soul, that through this peace it may become the dwelling of God . . .[43]

Although this passage has probably not been read through a pneumatological lens for some time, it stands in testament of Pico's sincere hope in December 1486 that "like earthly Mercuries," his contemporaries might find the enthusiasm and theological inspiration to unite the higher and lower aspects of human aspiration with the loftiest glories of God, and in so doing revitalize Christian thought and pedagogy during their century. Like Joachim of Fiore and the Franciscan Spirituals, who followed the encouragement of the Calabrian Abbot, the perceived project of recovery and innovation advocated by Ficino and Pico had clearly identifiable and highly creative pneumatological sensibilities. This is true regardless of whether or not modern and postmodern scholarship ever fully fathomed the presence of this subversive, yet highly creative, Spirit beseeching the believers of Christian reform and revitalization.

Throughout *The Oration*, Pico references the mystical theologies of Pythagoras and Plato; the magical theology of the Arabian alchemist al-Kindi, and of the Franciscan Roger Bacon, as well as the legendary Hermes Trismegistus; and the many miracles performed by Zoroaster, Moses, Enoch, and Jesus. His theological anthropology is rooted in a dynamic and optimistic view of human potential and individual free will as contrasted with created beings, like angels, or other creatures, such as animals and plants, whose mode of being was fixed when God created them:

> But upon man, at the moment of his creation, God bestowed seeds pregnant with all possibilities, the germs of every form of life. Whichever of these a man shall cultivate, the same will mature and bear fruit in him. If vegetative, he will become a plant; if sensual, he will become brutish, if rational, he will reveal himself a heavenly being, if intellectual, he will be an angel and the son of God. And if, dissatisfied with the lot of all creatures, he should recollect himself into the center of his own unity, he will there, *become one spirit with God*, and in the solitary darkness of the Father, Who is set above all things, himself transcend all creatures[44] (Emphasis added).

Despite his exuberant optimism for this "new philosophy" he was sharing with the Doctors of the Church, Pico's tone throughout *The Oration* is both diplomatic and humble. He acknowledges his youth, denounces the thought or title of being a "learned" *scholasticus*, and admits that the burden for proving the large number of propositions he has offered them rests on his shoulders alone. He was just twenty-three years old when he composed the *Oration* and the *900 Theses*. Nonetheless, he informs his interlocutors, and readers, that he knows a great many things, which others do not know, invokes Job, and declares: "The Spirit is in all men."

Finally, we come to the passages from *the Oration* that probably unnerved Pope Innocent VIII and sparked the concerns of the commission charged with investigating Pico's theological claims. Pico's timing was unfortunate because 1486 also witnessed the release of the notorious *Malleus maleficarum*, later known as the "Witches Hammer," which played a central role in the witch-hunts of the 1500s and 1600s. Two years earlier, Innocent VIII had issued the bull *Summis disiderantes*, declaring sorcery and witchcraft a heresy and raising suspicions across Europe about any sort of morally acceptable *theologia magica Christiana*. Nonetheless, Pico maintained that *Magia* has two forms and that he would be proposing certain theses in hopes of helping the Pope and Fathers of the Church better understand the dichotomies between "black" versus "beneficent" magic. He offers the usual medieval denunciation of black magic's emphasis on conjuring demons and malevolent spirits to assist in the magician's tasks, but then counters it with a very positive affirmation of "beneficent" magic, which "when thoroughly investigated" this other form of magic proves "to be nothing else but the highest realization of natural philosophy."[45] He then reviews the etymology of the term "magus" in ancient Persian and Greek sources before emphatically noting that: "the magician is the minister of nature and not merely its artful imitator."[46] Ficino, too, had once stated: "Nature is in all things a magician."[47] Pico lamented the undervalued status of "beneficent" magic in the world just as he detested the sinful sorcery and demonology of the dark arts. Pico writes:

> Moreover Fathers, the disparity and dissimilarity between these arts, is the greatest that can be imagined. Not the Christian religion alone, but all legal codes and every well-governed commonwealth execrates and condemns the first; the second, by contrast, is approved and embraced by all wise men and by all peoples solicitous of heavenly and divine things. The first is the most deceitful of arts; the second, a higher and holier philosophy. The former is vain and disappointing; the latter, firm, solid and satisfying. The practitioner of the first always tries to conceal his addiction, because it always redounds to shame and reproach, while the cultivation of the second, both in antiquity and in almost all periods, has been the source of the highest renown and glory in the field of learning.[48]

In this passage, Pico further claims that the kings of the Persians and Arabians taught their sons this "science of divine things" for political as well spiritual objectives so "that they might learn to rule their commonwealth on the pattern of the commonwealth of the universe."[49] This particular notion of reforming socio-political relations after the pattern of God's cosmic design and covenantal relations with humanity would have a noticeable impact upon the Rosicrucian and Masonic movements of the next two centuries. Just as in Ficino's project of recovery and synthesis, here in Pico's own words we have the merging of *prisca theologia* (ancient wisdom) with *theologia magica Christiana* (Christian magical theology).

Let us also recall that Hildegard of Bingen in the 1100s, along with a notable contingent of Scholastic theologians, believed that Antichrist would make use of the "diabolical arts" and try to deceive even the most educated and saintly among the clergy. Hildegard's contemporary, Hugh of St. Victor (ca. 1096-1141), maintained that Antichrist's demons would trick Christian teachers into making "the claim that magic, as an ally of philosophy, deserved a place among the blessed *artes liberales*,"[50] while degenerating "the minds of its followers toward every crime and abomination."[51] Despite the favorable opinions of "natural magic" (*magia naturalis*) ascribed to Albertus Magnus (1193-1280), Thomas Aquinas (1224-1274), Roger Bacon (ca. 1214-1292), and Pierre d'Ailly (1350-1420), similar cautions and condemnations abounded in the Scholastic treatises of the 1200s and 1300s. William of Auvergne (ca. 1180-1249) believed that demons relied on human "curiosity" as a snare and an entrapment defined as "the lust of knowing things which are unnecessary."[52] Pico, in contrast, positioned his propositions on magical theology in line with the admirable and pious legacies of Albertus Magnus, Thomas Aquinas, and Roger Bacon.

Pico and his friend and mentor, Ficino, saw themselves as devout reformers in the service of the Church and of Christian learning, and each of them was infused with a deep conviction in the promise and power of this "new philosophy" to transform both individual Christians and Christian society as a whole. In Pico's words:

> Just as that first form of magic makes man a slave and pawn of evil powers, the latter makes him their lord and master. That first form of magic cannot justify any claim to being either an art or a science while the latter, filled as it is with mysteries, embraces the most profound contemplation of the deepest secrets of all things and finally the knowledge of the whole of Nature.[53]

He reiterates that this new, magical philosophy offers much of practical value and is highly valuable as a testimony to both human potential and God's wondrous presence in Nature and in the universe. In perhaps the most eloquent yet ominous section of *The Oration*, Pico concludes his defense of *theologia magica*:

> Thus it draws forth into public notice the miracles, which lie hidden in the recesses of the world, in the womb of Nature, in the storehouses and secret vaults of God, as though she herself were the artificer. As the farmer weds his elms to the vines, so the 'magus' unites earth to heaven, that is, the lower orders to the endowments and powers of the higher. Hence it is that this latter magic appears

the more divine and salutary, as the former presents a monstrous and destructive visage. But the deepest reason for the difference is the fact that the first
magic, delivering man over to the enemies of God, alienates him from God,
while the second, beneficent magic, excites in him an admiration for the works
of God which flowers naturally into charity, faith and hope. For nothing so
surely impels us to the worship of God than the assiduous contemplation of His
miracles and when, by means of this natural magic, we shall have examined
these wonders more deeply, we shall more ardently be moved to love and worship Him in his works, until finally we shall be compelled to burst into the
song: 'The heavens, all of the earth, is filled with the majesty of your glory.'
But enough about magic. I have been led to say even this much because I know
that there are many persons who condemn it and hate it, because they do not
understand it, just as dogs always bay at strangers.[54]

Pico's "new philosophy" with its radical integration of natural philosophy and
theology under the auspices of the *Corpus Hermeticum's* Mercurial spirit started
an intellectual and pedagogical fire that burned throughout the Scientific Revolution and directly influenced the pneumatological sensibilities of later alchemists and Rosicrucian visionaries. One wonders how his ideas might have been
received if he had emphasized the Gifts of the Holy Spirit as opposed to the
mercurial gifts of the Christ-Hermes association?
    How effective and long lasting was this Humanist reformation of Christian
learning and theology advocated by Marsilio Ficino and Pico Della Mirandola?
Was their proposed integration of ancient Greek and Roman wisdom with Christian theology and Hermetic magic outside the bounds of practicality and accepted Christian doctrine? Ficino's colleagues elected him head of the Platonic
Academy at the Villa Careggi, and for several decades students came from afar
to study with him. When they left almost all of them took these new and often
radical Humanist insights with them wherever they went. The dissemination of
Humanism's conceptual and affective view was not only made possible by its
graduates, but also by secular intellectuals and learned clergy who became
pamphleteers, essayists, artists, civic leaders, and the entrepreneurs who opened
Europe's first publishing companies, like Aldus Manutius' Aldine Press in Venice. In this way, the "information revolution" of the Humanist recovery and
revitalization of the ancient wisdom traditions (*prisca theologia*), along with
Ficino's and Pico's mystical ideas about Nature and Spirit, reached beyond Florence to encompass all of Europe. In summary, Ficino and Pico advocated a
form of the medieval *theologia magica Christiana* that lay somewhere between
the former's *theologia Platonica* and the latter's *theologia Hermetica Christiana*. There was surely something intensely successful and appealing about Italian
intellectual life from the mid-1400s to the early 1500s that allowed pioneering
professional historians like Jules Michelet and Jacob Burckhardt later in the
1800s to build their academic careers on the study of modern individualism and
revolutionary ideals in their romanticized notions of a "civilization of the Renaissance in Italy."
    However, church authorities in Rome condemned Pico's *Oration* and sec-
tions of his *900 Theses* as heretical, and he fled to Florence seeking refuge with
the Medici and his friends at the Platonic Academy. In 1493 Pope Alexander VI

pardoned the charges of heresy against Pico, but the following year Pico died unexpectedly and prematurely at the age of thirty-three. Ficino outlived Pico by five years, passing away in 1499. With the death of *"il Magnifico,"* Lorenzo de Medici, in 1492 the entire Florentine Humanist project of recovery and innovation suffered the wrath of the Dominican friar Girolamo Savonarola and his fanatical followers who, after ousting Lorenzo's successor from power, rounded up artistic representations of the "new philosophy" around Florence, piled these in the city's central plaza and set them ablaze in their infamous "bonfires of the vanities."[55]

It is worth noting that Savonarola also regarded himself as a staunch reformer of Christian learning and pedagogy and that, as both Abbot at the monastery of Saint Mark's and Vicar-General of the Dominicans, he promoted reform efforts throughout the region and fostered cutting-edge New Testament and classical studies among his Dominican friars. In 1490, Pico had invited him to preach at Florence and Lorenzo the Magnificent promoted his reform efforts at Saint Mark's. He administered the sacrament of Last Rites at Lorenzo's bedside the day he died. He was even interested in Joachim of Fiore's prophecies of the Age of the Holy Spirit, and believed his reform minded and morally solid leadership of Florence might pave the way for the anticipated *renovatio* of the "new age."[56] For Savonarola and his devoted followers, the conceits and libertinism of Florentine Humanism had offended the limits of their late medieval moral sensibilities. After ousting the Medici from power, Savonarola became a political reformer and controlled Florence from 1494 to 1497. Hence the fiery creativity resulting from knowing God's majesty through the "new philosophy" advocated by writers like Ficino and Pico, and then fashioned into objects of beauty and decoration by Botticelli, Michelangelo, and Leonardo da Vinci under Medici patronage, were consumed in the flames of misunderstanding and apocalyptic fervor.

As for Savonarola, his luck ran out in the very heart of the Pentecostal season on May 4, 1497 when his highly antagonistic Ascension Day sermon led to riots and yet another "Bonfire of the Vanities," that incited the citizens of Florence into open revolt against him amidst calls for returning the Medici family to govern Florence. A year later, he was tried for heresy and treason, hanged from the gallows, and then burned at the stake on May 23, 1498 by an alliance of papal and secular forces. His ashes and those of his two closest collaborators were tossed into the Arno River.[57] Although the Protestant Reformation was still two decades away, these violent and ironic Florentine episodes illustrate the abiding urgency mingled with intense fear of change that late medieval and early modern Christians felt when confronting the demands of reforming Christian society, learning, and pedagogy. Lorenzo the Magnificent, Ficino, and Pico had envisioned a new era of human possibility and mastery over Nature, yet they all died before the wider dissemination of their ideas. Savonarola prophesied an impending Joachimist "regeneration" of Church and society as the millennial year 1500 approached, yet he suffered a humiliating death during the Pentecostal cycle of days at the hands of his opponents. *"What does this mean?"*

Ideas and religious idealism, no matter how inspirational or insightful, are only intellectual abstractions and cannot carry the same weight as the deep-rooted vigor of local practicing communities. Worldviews divorced from daily praxis and the shared rhythms of communal living are doomed to a short lifespan. Brown's theory of tradition warns us that:

> The on-going task of theological construction will falter unless it somehow has vital roots in practicing religious communities that allow it both to draw upon and contribute to the imaginative play within tradition. Whether or not he or she is a believer, the theologian is an artist as well as a critic of tradition, seeking to discern the varied conceptual possibilities apparent within the lived realities of a tradition, formulating and elaborating these potentialities, evaluating them in terms of the needs of the community, and the broader arenas of critical discourse, thus advocating some variants over others and, finally, serving in ways appropriate to the individual theologian's circumstance the integration of these reconstructions back into the felt practices of the community from which they originated.[58]

In the task of his own theological reconstruction as theologian and priest, historical scholar and philologist, magician and medical healer, Marsilio Ficino performed all of the above prescriptions for the Christian tradition he adored and lived. But the disconnect between the theological anthropology and cosmology Ficino's works espoused, and the daily practices and lived circumstances of communities across the rest of European Christendom, deprived the Florentine Humanism movement he espoused of the "vital roots" Brown contends are a necessity in "the ongoing task of theological construction."

I believe that what Ficino, Pico, and their colleagues and students at the Platonic Academy, as well as others among the wider ranks of Italian Humanism, actually stumbled onto was more than just a latent Christian Gnosticism in the *prisca theologia,* and far more than merely revived versions of Christian Hermeticism, alchemical magic, or Platonic theology. What re-entered Western Europe through the texts and teachings that Byzantine monks brought with them after the fall of Constantinople in 1453 was most likely the theological anthropology of Eastern Orthodox mysticism contained in the *theosis* tradition, a term that literally signifies the "deification" of the individual believer through the power of Holy Spirit.[59] If this were true, then it was a *theosis* commingled with Christian esoteric currents derived from alchemy and Hermeticism. Pico's optimism about the "divinity of humanity" bears an amazing resemblance to one of the key New Testament passages on the "deification of humanity" in 2 Peter 1:4 where Christians learn of their true call and election by the power of God and Christ to "become partakers of the divine nature." This dynamic mystical tradition, with ties to the Platonism of the Church Fathers, stretches from early Christianity to the contemporary revival of academic and popular interest in Eastern Orthodox spirituality. I have no way of proving this hunch in a manner acceptable to the standards of my profession as a historian, but the parallels are too obvious to rule out a fifteenth century Florentine, or even earlier Humanist, familiarity with either manuscripts espousing theōsis, or with doctrines about theōsis shared between refugee Byzantine monks and their northern Italian hosts at some point during the 1400s.[60] If this were true, and it is not merely plausible but *highly likely* given the similar emphases upon humanity's divine potential and spiritual gifts among these Florentine and Byzantine strands, then Eastern Orthodox pneumatology and beliefs about theōsis may have provided the *prima materia* for the *subversive fire* that stirred in the hearts of Renaissance Christians like Marsilio Ficino, Pico Della Mirandola, and artistic *virtuosos* like Leonardo da Vinci, Leone Battista Alberti, and Michelangelo. Hence, Renaissance Humanism's emphatic emphasis upon the "Divinity of Man," and the Promethean possibilities exemplified in the Hermetic magus capable of commanding Nature and Spirit by the Grace of God, found a place alongside the ideal of the *"Uomo Universale,"* whose education in the humanities (*artes liberales*) taught him about the spiritual dignity and limitless potential of the human person. As Christ foretold when promising to send the Paraclete: "Truly, truly, I say to you, he who believes in me will also do the works that I do; and greater works than these will he do, because I go to the Father."[61]

THE CHRISTIAN MONK AS MAGUS: ABBOTT TRITHEMIUS OF SPONHEIM

On the opposite spectrum of writers like Ficino and Pico, but related to their goal of reviving a Christian *theologia magica*, stands the life and work of Abbot Trithemius of Sponheim (1462-1516). Although virtually unknown among modern historians of Christianity, this Benedictine German monk advocated a monastic lifestyle of deep piety and vast erudition similar to the humanistic ideals of his younger Italian contemporaries. Trithemius' steadfast defense of *theologia magica* as the witch-craze gained momentum across Europe, and as Christendom neared the eve of the Protestant Reformation, provides one of the crucial links between the pneumatological sensibilities of Florentine Humanism in the late 1400s and that of the Rosicrucian manifestos of the early 1600s.

Although information about his early years is scanty, we know that he was born Johann Heidenberg about 1462, at Trittenheim on the Mosel river in Germany's rich wine growing region, the same village from which he derived his Latin appellation, Trithemius. His father died when he was a boy, and his mother later remarried a man whom he disliked considerably. Trithemius attended the University of Heidelberg until 1482 where he first excelled in Greek and later in Hebrew studies. He developed a genuine delight in the new humanistic curriculum of the times and integrated this emphasis in his later works on mystical theology, ecclesiastical history, and Christian magical theology in the tradition and style of Albertus Magnus. At Heidelberg, he studied with the most famous scholar of fifteenth-century northern Humanism, Johann Reuchlin. At twenty-one he became the Abbot of Sponheim and served there for nearly a quarter century until 1506 when he accepted a new position as Abbot of the Monastery of St. Jacob in Würzburg. Under his learned piety and leadership, from 1483-1506, the Monastery at Sponheim amassed one of the finest manuscript and book collections among all of the notable monastery libraries of the Northern Renaissance.

By the time of his death in 1516, he had authored an impressive number of works on esoteric Christian topics such as astrological prophecy, alchemy and Cabala, Pythagorean numerology, cryptography, and Christian magical theology. People came from far and wide to both converse and study with him at Sponheim. Among his students was the alchemist physician Paracelsus (1493-1541), who forms a significant link with the beginnings of modern chemistry and German Rosicrucianism, and the lay theologian and alchemist Heinrich Cornelius Agrippa (1486-1535), who will also significantly influence the Rosicrucians and the founders of modern chemistry.

As a key figure in the Renaissance discourse on *theologia magica*, scholars and historians have debated whether Trithemius' major influences derived from the Humanist faction of Ficino and Pico or from earlier strains of medieval mysticism. Despite the Florentine connections that Richard Auernheimer and Frank Baron contend were the primary magical influences on the Trithemian call for a revived *magnum miraculum Christianum*, the Abbots' statements in various works attest to his fondness for the style and legacy of the thirteenth-century German, scholastic Saint and Doctor of the Church, Albertus Magnus (1193-1280).[62] Albertus' defense of natural magic was legendary among clergy with similar interests, and, while Trithemius' fluency with Greek manuscripts no doubt granted him access to the *Corpus Hermeticum* and the Platonic Revival of the Florentine Academy, it was Albert the Great's emphasis on the nobility and integrity of the ancient traditions of "natural magic" that most appealed to him. For Albertus these esoteric traditions were best represented by the Persian "magi," who, by their knowledge of divine and cosmic truths understood the will of God, and traveled to Bethlehem to witness and honor the Incarnation of the Word in Jesus. Trithemius' attraction to a revitalized *theologia magica Christiana* was much inspired by these scholastic perspectives on natural magic.

Another key point he garnered from Albertus Magnus was the distinction between miracles performed by Moses and Jesus, or by the blessed saints of Christian history, versus the mundane operations of mere magicians and sorcerers. The primary distinction here rested on the sanctity of Moses' miracles, carried out by the Grace of God for the benefit of God's chosen people. This, in turn, was contrasted with the sinister machinations of Pharaoh's magicians. The former was superior to the latter by the very fact of the Hebrews' relational commitment to the one, true God of the Old Testament, by the fulfillment of the Mosaic covenant in Christ, and then further sanctified by the power of the Holy Spirit after Christ's Ascension and the Spirit's outpouring on the Day of Pentecost.[63] Trithemius' ability to read Hebrew also allowed him to draw from the tradition and wisdom of Jewish Cabala. Vestiges of his steadfast fascination with Albertus' teachings on "natural magic" are scattered throughout the Trithemian corpus.[64] In Albert's own words: "the magician (*magus*) is properly so-called from the word 'great' (*magnus*), because, having knowledge of all things from their necessary causes, and conjecturing from the effects of natural things, he sometimes exhibits and produces marvels of nature."[65] While this sounds a bit uncanny or bizarre to modern readers, this blending of scientific and spiritual concerns would provide a crucial stage in the development of modern consciousness about Nature and our ability to comprehend and control the natural realm for the benefit of humanity.

On the other hand as Aquinas' teacher and mentor, Albertus Magnus was famous for his piety and vast theological and scientific learning, a splendid combination of gifts that Trithemius himself emulated and sought to advance among his fellow monks during his tenure at Sponheim. The development and expansion of the impressive library which he meticulously oversaw for twenty-four years was clearly influenced by his esteem for both Albertus' and Aquinas' highly learned piety. The Sponheim Monastery library grew from an estimated fifty volumes in 1483 to over two thousand books and rare manuscripts by 1506 when Trithemius resigned from his position. His love of learning and books caught the attention of the Emperor Maximilian I (1459-1519) of the Holy Roman Empire, who eventually became his patron, and to whom he dedicated several of his major works. Trithemius apparently worked on his mystical and magical researches for years before daring to share them in a more public format.

Unfortunately for Trithemius, public and ecclesiastical fears about the presence of demons and fallen angels in the cosmos, along with steadily growing concerns about witches and sorcerers across Europe as the apocalyptic marker of the year 1500 approached, sullied responses to his cryptographic researches. In 1499, the same year Marsilio Ficino died, Trithemius' fondness for the magical arts led him into considerable controversy after a letter he sent to a Carmelite monk at Ghent, Arnold Bostius, led to insinuations of sorcery and black magic. Trithemius was already well known for his Greek studies and for his support of the liberal arts at Sponheim, but his proposed volume, entitled *Steganographia*, moved both his colleague Bostius and the French scholar Carolus Bovillus to accuse him of being a "demonic magician." Steganography is a form of spiritual communication aimed at transmitting secret messages from mind to mind across large distances without the use of writing.[66] The concerns and fears raised by his colleagues stemmed from the assistance of "angelic entities" in the transmission of steganographic messages, for which no one could be fully certain of either their "angelic" or "demonic" origin. Trithemius had stepped into the same quagmire as Pico Della Mirandola, a dangerous pit of magical speculation which, even Albertus Magnus and Thomas Aquinas maintained, required great caution and spiritual discernment concerning the identity of the principalities and powers being summoned by the Christian magus. Although Trithemius never finished this book, he invested considerable time and effort during his later years in studies of cryptography and esoteric communication, an endeavor for which we can be sure his Cabalistic background served him well. Trithemius would spend the remaining seventeen years of his life dealing with the fallout of these accusations, and his reputation would be questioned often among Roman Catholic and Protestant writers over the next three centuries. Following its eventual publication in Frankfort in 1609, the *Steganographia* was added to the Vatican's *Index of Forbidden Books*.[67]

Nonetheless, Trithemius serves as a link between the Florentine Humanism of Ficino and Pico and the Rosicrucian Enlightenment of Francis Bacon and J. V. Andrea. Noel Brann, one of the foremost contemporary experts on Trithemius, describes the dichotomous role the learned Abbot of Sponheim played then and now:

> Trithemius furnished to apologists of magic in the next two centuries a thoroughgoing Christian rationale for engaging in the occult arts. The posthumous image of the magical abbot for some was of one who had consorted with demons, whereas for others, just as committed as himself to the proposition that true magic represents a divinely sanctified branch of Christian theology, Trithemius helped reinforce the conviction that magic can just as easily obey the commands of God as those of the Devil. Finding in the great medieval scholastic Albertus Magnus one of his own favored paradigms for the union of magic with theology, Trithemius in turn became the foremost paradigm for others dedicated to the same goal.[68]

Early modern scientific reasoning emerged from a theological and philosophical fascination with "natural magic" as represented in the sort of *theologia magica Christiana* Trithemius advocated. Also, his less Platonic and more scholastic approach to the problem provided a link between Protestant and Catholic proponents of the scientific enterprise, whose joint aims advocated for human mastery over Nature. According to Brann:

> On both sides of the reformation divide . . . demonological extremists were to be found who demanded that true ecclesiastical reform must include the expurgation of magic as a primary component, with Trithemian magic being no exception to the rule. Fortunately for the legacy of Trithemius, however, also to be found on both sides of the Protestant-Catholic divide were others accepting of the abbot's thesis that religious reform, rather than excluding magic, should embrace it as one of its primary constituents. Despite their formal theological differences, Catholics and Protestants were jointly turning over the intellectual soil, which permitted magic to flourish on Christian ground. For these, with Trithemius an illuminating beacon, the Hermetic concept of the *magnum miraculum* coincided at bottom with such miracles as were performed by Moses, Christ, and the saints.[69]

Abbot Trithemius and his pupil Agrippa were well known to the Brotherhood of the Rosy Cross as precursors of their seventeenth century pneumatological and empirical program for reforming Christian learning and science.

AGRIPPA ON MAGICAL THEOLOGY AND THE HOLY SPIRIT

Before examining the pneumatology and utopian visions of the seventeenth century Rosicrucians, let us take a brief look at another important voice in the sixteenth century debate on the role of *theologia magica Christiana* in the reformation of Christian learning, Heinrich Cornelius Agrippa von Nettesheim (1486-1535). Lynn Thorndike in his *History of Magic and Experimental Science* downplayed Agrippa's part in the transition from magical theology to the modern scientific enterprise, but Thorndike was not reading these primary sources through a pneumatological and Pentecostal lens.[70] Indeed, Agrippa's work may represent a missing link between the Medieval and Renaissance strands of Christian Esotericism and the Rosicrucian Enlightenment of the 1600s. While most seekers of this elusive link have tended to focus on the prolific career of the famous and controversial physician, Paracelsus, Agrippa's conviction in the reality of the Holy Spirit and on the seminal qualities of the *"Quintessence"* for deciphering the secrets of Nature qualify him as the prototype of the Rosicrucian movement.

Agrippa was born in Cologne into a modestly wealthy family of the lower nobility. During his early studies and subsequent years teaching at the French University of Dole, Agrippa became despondent about the poor state of theological and scientific knowledge across European Christendom. He spent most of his later years lecturing and traveling through France, Germany, and Italy offering his services as itinerant theologian and unlicensed physician, classical grammarian, and legal scholar. According to several accounts, he served admirably as a soldier under Emperor Maximilian. Agrippa studied with Trithemius sometime around 1510 after the Abbot assumed his new post at the Monastery of Saint Jacob in Würzburg. Agrippa shared drafts of his masterpiece, *De occulta philosophia libri tres*, with his esteemed teacher and mentor, who praised the book for its learned wisdom from someone still as young as Agrippa, and emphatically warned him the book should be kept secret until completed so as to avoid a fate similar to the one that befell the Abbot's *Steganographia*.[71] Mindful of Europe's growing aversion to magical practices, Agrippa heeded his mentor's advice while writing and polishing the work over the next twenty years. He finally published this *magnum opus* of Renaissance *theologia magica Christiana* near the end of his life in 1531 and 1533.

The breadth and scope of Agrippa's *Three Books of Occult Philosophy* is so vast that a comprehensive analysis is beyond the scope of the present volume. However, Agrippa's pneumatological assumptions about Nature and the presence of Spirit throughout Creation shed considerable light upon his understanding of the Trinity and of God's relation to Nature. As the Psalmist praises God for making "the winds thy messengers, fire and flame thy ministers,"[72] so too Agrippa's three volume work is filled with pleas for a pneumatological revival based upon the miraculous gifts of magic. In a dedicatory letter to Archbishop Hermannus of Cologne, who as the Earl of Wyda was also a high-ranking official of the Holy Roman Empire, Agrippa refers to these volumes as "restoring" a much needed and useful "doctrine of antiquity." Indeed, Agrippa's *Three Books,* while vastly more detailed than Ficino's *Platonic Theology*, or Pico's *900 Theses*, or any of Trithemius' works, echoes and perhaps best summarizes the Renaissance call for a Christian revitalization of the ancient mystical tradition of *theologia magica.*

The publication of Agrippa's *De occulta philosophia* coincided with the fallout from the Diet of Augsburg's opposition to religious diversity and subsequent calls for the suppression of the heretical innovators of Catholic doctrine. Emperor Charles V's conflict with the German Protestant princes, who formed the Schmalkaldic League and supported Luther, did not help matters for anyone advocating theological innovations of Christian doctrine in the Holy Roman

Empire. In the opening preface, Agrippa expresses concern that some readers and censors might be disturbed by the book's title and "cry out that I teach forbidden arts, sow the seed of heresies, offend pious ears, and scandalize excellent wits; that I am a sorcerer, and superstitious, and devilish, who indeed am a magician."[73] However, in a time of political and theological turmoil across Germany and the territories of the Holy Roman Empire, when religious dissent or doctrinal innovation might cost a person his or her life, Agrippa also proffered for potential detractors and adversaries a stern defense of *theologia magica Christiana*:

> To whom I answer that a magician doth not amongst learned men signify a sorcerer, or one that is superstitious, or devilish: but a wise man, a priest, a prophet; and that the sybils were magicianesses, and therefore prophesied most clearly of Christ; and that magicians, as wise-men, by the wonderful secrets of the world, knew Christ the author of the world to be born, and came first of all to worship him; and that the name of magic was received by philosophers, commended by divines, and not unacceptable to the Gospel.[74]

Echoes of Ficino and Pico are evident in this passage. He references the tradition of the Three Magi who visited Jesus at the time of his birth. Elsewhere in this volume, Agrippa cites the works of others who were blessed with different gifts of the Holy Spirit like Hildegard of Bingen, Joachim of Fiore, Albertus Magnus and Thomas Aquinas, Roger Bacon, and Abbot Trithemius. He presents these famous scholars and clerics as exemplars who, as pious and devout Christians, understood and knew the power of magic. One gets the impression while reading Trithemius and Agrippa that the modern distinction between mystical theology and occult philosophy did not yet exist in the 1500s. Hence Agrippa's steadfast conviction that he, like his teacher Trithemius, was engaged in a *theologia magica Christiana* for the benefit of human existence, the alleviation of human ailments, and for the exaltation of God.

Although early modern scientists, like Robert Boyle and Isaac Newton, did not take Agrippa's premodern approach to alchemical operations very seriously, his emphasis upon figuring out the exact composition of matter was well ahead of its time, and was well known to the circle of scientists whose names have been linked to the founding of the Royal Society of London in 1660 that included Boyle. Agrippa's descriptions of the four elements (air, water, fire, and earth), and how to separate the elements in the laboratory drew from sources like the *Emerald Tablet,* the *Corpus Hermeticum,* and from Aristotle. Fire and earth he regarded as possessing certain superior qualities. He explains how these basic elements are present in all terrestrial and celestial things, and, in a manner reminiscent of Pythagoras and Plato, he believed the Spirit or Soul of the World (*Anima mundi*) somehow infused the elements with reality:

> The Soul of the World therefore is a certain only thing, filling all things, bestowing all things, binding, and knitting together all things, that it might make one frame of the world, and that it might be as it were one instrument making

of many strings, but one sound, sounding from three kinds of creatures, intellectual, celestial and incorruptible, with only one breath and life.[75]

Agrippa identified Nature's unfathomable mixing as the "Quintessence," (from Latin: *quinta essentia*) because it signifies the elusive yet unknown Fifth Element whose mystery and power lay beyond the physically observable and verifiable properties of the four basic elements. This Spirit is the "medium whereby celestial souls are joined to gross bodies, and bestow upon them wonderful gifts." In Agrippa's premodern, mythopoetic imagination, this *Quintessence* needed to be studied and uncovered for through its elusive operation functions the great mystery of the Triune God's relationship with humanity. "By this Spirit therefore every occult property is conveyed into herbs, stones, metals, and animals, through the Sun, Moon, planets, and through stars higher than the planets."[76] We are reminded here of Hildegard's naturalistic pneumatology that emphasized the "greening" of the Holy Spirit in Nature, and of Joachim of Fiore's mystical drawings of the Trinity in which Jesse Trees were combined with floral, triangular, and celestial images to depict the mysteries he experienced in his Pentecost visions. As the "divine kiss," or cohesive force of love between God the Father and Christ the Son, the Holy Spirit was clearly at the very heart of what Agrippa was trying to examine, identify, and harness:

> Now this Spirit may be more advantageous to us, if anyone knew how to separate it from the elements; or at least to use those things chiefly, which do most abound with this Spirit. For these things, in which this Spirit is less drowned in a body, and less checked by matter, do more powerfully, and perfectly act, and also more readily generate their like; for in it are all generative, and seminary virtues.[77]

He explains further that by the power of this *Quintessence*, the alchemists endeavor "to separate this Spirit into gold and silver."[78] Thus, what ancient and medieval alchemists had hitherto referred to as the Philosopher's Stone, Agrippa equates more clearly than anyone else in the 1500s with the power and mystery of the Holy Spirit as the *Anima mundi* (Spirit of the World), and a concept he borrowed from the *prisca theologia* and the Platonic *via antiqua* of Florentine Humanism. The energy, or *"quintessential fire"* that Agrippa and other Renaissance magicians believed lay concealed in matter was also synonymous with the spiritual gifts and sacred sciences, as he suggests throughout his *Three Books of Occult Philosophy*. These esoteric traditions he maintains were "acceptable to the Gospel," and their dissemination among the learned will benefit humanity and usher in a much needed reformation of Christian philosophical and scientific learning.

In comparison to most of his contemporaries Agrippa was not properly credentialed by any major college or academy, he practiced medicine without a license, and he never obtained a permanent chair at any important university. Unlike other legendary figures who lived and wrote in the same century, like the infamous alchemist and well-known pioneer of medicine Paracelsus, or the famous French prophet and physician Nostradamus, Agrippa's importance in the rise of experimental science from the debris of Medieval and Renaissance magical theology has been overlooked by most historians of European intellectual history, and he has remained virtually unknown among historians of Christianity.[79] However, Agrippa's examination of the origin and composition of the four elements and his faith in the ubiquity of the *Quintessence* as related to the Holy Spirit, along with the encyclopedic scope and utility of his *De occulta philosophia*, are among the most crucial links between the Italian revival of magical theology in the late 1400s and the pneumatological sensibilities of the Rosicrucian Enlightenment of the 1600s.

VEHICULA SCIENTIAE: FRANCIS BACON'S VISION OF PENTECOST

No discussion of the emergence of the Scientific Revolution would be complete without an overview of the life and career of its unwavering English champion and disseminator, Francis Bacon (1561-1626). He lived in an era of monumental changes in Christian civilization and for most of his sixty-six year span was very near the center of the most important events in early modern England. Since his death, nearly four hundred years ago, fantastic allegations about Bacon's mysterious double-life and life long need for secrecy generated much scholarly research and public investigations. One claim identifies him as the illegitimate son and heir of England's powerful Tudor monarch, Queen Elizabeth I (1533-1603), another identifies him as the real author behind the name and pen of William Shakespeare, while other rumors claim he was the chief editor of the first edition of the King James Bible (1611). Fanciful tales and legends aside, Bacon ironically did not uncover any new scientific principles, nor did he lay the foundation for any of the major modern scientific disciplines, as did Galileo and Kepler, or Boyle and Newton. Some historians of science are divided on whether Francis Bacon merits the title: "Father of Experimental Method."[80] Nonetheless, while "experimentation" was not unknown to Euro-Western science before Bacon, his plan for the renovation of knowledge called for both *Experientia literata* (Educated experiment) and an *interpretatio Naturae* (Interpretation of Nature), the novelty of which in the early seventeenth century rested upon the vigorous use of inductive reasoning to generalize axioms based upon empirical observation, which, in turn, would generate more experiments as fellow scientists across the world duplicated, and either verified or disproved, one's initial hypotheses.[81]

Francis Bacon's ambitious plans for the renovation of scientific learning, his calls for the establishment of a Christian fraternity dedicated to reforming education and improving the quality of human life through the advancement of science, along with his alleged ties to the Rosicrucian movement of the early 1600s, identify him as an important and pivotal figure in this study. Moreover, Bacon's vision of a Second Pentecost in *The New Atlantis* stands out as one of early modern Christianity's most intriguing examples of the liberative and transformative role of Pentecost and the Holy Spirit chronicled throughout this book.

Francis Bacon grew up in London as a member of the lower nobility in a family with strong ties to England's Tudor dynasty. He was a mere twelve years old when he entered Trinity College at Cambridge University. His distinguished career wavered between the intellectual pursuits of a scholar and the duties of serving as a high-ranking official in the courts of both Queen Elizabeth I and her successor King James I. During his education, Francis expressed disdain for the stultifying natural philosophy of the medieval Scholastics and for the erroneous conclusions of Aristotelian philosophy. He studied the classics and developed a passion for ancient languages, history and philosophy. "Knowledge is power" was one of Bacon's favorite sayings. The study of ciphers and cryptography fed his fascination for hermeneutic games and his uncanny desire for personal secrecy.[82] Bacon's erudition on classical and medieval thought was vast, as demonstrated by his familiarity with the Pre-Socratics, Plato and Aristotle, the Stoics and Skeptics of the Hellenistic world, medieval Scholasticism, Erasmus, and the Protestantism of Martin Luther.

Bacon was unfairly stereotyped as a closet atheist who vigorously pursued truth through empirical reasoning rather than through religious revelation. Over the centuries and to the late 1800s, he was often misquoted by both his admirers and detractors for whom "religious enthusiasm" had lost much favor after the derailment of the Puritan Revolution. However, Bacon was actually a devoted student of God's presence in Nature through the Holy Spirit of Christ. His passion for natural philosophy in the proper service of religious knowledge is expressed in his favorite quotation from Proverbs (25:2): "The glory of God is to conceal a thing, but the glory of a King is to find it out."[83] In the scientific utopia he created for the *New Atlantis*, Bacon reserved a special place for scientists as highly revered "Interpreters of Nature," a conviction he shares with many of the writers and visionaries discussed in this chapter. Bacon's deep certainty in the person of the risen Christ, and in the power of the Holy Spirit, recalls the *theologia magica Christiana* of his esoteric precursors in Italy and Germany:

> Our Saviour himself did first shew his power to subdue ignorance, by his conference with the priests and doctors of the law, before he shewed his power to subdue nature by his miracles. And the coming of the Holy Spirit was chiefly figured and expressed in the similitude and gift of tongues, which are but '*vehicula scientiae.*'[84]

Bacon's reference to Pentecost (Acts 2) and the "gift of tongues" as the "carriers of knowledge," or *vehicula scientiae*, reveals a belief of his that has seldom received any scholarly attention. This Pentecostal imagery demonstrates the persistence of the Pentecost story, as both liberative trope and repository of Christian tradition, even in the tumultuous times of early modern English reformism and revolt. In a moment, we will discuss his use of Pentecost in *The New Atlantis* as a significant literary and philosophical trope.

In a now lost work composed when he was about thirty-two, called *Temporis Partus Maximus* (*The Greatest Birth of Time*, ca. 1593-1594), Bacon envisioned a Golden Age of learning and unprecedented progress for the human spirit. He imagined England as the vital center of this forthcoming age of wonders, in which he outlined a plan of philosophical and reformist works that he called the *Instauratio Magna*, the Great Instauration.[85] He was quite aware of the legacy of alchemy and magic for the scientific enterprise he advocated, but lamented that such little progress had been made in expanding these mechanical and chemical horizons since the ancient and medieval sages had first turned their attention to the rational examination of Nature and the Cosmos. As a staunch supporter (and suspected family member) of the Tudor dynasty, Bacon's utopian dream of a world transformation was critical of what he and many of his Protestant contemporaries perceived as the Roman Catholic autocratic or "papist" tendency that stifled freedom of inquiry and prompted ecclesial abuses of power. He was, however, cognizant and somewhat fond of reforms promoted by the Jesuits who, in his own words, "quickened and strengthened the state of learning" among Roman Catholicism as "we say what notable service and reparation they have done to the Roman see."[86] Bacon's sense of historical consciousness clearly recognized the connections between the Renaissance, and the Protestant and Catholic Reformations as a "new spring of all other knowledges" in which the deeds of the Society of Jesus, founded by St. Ignatius of Loyola, and the promise of his own *Instauratio Magna* formed part of a much larger design meted out by Divine Providence.

Bacon again courted the support of Queen Elizabeth I, and her successor King James I, in a manner not unlike his ordained Roman Catholic, Italian Humanist predecessors, Ficino and Pico, who had courted the powerful Medici family to support and finance their reformist dreams in the late 1400s. In the dedicatory preface of *The Advancement of Learning* (1605; reprinted 1629), Bacon honored James I as a king who drinks from "the true fountains of learning" and who "standeth invested of that triplicity which in great veneration was ascribed to the ancient Hermes; the power and fortune of a King, the knowledge and illumination of a Priest, and the learning and universality of a Philosopher."[87] One wonders if this was merely a diplomatic ploy aimed at loosening a royal patron's purse strings, or an indication of King James' affinity for the Hermetic and magical traditions. Most likely it was the former and not the latter, for a few pages further Bacon's laudatory prose compares "the love and reverence towards learning which the example and countenance of two so learned princes," Queen Elizabeth and King James, to the twin stars Castor and Pollux whose "excellent light and most benign influence hath wrought in all men of place and authority in our nation."[88] Ironically, through the hubris and folly of Euro-Western patriarchy, Bacon's "Great Instauration" in time coalesced with the imperialist and millenarian agendas of the British Empire. Hence in the name of progress, and with the best of intentions, some of his ideas were carried aloft by imperialists who wreaked havoc and destruction upon the natural world and upon the indigenous and colonial inhabitants of the so-called "new worlds" which were then being explored and conquered by Spain, France, Portugal, the Netherlands, and Bacon's beloved England.

Beginning with *The Advancement of Learning* (1605) and culminating in *The New Organon: An Interpretation of Nature* (1620), Bacon took on Aristotle, the medieval Scholastics, and the alchemists of his day for not submitting their observations and conclusions about the natural world to more rigorous inductive analysis. He distinguished between speculative and applied science and critiqued the methods by which astronomers and alchemists arrived at their error-laden hypotheses and mystifying theories which he mocked as "the speculations of one who cares not what fictions he introduces into Nature, provided his calculations answer."[89] He describes "Astrology, Natural Magic, and Alchemy" as scientific pretenders "full of error and vanity," more akin to imaginative speculation than rational conclusions. He acknowledges their place in this history and then departs from where Ficino and Pico, as well as Albertus Magnus, Trithemius and Agrippa left off. To alchemy, especially, he gives credit for pushing natural philosophy forward for "assuredly the search and stir to make gold hath brought to light a great number of good and fruitful inventions and experiments, as well for the disclosing of nature as for the use of man's life."[90] In other words, it was not alchemy or astrology per se, or even the philosophy of the Schoolmen, that was to blame for the poor state of science and philosophy across Christendom, but rather it was the normative value assigned to religious and superstitious precepts about the physical causes and chemical operations of *Cowern* the natural world that concerned him most.

Francis Bacon was deeply convinced of the need to separate scientific inquiry from the domain of religion and the study of the Scriptures. Even as he steadfastly cautioned against what he called the "Idols of Superstition," and maintained that superstition was one of "the extremes of religion," it was actually his notion of science and religion, as two different yet complementary ways of knowing about God's Creation and humanity's place in the order of that Creation, that lay behind his call for a separation between the two. Bacon's historic awareness of Scholasticism's enthronement of Aristotelian categories into the structure of Christian metaphysics and theology fueled his passion for the separation of reason and faith. His understanding of multiple approaches to biblical exegesis was astounding. He warned his contemporaries that the future of scientific development and Christian learning was at stake since one could not read the Book of God as if it were the Book of Nature, nor vice versa. By confounding these dissimilar ways of knowing and relating the human realm to the divine realm, we might in time produce a "heretical religion" and debase the "divine mysteries," which are the precious gems concealed in the Holy Scriptures as "infinite springs and streams of doctrines to water the church in every part."[91] It was precisely because of this sort of transgression and deformation of knowledge that Bacon was so critical of the magical and alchemical traditions, and particularly those currents represented by Scholasticism and Cabala, Paracelsus and Agrippa.

In response to such an "ill-matched union, Bacon emphatically urges that we "give to faith that which is faith's." The school of Paracelsus and other currents of Esoteric Christianity that based their *theologia magica Christiana* on a natural philosophy derived from the Bible was for Bacon an endeavor fraught with peril:

For to seek heaven and earth in the word of God, whereof it is said, 'Heaven and earth shall pass, but my word shall not pass,' is to seek temporary things amongst eternal: and to seek divinity in philosophy is to seek the living amongst the dead, so to seek philosophy in divinity is to seek the dead among the living ... And again, the scope or purpose of the Spirit of God is not to express matters of Nature in the Scriptures, otherwise than in passage, and for application to man's capacity and to matters moral or divine.[92]

In defense of Bacon's "famous precept not to mix religion and science," Peter Urbach concludes that it "was founded, not on atheism, but principally, on what he thought was the unreliability of the Scriptures as a source for physical information, though he never expressed a doubt about their divine inspiration."[93]

In Book II of *The Advancement of Learning*, Bacon announced his hope for the establishment of an international fraternity of pious individuals dedicated to learning and improving the quality of human life around the globe. Although the Rosicrucian Manifestos announcing the work of the "secret" and "invisible" Brotherhood of the Rosy-Cross did not appear in Germany until 1614 to 1616, Bacon's description of this society in 1605 is often linked with the Rosicrucian Movement attributed to Johann Valentin Andreae.[94] Some have argued that Bacon was merely criticizing the various orders and universities throughout European Christendom for inadequately sharing data and knowledge with each other that should have been placed in the service of humanity. But clearly there is more to his choice of words than untrained eyes and ears can decipher. In words that inspired the founding of the Royal Society of London forty years later, Bacon stated:

> And surely as nature createth brotherhood in families, and arts mechanical contract brotherhood in communalities, and the anointment of God superinduceth a brotherhood in kings and bishops; so in like manner there cannot but be a fraternity in learning and illumination, relating to that paternity which is attributed to God who is called the Father of illuminations or lights.[95]

This famous passage from *The Advancement of Learning* has been read and interpreted since 1627 alongside Bacon's description of Solomon's House in *The New Atlantis*.[96] To that utopian work we now turn.

In late January 1621, King James I named Francis Bacon Viscount Saint Alban. Bacon had been serving as Baron Verulam and Lord Chancellor of England for several years. With such lofty titles, and fine land holdings around London, he was one of the most powerful aristocrats in England. He was at the pinnacle of his political career, but his luck ran out when he was accused of taking bribes in a legal proceeding. Bacon confessed to the charge, was incarcerated in the infamous Tower of London, then sentenced by the House of Lords on May 3, 1621 and stripped of his title as Lord Chancellor with a very hefty fine of £40,000. Falling from such an accomplished height and rank would break the spirit of most men and women in any age, but as luck would have it Bacon turned the next five years into one of nearly total concentration on his research and writing about the Great Instauration. He died on Easter Sunday, April 9, 1626, after apparently catching a cold while experimenting with the effects of refrigeration on the preservation of meat.

Among the various projects Bacon had been developing during the last few years of his life was a utopian novella, *The New Atlantis*, about a group of sailors departing from Peru and led off course by the shifting winds of the South

Sea who then land at an uncharted island where the inhabitants are governed by an order of scientist-priests known as Solomon's House. Bacon's close friend and pastor, William Rawley, took on the task of posthumously publishing this book the following year, which although left unfinished by Bacon's sudden passing was read widely during the 1600s.

The New Atlantis opens with the lost ship being approached by a messenger from the island bearing a scroll warning the visitors to this strange land that they are forbidden from staying past sixteen days unless permission is granted for an extension of time. The scroll is signed with a "stamp of cherubim's wings, not spread but hanging downwards and by them a cross."[97] To the great relief of the seafarers the inhabitants are Christians who know Hebrew, Greek, Latin and all of the other languages of the world, but, oddly enough, communicate with the wayfarers in Spanish. The men are then led to the Strangers House for medical quarantine and further assessment of their reasons for coming to the island. They are so well fed, and their sick are so well cared for, that they believe they are in heaven or in a land populated by angels: "we were apt enough to think there was somewhat supernatural in this island; but yet rather angelical than magical."[98] After three days the men are visited by the governor of the Stranger's House, a priest wearing a white turban "with a small red cross on the top," an eerie parallel to the Rosicrucian symbol of the "rosy cross"[99] associated with Andreae's movement in Germany. This official informs them that they have landed on the unknown and secret island of Bensalem.

The next day when the governor returns, the travelers ask him, who was the apostle that converted the people of Bensalem to the Christian faith. He tells them that Saint Bartholomew was the agent of that miraculous transformation. A few days later they learn that about 1,900 years ago, the legendary King Solomon founded the Order or Society known as the Brethren of Solomon's House. Thus, the two most significant events in the history of Bensalamite society, King Solomon's establishment of the Order and St. Bartholomew's apostolic mission to the island, are direct allusions to Bacon's plan for a universal reformation of Christian learning that he believed was needed for "the enlarging of the bounds of Human Empire, to the effecting of all things possible."[100]

The first event explained in the narrative is the conversion of Bensalem "about twenty years after the Ascension of our Saviour," on a cloudy but calm night in a city on the eastern coast of their island called Renfusa (meaning: "sheep natured").[101] That night "a great pillar of light" with a cross of light appeared at sea. People from the city approached the column of light in small boats, but were prevented from getting too close by some type of force field that bound the boats in place. A member of the ancient society of Solomon's House, in one of the boats, "who having awhile attentively and devoutly viewed and contemplated this pillar and cross" fell down upon his face, rose to his knees and with outstretched arms and hands prayed thus:

> Lord God of heaven and earth, thou hast vouchsafed of thy grace to those of our order, to know thy works of creation, and the secrets of them; and to discern (as far as appertaineth to the generations of men) between divine miracles, works of nature, works of art, and impostures and illusions of all sorts. I do

> here acknowledge and testify before this people, that the thing which we now
> see before our eyes is thy Finger and a true Miracle; and forasmuch as we learn
> in our books that thou never workest miracles but to a divine and excellent end
> (for the laws of nature are thine own laws, and thou exceedest them not but
> upon great cause), we most humbly beseech thee to prosper this great sign, and
> to give us the interpretation and use of it in mercy; which thou dost in some
> part secretly promise by sending it unto us.[102]

His boat then became unbound, and as this member of Solomon's House got
closer to the pillar and cross of light, the entire structure burst apart into a star-
like blaze that slowly dissipated, leaving only a small ark of cedar floating on
the sea, which once taken aboard by the man, opened on its own and revealed a
Book and a Letter.

The Book was a collection of the canonical texts of the Old and New Testaments, but Bacon tells readers that some other yet unwritten books were also
part of this collection. The Letter, announcing "salvation and peace and good-
will, from the Father, and from the Lord Jesus," was written and signed by Saint
Bartholomew, one of the original twelve Apostles who tradition tells us was
among the first to recognize Jesus as the Savior. After Pentecost, Bartholomew
preached the Gospel in Arabia and India until his martyrdom. Bacon's religious
imagination creates a Second Pentecost in the world of this little utopian novella
when the Book and the Letter, "wrought a great miracle, conform to that of the
Apostles in the original Gift of Tongues. For there being at that time" in Bensalem "Hebrews, Persians, and Indians, beside the natives, every one read upon
the Book and the Letter, as if they had been written in his own language."[103] We
are reminded of the Pentecostal inquiry from the Book of Acts: *What does this
mean?*

What this means, at least for our examination of pneumatology and Pentecost in early modern Christianity, is that for pious advocates of scientific
progress like Francis Bacon the "tongues of fire" described in the Acts of the
Apostles were understood as both "carriers of knowledge" (*vehicula scientiae*)
and arbiters of communication and relationality between humans and their Creator. Even though Bacon called for separating the domains of science and religion, for him the Holy Spirit was a bridge connecting the province of religious
learning about Divinity with the province of scientific learning about the natural
world. We are, once again, in the presence of the Holy Spirit, which believers
identified as the empowering and liberating countenance of the Triune God,
inspiring creativity and wisdom among men and women that they may study and
come to recognize and know the Word of God in the natural order of Creation.
That Bacon would even dream of connecting his joint program of reforming
Christian learning and advancing experimental science to the story of Pentecost
reveals the persistence of the spiritual traditions about the Holy Spirit surveyed
in this volume's earlier chapters. Nearly five centuries after Hildegard of Bingen's formulations about the Holy Spirit in Nature, and Joachim of Fiore's
prophecies about a universal transformation in the coming Age of the Holy Spirit, the quest for the Finger of God in Nature still dazzled the curiosity of Christian seekers like Bacon and many of his contemporaries.

The epistemic and socio-political question of who in society mattered most as a religious authority was a key issue for Francis Bacon and his colleagues. Just as the discernment of malevolent or beneficent spirits was a central concern to the advocates of Christian magical theology in the centuries before Bacon's era, the discernment and examination of miracles became a central concern of the advocates of science in the 1600s after Bacon. This may seem bizarre to us in the twenty-first century, but as Jerry Weinberger points out, "one of Bacon's concerns in telling this story is to establish the veracity of miracles," which "can be faked or explained away as misunderstood natural phenomena." The Bensalamite's response to this conundrum "is to rely not just on the internal evidence of the experience of faith, but also on the power of science to determine that an apparent miracle is not a natural, artificial, or illusory or deceitful event."[104] The veracity of religious belief, and the long awaited reform of Christian learning and science in Bacon's England, was such that he and his contemporaries believed firmly in the application of reason to the validation of miracles. He believed the integration of reason and faith had been botched by Scholasticism, magical theology, and the school of Paracelsus. No matter how naïve and misguided the Baconian quest for the conquest of Nature may seem to us in our time, Bacon's scientific enterprise sought not so much the earlier integration of rational inquiry and faith, but pointed toward a new way of knowing and relating both natural and supernatural causes. As observed by Peter Harrison:

> All of this amounted to the construction of a quite new framework within which the claims of the truth of the Christian religion were to be tested. A consequence of this development, and not necessarily one intended by the relevant agents was the promotion of a conception of religious truth as something that was to be established on rational grounds, as it were, independent of preexisting religious commitments. Religious truths were to be tested in a public and putatively neutral arena. As an indication of this transition, the ability to discern the genuine miracle was no longer a spiritual gift associated with personal piety or religious maturity, although Bacon retains an element of this, but was rather to do with competence in the procedures of experimental philosophy
> If experimental natural philosophers could make good their claim to be arbiters of religious truth, they could, in principle at least, ameliorate one of the fundamental problems of early modern Europe, that of distinguishing genuine from spurious religion.[105]

Or as Bacon's optimism expressed it through the voice of one of the Fathers of the College of the Six Days Work describing the riches of Solomon's House: "The End of our Foundation is the knowledge of Causes, and secret motions of things; and the enlarging of the bounds of Human Empire, to the effecting of all things possible."[106] Little did Bacon and his continuators realize how drastically their quest for "Dominion over Nature" would enhance human life over the next few centuries while simultaneously polluting Nature and enslaving human bodies.[107]

The epochal split between the religious worldview of the Middle Ages and the new sensibilities and commitments of the scientific outlook, with its attendant "modernist" epistemological crisis, was fully underway by the time of

Francis Bacon's passing in 1627. Over the next few decades the Baconian corpus, along with the specter of Solomon's House from *The New Atlantis*, became
a major encouragement to the circle of scholars who became founders of the
Royal Society of London. Bacon's work apparently also influenced another
movement well versed in the currents of Esoteric Christianity, which might have
been active on the continent since at least 1614, and maybe as early as the turn
of the century around 1604, —the Fraternity of the Rosy-Cross.

"THE HOUSE OF THE HOLY SPIRIT:"
SCIENCE AND ROSICRUCIANISM

Given the nearness in time of Francis Bacon's major publications (ca. 1605-
1627) to the release of the Rosicrucian Manifestos in Germany, France, and the
Netherlands (ca. 1614-1623), it is not surprising that Bacon's name is linked
with the Rosicrucians. Nor is it a shock, given the Masonic emphasis on the
"wisdom of King Solomon," to hear of theories and legends exploring alleged
connections between Bacon and Freemasonry. However, the parallels between
Bacon's Great Instauration as set forth in his *New Atlantis* and the universal reformation announced in the Rosicrucian Manifestos seem to be more than a
coincidence. These three manifestos took the form of two spectacular declarations and a mysterious alchemical allegory known as the *Chymische Hochzeit* or
The Chymical Wedding of Christian Rosenkreutz.
    The first manifesto, the *Fama Fraternitatis*, appeared in Germany in 1614
and caused a stir across Europe by announcing the existence of a secret order of
learned Christians dedicated to the old alchemical goal of deciphering and mastering the secrets of Nature.[108] This initial ruckus was followed in 1615 by The
Confessio Fraternitatis, a document addressed to all the learned of Europe that
explained a little more about the origins and goals of the Rosy Cross Fraternity.
The *Confessio* is the only one of the Rosicrucian manifestos with an overtly polemical tone, as it is quite critical of the Papacy's powerful role in Christendom.
And finally in 1616, the brethren released the much lengthier literary work, the
Chymical Wedding, attributed to Johann Valentin Andreae, whom we will discuss later in this chapter. The story is an allegory of spiritual transformation in
the guise of a mystical marriage between a king and queen carried out over sev-
en days. In the symbolism of the marriage rites, alchemy and magical theology
receive ample expression. In summary, while revealing the Order's existence
and explaining its new paradigm about humanity's place in the cosmos, each of
these Rosicrucian texts expresses unmistakable pneumatological ideas and sentiments. But each text also offers a bold theological reconstruction of Christian
tradition with the most intriguing theme being the designation of the home built
by Christian Rosenkreutz as the "House of the Holy Spirit." A complete analysis
of all three documents is not necessary because the most significant references
to the Holy Spirit are found in the first Rosicrucian Manifesto, which we will
examine.
    The *Fama Fraternitatis* (1614) proclaims the unveiling of the Order of the
Rosy Cross after a period of intentional secrecy, and ardently calls for a univer-

sal reformation of Christian learning and science; an entreaty for the revitalization of Euro-Western knowledge that sounds a lot like the revival of philosophy
and theology advocated by the Italian Humanists Ficino and Pico, and much like
the magical theology of Trithemius and Agrippa. Here is a reformist agenda
Francis Bacon would have backed wholeheartedly. The *Fama* openly criticizes
Europe's most learned for holding on to the outdated theories of Aristotle and
Galen. It suggests bringing together the various intellectual and theological factions of Europe so that by uniting for the advancement of knowledge and piety
"they might, out of all those things which in this our age God doth so richly bestow upon us, collect *Librum Naturae* or a perfect method of all arts."[109] In other
words, deciphering the secrets contained in the Book of Nature will lead to the
perfection of scientific knowledge, advancement of the medical arts, and the
revitalization of the liberal arts.

The *Fama* introduced Europe to the story of *Brother C. R.*, a.k.a. Christian
Rosenkreutz, the founder of the Fraternity who was born in 1378, and grew up
in a German monastery where he studied Latin and Greek since age five, and
then left for the Holy Land when he came of age. Eventually he discovers that
Jerusalem is not the only sacred site where spiritual treasures await people of
noble spirit and finds his way to Damascus at age sixteen to study with the Masters of Arabia. In Damascus he learned much about mathematics, physics, magic, alchemy and Cabala, and studied the Arabic and Hebrew tongues. From there
he traveled and studied in both Egypt and Fez before sailing back to Europe by
way of Spain.

Here we find another allusion to the transmission of Islamic knowledge
from the Arabian Near East and North Africa culminating in Andalusia; a trajectory analogous to, yet slightly different from, that recounted in Wolfram von
Eschenbach's *Parzival* exactly four hundred years before these Rosicrucian
texts. Modern readers will surely be put off by the narrators' late medieval ignorance of Arab culture and Muslim beliefs, and by his anti-Jewish prejudices,
but the *Fama* praises all of these non-Christian cultures and faith traditions for
their superior integration of learning and faith, which the authors of the *Fama*
considered so absent among European Christianity. Taking a cue from the Arab
and Jewish medical traditions of the Middle Ages, Brother C. R. and his followers will vow to heal and cure the sick, *gratis*, as an act of love and compassion
for others, a notion most likely influenced by how the *Fama*'s author or authors
understood the concept of the *elixir* as borrowed from Arabian alchemy. Commenting on the views of another Rosicrucian, Count Michael Maier, about the
elixir of longevity and health, B. J. Gibbons points out that: "The elixir in Western alchemy functions primarily as allegory" as "the great and glorious medicine
for all passion, pain, and sorrow," which "is none other than Christ."[110]

When Brother Christian Rosenkreutz arrived in Spain from his studies at
Fez, he was eager to share the fruits of his studies and earnestly hoped that:

> The learned of Europe would highly rejoice with him and begin to rule and or-
> der all their studies according to those sound and sure foundations. He therefore
> conferred with the learned in Spain, showing unto them the errors of our arts
> and how they might be corrected, and from whence they should gather the true

inditia of the times to come, and wherein they ought to agree with those things that are past; also how the faults of the Church and the whole *philosophia moralis* was to be amended. He showed them new growths, new fruits and beasts, which did concord with old philosophy, and prescribed them new *axiomata*, whereby all things might fully be restored.[111]

But in a mood reminiscent of the Papal Commission charged by Pope Innocent VIII with investigating Pico Della Mirandola's *900 Theses*, the *Fama* informs us that Spain's ecclesiastical and intellectual elite rejected the harmonious wisdom (*harmonia*) Brother C. R. brought back from Arabia and Africa:

> But it was to them a laughing matter; and being a new thing unto them, they feared that their great name should be lessened if they should now again begin to learn and acknowledge their many years' errors to which they were accustomed . . .[112]

Brother C. R. then took his message to the learned of other European nations, hoping that they would accept and apply the infallible *axiomata* he had derived from the Arabians, but to his great disappointment was met with similar indifference and rejection.

Wearied from so much traveling and the unexpected dismissal of the gifts he had hoped to share with fellow Christians across Europe, Brother C. R. returned to Germany and began building "a fitting and neat habitation, in which he ruminated his voyage and philosophy...in a true memorial. In this house he spent a great time in the mathematics, and made many fine instruments, for the benefit of all fields of his art."[113] This affinity for mathematical reasoning and its application to the study of the cosmos is one of the main differences between the reformist agendas of the Baconian and Rosicrucian systems.

After five years, Christian Rosenkreutz again gave much thought to "the wished-for Reformation." Mindful of the world's former rejection, however, Brother C. R. chose instead three highly esteemed brethren from his former cloister, and shared with them all that he had learned on his travels through Africa and Arabia; information that made up significant aspects of the mysterious "house" he had built recently by application of these tenets. Hence, the *Fama* informed its readers in 1614 that the Fraternity of the Rosy Cross began with just these four original members, and shortly thereafter expanded to eight members who agreed to disperse clandestinely abroad and share the Order's *axiomata* about Nature and the cure of the sick with the rest of world. The "house" mentioned here is not a typical dwelling of the 1600s, or of any other historical moment, for on the next page we learn that this invisible and movable dwelling is called *Sancti Spiritus*, or as identified elsewhere in the Rosicrucian corpus, "the House of the Holy Spirit".[114] The brethren agreed to meet every year on a specified date at *Sancti Spiritus* and that their Fraternity should remain secret for one hundred years. The text also implies that its authors were German Lutherans. As readers and interpreters of this text, we are led to ponder not only the actual location and surroundings of this inscrutable "house," but its imaginal location and divergent pneumatological meanings as well. *What does this mean?*

Before attempting to explain the confounding use of allegory in the *Fama,* a brief examination of the tomb of Rosenkreutz and the chronology cited in the Rosicrucian manifestos will help us fathom the meaning of the "House of the Holy Spirit." The tomb's seven sided structure, no less mysterious than any other aspect of the text, consisted of a ceiling, walls, and floor covered with strange and undisclosed markings. The ceiling was "divided according to the seven sides in the triangle" with an extremely bright artificial sun, or man-made light, in the center. Every side or wall was divided into ten squares, each with its own door for storing a chest, and each chest was filled with sacred books or special instruments. The floor was also "parted in the triangle" like the ceiling. Three sacred books containing the Order's wisdom are mentioned as part of the tomb's contents, each referred to by the first initial of its title yet presumably unknown to the rest of Europe. A Bible is also unearthed and praised as one of the Order's finest treasures. We learn also of the Order's reverence for alchemy, and for the medical legacies of Paracelsus. The *Fama's* persistent veneration of Paracelsus forms a sharp distinction with Bacon's caution about alchemy, and his unfavorable appraisal of Paracelsus. Elsewhere in the Rosicrucian documents we detect echoes of Ficino's and Pico's theological anthropology, along with a persistent veneration of Agrippa's *De Occulta Philosophia.*

Upon opening the tomb, the body of Christian Rosenkreutz was found intact and devoid of decay. In his hand, Brother C. R. held a manuscript with an explanation of his life story in the form of a curious eulogy comparing his existence, and the Order of the Rosy Cross, to a grain buried in the breast of Jesus Christ that at the appointed time would ripen and bear fruit. A brass plate around the altar declares the structure of the tomb as a "compendium of the Universe" (*Hoc universi compendium unius mihi sepulchrum feci*). This is followed by the phrase "*Jesus mihi omnia,*" or "*Jesus is my all.*"[115] The plate contained four more Latin phrases alluding to natural philosophy, the liberty of the Gospel, and the greater glory of God.[116]

The *Fama* states that Christian Rosenkreutz was born in 1378, lived for 106 years, and was buried in this hidden tomb inscribed with the Latin words: "*Post 120 annos patebo,*" meaning "After 120 years, I shall be opened."[117] Apart from the tomb's architectural décor and Latin inscriptions, such careful use of dates and years suggests that the author, or authors, wanted readers of this manifesto to calculate the number of years mentioned, and uncover a revelatory marker of some significant date in the future. Despite the appearance of the *Fama* in 1614, working out the numbers leads us to the fateful year of 1604 (1378 + 106 = 1484 + 120 = 1604). Like other researchers and commentators before me, I contend this is not a coincidence. In a manner of expectation similar to the years 1499 and 1500, many European Protestants and Roman Catholics living around the turn of the seventeenth century interpreted 1604 as an apocalyptic marker of great cosmological significance.

The year 1604 corresponded with the discovery of a very bright new star in the constellation of Serpentarius by the Lutheran astronomer Johannes Kepler (1571-1630). Kepler was a student of the Hermetic and alchemical traditions, as well as a devoted follower of Christ's teachings. He also served as Imperial Mathematician at the Court of the Holy Roman Emperor, Rudolph II (1552-1612). Kepler published his findings two years later in *De Stella Nova* (1606), which caught the attention of another rising star in the Scientific Revolution, Galileo (1564-1642). The *Confessio* of 1615 mentions "some new stars, which do appear and are seen in the firmament in Serpentario and Cygno," and which signify "powerful *signacula* of great weighty matters." Four years earlier William Jansonius had discovered another supernova in the constellation Cygnus, the Swan, whose significance to the Rosicrucian movement will be discussed below.[118]

Let us also recall that Francis Bacon published *The Advancement of Learning* with its plea for "the formation of a fraternity of learning and illumination"[119] based on knowledge of God and Nature in 1605. And curiously enough the visitors to the *New Atlantis* are greeted by an emissary from Solomon's House wearing a white turban with a *red cross* in the center, and are handed a scroll "signed with a stamp of cherubim's wings, not spread but hanging downwards, and by them a cross."[120] The Rosicrucian *Fama* concludes with the Latin phrase, "*sub umbra alarum tuarum Jehova,*" which in English reads: "Under the shadow of thy wings, Jehovah."[121] Curiosity compels our minds and hearts to repeat the ancient Pentecostal question: "*What does this mean?*"

The precise meaning of the Rosicrucian affinity for the Holy Spirit and its corresponding Trinitarian implications are perhaps unknowable. The cryptographers among the Order's devotees did a masterful job of allegorically cloaking their exact meanings. The text of the scroll that Brother C. R. held in his hand concludes with the statement: "*Ex Deo nascimur, in Jesu morimur, per Spiritum Sanctum reviviscimus*" which translates as: "We are born from God, in Jesus we die, by the Holy Spirit we are reborn."[122] As with the Arthurian, Holy Grail, and Joachimist allegories discussed in earlier chapters of this book, the intent of this allegory alongside enigmatic texts within texts suggests that the pneumatological aspects of communication and religious revitalization may be at work here. The first possible aspect is that of communication because of the Holy Spirit's role in fostering exchanges of both relationality and intimacy between individual believers and the other two Persons of the Trinity. The second possible aspect is that of renewal, or revitalization, because of the Holy Spirit's power to promote the process of moving from potentiality to actuality, known in traditional theological discourse as the Spirit's movement towards the fullness of all things. This aspect of Christian tradition, as we discussed in previous chapters, had proven its inspirational utility in reformist and visionary subversions of excessively dominant or reactionary ecclesiastical and socio-political paradigms. In its role of empowering Christians for ecclesiastical leadership and renewal, the Spirit opens human hearts and minds towards the possibilities of theological reconstruction among the different elements of Christian tradition, such as canon, doctrine, and ritual; daily and liturgical prayer, worship practices, pedagogy, and ecclesiology. In the case of the Rosicrucian manifestos, the perceived urgency to reform Christian learning in ways capable of integrating scientific knowledge about Nature with theological precepts motivated the second aspect of these pneumatological visions. It should be noted that the intensity of the Ro-

sicrucian outburst was fueled by the seventeenth century's nagging awareness
that European Christendom's project of reform and recovery had been under
way since before the Florentine Renaissance of the 1400s, but its fruition had
been delayed by the deficiencies of human nature and the perceived failures of
both Church and State to achieve genuine and long lasting reforms.

During the nearly two hundred years leading up to the celestial signs of
1600 and 1604, the pneumatological visionaries of the Florentine Renaissance,
and the Protestant and Catholic Reformations after them, had called out for very
similar transformations of Christian piety and learning. Many like Abbot Trithemius believed the great renovation leading to Christ's Second Coming would
begin soon after 1500. The depiction of "the House of the Holy Spirit," printed
in Daniel Moegling's *Mirror of Rosicrucian Wisdom* (*Speculum Sophicum Rho-
do-Stauroticum*) leaves little doubt about the Rosy Cross' awareness of the two
supernovae. Moegling published the work in 1618 under the pseudonym Theo-
philus Schweighardt and embellished its frontispiece with a fantastic drawing of
a building on wheels surrounded by a myriad of symbols and cryptic Latin
phrases. At the top of the drawing are three images that shed light on our discussion. In the center is the name "Jehovah" in Hebrew letters amidst a cloud with
outstretched wings and the "Finger of God" emanating from the bottom of this
cloud pointing to the building below known as *Sancti Spiritus*. In the upper left
hand corner is a star with the figure of Serpentarius, the Serpent-Bearer associated with Hermetic alchemy and healing, and the date "1604" below the figure, thus alluding to Kepler's new star and the opening of Christian Rosenkreutz's tomb in 1604. In the upper right hand corner is another star with the
figure of a Swan representing Cygnus, alluding to the new star of 1600. These
symbols are a clear indication of the apocalyptic dimensions of the new order of
pious and learned reformers that were believed to have emerged from this so-
called *domus Sancti Spiritus*. We are forced to ponder yet another possibility,
but one we cannot prove with total certainty. If the Brethren of the Rosy Cross
were not just the heralds of a Protestant reform movement, but signaled the advent of an Age of the Holy Spirit, then the Rosicrucian Manifestos and symbols
must also recall the twelfth century *magnus propheta*, Joachim of Fiore, who
prophesied and wrote about the coming of a world transformation of spiritual
liberty and learning in the Age of the Holy Spirit.

This now requires consideration of what might be the most unexpected cor-
relation in the entire ensemble of primary sources surveyed in the present book.
Is it possible that the designation of the Rosy Cross Fraternity as "The House of
the Holy Spirit;" the Order's noble ideals of social service, of curing the sick
without payment, and nurturing both personal piety and intellectual learning;
and the Brethren's renunciation of violence and warfare were all inspired either
directly, or indirectly, by the Joachimist visions foretold in the Calabrian Abbot's prophetic works: the *Psalterium decem Chordarum*, *Liber Concordie*, and
the *Expositio in Apocalypsim*? Before his death in 1202, Joachim prophesied the
rise of a new order of learned and spiritual brothers about the year 1260 whose
enlightened leadership would abolish the need for the hierarchical church of his
times. While many believed his visions dealt with the rise of the Spiritual Fran-

ciscans in the latter half of the 1200s, most European Christians, following the Fourth Lateran Council's denouncement of his work as heresy, dismissed the dates revealed in his visions and calculations. Nonetheless, while I am not the first researcher to point out these connections, the evidence for a Joachimist ideological connection with the Rosicrucian image of the "House of the Holy Spirit" merits further study and investigation.

In the late 1500s, a brief revival of Joachimist enthusiasm surfaced among at least four German Protestant writers who influenced the apocalyptic tone of the Rosicrucian manifestos. First among these was Adam Nachenmoser's *Prognosticum Theologicum* (1588), which sought to recalculate Joachim's fateful year of 1260 by counting the years from the baptism and death of Emperor Constantine the Great in 327 CE, instead of following Joachim's method of counting the generations of Hebrew and Christian patriarchs. Of course, this was historically incorrect since Constantine actually died on May 22, 337 CE, which was Pentecost Sunday. Nonetheless, following this strategy we derive the year 1587 (327 + 1260 = 1587). Nachenmoser believed that the period from 1587 to 1600 would witness the "labor pains" of the new age. The *Fama* cryptically asserts that: "Europe is with child and will bring forth a strong child who shall stand in need of a great godfather's gift."[123] Next was Julius Sperber, who later became a leading apologist for the Rosicrucian cause, and whom Christopher McIntosh includes among the group of "people who saw themselves as the founders of Joachim's new order."[124] In his *Book of Wonders* (ca. 1600), Sperber compares both the astrological aspects and the general mood of the period from 1500 to 1600 to the cosmological and socio-political aspects of the first century BCE just before the birth of the Savior. Sperber believed that a Joachimist transformation of Christianity, and of the whole world, was about to happen, and that it would witness Roman Catholicism being superseded by a new religious ethos governed by the Holy Spirit. Third, we have the example of the Protestant pastor Heinrich Vogel's *Revelation of the Secrets of Alchemy*, published not coincidentally in 1605, which foresaw the arrival of the Anti-Christ just as Christians rediscovered the lost secrets of alchemy. Finally, we have the extremely influential yet relatively unknown *Naometria,* by the Tübingen educated Simon Studion, which interestingly enough is dated 1604. The work never appeared in print, but as McIntosh asserts, it "must have been circulated widely in manuscript" form.[125] Studion adheres to Joachim's method of calculating the Biblical generations and concludes that the next to last of these extended from 1560 to 1590 so that the final generation lasting from about 1590 to 1620 would see the advent of the Age of the Holy Spirit. Simon Studion's *Naometria* and the discovery of Christian Rosenkreutz's tomb in the *Fama Fraternitatis* are both dated 1604. This, in turn, coincided with Kepler's supernova in the constellation Serpentarius, plus the eerie astrological conjunctions of Jupiter and Saturn in Sagittarius for that same year, and the discovery of yet another star in the constellation Cygnus four years earlier. As a dear friend of mine used to say: "The magic of believing is believing." Hence, the *Fama* served as both a mission statement of Rosicrucian ideals and as a cosmic key for reading the portents about the impending transformation of Christianity and the world by the Holy Ghost's intercession:

> For like as our door was after so many years wonderfully discovered, also there shall be opened a door to Europe (when the wall is removed), which already doth begin to appear, and with great desire is expected of many.[126]

However, when Studion's Joachimist apocalyptic marker of 1620 came and passed without the long awaited transformation of Church and State, more than a few adherents among the Brethren of the Rosy Cross went through a period of disillusionment and reappraisal.

Far from a rebirth of Christian piety and learning by the power of the Holy Ghost, what revealed itself across the European continent was the devastation of the Thirty Years' War from 1618 to 1648. This acutely violent struggle involved the Roman Catholic Hapsburg's of Spain, Austria, and the Holy Roman Empire against their anti-Hapsburg, and increasingly Protestant, provinces throughout Germany, the Netherlands, and Bohemia. At stake were the imperial claims of Spain and the Holy Roman Empire versus the assertions of religious liberty and territorial sovereignty by the German and Dutch provinces.

While all of Europe waited anxiously for the fragile truce between Spain and the Netherlands set to expire in 1621, England's James I had arranged for his daughter, Princess Elizabeth (1596-1662), to marry Frederick V of the Palatinate (1596-1632) back in February 1613. The marriage was seen across Europe as a signal that under King James I, Britain would protect the German Protestant Union from the aggressive designs of the Roman Catholic House of Hapsburg. As Elector Palatine of the Rhine, Frederick was one of the most important secular leaders in the Holy Roman Empire. His role in Bohemia's growing Rosicrucian movement from 1614 to 1618, along with more than a few alleged English Renaissance ties to Hermetic and alchemical currents among German Protestants, has been well documented.[127]

As fate would have it, however, the Protestant Union deposed King Ferdinand II as head of the Holy Roman Empire and elected the young and idealistic Frederick V as King of Bohemia, which he accepted under the erroneous assumption that his father-in-law, England's King James I, would intervene militarily. McIntosh observes that Frederick "may have done so in the belief that he was stepping into the new age" foretold by German Joachimist sympathizers like Simon Studion.[128] King James opted to distance himself from the conflict. After the Bohemian forces were obliterated west of Prague by the Imperial army and its Catholic allies at the Battle of the White Mountain on November 8, 1620, King Frederick and Princess Elizabeth were forced into exile for the rest of their lives. Following this decisive battle, movements of the Holy Spirit like the Moravian Brethren suffered to the point of seeing their leaders and teachers brutally executed in public as an act of terror to discourage all potential subversives and revolutionaries from continuing their activities. Thus began the great conflagration of the Thirty Years' War in Central Europe, which dashed the pneumatological hopes of so many across the Continent. There could be no Second Pentecost, and no Age of the Holy Spirit, amidst such violence and lack of grace.

By 1625, Spain and its allies expanded the war throughout most of Western Europe to the point of drawing in France, Sweden, and Denmark. The long and costly war was finally concluded by the Treaty of the Pyrenees, between Spain and France, and by the Treaty of Westphalia between the Hapsburgs and their Protestant rivals. After three decades of so much violence in the name of religion, the religious idealism of the Rosicrucian Manifestos was tempered by the folly of unrestrained imperial and sectarian ambitions. Ironically, due to its emphasis on alchemy and magic, the Fraternity of the Rosy Cross also became a target of the witch-craze that swept through Protestant and Catholic Europe from 1623 until the end of the century. Sometimes God's fiery wisdom proposes to revitalize humanity's fortunes, but humanity's shortsightedness disposes the promise of God's empowering vision, and the long-awaited epoch of Holy Ghost recedes yet again into the *not-yet* of the future.

JOHANN VALENTIN ANDREAE'S CHRISTIANOPOLIS, (1619)

A complete assessment of Rosicrucian history, and other original sources attributed to the movement, is beyond the scope of the present study, and for this reason I have intentionally omitted the lives and careers of well-known figures associated with the Rosy Cross Fraternity like the Englishman Robert Fludd (1574-1637) and the German Michael Maier (1568-1622).[129] However, the most significant figure in the Rosicrucian uproar on the continent was the Lutheran theologian and university professor, Johann Valentin Andreae (1586-1654), whom many still believe wrote the Order's manifestos.

Known to his German contemporaries as "the Phoenix of the Theologians," Andreae's early involvement and support of the Rosy Cross movement was probably muted in his later years by the effect of the Thirty Years' War, and by the growing European witch-craze that equated Rosicrucian claims and practices with black magic, sorcery, and demonology. Practically unknown today among students of European intellectual history or church history, Andreae was well versed in the leading theological and philosophical currents of his day. John Warwick Montgomery describes him as one of the leading proponents of Lutheran orthodoxy in seventeenth century Germany, and as one of the leading voices in that century on the relation of scientific learning to Christian piety.[130] Although Andreae's precise role in the composition of the Rosicrucian manifestoes and in the movement's origins remains controversial among scholars, his prolific output of theological and literary works, and his lifelong devotion to the integration of Christian piety and scientific learning, was profoundly inspired by the Holy Ghost and aimed at the liberation of humanity from sin and suffering.

In his autobiography at age forty-two, Andreae admitted writing the *Chemical Wedding of Christian Rosenkreutz* (1616), but of becoming disenchanted later with the proliferation of so many charlatans claiming to be Rosicrucians while spinning webs of secretive, magical nonsense and continually misrepresenting what being "brothers of Christ" really meant. For a long time historians thought Andreae had made the whole thing up as part of an elaborate hoax or prank. Scholars still follow Arthur Edward Waite and Frances Yates' leads by focusing on the meaning of Andreae's frequent use of the Latin term *ludibrium* alongside his references to the Rosy Cross, such as "the ludibrium of the vain *Fama*" and "the ludibrium of the fictitious Roscicrucian Fraternity." Yates observed that such derogatory instances from Andreae's *Vita* should be read with an eye toward multiple meanings since in Elizabethan England "a *ludibrium* could be a play, a comic fiction."[131] Peter Arnold also suggested a *sensus spiritualis* reading of the term since in French *ludibrium* can mean a "farce" or "prank," which might have been Andreae's way of detracting attention from his involvement in a reform movement that genuinely scared both nobles and commoners alike during the first half of the 1600s. Indeed, men and women from all walks of life were already on edge over the hostilities unleashed by the Thirty Years, War.[132] Other scholars, like John Warwick Montgomery, believe that Andreae's use of the term was contemptuous, as well as indicative of his low esteem of the movement, after its failure to manifest the finer ideals and expectations called for in the first two manifestos, whose composition he denied.[133] I have no doubt each of these fine scholars perceived a fragment of the truth, but as for me, "plausible deniability" about his role in a reformist secret society would seem a wise course of action during the most turbulent years of the Thirty Years' War, from 1625 to 1645, when the middle aged Andreae was completely focused on his career as a theologian and university professor.

Andreae's hopes for a reformation of Christian society, learning, and piety were expressed earlier when he was thirty-three in his utopian novella, *Christianopolis* (1619). A literary work about an ideal Christian Republic in which science, faith, and politics collaborate for the benefit of humanity, and which may have provided the inspiration for Bacon's *New Atlantis* (1627). Andreae's novella influenced the founders of the Royal Society and earned its author a secure place in the annals of utopian literature. Contemporary readers will be disappointed by Andreae's anti-Islamic views, excess of Christian exclusivity, subordinate views of women's roles in marriage, and by his Protestant versus Roman Catholic polemics. But these stern views and prejudices are not surprising given the strict gender roles, military violence, and religious intolerance that characterized the 1500s and 1600s through the end of the Thirty Years' War. His answer to the discomfort and unfulfilled promises of early seventeenth century European Christendom was the construction of an ideal state where the citizens study the teachings of Christ, the inner meaning of the Holy Scriptures, and the Secrets of Nature.

As the story opens, the narrator describes his decision to venture forth on a voyage "upon the Academic Sea," aboard a ship named "Phantasy," in search of knowledge until a strong storm destroyed their vessel and shipwrecked him alone on this "triangular shaped island." For the inhabitants of Christianopolis, their faith in Christ and their commitment to learning are the guiding lights of this civilization. The clergy are married and devote much time to contemplation and scientific learning. The fruits of scientific investigation, carried out in magnificently equipped laboratories, represent the most heroic and esteemed achievements of this idealized Christian community, in which chemistry is given the loftiest place in the pantheon of Christianopolis' sciences.

Book XXVIII of *Christianopolis* details the religious beliefs of this fictional society in what looks and sounds just like a church mission statement reminiscent of the Nicene Creed as used by seventeenth century Lutherans. The text, inscribed in golden letters on tablets of stone, explains the role of the Trinitarian Persons in the ideals of the State, and in the moral fabric of society, and then has this to say about the Holy Spirit:

> We believe with our whole heart in the Holy Spirit, our Comforter and Teacher by whom we are sanctified, enlivened, and equipped, after we go from freedom to doing good, by whom we are made wise beyond nature, armed against nature, and put at peace with her; by whom we grow warm, are united and divided into languages; by whom we see and hear the past, present, and future properly correlated; by whom we look into the Word of God.[134]

Later in the narrative, Andreae treats readers to a summary of the system of education used in Christianopolis, based on a revived and expanded model of the Seven Liberal Arts, whereby the Holy Spirit is given a very special role in theological and philosophical studies:

> This, first of all, teaches the mode of expression of the Holy Ghost in the Holy Scriptures; their strength, elegance, efficacy, and depth, that the student may know what is meant by this or that diction and this or that combination of words; and that they may learn to admire this sort of language more than all the eloquence of this earth. Then they are urged toward a devout imitation of this divine speech that, when they shall have collected for themselves from their [youthful] days a mighty treasure of holy thoughts, they may know how to adapt them also to the needs of mortals, and may learn to speak to others with the same Spirit, the same words with which the apostles of Christ preached the Gospel to the people.[135]

There is a remarkable and persistent cadence throughout the narrative about the human heart and mind developing an intimate acquaintance with the Holy Spirit, which contemporary scholarship and readers are not accustomed to equating with the Lutheran Reformation, or with the scientific mysticism of the Rosicrucian Enlightenment.

The leaders and inhabitants of Christianopolis place a high priority on the theory of mystical correspondences (*harmonia*) between heaven and earth, and on the doctrine of signatures (*significatio*), which Andreae describes as inspired and nurtured by the "school of the Spirit." In the opening lines the narrator states that: "One might think that here the heavens and the earth had been married and were living together in everlasting peace."[136] This seems to have been Andreae's way of alluding to the Hermetic dictum "As Above, So Below," which lies at the core of esoteric notions about terrestrial and cosmic correspondence. Astronomy, astrology, sacred geometry and arithmetic are described as essential to knowledge of humanity's place in the order of Creation.

There are no overtly Pentecostal themes in Andreae's *Christianopolis*, like the Second Pentecost that occurs in Bacon's *New Atlantis*. Although the narrative's utopian ideals and political structures contain considerable millenarian ramifications, there are no veiled or obvious references to Joachimist millennialism. There is, however, an allusion to the Rosy Cross, as the narrator, after being shipwrecked, is being examined by the Prefect of the Guard before being allowed to enter Christianopolis. The guard asks the stranger if he is "one of those whom the citizens of the community would not tolerate among them but would send back to the place from which they had come" such as those "impostors who falsely call themselves the Brothers of the Rosicrucians, and other like blemishes of literature and true culture, whom this city has never ceased to suspect."[137] From the tone of this disclaimer, it appears that Johann Valentin Andreae was already at work distancing himself from the specter of the Rosicrucian manifestos when he wrote this story, or perhaps we have here just another example of plausible deniability given the political dangers of challenging the status quo in the early 1600s.

SCIENCE & SPIRIT IN LATE SEVENTEENTH CENTURY EUROPE

Although this historical survey of medieval and early modern conceptions of the Holy Spirit and Pentecost covers five centuries of Western European and Christian intellectual history, our discussion concludes in the same domain that our review of the primary sources began in Chapter Two, —in the realm of *Natura*, the natural world, where Christians through the ages located, felt, heard, tasted, saw, and witnessed the presence of God and the living Jesus through the Holy Spirit. The seventeenth century view of Nature and humanity's place in the order of Creation was markedly different from the views of Nature expressed nearly five hundred years before by Hildegard of Bingen, Joachim of Fiore, or Francis of Assisi. However, just as Albert Einstein perceived the details of Relativity Theory, and, then near the end of his distinguished career, pondered the mysteries of the Unified Field Theory by working out mathematical equations on his chalkboard at Princeton University, so too did many ancient, medieval, and early-modern magicians believe the language of mathematics and geometry revealed something about the nature of God and the Cosmos. This feature of the Euro-Western scientific tradition, which probably goes all the way back to Pythagoras and Plato, and even further back to Egypt and Mesopotamia, took on a new meaning with the emergence of modern astronomy and physics.

However, while arithmetic and geometry served many of the empirical needs of early modern scientific observation and measurement in fields like astronomy, cartography, thermodynamics, and physics, the elusive chemical properties of Spirit and Matter held center stage among most of the pioneers of early modern chemistry. These were the pioneering trailblazers of chemistry, who emerged from medieval alchemy and Rosicrucianism, pioneers like Johannes Baptista von Helmont, who described himself as a "philosopher of fire," and Robert Boyle (1627-1691), who sought to comprehend and manipulate "those ponderable fire particles" for the enlargement of human industry and the improvement of human life. Very few people today have ever heard of the field of *pneumatic chemistry*, but in the late 1600s it represented the bold new frontier for the fulfillment of the Scientific Revolution inspired by Francis Bacon's life and works. To this frontier's new vistas we must add the objective of reading and mastering the Book of Nature expressed in the Rosicrucian Manifestos and in works like Andreae's *Christianopolis.* The theme of "deciphering the secrets of Nature" and achieving "Dominion over Nature" that developed from the mid-1400s to the late 1600s, among Italian Humanism, Christian magical theology, Baconianism, and the Roscicrucian Enlightenment, culminated in the official founding of the "Royal Society of London for the Improving of Natural Knowledge." The fraternity that formally became the Royal Society in 1660 under King Charles II had its beginnings in a benevolent circle of scientific inquiry and collegial sharing, led first by Theodore Haak (1605-1690) as early as 1645, and then later by Robert Boyle. The group usually met at London's Gresham College and included other notable figures associated with founding the Royal Society like Benjamin Worsley (1618-1673), Samuel Hartlib (1600-1662), Sir Christopher Wren (1632-1723), Robert Hooke (1635-1703), Sir Robert Moray (1609-73), and Elias Ashmole (1617-1692). Boyle referred to the group as "The Invisible College," a term that shows the abiding influence of Bacon's Great Instauration and the fraternity of Solomon's House depicted in *The New Atlantis.* The frontispiece to Thomas Sprat's *History of the Royal Society* (1667) depicts Francis Bacon and Robert Boyle. Both men were loyal supporters of the Royalist cause, and ardent advocates of the "new experimental philosophy" for the advancement of knowledge, and both were devout Christians.

Bacon had argued emphatically for the separation of faith and reason in scientific matters so as not to hinder or deform the Christian faith. But he never imagined the coming golden age of scientific achievement as being anything but an era complemented by the *vehicula scientiae* in his vision of a Second Pentecost set forth in *The New Atlantis.* Boyle had argued emphatically for the improvement of the old alchemical errors in the pioneering field of chemistry, which he discussed in *The Sceptical Chymist* (1661) and developed throughout the remainder of his long and distinguished career as a scientist. Boyle knew quite a bit about alchemy and the Hermetic tradition. Modern Rosicrucians consider him a member of their Rosy Cross Fraternity, and his name appears on the infamous Priory of Sion list featured in Dan Brown's popular novel, *The Da Vinci Code.* But Boyle never imagined a scientific community in which religious or spiritual questions were banished from the arena of empirical discourse as "unverifiable subjectivities," a conviction well attested to by endowing the Boyle Lectures in his will with the aim of defending the Christian religion against atheism and discussing the existence of God from a scientific perspective.

In the intellectual and revolutionary climate of the 1700s an increasing mistrust between the domains of science and theology emerged, a trend accompanied by increased suspicion against the "enthusiast" claims of visionary religious writers and reform movements across England following the Puritan Revolution of 1640-1660. In Germany, as in Great Britain, concern about the "enthusiasts" was sometimes mingled with anti-Catholic or anti-Jesuit polemics, which prevented the altruistic sharing of knowledge called for in the Baconian and Rosicrucian agendas for reforming Christian learning throughout Europe. In the lives

Those ponderable fire particles... 243

and careers of many eighteenth century scientists, like Isaac Newton in physics, or Anton Lavoisier in chemistry, the notion of a mechanistic, verifiable universe that could be known by deciphering mathematical formulae or by unearthing the chemical basis of an element, began gazing with new eyes upon a Cosmos whose celestial motions, basic substances, and energy fields could be discovered and then mapped by the application of fixed, natural Laws. In such a state of affairs, the kingdom of pneumatology and the creative imagination of Pentecost became little more than an "unverifiable subjectivity."[3] As the seventeenth century unfolded into the eighteenth century and beyond, the paradigm of Enlightenment Modernism, "the Age of Reason," decided which ways of knowing and relating the human to the Divine realms, if any, were worthy of serious academic and scientific investigation. Today, hardly anyone in the academic community, and scarcely anyone in the community of church-goers and clergy, is aware of the profound impact that Esoteric Christian currents like alchemy, magical theology, Hermetic philosophy, or Rosicrucianism had on the development of modern consciousness and the Scientific Revolution. But even fewer people in either academia, or in the various Christian denominations possess any knowledge of the role that conceptions of Pentecost and the Holy Spirit played in the rise of modern science. The early modern proto-scientific quest to understand the power and presence of the Holy Spirit through significations like "*ethereal fire,*" or through the ambiguity of Agrippa's *Quintessence* is largely unknown today. The investigation of this fiery and mysterious reality, that intrigued early Rosicrucian and Masonic sympathizers, eventually ceded its place in the history of ideas to the mysterious and elusive powers of electromagnetic energy. By the time Newton's Laws became known to the educated public, the would-be Christian theologian turned scientist, and distinguished President of the Royal Society of London, had been dubbed by some of his detractors as "the last alchemist."

NOTES

1. From *The Two Bookes of Francis Bacon. Of the proficience and advancement of Learning, divine and humane,* Book I (1605 Edition) in Helen C. White, et. al., *Seventeenth Century Verse and Prose, Vol. I: 1600-1660.* Second Ed. (New York: Macmillan, 1971), 62; see also *Francis Bacon, The Major Works.* Brian Vickers, Ed. (Oxford University Press, 2002), 123-124.
2. John Polkinghorne, *Belief in God in an Age of Science.* (New Haven: Yale University Press, 2005), 117-118.
3. Caroline Walker Bynum, "Introduction: The Complexity of Symbols," in *Gender and Religion: On the Complexity of Symbols,* Eds. C. W. Bynum, Stevan Harrell, and Paula Richman. (Boston: Beacon Press, 1986), 15.
4. Justo González, *The Story of Christianity; Volume I: The Early Church to the Dawn of the Reformation.* (San Francisco: Harper, 1984), xvi.
5. Ibid.
6. J. R. Partington, *A Short History of Chemistry.* Third Ed. (New York: Macmillan, 1957), 46.
7. Frances A. Yates, *The Rosicrucian Enlightenment* (London: Routledge, 1972), 226.

8. B. J. Gibbons, *Spirituality and the Occult: From the Renaissance to the Modern Age* (London: Routledge, 2001), 73.

9. Lynn Thorndike, *A History of Magic and Experimental Science, 8Volumes.* (New York: Columbia University Press, 1929-1958), V. I, 2.

10. The authors of this study add: "There is little doubt that this tradition could also be found in the province of earlier alchemy as well, but it is not our present brief to present a history of the discipline from its origins," in *Alchemy Tried in the Fire: Starkey, Boyle and the Fate of Helmontian Chymistry* (Chicago: University of Chicago Press, 2002), 38, fn. 7.

11. For a slightly more thorough yet concise history of the esoteric traditions described in this chapter, see any of the following: Michael D. Bailey, *Magic and Superstition in Europe: A Concise History from Antiquity to the Present* (Lanham: Rowan and Littlefield, 2007), 9-193; Arthur Versluis, *Magic and Mysticism: An Introduction to Western Esotericism* (Rowan and Littlefield, 2007), 11-96; see also Book One, Part Two of Antoine Faivre's *Access to Western Esotericism* (Albany: SUNY Press, 1994), 49-110; and for a classic overview of esoteric currents in the Renaissance period see D. P. Walker, *Spiritual and Demonic Magic from Ficino to Campanella* (1958; reprinted, University of Notre Dame Press, 1975).

12. Antoine Faivre, *The Eternal Hermes: From Greek God to Alchemical Magus* (Grand Rapids: Phanes Press, 1995), 71.

13. Antoine Faivre, *Access to Western Esotericism*, 4-5.

14. For more on *theosis* see Georgios I. Mantzaridis, *The Deification of Man: St. Gregory Palamas and The Orthodox Tradition.* L. Sherrard, Trans. (Crestwood: Saint. Vladimir's Seminary Press, 1984), 7-39.

15. B.J. Gibbons, 142.

16. Ibid.

17. Manfred Lurker, *Dictionary of Gods and Goddesses, Devils and Demons.* Trans. G. L. Campbell. (London: Routledge and Kegan Paul, 1987), 150-151.

18. It is important to distinguish between the two forms of esotericism exhibited among ancient Egypto-Greek Hermetic texts. On the one hand there was the "Technical Hermetica" or "Books of Thoth," which contained mostly spells, astrological formulas, recipes for alchemical stews, and genealogies of both beneficent and malevolent spirits. These comprised the oldest portions of the Hermetic writings with far more ancient roots in pre-Hellenistic Egyptian folk magic and the prehistoric legends of Thoth. On the other hand, there was the much more popular "Philosophical Hermetica," represented by the *Poimandres, Asclepius,* and the *Corpus Hermeticum* texts.

19. Antoine Faivre, *The Eternal Hermes*, 17.

20. See Howard R. Turner, *Science in Medieval Islam* (Austin: University of Texas Press, 1995), 189-194.

21. This is quite doubtful because *The Emerald Tablet* might be the oldest text among all of the known Arabian alchemical treatises, and it has always been connected with the ancient Hellenistic sage Apollonius of Tyana. No other alchemical treatise or Hermetic text has remained as influential as, or more consistently popular, into modern times than the *Emerald Tablet.* Despite all of its legendary accretions and mysteries, it is also an incredibly simple text of less than thirty lines in length when translated into English.

22. For a detailed and insightful analysis of the relationship among Hellenistic cosmology, musical harmonies and the seven vowels, and Hermetic philosophy see Joscelyn Godwin, *The Mystery of the Seven Vowels: In Theory and Practice* (Grand Rapids: Phanes Press, 1991), 19-33; 57-75.

23. As cited in Antoine Faivre, *The Eternal Hermes*, 25.

24. See Richard Morris, *The Last Sorcerers: The Path from Alchemy to the Periodic Table* (Washington, D.C.: Joseph Henry Press, 2003), 66-67.

25. I have intentionally chosen not to reproduce the entire text of the *Emerald Tablet* here, a work with many different Medieval Latin versions and Arabic texts which I have been working with since the early 1990s. Today there are literally dozens of versions available on the internet, some coming from very unsophisticated "new age" sites and unprofessional sources. The text quoted here is based upon the Medieval Latin text of the *Tabula Smaragdina* (ca. 1140) from Heinrich Khunrath's, *Amphitheatrum sapientiae aeternae.* (Hanau, 1609). See also the first edition (1602) of Khunrath's work discussed in Stanislas Klossowski de Rola, *The Golden Game: Alchemical Engravings of the Seventeenth Century* (New York: George Braziller, 1988), 36, plate 8; 42-43, fn. 8.

26. Petrus Bonus, *La Pretiosa margarita novella* (Venice: Aldine Press Edition, 1546); English trans. by Arthur Edward Waite, *The New Pearl of Great Price: A Treatise Concerning the Treasure and Most Precious Stone of the Philosophers* (London: James Elliot, 1894).

27. Ibid.

28. In *La Pretiosa margarita novella*, from the *Bibliotheca chemica curiosa* (Geneva, 1702) 42-43; as cited in S. K. de Rola, *The Golden Game: Alchemical Engravings of the Seventeenth Century,* 16, fn. 33; 22.

29. Ibid.

30. Maureen Quilligan, *The Language of Allegory: Defining the Genre* (Ithaca: Cornell University Press, 1979), 26.

31. Stephen A. McKnight, *The Modern Age and the Recovery of Ancient Wisdom: A Reconsideration of Historical Consciousness, 1450-1650* (Columbia: University of Missouri Press, 1991), 1.

32. Ibid. 24.

33. Ibid. 59.

34. Ibid. 47.

35. As quoted in Ibid. from Book 13, Chapter 4 of Ficino's *Theologia Platonica de Immortalitate Animorum* (Basel, 1561), and based upon quotations in Charles Trinkaus, *In Our Image and Likeness: Humanity and Divinity in Italian Humanist Thought.* 2 vols. (Chicago: University of Chicago Press, 1970), v. 2, 486.

36. *Boundaries of Our Habitations*, 118.

37. See Eugenio Garin, *Giovanni Pico Della Mirandola: Vita e dottrina* (Firenze, 1937); *Giovanni Pico della Mirandola* (Parma, 1963).

38. As cited in S. A. Farmer, *Syncretism in the West: Pico's 900 Theses (1486): The Evolution of Traditional and Philosophical Systems.* Medieval and Renaissance Texts and Studies, Vol. 167 (Tempe: Arizona State University, 1998), 19.

39. Giovanni Pico Della Mirandola, *Oration on the Dignity of Man.* Trans. by A. Robert Caponigri. (Washington, DC: Regnery Publishing, 1956), 3-4.

40. Ibid. 20.

41. Ibid. 21.

42. Ibid.

43. Ibid. 21-22.

44. Ibid. 8-9.

45. Ibid. 53.

46. Ibid. 56.

47. As quoted in Stephen McKnight, *The Modern Age and the Recovery of Ancient Wisdom*, 58.

48. Ibid. 53-54.
49. Ibid. 55.
50. As cited in Brann, *Trithemius and Magical Theology*, 19.
51. Hugh of St. Victor, *Didascalicon* (lib. VI, cap. 15 in J. P. Migne, Ed. *Patrologiae cursus completus...Series latina*, 1844-1905) as quoted in Noel Brann's *Trithemius and Magical Theology*, 19, fn. 22.
52. Ibid. 22.
53. *Oration on the Dignity of Man*, 56-57.
54. Ibid. 57-58.
55. See the fine recent work of Lauro Martines, *Fire in the City: Savonarola and the Struggle for the Soul of Renaissance Florence*. (New York: Oxford University Press, 2006).
56. For a discussion of Savonarola's Joachimist influences and apocalyptic motivations see Donald Weinstein, "Savonarola, Florence, and the Millenarian Tradition," *Church History*, Vol.27, No.4 (Dec. 1958): 298-305.
57. See Martines, *Fire in the City*, 254-281.
58. *Boundaries of Our Habitations*, 119.
59. For more on *theōsis* see the following works: Michael J. Christensen and Jeffrey A. Wittung, Eds. *Partakers of the Divine Nature: The History and Development of Deification in the Christian Traditions* (Madison: Fairleigh Dickinson University Press, 2007); Stephen Finlan and Vladimir Kharlamov, Eds. *Theōsis: Deification in Christian Theology* (Eugene: Pickwick Publications, 2006); Vladimir Lossky, *The Mystical Theology of the Eastern Church* (Crestwood: Saint Vladimir's Seminary Press, 1997); Georgios I. Mantzaridis, *The Deification of Man: St. Gregory Palamas and The Orthodox Tradition*. L. Sherrard, Trans. (Crestwood: Saint Vladimir's Seminary Press, 1984), 7-39; Panayiotis Nellas, *Deification in Christ: Orthodox Perspectives on The Nature of the Human Person* (Crestwood: Saint Vladimir's Seminary Press, 1987), 15-91; 199-237; Norman Russell, *The Doctrine of Deification in the Greek Patristic Tradition* (Oxford University Press, 2005); Lars Thunberg, *Man and the Cosmos: The Vision of Maximus The Confessor* (St. Vladimir's Seminary Press, 1985), 51-91.
60. For an informative and thought-provoking study of the Byzantine Empire's influence on Latin Christendom see Colin Wells, *Sailing from Byzantium: How a Lost Empire Changed the World* (Delacorte Press, 2006); and Deno John Geanakoplos, *Constantinople and The West: Essays on the Late Byzantine (Palaeologan) and Italian Renaissances and the Byzantine and Roman Churches*. (Madison: University of Wisconsin Press, 1989), 3-67; 91-113.
61. See John 14:12.
62. See the range of essays in the volume by Richard Auernheimer and Frank Baron, Eds. *Johannes Trithemius: Humanismus und Magie im vor reformatorischen Deutschland*. Bad Kreuznacher Symposien I, 1985 (Munich: Profil, 1991).
63. For more on miracles in Christian history see Peter Harrison, "Miracles, Early Modern Science, and Rational Religion," *Church History* 75:3 (September 2006): 493-510; Benedicta Ward, *Miracles and the Medieval Mind: Theory, Record, and Event, 1000-1215* (Philadelphia: University of Pennsylvania Press, 1982); and John Hardon, "The Concept of Miracle from St. Augustine to Modern Apologetics," *Theological Studies* 15 (1954): 229-257.
64. Trithemius' references to Albertus Magnus appear in works like his ill-fated and unfinished *Steganographia* (ca. 1499), *De septem secundeis* (1508), his autobiographical *Nepiachus,* in his ecclesiastical and political history of France and Germany, *The Annals of Hirsau* (ca. 1514), and in the famous *Polygraphia* (ca. 1516).

65. Albertus Magnus, *Commentarius in Evangelium secundum Matthaeum*, (cap. 2 in *Opera omnia*, edited by P. Jammy , IX, 24; 1651) as quoted in Noel L. Brann, *Trithemius and Magical Theology: A Chapter in the Controversy over Occult Studies in Early Modern Europe* (Albany: SUNY Press, 1999), 23, fn. 33.

66. See David Khan, *The Code Breakers: The Story of Secret Writing*, Second Ed. (1967; MacMillan, reprinted 1974), 130-37; or the substantially improved revised edition *The Code Breakers: The Comprehensive History of Secret Communication from Ancient Times to the Internet* (New York: Simon and Schuster; Rev. Ed., 1996), 81-83; 91-93; 130-137; 519-526.

67. For an overview and analysis of theological and historical appraisals of Trithemius' works and legacy in the centuries after his death see Brann's *Trithemius and Magical Theology*, 157-254.

68. Ibid. 10-11.

69. Ibid. 252.

70. Thorndike, *History of Magic and Experimental Science*, Vol. V: 8, 127.

71. See Letter 24 of Book I in the Epistolarum of the Latin *Opera* of Agrippa's works, 2:623-624.

72. See Psalm 104:1-5.

73. In Donald Tyson, Ed. *Three Books of Occult Philosophy Written by Henry Cornelius Agrippa of Nettesheim.* James Freake, Trans. (St. Paul: Llewellyn Publications, 2003), li.

74. Ibid. li.

75. Ibid. 421.

76. Ibid. 44.

77. Ibid. 44-45.

78. Ibid.

79. Although studies like Allen G. Debus' *Man and Nature in the Renaissance* (Cambridge University Press, 1978) assign a significant place to Paracelsus in the rise of scientific reasoning from medieval alchemy (see pp.14-34), I have intentionally omitted a special section on the life and works of Paracelsus from this book's historical narrative because so many of the English and German authors surveyed in this chapter were sharply critical of his conclusions in both alchemy and natural philosophy. For a more detailed analysis of Paracelsus and his critics see Debus' more recent study, *The French Paracelsians: The Chemical Challenge to Medical and Scientific Tradition in Early Modern France* (Cambridge University Press, 1992). Given my aim of examining conceptions of Pentecost and the Holy Spirit in the context of early modern esoteric, scientific, and religious ideas aimed at deciphering Nature's secrets, I regard Agrippa's influence and interest in the Spirit as the more significant one of the sixteenth century alchemists.

80. For a good summary and analysis of Bacon's experimental method and general ideas about science see Peter Urbach, *Francis Bacon's Philosophy of Science: An Account and a Reappraisal* (La Salle: Open Court, 1987), 17-82; 149-192.

81. See *The Advancement of Learning*, Bk. II, in *Francis Bacon: The Major Works* (London: Oxford University Press, 2002), 222, fn. 636.

82. Bacon's drive for secrecy, and the vast multi-volume compendium of ciphers he left behind, is one of the most perplexing aspects of his personal and professional life. This becomes all the more perplexing when we recall that, for both the sake of sharing scientific results and disseminating knowledge that might benefit humanity, he sternly opposed any form of secrecy in the scientific enterprise. However, the symbolic parallels between Bacon's use of certain motifs in *The New Atlantis* (1627) and the symbolic systems of both the Rosicrucians and Freemasons I believe are not mere coincidences and

point to something worth investigating and understanding in the Baconian corpus. On the other hand, the more mysterious sides of Bacon's personality and works are most likely the root causes for many of the preposterous and sometimes bizarre speculations and legends about his true identity, one of which even claimed that he faked his death, emigrated to Germany, and then lived to the ripe old age of 133 as Johann Valentin Andreae while leading the Rosicrucian Enlightenment and teaching at the University of Württemburg until 1654.

83. Note for instance the Trinitarian stance expressed in the opening lines of Bacon's *Confession of Faith* (1641; reprinted 1648, 1657): "I believe that nothing is without beginning but God; no nature, no matter, no spirit, but one only and the same God. That God as he is eternally almighty, only wise, only good, in his nature, so he is eternally Father, Son, and Spirit, in persons," *Francis Bacon: The Major Works* (Oxford University Press, 2002), 107; fn. 560-67.

84. *The Advancement of Learning*, Bk. I, in *The Major Works*, 152.

85. For a comprehensive discussion of Bacon's plan and its relation to the wider contexts of the seventeenth century see Charles Webster, *The Great Instauration: Science, Medicine and Reform, 1626-1660* (London: Duckworth, 1975), 1-31; 100-245.

86. *The Advancement of Learning*, Bk. I, *The Major Works*, 152-53.

87. Ibid. 121-22.

88. Ibid. 131.

89. From Bacon's *A Description of the Intellectual Globe* (ca. 1612) as cited in Peter Urbach, *Francis Bacon's Philosophy of Science*, 32.

90. *The Advancement of Learning*, BK. I, 143.

91. From *The Advancement of Learning*, BK. II in *Francis Bacon: The Major Works*, 296; see also *De Augmentis Scientiarum* (ca. 1623) as cited and discussed by Urbach in *Francis Bacon's Philosophy of Science*, 102-05.

92. *The Advancement of Learning*, BK. II, 295, fn.674-75.

93. Urbach, 106.

94. For more on the possible connections between Francis Bacon and J. V. Andreae see Yates, *The Rosicrucian Enlightenment*, 118-129; and Christopher McIntosh, *The Rosicrucians: The History, Mythology, and Rituals of an Esoteric Order*. Third Rev. Ed. (York Beach: Samuel Weiser, 1997), 39-41.

95. *The Advancement of Learning*, Bk. II in *The Major Works*, 174.

96. For more on the possible connections among these secret societies and fraternities, the Puritan position on founding a "universal college" for the advancement of piety, and Bacon's influence on the founders of the Royal Society around 1661 see Charles Webster's *The Great Instauration*, 32-99.

97. *New Atlantis* in *The Major Works*, 458.

98. Ibid. 466.

99. Ibid. 462.

100. Ibid. 480.

101. As defined by Jerry Weinberger, "On the Miracles in Bacon's *New Atlantis*," in *Francis Bacon's New Atlantis: New Interdisciplinary Essays*. Bronwen Price, Ed. (Manchester: Manchester University Press, 2002), 107.

102. *New Atlantis* in *Major Works*, 464.

103. Ibid. 465.

104. Weinberger, 112.

105. Peter Harrison, "Miracles, Early Modern Science, and Rational Religion," *Church History* 75:3 (September 2006): 506-07.

106. *New Atlantis* in *Major Works*, 480.

107. For a concise discussion of seventeenth century scientific and religious discourses on agricultural improvement, medicine and the "Prolongation of Life," and "Dominion Over Nature" see Webster 246-483.

108. Although the first printed Latin copies of the *Fama Fraternitatis* appeared in Germany in 1614, some scholars surmise that manuscript copies of the manifesto might have been in private circulation as early as 1604. Copies of the *Fama* were published for decades during the 1600s in German, Dutch, French, and English translations. Thomas Vaughn (1622-1666), writing under the pseudonym Eugenius Philalethes, published the first known English translations of the Rosicrucian Manifestos in 1652 as *The Fame and Confession of the Fraternity of R: C: Commonly of the Rosie Cross. With a Preface annexed thereto, and a short Declaration of their Physicall Work* (London: Printed by John Macock for Giles Calvert, at black spread Eagle at the West end of Pauls, 1652), Original in the Folger Shakespeare Library. All subsequent quotations of this work are taken from the edition of Thomas Vaughn's translation printed in *"Fama Fraternitatis*, or a Discovery of the Fraternity of the Most Laudable Order of the Rosy Cross," *Rosicrucian Digest*. Vol. 83, No. 1 (2004): 13-20.

109. Ibid. 13.

110. From Michael Maier's "A Subtle Allegory Concerning the Secrets of Alchemy," (ca. 1614) in B. J. Gibbons, *Spirituality and the Occult: From the Renaissance to the Modern Age*, 73.

111. Ibid. 14-15.

112. Ibid. 15.

113. Ibid.

114. Ibid. 16.

115. Ibid. 18.

116. The four Latin phrases cited at this stage in the *Fama Fraternitatis*, in the order each occurs in the text, are: 1) *Nequaquqm vacuum*, meaning that "A vacuum exists nowhere;" 2) *Legis Jugum*, "The yoke of the Law;" 3) *Libertas Evangelii*, "The liberty (or freedom) of the Gospel;" and 4) *Dei Gloria intacta*, signifying "The whole (or complete) Glory of God."

117. Ibid. 17.

118. For more scientifically oriented views of the astronomical discovery of these two supernovae see the historic studies by Edmond Halley, "A Short History of the Several New-Stars That Have Appear'd within These 150-Years; With an Account of the Return of That in Collo Cygni, and of Its Continuance Observed This Year 1715," *Philosophical Transactions of the Royal Society of London (1683-1775)*. Vol. 29 (1714-16) 354-356; and J. Norman Lockyer, "On the Causes which Produce the Phenomena of New Stars," *Philosophical Transactions of the Royal Society of London, A*. Vol. 182 (1891) 397-448.

119. *The Advancement of Learning*, Bk. II; *The Major Works*, 174.

120. *The New Atlantis* in *The Major Works*, 458, 462.

121. From the version printed in *Rosicrucian Digest*. Vol. 83, No. 1 (2004): 20.

122. Ibid. 19.

123. Ibid. 17.

124. Christopher McIntosh, *The Rosicrucians: The History, Mythology, and Rituals of an Esoteric Order*. Third Rev, Ed. (New York: Samuel Weiser, 1997), 15.

125. Ibid. 17.

126. *Rosicrucian Digest*. Vol. 83, No. 1 (2004) 17-18.

127. For more on the possible role of Frederick V, Elector Palatine and his father-in-law, King James I of England, in the Rosicrucian movement of the early 1600s and the

events leading up to the Thirty Years War see Yates, *The Rosicrucian Enlightenment*, xii-xv, 1-29, 70-90.

128. McIntosh, *The Rosicrucians*, 27.

129. For an outstanding account and analysis of Maier's career, works, and key role in these pivotal years of early modern European political, intellectual, and religious history see Hereward Tilton, *The Quest for the Phoenix: Spiritual Alchemy and Rosicrucianism in the Work of Count Michael Maier, 1569-1622* (Berlin: Walter de Gruyter, 2003), 69-214.

130. See Volume I: "Andreae's Life, World-View, and Relations with Rosicrucianism and Alchemy," of the very fine study by John Warwick Montgomery, *Cross and Crucible: Johann Valentine Andreae (1586-1654), Phoenix of The Theologians* (The Hague: Martinus Nijhoff, 1973), 13-22.

131 In Yates' *Rosicrucian Enlightenment*, 50; see also 140-144; 167-168.

132 Peter Arnold, *Histoire de Rose-Croix et les Origines de la Franc-Maçonnerie* (Paris, 1935), 50.

133. For more on this controversy see J. W. Montgomery's *Cross and Crucible, Vol. I.*, 158-252 wherein the author compiles an extremely erudite description and analysis of the reasons for and against Andreae as the author of both the *Fama* and the *Confessio*. He concludes that Andreae did not write the first and second manifestos and actually became an ardent opponent of the Rosicrucians, whose mistaken views of Christian reformism the young Andreae attempted to correct and critique by writing the *Chemical Wedding* and *The Tower of Babel* just a few years later. Based upon a very thorough review of the extant primary sources for Andreae's life and career, and the history of interpretation on Andreae's Lutheranism and Hermetic interests, Montgomery's views are an indispensable aid to understanding Andreae and his context. But Montgomery's conservative zeal for defending Andreae's Christian integrity and clearing his reputation from any association with occultist and esoteric currents is a bit overdone and ignores the rich medieval tradition of accepted Christian magical theology, and Esoteric Christianity, that preceded the early modern Lutheran interest in alchemy and Hermetic natural philosophy.

134. Johan Valentin Andreae, *Christianopolis: An Ideal State of the Seventeenth Century (1619)*. Trans. Felix Emil Held. (New York: Oxford University Press, 1916), 176.

135. Ibid. 240.

136. Ibid. 143.

137. Ibid. 145.

CHAPTER 6
CLOSING REFLECTIONS:
THE ECSTASY OF COMMUNICATION

And the Spirit of the Lord shall rest upon him, the spirit of wisdom and under-standing, the spirit of counsel and might, the spirit of knowledge and the fear of the Lord.

Isaiah 11:2

Our quarrel is altogether about words.

John Wesley to Count Zinzendorf, ca. 1745

But the witness of God's Spirit in the human spirit is symbolized by *imagina-tion*, without which there could be no sense of sin, no repentance and contrition, no tenderness and sympathy, no love and no hope.

Howard Thurman, *Deep is the Hunger,* 1951[1]

Traditions are processes of creating, sustaining, and recreating viable individual and communal identities. Those who inhabit traditions follow their ideas, try their arguments, contemplate their symbols, enter their stories, occupy their structures, enact their rituals, feel their sensibilities, and so on, and in so doing they ask and answer, ever anew, who they are and what they are for in relation to their community, their world, and their vision of the nature of things. Traditions are processes of identity making and remaking.

Delwin Brown, 2003[2]

Throughout this volume we have read the ancient Pentecostal refrain, rhetorically inserted in the New Testament text of the Book of Acts: "*What does this mean?*" In this concluding chapter we will both summarize the foregoing histo-riographic narrative and attempt a reflective overview that humbly considers the age-old question of what these divergent pneumatological ideas and sensibilities might mean. Borrowing the title of a book by controversial French theorist Jean Baudrillard (1929-2007) for the concluding chapter of a book about Pentecost and the Holy Sprit will no doubt disturb pastoral readers of this historical work even as it will surely interest academic aficionados of postmodern critical theory.[3] However, this narrative ploy is not intended to set the stage for a Bau-drillardian interpretation of the pneumatological movements and Christian vi-sionaries surveyed throughout the book. Such a stance can neither effectively account for, nor accurately interpret, the range of spiritual expressions examined in the preceding chapters. Besides such a standpoint would not have appealed to an ardent critic of modern mass media, technological illusion, and economic globalization like Jean Baudrillard whom many believe inspired Laurence and Andrew Wachowski's classic film *The Matrix* (1999).

The "ecstasy of communication" signified here harkens back to the very beginning of this study when we set out to recover medieval and early modern Christian conceptions of Pentecost and the Holy Spirit, as ways of commemorating and meditatively reliving the story of Pentecost. While the social logic of medieval and early modern pneumatological ideas and sensibilities has not received much academic or historiographic attention among modernist or postmodern scholars, one cannot come away from this story without noticing that throughout the history of Christianity fostering "communication" and "intimacy" has been the most persistent and noticeable role believers ascribed to the Holy Spirit. This observation holds whether the communication and intimacy is posited as occurring among the three Persons of the Trinity, or between human persons and any one of the Divine Persons, or among Christians of like mind coming together in any of their varied forms of praxis. We have noted both esoteric and exoteric dimensions of this form of communication as exemplified among the movements, writers, and visionaries discussed throughout the preceding chapters. Although not the primary objective of these closing reflections, before concluding this chapter, we will ponder whether Jean Baudrillard's ideas about human communication and global interaction might complement our postmodern understanding of the imagination of Pentecost and the quickening of the intellect and heart under the aegis of the Holy Spirit. Thus, I offer this concluding chapter as both a historiographic and theological reflection on the bewildering range of themes and possibilities suggested in the context of recovering a few vignettes from the story of medieval and early modern conceptions of Pentecost and the Spirit.

An effective framework for assessing the broader meanings of the wide-ranging figures and movements of the Spirit examined throughout this book is to the address the mystical or supernatural nature of the subject matter contained in the texts and lives we examined from the 1100s to the 1600s. There is an experience of ecstasy or an ecstatic dimension that is activated by spiritual communication, relationality, and intimacy when individual seekers access the force field of the Third Person of the Trinity. These supernatural communications and metaphysical interactions take on a spiritual luminosity that knows no boundaries and follows no set telos, a feature which accounts for the diverse, and often subversive, ways that Pentecost shows up throughout the history of Christianity. For thousands of years images of fire, water, and wind served both the Jewish and Christian traditions as effective metaphors and alluring symbols for expressing the ineffable mystery of the Spirit of God. As demonstrated in the lives and historical documents of the men and women surveyed throughout this book, these perplexing patterns of the Divine presence were "real" to these people, regardless of whether or not our limited materialistic modern and postmodern epistemologies recognize them as "real."

Furthermore ecstatic states of consciousness, and other forms of religious experience, presuppose a certain degree of shared intimacy between the human "subject" and his/her particular object of divine veneration, which for most of the protagonists in this study was the Third Person of the Trinity. As discussed in the opening chapter, unexamined assumptions about the unverifiable and subjective quality of pneumatological ideas and religious experience among the various fields and sub-fields of historical research diminished the perceived value, or intellectual desirability, of researching and writing about so-called "spiritual" themes and content such as long forgotten conceptions of Pentecost. No doubt this state of affairs generated more than a few silent spaces and blindspots in our modern and postmodern understanding of interiority in the history of Christianity.

Nonetheless, we began our inquiry into these lost memories and blind spots by posing several fundamental questions. What about Pentecost, and the Euro-Western religious imagination, allows Pentecost to show up in a variety of literary and theological forms throughout Christian history? Why have so many Christian thinkers and visionaries revisited the story of Pentecost as an act of *theological reconstruction* aimed at revitalizing Christian traditions as well as subverting dominant ecclesiastical paradigms or oppressive political structures? What is the relationship between the miraculous communication signified in the biblical story of Pentecost and the empowering presence of the Holy Spirit in Christian teaching and learning? Our inquiry was also grounded in the conviction, based on close readings of primary sources spanning five centuries that these Pentecostal legacies functioned in two significant ways.

First, in the worldviews of both clergy and laity the story of Pentecost, as set forth in Acts 2, manifested as a *recurring literary or prophetic trope* in Christian symbolism and local canonical traditions dealing with pneumatological concerns, a text that contained great creative and liberative potential. Secondly, the story of Pentecost served as a *source of inspiration* or *repository of tradition* for ecclesiastical reformers and visionaries across the varied times and places of Christian history. In each of these instances, the meditative piety practiced by both clergy and laity, who literally lived the days and months of the year within the Christian liturgical calendar, amounted to living one's life in an extended meditation on the life of Jesus Christ with its two greatest fulfillments coming in springtime: Ascension Day and Pentecost Sunday. Finally we read the sources and interpreted the various pneumatological changes and movements from the late 1100s to the late 1600s through the critical lens of theologian Delwin Brown's *theory of tradition*, also known as *constructive historicism*, which understands theology and religious ideas as located in particular times and specific places yet engaged in "the creative reconstruction of inherited symbols" and in "the construction of a tradition's future from the resources of its past." Brown's notion of the on-going task of theological construction from the resources of any given religious tradition's past correlated almost precisely with the continuities and discontinuities I detected in the original sources examined throughout this book. Brown's theory is so simple, so aesthetically and intellectually uncomplicated, yet so very accurate in describing the innovations and revitalizations of Christianity through the centuries that one is left wondering why more church historians have not employed it as a critical and evaluative lens.

The outcome of this multi-pronged historical inquiry brought two primary features of Pentecost and the Holy Spirit into clearer focus: *ecstatic visions* and *supernatural communication.* These features should not be treated as normative to Christian faith and thought, but rather as dynamic and creative tendencies of the Christian ethos with no set telos or ideological rigidity. Indeed, a historicist reading of medieval and early modern conceptions of the Pentecost story and the work of the Holy Spirit in primary source accounts of ecstatic piety, ecclesiology, and reformist or visionary movements serves to highlight what leading theologians like Moltmann, Kärkkäinen, McDonnell, and Pannenberg have been stating about such historically situated manifestations of the Spirit across time and place. This interplay of ecstatic visionary experiences alongside the related theme of supernatural communication, as evidenced in the lives and works of the Christian thinkers and visionaries surveyed in this study, reminded me of the phrase "*the ecstasy of communication.*" However, medieval and early modern conceptions of the story of Pentecost were as much about the *ecstasy of communication* among individuals and communities as about the descent of the Holy Spirit into the hearts and minds of Christian believers. These pneumatological conceptions were also about upholding ecclesiastical tradition, and if necessary also about subverting tradition in order to breathe new life into rigid structures of power and sometimes corrupt institutional structures. These conceptions were also as much about understanding the Almighty's invisible imprint in Nature as about generating new ways of knowing and communicating across cultural boundaries and rigid worldviews in need of being shaken by mighty winds and prophetic tongues of fire.

In addition, this historiographic inquiry yielded four characteristic ways that Christian thinkers and visionaries conceived and claimed to have experienced the Holy Spirit's acts of intercession and transformation. These "Acts of the Spirit" manifested in both their personal lives and in wider realms such as that of the *ecclesia* and the *civitas*, as well as those of the *Imperium* or of the *mundus.* Despite the complexity of articulating anything uniform about the transformative powers historically ascribed to the Holy Spirit, I will discuss the following four distinctive pneumatological traits: 1) The tension between *anamnesis* (remembrance) and *amnesia* (forgetfulness) in the commemoration of Christian pneumatological traditions; 2) The relationship between Spirit and Nature throughout the history of Christian pneumatology; 3) The *subversive* function of pneumatological claims trumping preconceived ideas of authority and exclusivity; and 4) The empowerment of individual believers for prophetic leadership and various types of reformism. A discussion of each of these four qualities followed by an analysis of the dynamics of *ecstasy* and *communication* is the primary focus of this closing chapter. However, before moving on to these broader assessments, we will briefly review the research outcomes of the medieval and early modern periods, people and movements, texts and locations surveyed in this historical narrative.

SUMMARY OF RESEARCH FINDINGS

As noted at the outset, establishing the historical reality of the Pentecostal legacies and pneumatological sensibilities exhibited within and among various medieval texts and literary traditions, was imperative to demonstrate their longevity
across time and place and to examine the social-logic by which these conceptions served various communal and religious functions. We acknowledged that
most of the primary sources available for this study were coded texts open to
multiple meanings for both the author and the intended audience, a feature that
also rendered the interpretation problematic for contemporary historians. Micro
studies of an era in church history, or of a major historical figure, are fine for
incrementally advancing medieval and early modern studies. But in the history
of Christianity, as well as in European intellectual history, sometimes wider
thematic studies are more effective at showing the trans-local processes and
broader trajectories of intellectual and cultural history. The period from the
twelfth to the seventeenth century seemed especially fruitful given the rich yet
highly perplexing references to Pentecost and the Holy Spirit nearly everywhere
one looked discerningly, or whenever one read carefully through the primary
pneumatological sources. A multi-volume study of medieval and early modern
conceptions of Pentecost and the Holy Spirit is perhaps an objective worth pursuing someday.

However, in order to effectively demonstrate the liberative and volatile characteristics fostered by pneumatological ideas and sensibilities, and which I refer
to as *subversive fire*, a series of vignettes compiled into one volume was the best
forum for bringing these nearly forgotten Pentecostal tendencies and trajectories
to the attention of academic colleagues and interested ministerial readers for
further study, debate, and reflection. Now at the conclusion of this project of
historical recovery and exposition, these vignettes on the selected writers, dissenters, visionaries and reformers from each of these periods who were tinged
with the flames of the Spirit during Pentecost, proved to be an effective and manageable strategy for encapsulating five centuries of historical materials.

In Chapter Two we examined the syncretism of pre-Christian, pagan fertility traditions alongside the image of the Holy Spirit and Pentecost detected
among the numerous medieval celebrations and ritual practices usually celebrated during the so-called "merrie month of May." We concluded that the numerous references to Pentecost throughout the stories of King Arthur and the quest
for the Holy Grail highlight a convergence of pre-Christian religious traditions
concerning the months of May and June with medieval Christian traditions of
pneumatology and the Feast of Pentecost during the same two months of the
liturgical year. This examination shed light on medieval conceptions of Pentecost as related to *Natura* (Nature), and on the ways in which Christian clergy
and laity in Western European societies associated the annual springtime rebirth
of flora and fauna more with Pentecost than with Easter due to the "greening"
that accompanies May and June's warmer temperatures. When compared with
our contemporary experience of climate patterns in the Northern Hemisphere
during the annual Easter to Pentecost cycle, the contrast with the Middle Ages

seems so stark that the effects of the alleged "Little Ice Age" on European temperature patterns in March and April of each year from 1100 to 1700 warrants being both mentioned here and subjected to further investigation.

For medieval Europeans there were essentially two major traditions that almost always overlapped in the "merrie month of May." One was the Christian feast of Pentecost or Whitsuntide. The other one honored the great Mother Goddesses of Nature and her ancient fertility rites rooted in Celtic and Germanic traditions much older than Christianity itself. Vestiges of the Divine Feminine's power to connect humanity and Nature survived well into Christian times and thrived in the medieval countryside and rural areas where the influence of Christian pedagogy and clerical pressure for conversion was less severe than in the growing urban areas of the Middle Ages. These naturalistic beliefs represent the indigenous peoples and cultures of pre-Christian Europe, some of whom like the Celts, and their Druid priests and priestesses, predated the arrival of Greek colonists and the expansion of the Latin tribes into Western Europe. Vestiges of this rich heritage of spiritual practices and naturalistic beliefs survived well into the early modern period in a variety of ways, such as the knightly class' horse riding tradition of "going-a-maying" on the eve of May's first full moon; in the reverence for Hawthorne trees and sacred groves in May and June; in the widespread Maypole celebrations across Britain and continental Europe that extended into the late 1600s; in the Pentecostal imagery of chivalric romances like Wolfram's *Parzival* (ca. 1200) and Malory's *L'Morte d'Arthur* (1485); and in the depiction of shamanic characters like Merlin or Morgan Le Fay in the Arthurian and Grail sagas.

On the other hand, we cannot ignore that, according to most chroniclers and bards, King Arthur pulled Excalibur from the stone during the season of Pentecost. In other accounts of the legend, it was the ancient Mother Goddess of flora and fauna personified as the Lady of the Lake who confers Excalibur, the "Sword of Power," upon the reluctant boy who would be King of Britain. After forging peace out of the chaos of feudal warfare, King Arthur founded the Round Table fraternity on Pentecost. Some of King Arthur's valiant quest knights, who were the focus of fantastic legends about their own exploits passed down in song or story through the centuries, almost always experienced their visions of the Holy Grail during Holy Week or Pentecost. Herein lays the irony of the calendar systems echoed in these examples of literary syncretism and cultural diffusion: calendars are instruments of cultural domination and religious conversion as well as systems of earthly and celestial time keeping. In this instance, the overlapping of pagan fertility festivals with major Christian feast days onto the liturgical calendar represents the forgotten remnants of the immense tribal migrations of the sixth, seventh, and eighth centuries. These migrations were accompanied by Christian conversions of Celtic and Germanic tribal chieftains during the same Early Medieval period, which by the late 1100s began generating the much more Christianized literary corpus of Arthurian sagas attributed to Chretien de Troyes, Wolfram von Eschenbach, Marie de France, and a host of others.

Precisely when Celtic and Germanic pagan religion began undergoing a creative and subversive adaptation of Christianity was hardly the point of the analysis and discussion presented in the second chapter. Reflecting back on that chapter's historiographic objectives, I am reminded of Delwin Brown's discussion of how African religion was adapted in the African American slave experience which enabled the emergence of African American Christianity from the roots of a far older tradition carried in the hearts and minds of an oppressed people who refused to forget who they were and where they had come from. "The point is that in each step of this quite extraordinary series of transformations . . . something new was integrated into an inherited mythos in such a way as to reconstruct that inheritance, thus providing the ground for the next alteration. It only remains to add that this process was not exclusively, or even primarily, a matter of continuously reconstructing beliefs. Central to these successive reconstructions of inheritance was a constantly developing material conjuration, a complex of felt relationships and a system of practices involving magic, medicine, and witchcraft integrated for the community through ritual."[4] Such competing conceptions of temporality and of humanity's place in the cosmos, also represented a cultural fault line between the Roman Church of Western Europe and the much older, pre-Christian time-reckoning practices of Europe's indigenous tribes and peoples whose experience of time was more attuned with lunar and agricultural cycles than with the *imitatio Christi* of the liturgical calendar. All of which, serves to highlight not only the adaptations of pagan beliefs and lore, which were adapted into the Arthurian and Grail traditions, but also the second major medieval celebration cycle that coincided with the fertility traditions of the "merrie month of May," and which were adapted over the centuries alongside Christendom's Feast of Pentecost.

The experience of time documented among saint's lives and rules for monastic orders throughout the Early and High Middle Ages was synonymous with the Christian liturgical calendar that began each year with Advent in late November or early December, and then culminated each spring with the outpouring of the Holy Spirit on Pentecost Sunday in May or early June at the latest. One's participation in liturgical ritual and worship, and the rhythmic cadences of daily contemplative prayer and periodic fasting, amidst the alternating passage of ordinary time and festal jubilation had a profound effect on individual and collective spirituality. In this second chapter we also took a cursory look at Hildegard of Bingen's dynamic conception of Nature and the Holy Spirit's sanctifying and comforting presence in the natural world, which could be read as a pneumatological aesthetics of Nature nurturing humanity through Divine Grace. Among devout clergy and educated laity, living the monthly cycles of the sun and moon through the Christian liturgical calendar was like living in an extended, existential meditation on the *imitatio Christi*. Thus, providing a window into the pneumatological sensibilities of medieval Christian men and women for whom the fifty-day Pentecost cycle of their liturgical calendar witnessed Nature's revitalization, generated by the "greening" that accompanied the onset of spring, an annual process that also revitalized one's inner longings in deep prayer and personal piety. These acts of commemoration and regeneration were carried out in remembrance of that first outpouring of their Savior's fiery breath on Pentecost so many centuries before their own time yet ever open and overflowing with hope and joy, and possibility.

In Chapter Three we then looked at the pneumatological imagery and sensibilities in the monastic career and prophecies of Abbot Joachim of Fiore (d. 1202), whose ecstatic visions and supernatural insights on Pentecost Sunday of either 1188 or 1189 generated one of the most influential and highly contested prophecies for the future history of Christianity. As was customary among Christian visionaries before and after him, Abbot Joachim divided the history of Salvation into three distinct but interdependent phases. For Joachim, however, the third and final stage of history would commence around 1260 or 1265, and would usher a universal transformation of church and society through the agency of the Holy Spirit. The institutional, hierarchical Church would be rendered obsolete by God's outpouring of divine love and energy in the Age of the Holy Spirit. We also examined Joachim's following among the Franciscan Spirituals, some of whom believed they were the world-transforming "Spiritual Order" prophesied by the Calabrian Abbot. Indeed, the Fraticelli believed they were protecting the sacred order founded by St. Francis of Assisi from corruption and betrayal at the hands of an ecclesiastical leadership who had become too worldly and greedy.

We also examined the little known story of Guglielma of Milan and her followers who believed she was the incarnation of the Holy Spirit and would soon usher in the prophesied apocalyptic *renovatio* of the male dominated Roman Church. Her followers believed the new Church of the Holy Spirit would feature female cardinals and bishops led by a woman Pope who would authorize the composition of a "Third Gospel" beyond the New Testament scriptures. Eventually the Dominican inquisitors operating out of Milan and its surrounding towns and villages arrested the ring leaders and tried them for heresy. The Inquisition then exhumed and burned Guglielma's body, destroyed her relics, and disbanded her remaining followers in terror after burning the leading Guglielmites at the stake. Reviewing this tragic incident suggests that there was an emerging medieval feminist pneumatological movement in northern Italy during the late thirteenth century which by the beginning of the fourteenth century seems to have either disappeared through persecution or to have been forced either underground or deeper into the countryside. Medieval ecclesiastical and social perceptions about the Holy Spirit's role in gender relations and in the empowerment of medieval religious women who claimed to have received either ecstatic visions or supernatural communication is an area in need of further investigation.

And finally, in this third chapter, we reviewed the tragic incident of rebellion led by the Roman Tribune Cola di Rienzo across Italy against the perceived excesses of the Papacy and the Holy Roman Empire, a seizure of power that erupted on Pentecost Sunday May 1347 and culminated in war and death among his followers and his opponents just before the outbreak of the Black Death in Italy. The visions and hopes espoused among these figures' lives and written works, and in their struggles with contentious opponents, suggest that in their collective and individual cries for ecclesiastical justice and political integrity the theme of a *plena Spiritus libertas*, mentioned by Joachim of Fiore and others besides him, was more than just the passing fancy of few misguided Christian heretics. This chapter's tragic vignettes of ecstatic Pentecost visions turned uncharacteristically violent reveals the danger of misinterpreting pneumatological visions, supernatural communication, and the creative potentialities inherent in the story of Pentecost. Despite persecution and violence, perhaps something of the Triune God's propensity towards human empowerment, fullness, and liberation is revealed through the communicative and ecstatic manifestations of the Third Person of the Trinity. We will return to the pneumatological implication of these three themes later in this concluding discussion.

Ironically, some of the subversive visionaries and ecclesiastical nonconformists surveyed in this third chapter were contemporaries of the two most important and prolific mainline theologians of the Western Latin Church in the High Middle Ages, the Dominican Thomas Aquinas (1225-1274) and the Franciscan Bonaventure (1221-1274), each of whom in their day were steadfast critics of the rising tide of Joachimist sympathizers and destabilizing movements of the Spirit. Contrary to modern and postmodern rationalist misconceptions of the mystical qualities of the Thomistic corpus, Aquinas was also acutely inspired by the Holy Spirit and sought to harmonize the theological naturalism he learned from his mentor, Albertus Magnus (ca. 1206-1280), with the philosophical naturalism of Aristotle, and then grafting this naturalistic view of things and human flourishing onto Christianity's Platonic and Augustinian views of the human person. A synthesis of reason and faith, of the heart and the mind, that contemporary Christians of all denominations would do well to revisit regardless of any medieval prejudices in the Thomistic corpus that might offend our postmodern thinking and sensibilities. Similar positive appraisals of Bonaventure's theological anthropology remind us that the "high voltage" ecstatic visions and supernatural communication reported from the realm of the Divine sometimes generate pneumatological radicalism leading to outbreaks of death and destruction while claiming a providential mandate "to purify by fire." No Christian community of the medieval or early modern eras could long tolerate the euphoria or destabilization of such "wild-fire" movements before turning its own believers over to secular and military authorities as in the case of Cola di Rienzo's Pentecost 1347 eruption of revolutionary zeal, apocalyptic propaganda, and regional warfare.

Chapter Four examined how both Protestant and Roman Catholic leaders sought to impose structures of authority and control against a rising propensity towards the fullness of human potentiality and spiritual liberation as movements of the Spirit proliferated during the Reformation and Early Modern periods. We discussed the role of pneumatological ideas among the Protestant and Roman Catholic Reformation movements of the 1500s and early 1600s by looking into the Pentecost visions of two of the major figures of the Radical Reformation: Thomas Müntzer and Michael Servetus. We looked at Martin Luther's and John Calvin's little understood relation to the Holy Spirit, and how their political assumptions about religious authority, and deep suspicions about "enthusiast" factions within the ranks of the Protestant Reformation, led to their respective quarrels with Müntzer and Servetus. We then saw similar manifestations of these pneumatological tendencies and suspicions arise among Radical Reformers as the same old patterns and ecclesiastical tendencies towards power, exclusion, and persecution resurfaced among the Lutheran and Calvinist wings of the Reformation.

Although in the Reformation, we again encountered the problems of sectarian nomenclature, competing Christian ideologies of leadership and authority, and mistrust of "enthusiast" factions claiming normative or authoritative spiritual experiences, the role of meditative practices associated with the feast of Pentecost and the image of the Holy Spirit's empowering gifts was no less subversive of teleological assumptions or rigid structures of authority and canonical interpretation than in the chapters covering the earlier medieval periods. In numerous ways, both the Protestant and Roman Catholic Reformations best exemplify Brown's theory of religious traditions fostering the reconstruction of inherited symbols and theological resources from the past as well as my own arguments that the story of Pentecost functioned as both a repository of Christian ecclesiastical and spiritual traditions and as a recurrent liberative trope among reform minded Christian visionaries and writers.

In the case of the Catholic Reformation, Spain's domination of the Papacy after 1492, its brutal conquest of Italy in 1527 that lasted for three centuries, and its steadfast persecution of anyone hinting at Illuminism (Alumbrados) or smelling of Lutheranism, considerably muted the pneumatological imagery and spiritual rhetoric of Roman Catholic reformers. For example, at some point in each of their careers, figures like Teresa of Ávila, John of the Cross, and Ignatius of Loyola, walked a fine line between liberty and imprisonment for fear of their ministerial ideas or reformist activities. This does not mean that their personal lives and religious works were any less touched by the Spirit's fiery inspiration, but it does mean that shrewdly diplomatic clergy like themselves needed to be very careful about their rhetoric of personal experience and spiritual illumination even if they each claimed to have a special relationship with the Third Person of the Trinity. A nation as obsessed with autocratic rule, and as anxious about religious heterodoxy, as Spain was from 1470 till the end of the Spanish Inquisition in 1834, was also fairly predisposed against pneumatological subversions of power and the liberative voice of the Spirit within its borders and throughout its vast colonial empire. But just as water, wind, or fire cannot be easily contained so too the Spirit defies any set telos or rigid boundaries within which Scholastic theologians or ecclesiastical authorities believed the Spirit must act (*potentia absoluta*). In time Ignatius of Loyola's Pentecost vision about the life and piety of Jesus, received while laying in a hospital bed after being wounded in a military battle, blossomed into reality as the Jesuits became the quintessential defenders of social justice, spiritual liberty, and Roman Catholic learning across the Spanish Empire until their temporary Papal expulsion from many of the Spanish and French colonies in the 1700s.

Finally in Chapter Five we surveyed the pneumatological aspects of several Christian Esoteric currents that inspired the theological anthropology of the Florentine Renaissance and the Scientific Revolution's aims of achieving mastery

over Nature and promoting the healing arts for the alleviation of human suffering. During the translation projects of the Twelfth Century Renaissance, practical and philosophical alchemy along with naturalistic magical practices and
Neoplatonism dating back to Hellenistic and Arabian Alexandria re-entered Europe. This trajectory, along with the possible accretion of Eastern Orthodox
pneumatological and mystical influences that reentered European intellectual
life after the fall of Byzantium in 1453, helped inspire the now nearly forgotten
tradition of Christian magical theology (*theologia magica Christiana*), which
was the crucial link between ancient and medieval views of Nature and the human person and the early modern paradigms of Humanism and scientific
progress. Among the adherents and practitioners of this *theologia magica Christiana* we find such notable figures as the Dominican St. Albertus Magnus (d.
1280), the Franciscan Roger Bacon (1214-1294), the Italian Humanists Marsilio
Ficino (d. 1499) and Pico Della Mirandola (d. 1494), and the Jesuit Athanasius
Kircher (1601-1680) as well as lesser known esoteric writers like the Germans:
Abbot Trithemius of Sponheim (d. 1516), Heinrich Cornelius Agrippa (d. 1535),
and Paracelsus (d. 1541). These esoteric and theological writers and their proto-
scientific concerns, along with a host of others whose lives and works are
beyond the scope of this book, represent a forgotten and neglected chapter in the
history of pneumatology for it was their conviction in the abiding presence of
the Holy Spirit in Nature (*Natura*), along with a mighty host of lesser spirits in
need of proper Christian discernment, that stimulated a sizable portion of Western Europe's early modern efforts at scientific rationalism. Late Renaissance
proto-scientific works, like Agrippa's *De Occulta philosohia* (ca. 1531/1533) or
Bacon's *New Atlantis* (1627), conjured up a profound curiosity among contemporary readers about Nature's unknown properties, such as the chemical
processes in plants and stones and the human body, or the electromagnetic properties in lightning, as well as the energies contained in the very air people
breathed or in the waters they drank. Not for nothing did the first few generations of spiritually curious scientific pioneers, like Jan Baptiste van Helmont call
themselves, "philosophers of fire" (*philosophus per ignem*).[5] Such an appellation suggests that, among scientific seekers like van Helmont, it represented a
vocational and religious attitude highlighted by their desire to understand this
mysterious presence or force field, and then someday harness the power of the
Holy Spirit, which they often identified as the *ethereal fire* or as the *Quintessential Fire* permeating Nature and the heavens above. This may seem like pure
hubris to Christian believers today, but in the Early Modern era this was the outgrowth of centuries of Scholastic and Humanistic claims about the human intellect's ability to gain knowledge of the great treasures God had concealed in the
material world, and how these riches, if released like an Arabian spirit from a
bottle of medicinal elixir, might alleviate human suffering through medicine or
improve human industry through science and technological innovation.

Indeed, for English scientific pioneers like Francis Bacon (1561-1626) and
Robert Boyle (1627-1691), it was their critique of alchemy's haphazard claims
and magical superstitions, and neither atheistic materialism nor rationalist disdain for Christian beliefs, that motivated each man's life long quest to under-

stand the mystery of the Holy Spirit's presence in Nature and in the unique powers God had concealed in the natural world. Bacon's utopian novella, *The New
Atlantis*, called for a Second Pentecost based upon the tongues of fire as the *Vehicula scientiae* (carriers of knowledge) of the new scientific and experimental
paradigm. Boyle's *Skeptical Chymist* (1661) sharply criticized the fanciful
claims of alchemy even as he defended Christianity against the rising tide of
rationalist materialism while pursuing the mystery of Spirit in Nature by investigating what he and others called *"those ponderable fire particles."* The culmination of these lines of scientific development is often seen as the founding of the
Royal Society of London for the Improvement of Natural Knowledge in 1660,
the same year as the English Restoration of the monarchy under Charles II.
Boyle and all those who played a key role in the Royal Society's founding from
the remnants of their earlier group, the Invisible College, acknowledged their
indebtedness to Francis Bacon's works and career. In the aftermath of the Puritan Revolution's enthusiast excesses and political violence, English scientists
and fellows of the Royal Society developed a deep mistrust of researchers who
mingled scientific questions with spiritual inspiration. As a result a deep chasm
opened up between the empirical study of Nature and the Cosmos and the much
older Christian spiritual traditions that sought to study and understand Nature
and heaven's *"ethereal fire."*

   Back on the European continent, however, the situation for the advocates of
preserving pneumatological consciousness aligned with scientific learning was
not much better. The appearance of the Rosicrucian manifestoes in Germany
from 1614 to 1616, and later in France from 1619 to 1625 caused a huge com-
motion among the educated laity and clergy, which in time was accompanied by
fantastic conspiracy theories and tales of political revolution led by the fraternity's undercover Illuminati. Calling itself, the House of the Holy Spirit, the mysterious Brotherhood of the Rosy Cross announced its designs to the world and
promised a new era of scientific achievement and harmony among the nations of
the world. Some of the order's members intentionally tied their esoteric movement all the way back to the prophecies of Joachim of Fiore (d. 1202) and then
projected their achievements forward to an apocalyptic era of unprecedented
learning and human liberty based upon scientific principles and the gifts of the
Holy Spirit that was to have begun sometime between 1604 and 1622. The
movement was linked with Lutheran orthodoxy, the humanistic ideals of Ficino
and Pico, and Hermetic-alchemical principles borrowed from Abbot Trithemius,
Agrippa, and Paracelsus. Some anti-Catholic biases aimed at the Jesuits and the
Hapsburg dynasty, which at the time ruled Spain and the Holy Roman Empire,
also characterized the movement's rhetoric. Although Rosicrucianism went
through various transformations in the late 1600s and early 1700s, some of
which led directly to the formation of English, Scottish, and French Freemasonry, the noble ideals and lofty promises of the brethren's manifestoes were dealt
a serious and disillusioning blow by the disastrous events and deadly outcomes
of the Thirty Years' War from 1618 to 1648, which further convinced European
Christians of the dangerous excesses of pneumatological enthusiasts.

In summary, negative attitudes towards religious heterodoxy propagated by the Hapsburg dynasty's exacerbation of Protestant versus Catholic factional turmoil across continental Europe was a major obstacle to the advancement of learning and science advocated by the Rosicrucians. While England opted against direct involvement in the Thirty Years' War the situation on the other side of the English Channel was not much better. Deeply entrenched suspicion of pneumatological movements and "enthusiast" writers, aroused throughout Great Britain by the excesses of the Puritan Revolution, became juxtaposed against the Restoration monarchy's predilection for rationalist modes of thinking. The combination of these factors produced a Western European intellectual life that became increasingly estranged from the pneumatological sensibilities and Pentecostal traditions illustrated in previous centuries. No doubt this had much to do with the demise of the medieval worldview and the early modern devaluation of its corresponding cosmological sense of time and eternity. This growing sense of amnesia about pneumatological tradition across European Christendom also had much to do with a desire among the emerging Protestant denominations and nation-states of the 1600s to move away from the old feast days of the Christian liturgical calendar, which was increasingly regarded as an outdated and superstitious Roman Catholic calendar. The social desire and political need to construct new "national" holidays commemorating the historical events and literary heroes of the modern nation-state rapidly accelerated across Europe in the late 1600s and 1700s, and then spread throughout Europe's former and current colonies during the 1800s. After all, in England the Puritans outlawed all Maypole celebrations and fertility dances around sacred Hawthorne groves in May and June with the aim of permanently quenching all such lingering pagan savageries. As far eastward as the German Rhineland Maypoles were also toppled during the Protestant Reformation and then further demolished during the disruptions of the Thirty Years' War. As is well known to any Latin American or Hispanic American person fairly aware of his/her cultural and religious heritage, despite the violence and oppression of Spain's colonial administration system, Roman Catholicism proved far more effective and skillful at allowing (or ignoring) the syncretism of indigenous and Christian symbol systems and traditions at the local level than was permitted by European Protestant nation-states throughout their colonial possessions in the Americas, Africa, and Asia.

BETWEEN TRADITION AND PNEUMATOLOGICAL FULLNESS

We now come to the discussion of several distinctive features, culturally and temporally situated, that emerged from this examination of the Holy Spirit and Pentecost in conjunction with the figures and spiritual movements ranging from the 1100s through the 1600s chronicled in this book. Among these features we find an *anamnesis* of the Holy Spirit through liturgical and ritual observances of Pentecost mingled with notions about the Spirit as a "force field" in Nature and the Cosmos. This comingling led to the emergence of a "syncretistic pneumatology" as Christianity encountered other tribal, ethnic, and cultural systems wherein spirit entities and various naturalistic energies were regarded as sacred. This leads to considerations of the symbolic and moral role of the Holy Spirit as a "subversive fire" in the on-going work of personal and societal liberation both within the ecclesia of all Christian believers and in the wider society. Each of these features about the story of Pentecost and the Holy Spirit requires careful consideration, and yet each of these trajectories emerge from the Holy Spirit's perceived and signified propensity towards promoting and generating ontological and existential fullness as Third Person of the Trinity (given the role of *potentia absoluta* versus *potentia ordinata* in medieval and early modern understandings of God's Will). The four distinctive and interconnected pneumatological traits are: 1) The tension between *anamnesis* (remembrance) and *amnesia* (forgetfulness) in the commemoration of Christian pneumatological traditions; 2) The relationship between Spirit and Nature throughout the history of Christian pneumatology; 3) The *subversive* function of pneumatological claims trumping preconceived ideas of authority and exclusivity; and 4) The empowerment of individual believers for prophetic leadership and various types of reformism.

First by unearthing so many long forgotten ways of imagining and commemorating the story of Pentecost and the presence of the Holy Spirit among widely differing, temporally distant Western European local and trans-local Christian traditions, figures, and movements, we are in the domain of ecclesiastical "memory." Here *memoria* implies not only our historiographic recovery of these stories, symbols, and beliefs, but also implies the remembrance and revitalization of these traditions by the medieval and early modern protagonists whose lives and works, hopes and visions we have examined and made known in the present. The closely related ancient Greek word, "*anamnesis*," is usually translated as "recollection" or "remembrance," but also signifies "the ability to recall past events or occurrences." One might easily assume that both "recollection" (in its meditative or contemplative dimension) and "remembrance" (in its temporal and historical dimensions) is what Jesus, and the Gospel writers, had in mind when the phrase, "Do this in remembrance of me," was recorded in the New Testament. In other words, "Do this in *anamnesis* of me," or both "in remembrance" and "in recollection" of Him whose Holy Spirit was later given forth freely and abundantly on the day of Pentecost.

I have no doubt that the seven-times-seven-weeks of Whitsuntide leading to the liturgical calendar's Feast of Pentecost functioned among medieval and early modern Christians as a two-fold anamnesis whereby the historical event of the first Pentecost was liturgically remembered and wherein the individual Christian believer simultaneously went forth into deeper recollection and communion with God and self, with Nature and self, and with empathy and love for all one's brothers and sisters in society. Saint Francis of Assisi's famous compassion and love for humans, animals and birds, and plants can be read and understood through this pneumatological lens just as Holy Communion or Easter Sunday services were an anamnesis of God's redemptive act in time and space through the sacrifice of Jesus. Hence all Pentecost celebrations and practices functioned as an *anamnesis* of the Church's founding moment and of the miraculous outpouring of spiritual power upon those who wished to serve Christ's Church in the world. These two-fold tendencies of meditative recollection and remembrance are evident in the pneumatological ideas and feelings noted in the historical record from Hildegard of Bingen to the Radical Reformation, from Joachim of Fiore's Pentecostal visions to the ideals of the Rosicrucian Renaissance, from the pre-Christian naturalism of the Arthurian and Grail sagas to the theological naturalism of Thomas Aquinas, and from the ecclesiastical reformism of the Franciscan Spirituals to the evangelical and pedagogical reformism of the Jesuits. Even Francis Bacon's utopian vision of a Second Pentecost through the gifts of scientific knowledge was firmly anchored in the scriptural and epistemological resources of the past. Hence, the potency (*potentia*) of acts of remembrance and recollection resides in their power to trigger creative reconstructions of the tradition's inherited symbols and beliefs, a feature of religious traditions well articulated in theologian Delwin Brown's historicist framework.

However, in the centuries since the Enlightenment's revolt against ecclesiastical tyranny and religious superstition, and since the rise of logical positivism among the humanities and social sciences in the late 1800s, an abiding *theological amnesia* emerged. This loss of cultural and religious memory concerning Christianity's Pentecostal and pneumatological legacy gradually developed among the laity across almost all Christian denominations, as well as among those of us who research and teach about the history of Christianity. This loss of memory set in as well among the ranks of Christian clergy across all denominations, although for some with strong enthusiast or charismatic factions this was less so than for others. This is not to say that Pentecostal visions and pneumatological concerns vanished from the hearts and minds of Euro-Western Christians after the Enlightenment. Concern for the Spirit is a theme that abounds in the treatises and theological discourses of the eighteenth, nineteenth, and twentieth centuries. But new attitudes towards religion and spirituality among Euro-Western, and later American, intellectuals after 1750, accompanied by modernity's increasing secularization and industrialization from the mid-1800s through the late 1900s, effectively closed the cosmological skylights, calendar cycles, and liturgical practices within which the Pentecostal and pneumatological trajectories discussed throughout this book had their origins and imaginative vitality.

The cumulative effect of these socio-political clashes and cultural shifts was a steady decline in naturalistic and symbolic expressions of the Holy Spirit noted in numerous medieval sources, as well as a steady decline in the liturgical and canonical traditions associated with the seven-times-seven days of Pentecost. This "pneumatological deficit," identified by Kärkkäinen and other contemporary writers on pneumatology,[6] has been a feature of mainline Protestant and Roman Catholic religious practices for most of the nineteenth and twentieth centuries. No amount of Romantic idealism about Nature and Spirit, or nostalgia for the medieval past as in the proliferation of European Holy Grail societies and North American Masonic fraternities, was able to revive the realities of these traditions. By the mid-1800s and early 1900s most Euro-Western Christians no longer lived in the space-time reality or meditative spirituality of the medieval liturgical calendar. One is reminded here of Emile Durkheim's musings about

his society's loss of religious beliefs and traditions: "The old gods are dead and new one's not yet born."

Nonetheless, such nostalgic wistfulness is slightly misleading for even amidst the paradigm shifts and cultural changes noted beyond the outer edges of the centuries examined in this book, we find remarkably resilient examples of pneumatological movements and Pentecostal expression. For example, throughout the late 1600s and 1700s German Pietism served as one of the most important spiritual developments in the intellectual history of Christianity. From its roots in the earlier Moravian movement, Pietism witnessed and fostered the *subversive fire* of Christian pneumatological liberation noted among the medieval and early modern sources in this study, and in time had both direct and indirect effects on modern thinkers like John and Charles Wesley, Schleiermacher, and Hegel. Influenced by the piety and convictions of Moravians like Peter Böehler (1712-1775) and William Holland (d. 1761), Charles Wesley's (1707-1788) conversion experience took place on Pentecost Sunday May 21, 1738; an initiation into "heart holiness" that he immediately shared with his brother, John, who reported having an equally significant experience several days later. The fact that the Moravian Church of the Wesley's day was intentionally connected to the tragic demise of the Moravians in Bohemia, who in 1619 supported the Elector Frederick of the Palatinate against the Spanish Hapsburgs and the Holy Roman Empire and were violently defeated at the Battle of the White Mountain that started The Thirty Years' War, is not that surprising when we recall the close ties that existed among seventeenth and eighteenth century pneumatological movements. Indeed as far back as the 1400s the Moravians were originally known by appellations like "The Brethren of the Law of Christ" or as the *Unitas Fratrum*, phrases that sound eerily similar to the themes and ideals of the Fraternity of the Rosy Cross.

Similarly influenced by Pietism's Moravian currents in Great Britain through Böehler, and then in the American colonies while conducting missionary work in Georgia, John Wesley (1703-1791) began a dialogue with the Moravian minister August Gottlieb Spangenberg (1704-1792) that changed his life. On one occasion Spangenberg asked the restless and spiritually troubled John: "Does the Spirit of God witness with your spirit that you are a child of God?" The young Wesley was baffled and fumbled for an adequate answer in the face of the Moravian Brethren's deep piety and peace of mind. John's famous "Aldersgate Street experience" happened on Wednesday May 24, 1738, three days after Pentecost Sunday. The thirty-four year old John Wesley reluctantly attended an evening worship service in London where his heart was moved deeply while listening to the minister's reading of Luther's preface to Romans and explanation of God's redemptive transformation of the human heart through Christ and the Holy Spirit. The person reading that night at Aldersgate is believed to have been the English Moravian pastor, William Holland who had also influenced John's brother, Charles. Hence from this seminal encounter, and the brief theological interactions that followed, sprang the movement known today as Methodism, which under the influence of John Wesley's very close friend and chosen successor John Fletcher (1729-1785) developed a dynamic theology of

Pentecost and the indwelling of the Holy Spirit in the hearts of Christ's followers. John Wesley's aim of being "methodical" in his approach to personal holiness and Christian learning probably led him and his fledgling movement to tap
into the meditative practices and liturgical reminiscences of Pentecost and the
Holy Spirit. This is precisely how I contend that deep prayer and liturgical praxis also inspired and empowered so many of the figures and movements discussed elsewhere in this book. All of which further illustrates how acts of remembrance or liturgical commemoration still kept the pneumatological embers
of Pentecost going just before the emergence of the Enlightenment.

Secondly, the emergence of a "syncretistic pneumatology" in the early
Middle Ages as Christianity encountered other tribal, ethnic, or cultural systems
wherein spirit entities and various naturalistic energies were regarded as sacred
had the effect of supplementing and transforming the Christian pneumatological
paradigm. The eerie syncretistic parallels among pre-Christian conceptions of
the Divine Feminine's presence in Nature, Christian conceptions of Pentecost,
and the symbolic realm of Arthurian and Holy Grail literature lead us to consider the historic relationship posited between the Holy Spirit and Nature. Despite
the disastrous effects of conquest and conversion on the Celtic and Germanic
peoples of Europe, as Brown's notion of "traditioned ingenuity" informs us,
when "threatened from without" the Celts and others, "reached back into their
own inheritance, drew out this particular symbol, elevated it, and made it the
center of their reorganized system of meaning."[7] Hence, when German scholars
rediscovered Wolfram von Eschenbach's thirteenth century chivalric classic in
the late 1780s, they figured the reason so many copies of the work lay forgotten,
in dusty and moldy old German monastery libraries, was due to its perceived
medieval, and hence Roman Catholic, provenance during the contentious paradigm shifts of the Protestant Reformation after the 1520s. However, an epic
poem such as *Parzival*, in which all of the major narrative events and spiritual
transformations occur over seven Pentecosts, calls out for an understanding of
its bewildering time sequences aligned with Nature's cycles of fertility, death,
and rebirth while probing deeper than the surface fancies of chivalric lore and
courtly romance might lead us to believe about this legend's social logic and
thematic structure. While missing the exact meanings of the Pentecostal imagery
in the construction of which Wolfram invested so much energy and creativity,
most nineteenth and twentieth century interpreters of *Parzival* focused on the
narrative's implied heroic individualism or on the main character's spiritual
transformation divorced from the liturgical and cosmological implications of the
Pentecost cycle.

By contrast, in the post-September 11th milieu of war and intolerance,
twenty-first century readers of *Parzival* find fresh insights about reconcilia-tion
and kinship among the Children of Abraham, insights originally intended by
Wolfram for a thirteenth century audience then quite familiar with the Crusades
and the persecution of religious minorities in a story set within the transformative piety of the liturgical calendar's Pentecostal period of the year. In an odd
way, the character of Parzival too was a seeker of lost memory and experienced
a powerful anamnesis of the Spirit at Pentecost. We can only wonder at how

these themes and remembrances were experienced by Wolfram's audiences and readers since in the history of Christianity, the "Gift of Tongues" at Pentecost also raises questions of inter-religious dialogue and religious toleration. It was not medieval chivalric exuberance, nor the heroic individualism of the 1800s, but something as simple as deep piety and personal humility that finally allows the naïve and itinerant young knight, Parzival, to ask the healing question of the Wounded Fisher-King on Pentecost week. This act of compassion allows Parzival to finally take his place as King of the Grail-Family at their mysterious castle perched atop the Mount of Salvation; a family whose heraldic crest featured a turtle-dove, the ancient Jewish and medieval Christian symbol for the Holy Spirit. This is an image of the Holy Spirit and of the Pentecost story capable of combining Celtic and Germanic elements alongside Christian, Jewish, and Islamic elements in ways that reveal the dynamic and imaginative possibilities of Pentecost and the Spirit.

Looked at from this angle, Wolfram's Grail-Castle appears as yet another "House of the Holy Spirit" imagined four hundred years before the *Domus Sancti Spiritus* of the Rosicrucian manifestos of the early 1600s. The actuality of this cultural and theological amnesia is further attested by the fact that under the influence of modern German nationalism scores of Wolfram scholars and Grail-legend connoisseurs from the 1780s to the mid-1900s sought to sterilize the *Parzival* saga of its disturbing Semitic elements. We eventually learn of the story's origins from the pen of a learned Moor in Toledo who obtained it from a pious Jew descended from King Solomon. One can only imagine the reaction of German and Austrian audiences, who came of age in a nationalistic society that detested racial mixing, when Parzival and his Moorish half-brother gaze into each other's eyes near the story's dramatic climax on Pentecost Sunday and realize that, while the Muslim's mother was "black" and the Christian's mother was "white," they were both born of the same father who died prematurely for his love of knight-errantry and crusading.

If the Holy Spirit as the "Divine Kiss," or *vinculum pacis*, among the three Persons of the Trinity may indeed be likened to the energy of attraction and intimacy then Wolfhart Pannenberg's notion of the Holy Spirit as a "force field" helps us better understand the naturalistic pneumatology and attitude about the Holy Spirit's presence in Nature that we find in medieval and early modern currents of thought. Among these currents we have the pneumatological naturalism of Hildegard of Bingen, or the naturalism of an Albertus Magnus or Francis of Assisi, or the views of Nature expressed in Christian alchemy, Hermetic lore, and Christian magical theology, and finally among the pioneers of the Scientific Revolution. No matter how naïve or destructive their enterprise proved in the log run, who wanted to read and decipher the Book of Nature for the alleviation of human suffering and expanding the bounds of human industry. We are reminded too that Christian theological discourse focused for too long on the human to the exclusion of animals and birds, plants, the oceans, and the earth. The medieval and early modern vignettes we looked at, and read, remind us that there was a pre-modern social logic convinced that Nature and the earth possessed "consciousness" and that, human beings as contemplative and embodied terrestrial creatures were partakers of both a material as well as a spiritual inheritance.

Third, just as in formulating a theory of tradition Delwin Brown asked: "What explains the creativity or transformation that continuously characterizes traditions?" Or, "How do we account for . . . the persistent power of the past in the formation of the present?"[8] The *subversive* function of pneumatological claims trumping preconceived notions of authority and exclusivity is a historic trajectory in the history of Christianity that cannot be separated too neatly from the domain of religious interiority and mystical experience. Contemplation happens through bodily actions aimed at stilling the mind and allowing the soul's voice to emerge from the materiality of one's physical frame and from the noisiness of one's daily routines. From a Scholastic perspective, just as the Incarnation of the Son functioned as a restoration (*restauratio*) of the human to the Father, and vice verse, one of the most vital functions of the Holy Ghost was perceived as infusing particularity (Nature) with divinity as the breath of God through the Son.

The second and third features cited above about pneumatological ideas and sensibilities opened the theological imaginations of both Christian believers and pagan shamans to the possibilities of both socio-cultural accommodation and spiritual resistance to the ever-increasing tide of early medieval conversions and regional conquests sanctioned by the Latin Church. It is precisely in this much more contested domain of resistance that the Spirit's propensity towards the fullness of all things, which, neither espouses nor possesses any set telos other than this drive towards empowerment, that we come to an understanding of the story of Pentecost as both a traditioned and liberative trope in the long history of medieval and early modern Christianity. Just as in the realm of Nature "need" calls forth "action" through natural events and processes, so too in the realm of the human person "need" calls forth "action" as resistance to social injustice and oppression as well as against stagnation and the lack of imaginative play with the resources of the Christian tradition.

Fourth, the feature of pneumatological subversion, as has already been suggested by the foregoing examples and conversation, is inextricably tied to the pneumatological empowerment of individual believers for prophetic leadership and various types of reformism. This is true regardless of whether or not the cultural or socio-political effects of pneumatological ideas and sensibilities emerging at any time from the prophetic and liberative power of the Pentecost story results in either positive or negative outcomes, or whether movements of the Spirit either succeed or fail to accomplish their transformational objectives. For example, as a reform movement within the Friars Minor, the Franciscan Spirituals did not win the battle for control of their beloved monastic order, and Cola di Rienzo's Pentecost revolution did not liberate Rome or Italy from the control of the Holy Roman Empire. I am not suggesting theologies that either makes no mention of enthusiast or ecstatic experiences, or theologies that offer extreme caution of the high voltage effects of such experiences, are necessarily always wrong. I am, however, claiming that overlooking the role of pneumatological ideas and sensibilities in effectively transforming persons in this world who wish to transform or revitalize church and society posits an incomplete history of Christianity regardless of the negative or unsuccessful outcomes of radical Christian reform and revitalization movements. Perhaps it is the particularity of the social justice concerns of a given person or community that triggers the need for a divine infusion of pneumatological vitality and power. Perhaps this is how the Holy Spirit manifests in the lives and careers of reform minded visionaries and writers concerned with social change and human transformation. And, since "hierarchy" implies "holy order," reflecting on the birth of the Christian church each year during the seven-times-seven-days of Pentecost was particularly disturbing if the ecclesiastical state of affairs in one's respective homeland or historical moment was perceived as dysfunctional, corrupt, and oppressive; in which case the story of Pentecost then offered an imaginative and liberative reminder of human potential and spiritual power for subverting the ecclesiastical, socio-political, or educational "disorder" of the times. One never knows how historic events or religious movements will unfold over time, but the really significant issue here is the high degree of self-confidence and vocational empowerment, generated by both pneumatological experience and remembrances of the Pentecost story, which historically motivated Christian men and women to carry out perceived ecclesiastical reforms and at times much wider social, political, or pedagogical agendas of revitalization for the benefit of the community's members.

BETWEEN ECSTASY AND COMMUNICATION

I will revisit Jean Baudrillard's critique of humanity's modern and postmodern predicament at the end of this concluding chapter. However, what is understood in this concluding discussion by the "*ecstasy of communication*" denotes two characteristics of the Holy Spirit's role in the Trinity and in theological discourse, insights that emerge from the foregoing survey of Christian conceptions of Pentecost and pneumatological experiences spanning the period from the 1100s to the 1600s. These two characteristics are the Spirit's theologically ascribed role of fostering intimacy and relationality through "ecstasy," and the Spirit's scriptural role of facilitating "communication" as the Paraclete or Divine Intercessor between the human and the Divine realms.

First as a manifestation of God's abiding love and ineffable presence in the order of things, religious or spiritual "ecstasy," derives from the ancient Greek term "*ek-stasis*," and literally means, "standing outside." This implies a moving or going outwards towards the other two Persons of the Holy Trinity. In metaphysical terms, this reminds us of early Christian and medieval conceptions of the Holy Spirit as the "divine kiss" that binds the other two Persons of the Triune God, Father and Son, to each other in perpetual love and intimacy. In human epistemological and ethical terms, this implies an embracing of the terrestrial and embodied "Other" just as Christ commanded his followers to love one another unconditionally as God loves them. It also implies an embracing of both the heart and the intellect through the intimacy of deep prayer and personal piety that is sometimes accompanied by pneumatological revelations. Theologian

Edith Humphrey refers to this "ecstasy" as an "abandonment of self as one goes out to the other;" an "ecstatic movement which, it seems, enables the mysterious *intimacy* shared between the Divine Persons. Or, perhaps is it the other way around," as Humphrey asks, "does their shared intimacy allow for their ecstatic freedom? Intimacy and ecstasy, at any rate, are mutual states, each nourishing or attending the other."[9] Intimacy generates empathy and harmony between people while ecstatic experience stimulates all of our senses and quickens the imagination. Speaking as the bright morning star in the closing verses of Revelation Jesus states: "The Spirit and the Bride say, 'Come.' And let him who hears say, 'Come.' And let him who is thirsty come, let him who desires take the water of life without price" (22:16-17). The "quickening" of one's theological imagination is one of the modes of knowing and relating which allows Pentecost to show up in such creative and divergent ways across the varied landscapes and periods of the history of Christianity. And, this dimension of imaginative play, from within the resources of this particular religious tradition, engages and activates the affective aspects of one's faith as the process of theological construction and *re-construction* motivates and provokes *renovatio, reforma,* and seemingly endless permutations of pneumatological ideas and sensibilities.

Hence the *ethereal fire* that touched and filled the hearts of Hildegard of Bingen, Thomas Aquinas and Bonaventure, and Julian of Norwich during Pentecost also inspired ecstatic visions of freedom and human possibility in Joachim of Fiore and the Franciscan Spirituals, and in rebellious spirits like Cola di Rienzo, Thomas Müntzer, and Michael Servetus. We see the same exuberance of purpose manifested in the *Quintessential Fire* sought by Humanists, alchemists, magicians, and scientific pioneers like Ficino and Pico in Italy, Agrippa and Trithemius in Germany, or Francis Bacon and Robert Boyle in England. In the high-voltage moment of the human encounter with the Divine, "ecstasy" and "intimacy" collide in ways that sometimes unhinge the conscious mind, at which point the seeker, contemplative, or reformer is seriously in need of those angelic reassurances echoed throughout the Hebrew and Christian scriptures: "Be still; do not be afraid." Little wonder then that after the so-called "Chemical Revolutions" of Robert Boyle and Antoine Lavoisier (1743-1794), and after the rise of Newtonian "laws" in physics, the Fraternity of the Rosy Cross eventually turned its interest in the Holy Spirit to the study of electromagnetic vibrations as the underlying mystery of that elusive yet quintessentially ever-present *ethereal fire,* which was known to pre-modern seekers as the Holy Ghost.

Secondly, as a manifestation of humanity's bond with God through the *Imago Dei* (Genesis 1:26-27) and the Incarnation of Christ, "communication" here implies the "communion" of individual human persons with each other as well as with the other two Persons of the Trinity. Indeed a "common-union," and a "mutual participation" as attested by the Latin root of the word "communication," whereby scriptural interpretation, empowerment and liberation, and theological imagination are all activated by an influx of that mysterious *ethereal fire* symbolized in the "tongues of fire" that descended upon the heads of those gathered at the first Pentecost. In this way receiving the gifts and fruits of the Spirit is an act of God's divine mercy, a mutual participation in the alleviation of human suffering and in the fulfillment of human potential. Looked at from this perspective, learning and teaching in the Christian community then assume more than just a socio-cultural or political role, but become ways of fostering holiness and piety in the wider world so that all members of the Christian community, male and female; rich and poor; clergy and laity alike may be empowered to become partakers of the Divine Nature through the on-going presence of the Holy Spirit in the ecclesial community.

Hence "communication," whether esoteric or exoteric, is not just the responsibility of God's Will or Divine Grace, or the result of Christ sending forth the Holy Spirit on Pentecost, but becomes a veritable virtue of the human intellect and heart so that each of these modalities, in its own way of knowing and relating, also wonders at the infinity of the cosmos and begins reading the Book of Nature; a text wherein we eventually learn that men and women can create order out of disorder just as the Spirit of God moved over the face of the waters on the first day of Creation (See Genesis 1:1-2). We are reminded here of the Church Fathers' fascination with pagan deities like the Egyptian Thoth, or the Greek god Hermes and the Roman god Mercury, who, as initiators of the gift of literary interpretation and as messengers of the pagan pantheon of heaven, signified for Early Christians the universality of the human predisposition towards pneumatological consciousness and sensibility. The Spirit's role in the "arts of communication" also reminds us of the numerous references to the "Divine Names of God" that abound among Jewish, Islamic, and Christian mysticism, and of the medieval notion of learning one's "abc's without the use of black magic" as cryptically cited in Wolfram von Eschenbach's *Parzival*.[10] It is also reminiscent of the so-called "grammars of the spiritual life" found among late medieval and early modern catechetical texts composed by visionaries and reformers from across European Christendom like the *Ejercitatorio de la vida Espiritual* published in 1500 by García Jiménez de Cisneros, who was Abbot of the Monastery of Montserrat in Catalonia and a cousin of Cardinal Cisneros of Toledo,[11] or like Francisco de Osuna's contemplative and controversial manual published in 1527, *Tercer abecedario espiritual*.[12]

The "ecstasy of communication" also echoes in the paradoxical words and concepts of Jean Baudrillard who passionately critiqued the explosion of modern mass media portals and platforms, and who had no interest in pneumatological movements or church history: "What if the modern universe of communication, of hyper-communication, had plunged us, not into the senseless, but into a tremendous saturation of meaning entirely consumed by its success, without the game, the secret, or distance? If information no longer had anything to do with an event, but were concerned with promoting information itself as the event? If history were only an accumulative, instantaneous memory with a past?"[13] One response to this conundrum is to re-enter, or theologically re-construct, the realm of interiority as evidenced in the outpouring of enthusiasm observed among both global and regional manifestations of Pentecostalism since the early 1900s, or as evidenced by the proliferation of New Age movements since the 1970s. But, as the history Christian conceptions of Pentecost demonstrates, the

273 Subversive Fire: The Untold Story of Pentecost

turn to interiority often brings other visionary perils and spiritual excesses in its wake.

In 1966 Thomas Pynchon published the postmodern classic, *The Crying of Lot 49*, a novel whose title is a direct allusion to the seven-times-seven-days of Pentecost. No matter how many times one reads this novel from cover to cover, it always ends up being about circuitous communications and the mystery of human narrativity.[14] *What does this mean?* Indeed, anyone who tries to uncover the structure of Pynchon's mysterious work will be confounded time and time again as the narrative questions itself on almost every page amidst all sorts of twists and turns through a seemingly endless series of wordplay, wacky symbols, and enigmatic signs. Some literary critics have dismissed the novel as meaningless and incapable of interpretation, a state of scholarly opinion that, over four decades after its publication, still persists among literary critics and scholars. *What does this mean?* All of which sets up Pynchon's novel as another example of the bewildering ways that Pentecost shows up across the pages of Western literary, cultural, and religious history.

Ironically, the Christian historical tradition records that the Roman Emperor Constantine the Great died at noon on the Feast of Pentecost. Since Constantine's life and political career has been vilified as well as praised for the ecclesiastical trajectories his religious and political reforms set in motion, it is only fitting to conclude with this reminder about the paradoxical and multivalent nature of all Pentecostal manifestations, sensibilities, and ideas. The question passed down over the centuries by the author of the Book of Acts: *What does this mean?* Might be more aptly rephrased as: *What is reality?* In the realm of pneumatology and Pentecost, *meaning* and *reality* are sometimes blurred as divergent forms of spiritual *ecstasy* and miraculous *communication* are poured forth from the divine force field as well as acted upon by believers commemorating, experiencing and channeling, and reimagining the *subversive fire* of the untold story of Pentecost. The medieval and early modern Christians whose lives and works we examined throughout the pages of this book were also figuring out the question of reality while experiencing the "ecstasy of communication" with the Trinitarian Persons through the intercession of the Holy Spirit.

NOTES

1. Howard Thurman, *Deep is The Hunger: Meditations for Apostles of Sensitiveness* (New York: Harper & Row, 1951; Reprinted Richmond, IN: Friends United Press, 1978), 166.

2. Delwin Brown, "Limitation and Ingenuity: Radical Historicism and the Nature of Tradition," *American Journal of Theology and Philosophy* Vol. 24, No. 3 (September 2003): 201.

3. See Jean Baudrillard, *The Ecstasy of Communication.* Semiotexte(e) Foreign Agents Series. Bernard and Caroline Schutze, Trans. (Brooklyn: Autonomedia, 1988), 11-28.

4. Delwin Brown, "Limitation and Ingenuity: Radical Historicism and the Nature of Tradition," 197.

5. As cited in J. R. Partington, *A Short History of Chemistry*. Third Ed. (New York: Macmillan, 1957), 46.

6. Kärkkäinen, *Pneumatology*, 17.

7. Brown, "Limitation and Ingenuity: Radical Historicism and the Nature of Tradition," 199.

8. Ibid. 201.

9. Edith M. Humphrey, *Ecstasy and Intimacy: When the Holy Spirit Meets the Human Spirit*. (Grand Rapids: Eerdmans, 2006), 4-5.

10. Mustard and Passage, 244; Lachmann, 232, Buch IX, 453.17.

11. Alistair Hamilton, *Heresy and Mysticism in Sixteenth Century Spain: The Alumbrados* (Toronto: University of Toronto Press, 1992), 12; 14.

12. See Mary E. Giles and Kieran Kavanaugh, Eds. *Francisco de Osuna: Third Spiritual Alphabet*. Classics of Western Spirituality. (Mahwah: Paulist Press, 1981).

13. Baudrillard, *The Ecstasy of Communication*, 103-104.

14. Thomas Pynchon, *The Crying of Lot 49* (New York: J. B. Lippincott Company, 1966).

SELECTED BIBLIOGRAPHY

Achinstein, Sharon. *Literature and Dissent in Milton's England.* Cambridge: Cambridge University Press, 2003.

Adam, Adolf. *The Liturgical Year: Its History and Its Meaning After the Reform of the Liturgy.* Trans. M. J. O'Connell. Freiburg: Verlag Herder, 1979. Reprinted New York: Pueblo Publishing, 1981.

Andreae, Johan Valentin. *Christianopolis 1619.* Originaltext und Übertragung nach, D. S. Georgi, 1741. Trans. Richard van Dulmen. Stuttgart: Calwer Verlag, 1972.

———. *Christianopolis: An Ideal State of the Seventeenth Century (1619).* Trans. Felix Emil Held. Germanic Literature and Culture Monograph Series, Julius Goebel, ed. New York: Oxford University Press, 1916.

Armstrong, Dorsey. *Gender and the Chivalric Community in Malory's 'Morte d'Arthur.* Gainesville: University Press of Florida, 2003.

Bacon, Francis. *The Major Works.* Oxford World's Classics. New York: Oxford University Press, 2002.

———. *The New Atlantis,* (1627). Dodo Press Edition, 2006.

Bailey, Michael D. *Magic and Superstition in Europe: A Concise History from Antiquity to the Present.* Lanham: Rowan & Littlefield, 2007.

Bainton, Roland H. *Hunted Heretic: The Life and Death of Michael Servetus, 1511-1553.* Boston: Beacon Press, 1960.

Barber, Richard. *The Holy Grail: Imagination and Belief* Cambridge: Harvard University Press, 2004.

Barbour, Reid. *Literature and Religious Culture in Seventeenth-Century England.* Cambridge University Press, 2002.

Baudrillard, Jean. *The Ecstasy of Communication.* Semiotexte(e) Foreign Agents Series. Bernard and Caroline Schutze, Trans. Brooklyn: Autonomedia, 1988.

Beeler, Stanley W. *The Invisible College: A Study of Three Original Rosicrucian Texts.* New York: AMS Press, 1991.

Benedetti, Marina. *"Io non somo Dio": Guglielma di Milano e i Figli dello Spiritu Santo.* Milan: Edizioni Biblioteca Francescana, 1998.

Bensaude-Vincent, Bernadette and Isabelle Stengers. *A History of Chemistry.* Deborah van Dam, Trans. Cambridge: Harvard University Press, 1996.

Billington, Sandra and Miranda Green, Eds. *The Concept of the Goddess.* London: Routledge, 1996.

Blair, Peter Hunter. *An Introduction to Anglo-Saxon England.* Third Ed. Cambridge University Press, 2003.

Bradstock, Andrew. *Faith in the Revolution: The Political Theologies of Müntzer and Winstanley.* London: Society for Promoting Christian Knowledge, 1997.

Brann, Noel L. *Trithemius and Magical Theology: A Chapter in the Controversy over Occult Studies in Early Modern Europe.* Albany: SUNY Press, 1999.

Brooke, Rosalind B. *Early Franciscan Government: Elias to Bonaventure.* London: Cambridge University Press, 1959.

Brown, Delwin. *Boundaries of Our Habitations: Tradition and Theological Construction.* Albany: SUNY Press, 1994.

———. "Limitation and Ingenuity: Radical Historicism and the Nature of Tradition," *American Journal of Theology and Philosophy* Vol. 24, No. 3 (Sept. 2003): 195-213.

Brown, Peter. "The Rise and Function of the Holy Man in Late Antiquity," *Journal of Roman Studies* 61 (1971): 80-101.

————. *The Cult of the Saints: Its Rise and Function in Latin Christianity.* Chicago: University of Chicago Press, 1981.

————. "The Rise and Function of the Holy Man in Late Antiquity," reprinted in *Society and The Holy in Late Antiquity* Berkeley: University of California Press, 1982.

————. *Authority and The Sacred: Aspects of the Christianisation of the Roman World.* New York: Cambridge University Press, 1996.

Bryant, Nigel. *The High Book of the Grail: A Translation of the Thirteenth-Century Romance of Perlesvaus.* Totowa: Independent Press, 1978.

Buckland, Patricia B. *Advent to Pentecost: A History of the Christian Year.* Wilton: Morehouse-Barlow Press, 1979.

Burgess, Stanley. *The Holy Spirit: Ancient Christian Traditions.* Peabody: Hendrickson Publishers, 1984.

————. *The Holy Spirit: Eastern Christian Traditions.* Hendrickson, 1989.

————. *The Holy Spirit: Medieval Roman Catholic and Reformation Traditions.* Hendrickson, 1997.

Burr, David. *Olivi and Franciscan Poverty: The Origins of the 'Usus Pauper' Controversy.* Philadelphia: University of Pennsylvania Press, 1989.

————. *The Spiritual Franciscans: From Protest to Persecution in the Century After Saint Francis.* University Park: Pennsylvania State University Press, 2001.

Castleden, Rodney. *King Arthur: The Truth Behind the Legend.* London: Routledge, 2000.

Cavaletti, Sofia. "The Jewish Roots of Christian Liturgy," (7-40) in *The Jewish Roots of Christian Liturgy.* Eugene J. Fisher, Ed. New York: Paulist Press, 1990.

Celtic Spirituality. Edited and Trans. by Oliver Davies with the collaboration of Thomas O'Loughlin. Mahwah: Paulist Press, 1999.

Chew, Sing C. *World Ecological Degradation: Accumulation, Urbanization, and Deforestation, 3000 B.C. – A.D. 2000.* Lanham: Altamira Press, 2001.

Chretien de Troyes. *Chretien de Troyes: Arthurian Romances.* W. W. Comfort, Trans. London: Everyman's Library, 1914.

Churton, Tobias. *The Magus of Freemasonry: The Mysterious Life of Elias Ashmole; Scientist, Alchemist, and Founder of the Royal Society.* Rochester: Inner Traditions Press, 2006.

Clark, Elizabeth. *History, Theory, Text: Historians and the Linguistic Turn.* Cambridge: Harvard University Press, 2004.

Cobb, Cathy and Harold Goldwhite. *Creations of Fire: Chemistry's Lively History from Alchemy to the Atomic Age.* New York: Plenum Press, 1995.

Cohen, Jeremy. *"Be Fertile and Increase, Fill the Earth and Master It": The Ancient and Medieval Career of a Biblical Text.* Ithaca: Cornell University Press, 1989.

Cohn, Norman. *The Pursuit of the Millennium: Revolutionary Millenarians and Mystical Anarchists of the Middle Ages.* Revised and Enlarged Ed. New York: Oxford University Press, 1970.

Collins, Amanda. *Greater Than Emperor: Cola di Rienzo (ca.1313-54) and the World of Fourteenth-Century Rome.* Ann Arbor: University of Michigan Press, 2002.

Congar, Yves. *I believe In the Holy Spirit.* New York: Crossroad-Herder, 1997.

Copenhaver, Brian P. *Hermetica:* The Greek *Corpus Hermeticum* and the Latin *Asclepius* in a new English Translation, with Notes and Introduction. New York: Cambridge University Press, 1992.

Cunliffe, Barry. *The Celtic World.* New York: McGraw-Hill, 1979.

Daniel, Randolph E. *Abbot Joachim of Fiore: Liber de Concordia Noui ac Veteris Testamenti.* Transactions of the American Philosophical Society: Volume 73, Part 8, 1983. Philadelphia: American Philosophical Society, 1983.

Davaney, Sheila. *Pragmatic Historicism: A Theology for the Twenty-First Century.* Albany: SUNY Press, 2000.

Debus, Allen G. *Man and Nature in the Renaissance.* Cambridge University Press, 1987.

Donnelly, Dorothy F. *Patterns of Order and Utopia.* New York: St. Martin's Press, 1998.

Douie, Decima L. *The Nature and the Effect of the Heresy of the Fraticelli.* Manchester: University Press, 1932.

Dreyer, Elizabeth A. and Mark S. Burrows, Eds. *Minding the Spirit: The Study of Christian Spirituality.* Baltimore: Johns Hopkins University Press, 2005.

Dreyer, Elizabeth A. *Holy Power, Holy Presence: Rediscovering Medieval Metaphors for the Holy Spirit.* Mahwah: Paulist Press, 2007.

———. "An Advent of the Spirit: Medieval Mystics and Saints" (pp. 123-162). In *Advents of the Spirit: An Introduction to the Current Study of Pneumatology.* Edited by Bradford E. Hinze and D. Lyle Dabney. Milwaukee: Marquette University Press, 2001.

Dubay, Thomas. *Fire Within: St. Teresa of Avila, St. John of the Cross, and the Gospel on Prayer.* San Francisco: Ignatius Press, 1989.

Durant, Will. *The Story of Philosophy.* New York: Simon & Schuster, 1961.

Ellis, Peter Beresford. *Celtic Myths and Legends.* New York: Carroll & Graff Publishers, 2002.

———. *The Celtic Empire: The First Millennium of Celtic History, 1000 BC – AD 51.* New York: Carroll & Graff, 2001.

———. *A Brief History of the Druids.* London: Constable & Robinson, 2001.

———. "The Fabrication of Celtic Astrology," *Astrological Journal* (Vol. 39, N. 4, 1997).

Esser, Kajetan. *The Origins of the Franciscan Order.* Aedan Daly and Irina Lynch, Trans. Chicago: Franciscan Herald Press, 1970.

Eurich, Nell. *Science in Utopia: A Mighty Design.* Harvard University Press, 1967.

Faivre, Antoine. *The Eternal Hermes: From Greek God to Alchemical Magus.* Joscelyn Godwin, Trans. Grand Rapids: Phanes Press, 1995.

———, *Access to Western Esotericism.* Albany: SUNY Press, 1994.

Feingold, Mordechai, Ed. *Jesuit Science and the Republic of Letters.* Cambridge: Massachusetts Institute of Technology Press, 2003.

Filotas, Bernadette. *Pagan Survivals, Superstitions, and Popular Cultures in Early Medieval Pastoral Literature.* Studies and Texts 151. Toronto: Pontifical Institute of Medieval Studies, 2005.

Findlen, Paula. *Athanasius Kircher: The Last Man Who Knew Everything.* New York: Routledge, 2004.

Fisch, Harold. "Teach Us to Count Our Days: A Note on Sefirat Haomer," (205-17). In *From Ancient Israel to Modern Judaism: Intellect in Quest of Understanding, Vol. I.* Edited by Jacob Neusner, E.S. Frerichs, and Nahum M. Sarna, Atlanta: Scholar's Press, 1989.

Fletcher, Angus. *Allegory: The Theory of Symbolic Mode.* Ithaca: Cornell University Press, 1964.

Fourquet, Jean. *Wolfram d'Eschenbach et le 'Conte del Graal:' Les divergences de la tradition du 'Conte del Graal' el leur importance pour l'explicacion du texte du 'Parzival.'* Paris: Sorbonne, 1966.

Francis of Assisi: Early Documents. 3 Volumes. Edited and Trans. by Regis J. Armstrong, *et. al.* New York and London: New City Press, 2000.

Frappier, Jean. *Chretien de Troyes: The Man and His Work.* Raymond J. Cormier, Trans. Athens: Ohio University Press, 1982.

Friesen, Abraham. *Thomas Muentzer, a Destroyer of the Godless: The Making of a Sixteenth-Century Religious Revolutionary.* Berkeley and Los Angeles: University of California Press, 1990.

Gibbons, B.J. *Spirituality and the Occult: From the Renaissance to the Modern Age.* New York: Routledge, 2001.

Gobry, Ivan. *Saint Francis of Assisi: A Biography.* Michael J. Miller, Trans. San Francisco: Ignatius Press, 2006.

Godwin, Joscelyn. *Athanasius Kircher's Theatre of the World: The Life and Work of the Last Man to Search for Universal Knowledge.* New York: Inner Traditions, 2009.

———. *Athanasius Kircher: A Renaissance Man and the Quest for Lost Knowledge.* London: Thames and Hudson, 1979.

Goergen, D. *Fire of Love: Encountering the Holy Spirit.* Mahwah: Paulist Press, 2006.

Goering, Joseph. *The Virgin and The Grail: Origins of a Legend.* New Haven: Yale University Press, 2005.

Goertz, Hans-Jürgen. *Thomas Müntzer: Apocalyptic Mystic and Revolutionary.* Edited by Peter Matheson. Jocelyn Jaquiery, Trans. Edinburgh: T. T. Clark, 1993.

Goffart, Walter. *Barbarian Tides: The Migration Age and the Later Roman Empire.* Philadelphia: University of Pennsylvania Press, 2006.

Goldstone, Lawrence and Nancy. *Out of the Flames:* The Remarkable Story of a Fearless Scholar, a Fatal Heresy, and One of the Rarest Books in the World. New York: Broadway Books, 2002.

Gómez-Ruiz, Raúl. *Mozarabs, Hispanics, and the Cross.* New York: Orbis, 2007.

González, Justo. *Acts: The Gospel of the Spirit.* New York: Orbis, 2001.

———. *The Story of Christianity, Volume I: The Early Church to the Dawn of the Reformation.* New York: Harper-Collins, 1984.

Goodman, Philip, Ed. *The Shavuot Anthology.* Philadelphia: Jewish Publication Society, 1974.

Green, Miranda, Ed. *Celtic Goddesses: Warriors, Virgins, and Mothers.* New York: George Braziller, 1996.

———. Ed. *The Celtic World* London: Routledge, 1995.

Gritsch, Eric W. *Reformer Without a Church: The Life and Thought of Thomas Müntzer, 1488-1525.* Philadelphia: Fortress Press, 1967.

Groos, Arthur. *Romancing the Grail: Genre, Science, and Quest in Wolfram's 'Parzival.'* Ithaca: Cornell University Press, 1995.

Hamilton, Alastair. *Heresy and Mysticism in Sixteenth Century Spain: The Alumbrados.* Toronto and Buffalo: University of Toronto Press, 1992.

Hasty, Will, Ed. *A Companion to Wolfram's Parzival.* Columbia: Camden House, 1999.

Haskins, Charles Homer. *The Renaissance of the Twelfth Century.* New York: Meridian Books, 1957.

Hendrix, Scott H. *Recultivating the Vineyard: The Reformation Agendas of Christianization.* Westminster John Knox, 2004.

Henisch, Bridget Ann. *The Medieval Calendar Year.* Pennsylvania State University Press, 1999.

Hernández, Albert. *Islam and the Holy Grail: 'Convivencia,' Allegorical Transformation, and Ecumenical Visions in Wolfram von Eschenbach's 'Parzival.'* UMI Dissertation Services, 2001.

Herren, Michael W. and Shirley Ann Brown. *Christ in Celtic Christianity.* New York: Boydell Press, 2002.

Herrera, R. A. *Silent Music: The Life, Work, and Thought of St. John of the Cross.* Grand Rapids: Eerdmans, 2004.

Hildegard, Saint. *The Letters of Hildegard of Bingen, Volume III.* Joseph L. Baird and Radd K. Ehrman, Trans. New York: Oxford University Press, 2004.

Hillar, Marian and Claire S. Allen. *Michael Servetus: Intellectual Giant, Humanist, and Martyr.* Lanham: University Press of America, 2002.

Hillar, Marian. *The Case of Michael Servetus (1511-1533): The Turning Point in the Struggle for Freedom of Conscience.* Texts and Studies in Religion, Volume 74. Lewiston: Edwin Mellen Press, 1997.

Hinze, Bradford E. and D. Lyle Dabney, Eds. *Advents of the Spirit: An Introduction to the Current Study of Pneumatology.* Milwaukee: Marquette University Press, 2001.

Hodges, Kenneth. *Forging Chivalric Communities in Malory's Le Morte Darthur.* New York: Palgrave MacMillan, 2005.

Hoffman, Bengt R. *Theology of the Heart: The Role of Mysticism in the Theology of Martin Luther.* Minneapolis: Kirk House Publishers, 1998.

Honig, Edwin. *Dark Conceit: The Making of Allegory.* Cambridge: Walker-De Berry Press, 1960.

Höpfl, Harro. *Jesuit Political Thought: The Society of Jesus and the State, c.1540-1630.* Ideas in Context, 70. Cambridge: Cambridge University Press, 2004.

Howels, Edward. *John of the Cross and Teresa of Avila: Mystical Knowing and Selfhood.* New York: Crossroad Publishing, 2002.

Hughes, H. Stuart. *Consciousness and Society: The Reorientation of European Social Thought 1890-1930.* Rev. Ed. New York: Vintage, 1977.

Hughes, J. Donald. *The Mediterranean: An Environmental History.* Nature and Human Societies Series. Santa Barbara: ABC-CLIO, 2005.

Humphrey, Edith M. *Ecstasy and Intimacy: When the Holy Spirit Meets the Human Spirit.* Grand Rapids: Eerdmans Publishing, 2006.

Hunter, Michael. *Robert Boyle (1627-1691): Scrupulosity and Science.* Woodbridge: Boydell Press, 2000.

―――. Ed. *Robert Boyle Reconsidered.* New York: Cambridge University Press, 1994.

Ignatius of Loyola. *Ignatius of Loyola: The Spiritual Exercises and Selected Works.* Edited by George E. Ganss, S. J. Mahwah: Paulist Press, 1991.

―――. *The Spiritual Exercises of St. Ignatius.* Anthony Mottola, Trans. New York: Doubleday/Image Books, 1989.

John of the Cross, *The Collected Works of St. John of the Cross.* Trans. by Kieran Kavanaugh and Otilio Rodriguez. Washington: ICS Publications, 1991.

―――. *The Poems of St. John of the Cross.* Third Ed. John F. Nims, Trans. Chicago: University of Chicago Press, 1979.

―――. *The Dark Night of the Soul and The Living Flame of Love.* Fount Classics Paperbacks. London: Harper Collins, 1995.

Kahane, Henry and Renée. *The Krater and The Grail: Hermetic Sources of the 'Parzival.'* Urbana: University of Illinois Press, 1965; reprinted 1984.

Kärkkäinen, Veli-Matti. *Pneumatology: The Holy Spirit in Ecumenical, International, and Contextual Perspective.* Grand Rapids: Baker Academic, 2002.

―――. *An Introduction to Ecclesiology: Ecumenical, Historical, and Global Perspectives.* Downers Grove: Inter Varsity Press, 2002.

Katz, Henry. *Wolfram von Eschenbach's 'Parzival:' An Attempt at a Total Evaluation.* Bern: Francke Verlag, 1973.

Kelly, Samantha. *The New Solomon: Robert of Naples (1309-1343) and Fourteenth-Century Kingship.* The Medieval Mediterranean: Peoples, Economies, and Cultures, 400-1500, Volume 48. Leiden: Brill, 2003.

Klaniczay, Gábor. *The Uses of Supernatural Power: The Transformation of Popular Religion in Medieval and Early Modern Europe*. S. Singerman, Trans. K. Margolis, Ed. Cambridge: Polity Press, 1990.

———. *Holy Rulers and Blessed Princesses: Dynastic Cults in Medieval Central Europe*. Eva Pálmai, Trans. Cambridge: Cambridge University Press, 2002.

Koetsier, Teun and Luc Bergmans, Eds. *Mathematics and the Divine: A Historical Study*. Amsterdam, The Netherlands: Elsevier, 2005.

Lachmann, Karl, Ed. *Wolfram von Eschenbach: Parzival, Studienausgabe, Mittelhochdeutscher Text nach der sechsten Ausgabe von K. Lachmann, Einfuhrung zum Text von Bernd Schirok*. Berlin: Walter de Gruyter, 1833.

———. *Wolfram von Eschenbach 'Parzival.'* Sixth Edition. Berlin: Walter de Gruyter, 1999.

Lacy, Norris, Ed. *A History of Arthurian Scholarship*. Cambridge: D. S. Brewer, 2006.

Lacy, Norris J. and Joan T. Grimbert, Eds. *A Companion to Chrétien de Troyes*. Cambridge: D. S. Brewer, 2005.

Laeuchli, Samuel. *Power and Sexuality: The Emergence of Canon Law at the Synod of Elvira*. Philadelphia: Temple University Press, 1972.

Leviton, Richard. *The Imagination of Pentecost: Rudolf Steiner and Contemporary Spirituality*. Hudson: Anthroposophic Press, 1994.

Leeman, Saul. "Shavuot – 'z'man matan torateinu,'" *Jewish Bible Quarterly* Vol. 25, No. 3 (1997): 173-76.

Loomis, Roger Sherman. *The Grail: From Celtic Myth to Christian Symbol*. New York: Columbia University Press, 1963.

———. *Studies in Medieval Literature: A Memorial Collection of Essays*. New York: Burt Franklin, 1970.

Maier, Paul. *First Christians: Pentecost and the Spread of Christianity*. San Francisco: Harper Collins, 1976.

Makiya, Kanan. *The Rock: A Tale of Seventh-Century Jerusalem*. New York: Vintage Books, 2002.

Malory, Sir Thomas. *Le Morte D'Arthur, Volume I*. Janet Cowen, Ed. New York: Penguin Classics, 1970.

———. *Malory's Le Morte D'Arthur*. Keith Baines, Trans. New York: Mentor Books, 1962.

Mantzaridis, Georgios I. *The Deification of Man: St. Gregory Palamas and the Orthodox Tradition*. L. Sherrard, Trans. Crestwood: St. Vladimir's Seminary Press, 1984.

Martin, Catherine Gimelli. *The Ruins of Allegory: Paradise Lost and the Metamorphosis of Epic Convention*. Duke University Press, 1998.

Martines, Lauro. *Fire in the City: Savonarola and The Struggle for the Soul of renaissance Florence*. New York: Oxford University Press, 2006.

Matheson, Peter. *The Imaginative World of the Reformation* Minneapolis: Fortress Press, 2001.

McCluskey, Stephen C. *Astronomies and Cultures in Early Medieval Europe*. Cambridge University Press, 1998.

McGrath, Alister. *Christian Theology: An Introduction*. Second Ed. Cambridge: Blackwell, 1997.

McGinn, Bernard. *The Calabrian Abbot: Joachim of Fiore in the History of Western Thought*. New York: Macmillan, 1985.

———. *Apocalyptic Spirituality:* Treatises and Letters of Lactantius, Adso of Montieren—Der, Joachim of Fiore, the Spiritual Franciscans, and Savonarola. New York: Paulist Press, 1979.

————. *The Harvest of Mysticism in Medieval Germany, (1300-1500).* Volume IV of *The Presence of God: A History of Western Christian Mysticism.* New York: Crossroad Publishing, 2005.

McKnight, Stephen A. *The Modern Age and the Recovery of Ancient Wisdom: A Reconsideration of Historical Consciousness, 1450-1650.* Columbia: University of Missouri Press, 1991.

Meigne, Maurice. "Concile ou collection d'Elvire," *Revue d'histoire ecclésiastique* 70 (1975).

Menocal, María Rosa. *The Ornament of the World: How Muslims, Jews, and Christians Created a Culture of Tolerance in Medieval Spain.* New York: Little, Brown & Co., 2002.

Moltmann, Jürgen. *The Spirit of Life: A Universal Affirmation.* M. Kohl, Trans. Minneapolis: Fortress Press, 1992.

Montgomery, John Warwick. *Cross and Crucible: Johann Valentin Andreae (1586-1654), Phoenix of the Theologians.* 2 Volumes. The Hague: Martinus Nijhoff, 1973.

Moorman, John. *A History of the Franciscan Order: From Its Origins to the Year 1517.* Chicago: Franciscan Herald Press, 1988.

Morris, Richard. *The Last Sorcerers: The Path from Alchemy to the Periodic Table.* Washington: Joseph Henry Press, 2003.

Müntzer, Thomas. *Revelation and Revolution: Basic Writings of Thomas Müntzer.* Trans. and edited by Michael G. Baylor. Bethlehem: Lehigh University Press, 1993.

Muraro, Luisa. *Guglielma e Maifreda: Storia di un'eresia femminista.* Milan: La Tartaruga, 1985.

Murray, Robert. "New Wine in Old Wineskins: XII. Firstfruits," *Expository Times 86* (March 1975): 64-68.

Mustard, Helen M. and Passage, Charles, Eds. and Trans. "Introduction" to *Wolfram von Eschenbach, 'Parzival:' A Romance of the Middle Ages.* New York: Vintage Books, 1961.

Musto, Ronald G. "Queen Sancia of Naples (1286-1345) and the Spiritual Franciscans," pp. 179-214. In *Women of the Medieval World: Essays in Honor of J.H. Mundy,* edited by Julius Kirschner and Suzanne Wemple. Oxford University Press, 1986.

————. "Franciscan Joachimism at the Court of Naples, 1309-1345: A New Appraisal," *Archivum Franciscanum Histroicum* 90 (1997): pp. 419-486.

————. *Apocalypse in Rome: Cola di Rienzo and The Politics of the New Age.* Berkeley: University of California Press, 2003.

Nellas, Panayiotis. *Deification in Christ: Orthodox Perspectives on the Nature of the Human Person.* Norman Russell, Trans. Crestwood: St. Vladimir's Seminary Press, 1987.

Newman, Barbara. *Sister of Wisdom: St. Hildegard's Theology of the Feminine.* Berkeley: University of California Press, 1987.

————. *From Virile Woman to WomanChrist: Studies in Medieval Religion and Literature.* Philadelphia: University of Pennsylvania Press, 1995.

————. "Did Goddesses Empower Women? The Case of Dame Nature," 135-155. In *Gendering the Master Narrative: Women and Power in the Middle Ages,* edited by Mary Erler and Maryanne Kowaleski. Ithaca: Cornell University Press, 2003.

————.*God and the Goddesses: Vision, Poetry, and Belief in the Middle Ages.* Philadelphia: University of Pennsylvania Press, 2003.

Newman, William R. and Lawrence M. Principe. *Alchemy Tried in The Fire: Starkey, Boyle, and the Fate of Helmontian Chymistry.* University of Chicago Press, 2002.

Nold, Patrick. *Pope John XXII and His Franciscan Cardinal: Bertrand de la Tour and the Apostolic Poverty Controversy.* Oxford Historical Monographs. Oxford: Clarendon Press, 2003.

O'Loughlin, Thomas. *Celtic Theology: Humanity, World and God in Early Irish Writings.* London: Continuum, 2000.

O'Malley, J. Steven. "The Warmed Heart in the German Idiom." In Richard B. Steele, Ed., *Heart Religion in The Methodist Tradition and Related Movements.* Lanham: Scarecrow Press, 2001.

Osler, Margaret J., Ed. *Rethinking the Scientific Revolution.* New York: Cambridge University Press, 2000.

Ozment, Steven. *The Age of Reform, 1250-1550: An Intellectual and Religious History of Late Medieval and Reformation Europe.* New Haven: Yale University Press, 1980.

Pérez-Higuera, Teresa. *Medieval Calendars.* London: Weidenfeld & Nicolson, 1998.

Perlin, John. *A Forest Journey: The Role of Wood in the Development of Civilization.* New York and London: W. W. Norton & Co., 1989.

Polkinghorne, John. *Belief in God in an Age of Science.* New Haven: Yale University Press, 1998.

———. *Science and the Trinity, The Christian Encounter with Reality.* Yale University Press, 2004.

———. *Exploring Reality: The Intertwining of Science and Religion.* Yale University Press, 2005.

Price, Bronwen, Ed. *Francis Bacon's 'New Atlantis:' New Interdisciplinary Essays.* Manchester: Manchester University Press, 2002.

Principe, Lawrence M. "Boyle's Alchemical Pursuits," (91-105). In Michael Hunter, Ed. *Robert Boyle Reconsidered.* New York: Cambridge University Press, 1994.

Pynchon, Thomas. *The Crying of Lot 49.* New York: J. B. Lippincott, 1966.

Quilligan, Maureen. *The Language of Allegory: Defining the Genre.* Ithaca: Cornell University Press, 1979.

Ratzinger, Joseph. *The Theology of History in St. Bonaventure.* Trans Zachary Hayes. Chicago: Franciscan Herald Press, 1971.

Reeves, Marjorie. *Joachim of Fiore and The Prophetic Future.* London: Sutton Publishing, reprint edition 1999.

Reeves, Marjorie and Beatrice Hirsch-Reich. *The 'Figurae' of Joachim of Fiore.* London: Oxford University Press, 1972.

Reeves, Marjorie and Warwick Gould. *Joachim of Fiore and The Myth of the Eternal Evangel in the Nineteenth Century* Oxford: Clarendon Press, 1987.

Regan, P. "The Fifty Days and the Fiftieth Day," *Worship* 55 (May 1981): 194-218.

Rockefeller, Steven and John C. Elder, Eds. *Spirit and Nature: Why the Environment is a Religious Issue.* Boston: Beacon Press, 1992.

Santmire, H. Paul. *The Travail of Nature: The Ambiguous Ecological Promise of Christian Theology.* Philadelphia: Fortress Press, 1985.

Schaya, Leo. "The Sinaitic Theophany According to the Jewish Tradition," *Studies in Comparative Religion,* V. 16, Numbers 3 and 4 (1984): 214-233.

Schweid, Eliezer. *The Jewish Experience of Time: Philosophical Dimensions of the Jewish Holy Days,* Ammon Haday, Trans. Northvale: Jason Aronson, 2000.

Scott, Tom. *Thomas Müntzer: Theology and Revolution in the German Reformation.* New York: St. Martin's Press, 1989.

Sheldrake, Philip. *Spirituality and History: Questions of Interpretation and Method.* Rev. Ed. New York: Orbis Books, 1998.

Shichtman, Martin B. and James P. Carley, Eds. *Culture and the King: The Social Implications of the Arthurian Legend.* Albany: SUNY Press, 1994

Spiegel, Gabrielle M. *The Past as Text: The Theory and Practice of Medieval Historio-graphy.* Baltimore: Johns Hopkins University Press, 1997.
Sorrell, Roger D. *St. Francis of Assisi and Nature: Tradition and Innovation in Western Christian Attitudes toward the Environment.* New York: Oxford University Press, 1988.
Stayer, James M. and Werner O. Packull, Eds. and Trans. *The Anabaptists and Thomas Müntzer.* Dubuque: Kendall-Hunt Publishing, 1980.
Steinberg, Theodore. "Counting the Omer: Two Perspectives," *Jewish Bible Quarterly* Vol. 24, No. 4 (1996): 262-264.
Stephens, James. *Francis Bacon and the Style of Science.* University of Chicago Press, 1975.
Stookey, Laurence Hull. *Calendar, Christ's Time for the Church.* Nashville: Abingdon Press, 1996.
Stressfeld, Michael. *The Jewish Holidays: A Guide and Commentary.* New York: Harper and Row, 1985.
Swanson, R. N. *Religion and Devotion in Europe, c.1215-c.1515.* Cambridge University Press, 1995.
Sweeney, Jon M. *Light in the Dark Ages: The Friendship of Francis and Clare of Assisi.* Brewster: Paraclete Press, 2007.
Talley, Thomas J. *The Origins of the Liturgical Year.* New York: Pueblo Publishing, 1986.
Tauler, Johannes. *Johannes Tauler: Sermons.* Classics of Western Spirituality. Josef Schmidt, Ed. Maria Shrady, Trans. Mahwah: Paulist Press, 1985.
Teresa of Avila. *Interior Castle.* E. Allison Peers, Trans. New York: Image Books, 1989.
———. *The Way of Perfection.* E. Allison Peers, Trans. New York: Image Books, 1991.
———. *The Life of St. Teresa of Avila by Herself.* J. M. Cohen, Trans. London: Penguin Books, 1957.
Tillyard, E.M.W. *The Elizabethan World Picture.* New York: Vintage Books, 1959.
Tilton, Hereward. *The Quest for the Phoenix: Spiritual Alchemy and Rosicrucianism in the Work of Count Michael Maier (1569-1622).* Berlin: Walter de Gruyter, 2003.
Thompson, Bard. *Humanists and Reformers: A History of the Renaissance and Reforma-tion.* Eerdmans Publishing, 1996.
Thorndike, Lynn, *A History of Magic and Experimental Science, 8 Volumes.* New York: Columbia University Press, 1929-1958.
Tocco, Felice, ed. "Il Processo dei Guglielmiti," *Rendiconti della Reale Accademia dei Lincei: Classe di Scienze Morali, Storiche e Filologiche,* ser. 5, Vol. 8 (Rome 1899): 309-470.
Trithemius, Johannes. *De septem secundeis intelligentiis sive spiritibus orbes post deum moventibus.* From *Opera Historica, quotquot hactensus reperiri potuerunt omnia.* Frankfurt: Typis Wechelianis, 1601.
Urbach, Peter. *Francis Bacon's Philosophy of Science: An Account and a Reappraisal.* La Salle: Open Court Press, 1987.
Valone, Carolyn. "The Pentecost: Image and Experience in Late Sixteenth-Century Rome." *Sixteenth Century Journal,* Vol. 24, No. 4. (Winter 1993), pp. 801-828.
Versluis, Arthur. *Magic and Mysticism: An Introduction to Western Esotericism.* Lanham: Rowan & Littlefield, 2007.
Voegelin, Eric. *The Ecumenic Age.* Baton Rouge: Louisiana State University Press, 1974.
Wallace, Karl R. *Francis Bacon on the Nature of Man.* University of Illinois Press, 1967.
Webster, Charles. *The Great Instauration: Science, Medicine, and Reform, 1626-1660.* London: Duckworth, 1975.

Weigand, Hermann J. *Wolfram's Parzival: Five Essays with an Introduction.* Edited by Ursula Hoffman. Ithaca: Cornell University Press, 1969.

―――. "Narrative Time in the Grail Poems of Chretien de Troyes and Wolfram von Eschenbach." *P.M.L.A.* 53 (1938): 917-950.

Weisman, Ze'ev. "Reflection of the Transition to Agriculture in Israelite Religion and Cult," (251-261). In *Studies in Historical Geography and Biblical Historiography*, (Supplement to *Vetus Testamentum*, v. 81). Edited by Gerson Galil and Moshe Weinfeld. Leiden and Boston: Brill, 2000.

West, Delno C. and Sandra Zimdars-Swartz. *Joachim of Fiore: A Study in Spiritual Perception.* Bloomington: Indiana University Press, 1983.

White, Lynn T. "The Historical Roots of Our Ecologic Crisis," *Science* 155 (1967): 1203-1207.

White, Ralph, Ed. *The Rosicrucian Enlightenment Revisited.* New York: Lindisfarne Books, 1999.

Whited, Tanara L., et. al. *Northern Europe: An Environmental History.* Nature and Human Societies Series. Santa Barbara: ABC-CLIO, 2005.

Wiederkehr-Pollack, Gloria. *The Jewish Festivals in Ancient, Medieval, and Modern Sources.* Brooklyn: Sepher-Hermon Press, 1997.

Williams, Charles. *The Descent of the Dove: A Short History of the Holy Spirit in the Church.* Grand Rapids: Eerdmans Press, 1939.

Williams, Michael. *Deforesting the Earth: From Prehistory to Global Crisis.* University of Chicago Press, 2003.

Wolf, Kenneth Baxter. *The Poverty of Riches: St. Francis of Assisi Reconsidered.* Oxford Studies in Historical Theology. New York: Oxford University Press, 2003.

Wood, Laurence W. *The Meaning of Pentecost in Early Methodism: Rediscovering John Fletcher as John Wesley's Vindicator and Designated Successor.* Pietist and Wesleyan Studies, No. 15. Lanham: Scarecrow Press, 2002.

Yates, Frances Amelia. *The Rosicrucian Enlightenment.* London, 1972.

Index

Renaissance (Italian) x, 10, 20, 41, 123, 147, 148, 164, 166, 169, 178, 187, 196,
    204, 206, 212, 215, 219, 221, 224, 261
    English 237
    Florentine 124, 139, 148, 192, 204-215, 235, 260
    Rosicrucian Renaissance 4, 21, 192, 265
    Twelfth Century 28, 29, 86, 87, 201, 261, 278
Renovatio 9, 13, 116, 123, 132, 147, 148, 158, 162, 164, 169, 184, 186, 213,
    258, 271
Restauratio 148, 164, 165, 186, 269
Reuchlin, Johann 215
Richard the Lion Heart, King 88
Robert de Boron 58
Robert the Wise of Anjou, King 115, 123, 143n66
Roger II of Sicily, King 87
Roman Catholic xi, xiii, 4, 12, 14, 17, 35, 49, 62, 84, 117, 139, 149, 150, 151,
    154, 155, 157, 158, 160, 162, 164, 166, 170, 173, 182, 186, 187, 193, 194,
    197, 217, 224, 233, 236, 237, 239, 259, 260, 263, 265, 267
Roman Catholicism 14, 150, 187, 236, 244, 263
Roman Empire 7, 28, 32, 37, 38, 44, 66, 122, 121, 124, 128, 131,
Romanticism 6, 16, 155
Rosenkreutz, Christian 230, 231, 232, 233, 235, 236, 238
Rosicrucian (aka: Rosicrucian Movement) xv, 4, 10, 13, 21, 23n4, 94, 192-194,
    197, 198, 208, 211, 212, 215-219, 222, 226, 227, 230-243, 248n82, 249n108,
    262, 263, 265, 268
Royal Society of London 15, 192, 220, 226, 230, 242, 243, 249n118, 262
Rudolph II, Emperor 234
Rupert of Deutz 94

S
Saintes-Marie-de-la-Mer, Church of 48, 49
Saladin 88
Salome, Mary 48-49
Sancia of Majorca, Queen 115, 118, 143n65-66
Santmire, H. Paul 47, 77n49
Sara-la-Kali, (servant of Mary Salome and Mary Jacobe) 48-49
Saramita, Andreas 119, 120
Savonarola, Girolamo 213, 246n56
Schwärmer (see also Enthusiasm or Enthusiasts) 13, 158
Schleiermacher, Friedrich 16
Scholasticism 29, 54, 117, 178, 179, 206, 207, 223, 225, 229
Scientific Revolution vii, xi, 10, 139, 148, 187, 191, 193, 194, 212, 222, 234,
    241, 243, 260, 268
Secretum Secretorum 202, 207
September 11th 18, 267
Seneca 124

Hawthorne trees 14, 40, 41, 42, 256, 263
Jesse Tress 95, 113, 221
Trevrizent (Parzival's uncle) 66, 67, 69, 70
Trimethemius of Sponheim, Abbot 169, 186, 215-218, 219, 220, 235, 261, 262
Trinity, Holy xiv, 29, 44, 51, 53, 59, 91-98, 100, 119, 132, 139, 141n20, 164,
    176, 178, 180, 182, 183, 186, 219, 221, 234, 252, 268, 270, 271
Trinity Sunday 51

U
Ubertino da Casale 109, 111, 112, 113, 114, 115, 116, 142n48, 142n50
Underhill, Evelyn 152
Urbach, Peter 226, 247n80, 248n89, 248n91, 248n93
Urban III, Pope 99
Urban IV, Pope 51, 52

V
Valdes, Francisco de 150, 175
Valdes, Juan de 150, 171, 179, 188n9, 189n50
Velázquez de Cuéllar, Don Juan 183
Vespasian, Emperor 124
Vetter, Ferdinand 151
Via Antiqua 206, 221
Via Moderna 145, 165, 206
Viriditas (see Greening of the Holy Spirit)
Vogel, Heinrich 236
Vogelin, Eric 37, 76n30, 89

W
Wachowski, Laurence and Andrew (*The Matrix*) 252
Wagner, Richard 80n92, 122
Waite, Arthur Edward 238, 245n26
Walter III of Brienne, Count 103
Welsh 7, 31, 34, 46, 51, 56, 57, 58, 64, 65, 67
Wesley, Charles 266
Wesley, John 4, 16, 25n31, 251, 266, 267
White, Lynn 46
Whitsuntide x, 12, 32, 57, 58, 67, 72, 73, 152, 153, 256, 264
Wiegand, Herman 68, 70
William of Auvergne 211
William of Conches 29
William the Conqueror, King 55
William of Malmesbury 33
William I of Sicily, King 88
William of Toulouse, Count 62
William of Tudela 62
Williams, Charles 8, 24n18

333

Witch 156, 217
  witch craft 210, 257
  witch craze 46, 156, 215, 238
  Witches' Hammer (*Malleus Maleficarum*) 210
  witch hunt 156, 210
Wolfram von Eschenbach 4, 6, 7, 10, 21, 23n10, 29, 33, 39, 50, 58, 59-71, 74, 79n79-83, 80n84, 80n86-88, 80n90, 80n92-94, 81n95, 81n99, 86, 157, 231, 256, 267, 268
  and Chrétien de Troyes' Grail stories 49, 57, 60, 63, 80n93
  treatment and portrayal of Muslims 10, 60-66
Wood, Laurence W. 25n31
Worsley, Benjamin 242
Wren, Christopher 242

Y
Yates, Frances Amelia 23n4, 192, 238, 239, 243n7, 248n94, 250n127, 250n131

Z
Zeus 1, 198
Zinzendorf, Count 251
Zoroaster 209
Zoroastrianism 38
Zosimos of Panopolis 200
Zwingli, Ulrich 154

Lightning Source UK Ltd.
Milton Keynes UK
UKHW010657151220
375173UK00001B/60